John Hine Mundy

THE REPRESSION OF CATHARISM AT TOULOUSE

The Royal Diploma of 1279

In 1279 the king of France issued a royal diploma which listed 278 citizens of Toulouse whose property had been confiscated for heresy; under this amnesty, the property was to be returned to the citizens or their heirs. The central focus of this study, then, is an edition of the royal diploma and the attempted identification of the 278 citizens, along with a list of the proctors who originally petitioned the king for the amnesty. Moreover, there are histories of twenty families whose scions were listed, based on the diploma and other surviving documents. All available material on these families is noted, and thus the histories concern the general history of Toulouse, not just its religious history.

Part One of the study comments on the nature of Catharism, on twelfth-century events and on the defeat of the Midi during the Albigensian Crusade (1209-1229). Orthodox repression from 1178 to the crusade is emphasized, including an important law against heretics issued by the count of Toulouse. Initially hardly aware of Catharism's teachings, the orthodox soon devised an effective propaganda linking or confounding usury with heresy.

Toulouse was absorbed by northern French power and ecclesiastical repression continued from 1229 until the publication of the amnesty of 1279. The diploma itself, therefore, is a form of treaty between monarch and town that finally removed the threat of property confiscation for past heresy.

The repression in the town of Toulouse was both severe and rapid, Catharism being irreparably doomed by the end of the 1230s, even before the Inquisition was itself well organized. The province having already been beheaded, the later extirpation of rural Catharism was a mere mopping up operation. By analysing the role of different social classes and groups, it becomes clear that the inquisitors aimed high, both women and the lower classes being underrepresented among the condemned. One thing is sure: noble or commoner, the town's well-to-do were deeply involved in Catharism. Although closely linked, families were not uniform in belief – some members were Cathar and others not. Before the repression, Toulousan society tolerated religious divergence.

Toulouse, Archives municipales, AA 34 3 [top]

Toulouse, Archives municipales. AA 34 3 [bottom]

STUDIES AND TEXTS 74

THE REPRESSION OF CATHARISM AT TOULOUSE

The Royal Diploma of 1279

JOHN HINE MUNDY
Columbia University

PONTIFICAL INSTITUTE OF MEDIAEVAL STUDIES

Acknowledgment

This book has been published with the help of a grant
from the Canadian Federation for the Humanities,
using funds provided by the Social Sciences and
Humanities Research Council of Canada.

CANADIAN CATALOGUING IN PUBLICATION DATA

Mundy, John H. (John Hine), 1917-
  The repression of Catharism at Toulouse

(Studies and texts, ISSN 0082-5328 ; 74)
Bibliography: p.
Includes index.
ISBN 0-88844-074-X

1. Albigenses - History.   2. Toulouse (France) - Church history.
3. Toulouse (France) - Genealogy.   I. France. Sovereign (1270-1285: Philip III).
Royal Diploma (1279).   II. Pontifical Institute of Mediaeval Studies.
III. Title.   IV. Series: Studies and texts (Pontifical Institute of Mediaeval
Studies) ; 74.

BX4891.2.M84 1985   284´.4   C84-099082-0

PRINTED BY UNIVERSA, WETTEREN, BELGIUM

Martha and John

Contents

PART THREE

Preface

The research contained in this book was begun in 1946, and the majority of the documents were photographed or examined in that year and 1947. Subsequent research was done on sabbatical in 1958 and thereafter, starting in 1969, in almost yearly brief trips to France, especially to Paris, Montauban, and Toulouse. Over the course of the years, time and money for research was provided by my longtime employer, Columbia University, and by grants and fellowships from the Social Science Research Council, the American Council of Learned Societies, the Fulbright Administration, the John Simon Guggenheim Foundation, the Institute for Advanced Study at Princeton, and the National Endowment of the Humanities.

Abbreviations

Maps

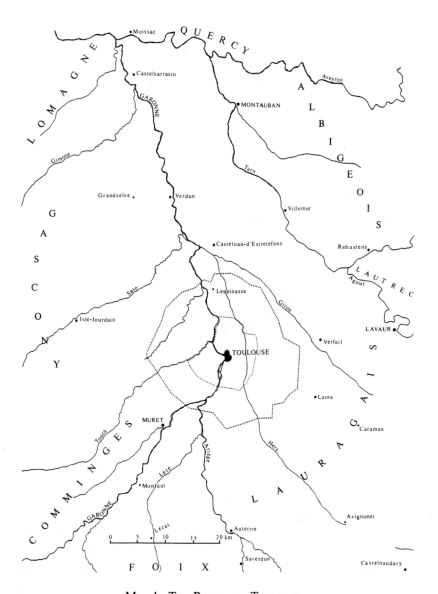

Map 1. The Region of Toulouse

MAP 2. TOULOUSE

This map is a traced sketch taken from the Plan Saguet of 1750. It is roughly aligned on a north-south axis, the most northerly gate of the Bourg being that of Arnaud-Bernard. The modern town differed from that of the twelfth and thirteenth centuries in many respects of which the following are the most notable:

Saint-Cyprien was not fortified until the Hundred Years War and therefore constituted a "barri" (Latin, *barrium*) similar to that of Saint-Michel to the south of the town at this time.

The broad bridge (now called the New Bridge) was not built until 1543-1614. By the end of the thirteenth century, there were four bridges, two of which are not shown on the map because of the uncertainty as to where they were exactly located. The missing bridges are those furthest north and furthest south. The former is the Bazacle Bridge, constructed from the early years of the thirteenth century, crossing the river from somewhere in or near the Bazacle to Saint-Cyprien, meeting land at a point further south than that of the eighteenth century barrage. The most southerly was the Comminges Bridge, begun in the late thirteenth century, crossing the Garonne from a site north of the mid-point of the Isle-de-Tounis and south of the Old Bridge.

The numbers on the map read from west to east and north to south:

1 Lascrosses Gate
2 Arnaud-Bernard Gate
3 Saint-Julien church in the parish of Saint-Sernin
4 The Bazacle, site of the famous mills, a small castle, and probably the head of the Bazacle Bridge
5 Saint-Sernin, the basilica of the canons-regular, and a parish church
6 Pousonville Gate
7 Saint-Pierre-des-Cuisines, a parish church and a priory of the Benedictines of Saint-Pierre of Moissac
8 Matabiau Gate
9 The Franciscans
10 The Taur, a parish under the patronage of Saint-Sernin
11 Saint-Nicholas, a parish under the patronage of the Daurade
12 The Dominicans
13 The Portaria, having, to its east a block away, the *Palatium* or Town Hall (the later Capitole), and, on its west, the church of Saint-Quentin under the patronage of Saint-Sernin. The Portaria was named after the remnants of a Roman gate that stood in this place. It was part of a dismantled wall that divided the City from the Bourg called the Saracen Wall.
14 The New or Daurade Bridge constructed in the twelfth century
15 The Bourguet-Nau
16 Saint-Pierre-Saint-Martin in the parish of the Daurade
17 The Villeneuve Gate in the quarter of the same name in the Bourg
18 The Daurade, a parish church, monastery, and priory of the Benedictines of Saint-Pierre of Moissac
19 Saint-Romain, a church in the parish of Saint-Étienne, given to the Dominicans in 1216
20 The Montardy Square
21 The Old Bridge
22 The square and market of La Pierre and the church of Saint-Pierre-Saint-Géraud in the parish of Saint-Étienne

23 The square and market of Montaygon and the church of Saint-Georges in the parish of Saint-Étienne

24 The Neuve Gate

25 The Dalbade parish church under the patronage of the Daurade

26 The street of Joutx-Aigues on which the synagogue was located

27 The church of Saint-Victor in the parish of Saint-Étienne and the square called Rouaix

28 The Baragnon Cross

29 The Hospital of Saint John of Jerusalem and church of Saint-Remésy

30 The cathedral and parish church of Saint-Étienne, and, across the cloister to the south, the church of Saint-Jacques

31 The Templars

32 The Carmelites

33 Saint-Barthélemy of the parish of Saint-Étienne (once Sainte-Marie of the Palace)

34 The Narbonne Castle (Château Narbonnais) or *Palatium*

35 Montgaillard Gate

36 Montoulieu Gate

37 Saint-Michel, a church in the parish of Saint-Étienne that derived its dedication from the chapel of the Château Narbonnais, and gave its name to the *barri* or quarter in which it was located. The church was not built until 1331.

Introduction

This monograph discusses and publishes a diploma issued by the king of France in August 1279.[1] This document listed citizens of Toulouse whose inheritances had been condemned to confiscation because of heresy, and consequently concerns the repression of heresy in that town. The diploma of 1279 has been commented on, but has not been used by historians of the repression of heresy in this region, even the most recent ones.[2] This is principally because the historians of Catharism, Waldensianism, etc. have concentrated either on the intellectual aspects of the divergent religions – and with magnificent and sometimes unanticipated results![3] – or on the institutional history of the police agencies of the church, especially the Inquisition sponsored by the popes.[4] The latter area is closer to the business of this monograph than is the intellectual history of these divergent religions. Nevertheless, I hope to add to the clarity of the general picture by using the diploma as a central piece in the history of the repression of heresy.

A reason is this. The careful examination by previous scholars of the activities of churchmen as inquisitors has led them to believe correctly

---

[1] The system of referring to documents, texts, and monographs may best be understood by examining the Bibliography (below, pp. 305-315) which is divided into three parts: unpublished archival documents, published primary sources, and secondary sources. The method of dating Toulousan documents is also explained there, but it may be noted that all dates seen in this text and its notes are modernized. The system employed in presenting the names of persons is explained at the beginning of Chapter 5.

[2] In the popular history of his town (*Toulouse*, p. 127), Philippe Wolff remarked that the publication of this diploma marked the end of the pursuit of Cathar heresy at Toulouse. Mr. Wolff's perceptive remark seems to be unique in the litterature.

[3] Note especially the general survey of Catharism by Borst, *Katharer*, of 1953, the rich survey of that religion and its Waldensian rival by Thouzellier, *Catharisme et Valdéisme*, in 1966, and the recent defense of Catharism as a religion by Duvernoy, *Le Catharisme: La religion des Cathars*, of 1976. To these may be added the wide variety of materials presented by the *Cahiers de Fanjeaux*, an annual publication of monographic articles and "essais de synthèse" initially inspired by the loyal spirit of the Dominican, Father Vicaire, the noted historian of Dominic Guzmàn and his order, Canon Delaruelle of the Institut Catholique de Toulouse, and Professor Wolff of the University of Toulouse.

[4] The diploma of 1279 is not studied in the older histories of the Inquisition, nor in recent ones, Dossat's *Inquisition* of 1959, for example, and Kolmer's *Ad capiendas vulpes* of 1982. Wakefield, *Heresy, Crusade and Inquisition* (1974) mentioned it but did not examine the families.

that the repressive machinery of the Inquisition did not reach maturity until the mid 1240s. To them, consequently, the back of Languedocian Catharism was not broken until the inquisitorial campaigns of the 1240s and 1250s. In spite of the truth of the assertion about institutional "maturity," it is the argument of this book that an examination of the information contained in the diploma of 1279 clearly shows that the basic victory of the Catholic over the Cathar church was won before the inquisitorial institution was fully developed. However immature their procedures, churchmen and their lay allies were able to behead the Cathar form of Christianity in Toulouse, the capital of western Languedoc, between 1229 and 1240. Deprived of its head, the small town and rural body of the Cathar faith, itself already severely shaken, was cut to pieces later on.

Other than the fact that recent historians have concentrated on the institutional history of the repression, another reason for the neglect of this diploma is probably that a lengthy list of some 278 individuals is too forbidding and uninteresting to tackle until the persons can be identified. The identification of as many persons and their families as presently possible has been undertaken in this study. Although, as the reader will see, the measure of the identification achieved does not enable us to know exactly what particular social elements were especially attracted to divergent religious thought, it certainly proves that the well-to-do, both knightly and burgher patrician, were heavily infiltrated by Catharism. The investigation of the families of Toulouse shows, furthermore, that many of the greater clans hit hard because of heresy survived the losses caused by imprisonment, death, and the confiscation of property. Oddly enough, the same was true of some of the smaller families as well.

A word about vocabulary. I will use the nouns "orthodoxy" and "heresy" and the adjectives derived from them, to define, on the one hand, the Catholic church, and, on the other, the Cathar church, and their members. This is not because, when speaking as an historian, I favor either one or the other side. I am also aware that, in spite of the great divergence of their faith from that of most other Christians of the time, including most of the other heterodox sects, the Cathars called themselves "Christiani." None of these meaningful considerations, however, make it possible for me to do away with the traditional terminology. To do so, one has to replace simple nouns and adjectives with whole phrases, and life is too short for that. There is also a traditional vocabulary attached to the history of heresy. One is the use of the verb "to relapse" to mean that a person, who had confessed heresy and abjured it, subsequently returned to it, as the inquisitors liked to say, "as a dog to its vomit." Also, although

I shall explain them when necessary, the technical vocabulary of the inquisitors will occasionally be taken over into mine. To the later inquisitors, in fact, the word "hereticus" had come to mean a member of the semi-priestly elite of the Cathar religion, a "perfectus," whereas the ordinary believers or "credentes" were not accorded that honor. As a result of this technical use of the word "hereticus," the verb "hereticare," which simply meant to become an heretic, technically came to mean to become a "perfectus." Anent the deathbed, for example, the word "heretication" refers to that mixture of a general or non-specific confession and a promise to sin no more which resulted in the Cathar becoming a "perfectus," a ritual sometimes called the "consolamentum." The only other technical term that will sometimes appear here is that of "adoratio." This is a word coined by the inquisitors to describe the salute to the Holy Spirit that occurred when the believers met the "perfecti."

Part One

History and Analysis

1

The Early History of Repression

A. The Circumstances and Nature of Toulousan Heresy

The nature of the repression studied in this book obviously partly depended on the character of the divergent religions or heresies involved. I am therefore encouraged to diverge briefly from the main theme of this essay to offer some introductory and brief observations about the relationship of Toulousan heresy to the machinery of repression.

One of the peculiarities of Toulousan heresy is that, although deeply implanted and intense, it was curiously monochromatic. The various ideologies of dissent describable as Waldensian and Poor Catholic had little hold in the Toulousain, serious vestiges of these sects being seen only to the east and south of that region.[1] Naturally, Waldes' teaching was known at Toulouse. The Dominican Inquisitor and chronicler, William Pelisson quaintly describes an "archimandrita magnus Valdensium" named Galvannus whose body was disinterred with obloquy from the Villeneuve cemetery in 1231.[2] We also know that a sister of the Fonte-vrault house of Lespinasse, the widow of Bernard de Turre, was broad-minded or indiscriminate enough to play with both the Waldensian and Cathar religions, and was condemned for it.[3] Lastly, very late in this history, Bernard Raymond Baranonus, a merchant who had resided at Bordeaux, was picked up for Waldensian divergence.[4] These few exceptions apart, however, it seems that the Waldensians had made little impression in Toulouse and its immediate environs, and indeed that the spokesmen for this movement had sometimes seemed to be the allies of the church in its battle against the Cathars. Although his polemical

---

[1] On Waldensians, see Dossat, "Les vaudois méridionaux d'après les documents de l'Inquisition," Selge, "Pauvres catholiques et Pauvres réconciliés," and Vicaire, "Les Vaudois et Pauvres catholiques contre les Cathars," all in *Cahiers de Fanjeaux* 2 (1967) 207-272.

[2] Pelisson, *Chronicon*, p. 88.

[3] No. **97** in the amnesty in Chapter 5 below and in the Turre family history in Part 3 below.

[4] See the family history of the Baranoni in Part 3 below, where one can see from his reading and attitudes his Waldensian-Protestant cast of mind.

preciosity caused him to attribute this alliance to the sheer ignorance of the orthodox clergy, the otherwise excellent historian William of Puylaurens remarked that the Waldensians did combat the Cathars.[5] A later source has the inquisitors eliciting evidence of a debate between the celebrated Cathar "perfectus" Isarn of Castres and the Waldensian Bernard Prima in about 1208 not far from Castelnaudary far south in the Lauragais. One aged witness from Avignonet speaking about events around 1221 remarked that the Waldensians attacked the Cathars, and were therefore welcomed in the churches, and he had himself given them charity.[6] Religiously or ideologically, Cathars and Waldensians seem to have been oil and water, but, in a really large city such as Milan, these two conflicting types of divergent thought coexisted. In the somewhat provincial world of Toulouse, in short, Catharism was the almost exclusive business of those who sought a religious experience different from the normal faith or orthodoxy of the Roman church.

In comparison with Toulouse and with western Languedoc, furthermore, north and central Italy and even Provence and maritime Languedoc were much richer in divergent thought and heretical institutions. In spite of the spotlight focused on western Languedoc by modern scholarship, these other areas boasted almost every conceivable variety of heresy, Cathars, Judaizers, Waldensians, etc. This great diversity distracted the aim of orthodox churchmen who consequently found it more difficult to repress heresy in these regions than in Toulouse and the Toulousain. The heretics of Italy, moreover, benefited from a political advantage. Although attacked by Catholic authority at the same time as those in Languedoc, Italy's divergent sects were treated more gently because the peninsula's towns, especially Milan, a community that James of Vitry called the very

---

[5] Puylaurens, *Chronica*, p. 24 "Et illi quidem Valdenses contra alios [Catharos] acutissime disputabant, unde et in eorum odium aliquando admittebantur a sacerdotibus ydiotis." "Idiota" does not mean "idiot," merely that the person was uninstructed. For his reference to Durand of Huesca, see note 12 below.

[6] The principal source is TBM, MS 609, fol. 136r (December 1246 [?]) where Michael Verger at Avignonet south of Toulouse said that circa 1221 "Valdenses persequebantur dictos hereticos [Catharos], et multociens fecit [ipse testis] helemosinam dictis Valdensibus, quando querebant hostiatim amore dei; et quia ecclesia sustinebat tunc dictos Valdenses, et erant cum clericis in ipsa ecclesia cantantes et legentes, credebat eos esse bonos homines." Most persons testifying had not really heard of Waldensians and knew little or nothing about them. The debate involving Prima was recorded in fol. 198r in December 1245 as taking place at Mireval Lauragais southwest of Castelnaudary, well to the south of Toulouse, 37 years before. The depositions of which these are examples were copied into MS 609 on the orders of William Bernard and Reginald of Chartres, inquisitors at Toulouse, sometime between 1258 and 1263. Although the vast bulk of the depositions derive from 1245-1246, the last is dated October 1258.

womb of heresy, were allies needed by the popes in their struggle with the empire.[7] For this reason, divergent religious thought was not only richer and more varied in northern Italy, but also longer lasting than was the case in Toulouse and western Languedoc.

Catharism was also more vulnerable to repression than other systems of divergent religious thought. I hasten to say that this was not because this cult was a weak or unattractive religion. Its highly spiritual or spiritualist doctrines, especially that of the transmigration of souls, clearly attracted the adhesion of certain kinds of religious minds. Furthermore, in spite of the ostensibly dour and anti-naturalist quality of Cathar moral doctrines, the severities of this faith fell heavily only on the "perfecti," the more or less monastic clergy of the cult.[8] These had to forego pleasurable foods, sexual relations, indeed, almost everything appealing to ordinary men and women in order to enjoy an almost wholly noncoercive mental power over others. On the other hand, the ordinary "credentes" or lay believers were, until their conversion or "consolamentum," an action often remanded to the deathbed, relatively free from moral suasion. They were not subjected to the confessional or penitential system that was growing at this very moment among the Catholics nor to the active and pressing social conscience of the Waldensians, their principal rivals among those of divergent thought at this period. Harder on their clergy than the others, perhaps, the Cathars demanded less of their adherents. As a result, Catharism's intense spiritualism combined fruitfully with the relatively undemanding morality imposed on the ordinary believer to make it a very appealing religion. All the same, its spiritualism exposed Catharism dangerously. As is well known, Catharism sought to explain the coexistence of good and evil by means of dualism, personifying or "divinizing" those qualities either in the extreme form of two coeternal deities or the more moderate one of two conflicting principles after Satan's fall. As a result, a vigorous dualism clearly set this faith apart from almost all other Christian communities or sects, orthodox or divergent.

Catharism's sharply defined identity was something never again to be repeated in the history of medieval Latin heterodoxy. As is seen in Bernard Gui's inquisitors manual, the members of other sects, notably the

---

[7] Vitry, *Lettres*, No. 1, pp. 72-73.

[8] To remind the non-specialist, those who had received the "consolamentum," a ceremony that obliged the penitent henceforward to eschew sex, eating meat, etc. and which was rather like a combination of baptism and the shriving of sins, were "perfecti" or, as the Cathars said, "the pure;" the "credentes" were the mere believers.

Waldensians, were difficult for ecclesiastical policemen to pin down.[9] The Cathars were simplicity itself. Movements of the Waldensian type were hard to identify and, in fact, possessed so substantial a measure of agreement with what seemed orthodox that it was well-nigh impossible to destroy them before their thought had taken very deep root.[10] Catharism may therefore be described as a religious divergence that could have grown up only in an age when an ecclesiastical police had not yet been established. Partly because it was so visible and consequently so open to attack, it was easily obliterated once an apparatus of repression was built.

Nor was the fate of this heresy determined only by its incapacity for disguise or camouflage; it also had much to do with its relative indifference to eliciting mass social support. Catharism, for example, appealed to those inclined to gnostic ideas and who shared the widespread hostility to the dominant church, but it lacked any express social appeal. The notion of the priesthood of all true believers, the consequent relative absence of hierarchy, the drive to restore on earth a simulacrum of apostolic community or communism, and a hope of realizing the spiritual equality of men and women were voiced by Waldensians and "left" Christian sects but not by the Cathars. Although the Cathar "perfecti" (as against the mere "credentes") lived out for themselves a version of the ideal community of the apostles, the general programs described above were far too earth-centered for their highly spiritual faith. The Cathars were not much exercised against or for poverty, and are never known to have attacked usury, a pejorative word used in the middle ages to describe any interest collected on capital, whether of goods or money, or, more generally, what a modern might think of as the "moral" aspect of "economic individualism." Because it expressed few of the ideas of brotherhood and community possessed in such abundance by the other secessionist Christian sects, neither social activists nor the plebs could find

---

[9] See Bernard Guy, *Practica inquisitionis*, ed. Douais, pp. 252-256 and ed. Mollat, 1: 64-69: "Valdenses sunt valde difficiles ad examinandum et inquirendum et ad habendum veritatem ab eis de erroribus suis propter fallacias et dupplicitates verborum ...." The Dominican inquisitor obviously does not say what I have above, and merely remarks that they are hard to trap, but he does not make the same observation about the Cathars and other sects.

[10] Even Vaux-de-Cernay, *Historia Albigensis*, 1: 18-19 remarks that, although the Waldensians "mali erant, set comparatione aliorum hereticorum longe minus perversi: in multis enim nobiscum conveniebant, in aliquibus dissentiebant." Their crimes were that they wore sandals "more apostolorum," that is, that they believed in apostolic poverty, took no oaths, altogether eschewed the sword, and espoused the priesthood of all true believers.

much in Catharism for them.[11] In addition, other than by its attack on the ecclesiastical hierarchy, Catharism was not of much use to the secular state, either republican or monarchical. Although attacking the Catholic clergy, it did not aim its artillery at the hierarchical principal of ecclesiastical organization as did the Waldensians and many later medieval "reformers." This astonishing lack of a social ideology created another aspect of the religious dualism described in the preceding paragraph. It had the advantage of setting intellectual and individual freedom against institutional and group authority in the strongest possible terms. Based on a revelation beyond the reach of rational proof and attracting no motivated or "servile" (because profitable to the adherent) adhesion of specific social groups or their leaders, this struggle between the Cathars and the ecclesiastical order or orthodoxy was among the purer ideological conflicts known to western history, a conflict that was, simply because of its astonishing purity, beyond hope of compromise. Unlike the Waldensians, no accommodating and useful Durand of Huesca returned to the orthodox, and no Bernard Prima from Catharism would be heard preaching to his onetime co-religionists.[12]

To these general perspectives must be added the history of the mounting repression of the Cathars. I have mentioned above that the ecclesiastical repression of heresy was slower and relatively less violent in northern Italy than in Languedoc. Having nothing to lose and much to gain in south France, Rome, usually aided by the northern French, early began to investigate the situation in that area, and slowly developed methods of repression and reconversion that were to end in the launching of the famous crusade against this region in 1209. A brief review of this history will be in order here.

B. PERSUASION AND FORCE

The spread of heresy in the region of Toulouse had long excited the interest of churchmen. A canon of a council held in Toulouse in 1119 had adverted to an aspect of the problem, and, in 1145, the famous Bernard of

---

[11] An ampler statement of this theme along with the citation of pertinent literature will be seen in my "Urban Society and Culture: Toulouse and Its Region," in *Renaissance and Renewal in the Twelfth Century*, pp. 238-243.

[12] Puylaurens, *Chronica*, p. 48 records a debate between the Waldensians and the orthodox, and remarks that Durand of Huesca (Osca) converted "et composuit contra hereticos quedam scripta." As an example of his work, see Thouzellier's *Une somme anti-Cathar: Le "Liber contra Manicheos" de Durand de Huesca*.

Clairvaux and a papal legate had been moved to visit the Toulousain and the town to preach and persuade. Somewhat charitably, the mission has been described as a success, but it seems pretty clear that the great preacher left little or no mark on the Midi.[13] His mission, however, did mark the Cistercians who, from that time on, were committed to leading the movement against southern French Catharism.

The next mission took place in 1178, and was precipitated by an invitation accorded the orthodox by the count of Toulouse. In 1177 Raymond v of Saint-Gilles wrote a letter appealing for help to Alexander, abbot of Cîteaux. He there stated that he was powerless in the face of a growing heresy that attracted the magnates in his domains who in turn, he opined, corrupted the people.[14] He also referred to an earlier appeal sent to the king of France, and there is evidence to show that the kings of both England and France had toyed with the idea of intervening in the south and repressing heresy there.[15] Perhaps not wishing to confuse the pursuit of heresy with the conflicting political ambitions of the Capetians and Angevins, who had several times invaded the principality of the counts of Toulouse in the past, the clergy appear not to have encouraged the intervention of these rival princes. They therefore answered Raymond's appeal themselves. True to past attempts by Rome and by the Cistercian order to defeat heresy by preaching, a group led by the Cistercian Peter of Pavia, cardinal priest of Saint-Chrysogon, and by the redoutable Henry (of Marsy or Marsiac), abbot of Clairvaux, arrived at Toulouse in August 1178. The clergy of England and France were represented by the archbishop of Bourges and the bishop of Bath, and that of the Midi by the metropolitan of Narbonne, of which Toulouse was suffragan. These churchmen were protected at Toulouse, and their will enforced by a group of secular notables headed by the count of Toulouse.[16]

It is worth noting that these events may be defined in more than merely religious terms. One perceives the fact that the mission of 1178 fitted

---

[13] For these events, see Griffe, *Les débuts de l'aventure cathare en Languedoc*.

[14] As recorded by the English historian Gervase of Canterbury, *Chronicle*, Rolls Series 78, 1: 270, the count stated that he wanted to crush Catharism, but that "ad tantum et tale negotium complendum vires meas deficere cognosco, quoniam terrae meae nobiliores, jam praelibata infidelitatis tabe, aruerunt, et cum ipsis maxima hominum multitudo a fide corruens aruit, unde id perficere non audeo nec valeo. Nunc igitur ad vestrum confugiens subsidium ...."

[15] Gervase again quoting the count in ibid., p. 271: "Ad quod peragendum dominum regum Francorum accersiri vestris ex partibus persuadeo, quia per ipsius praesentiam tanta male finem suscipere suspicor."

[16] The viscount of Turenne in the Limousin and a Raymond of Castelnau. Who the latter was is not known with any certainty.

neatly, in the manner of a prologue, into a troubled political and social crisis in Toulouse that ran from the late seventies until 1189. In 1178, Count Raymond, who had hitherto busied himself somewhat unsuccessfully in southern and eastern Languedoc combating the spread of Catalan-Aragonese power, returned to Toulouse to reassert his fading authority there at the expense of the consuls, the count's quondam council whose growing independence had been remarked for sometime. The count's success was real and effected the re-establishment of his power by about 1181. His intervention was made possible by divisions within Toulouse itself: conflicts derived, probably, from rapid economic growth. This social malaise and the count's effort to restore his power over the town coincided with the beginning of the ecclesiastical attack on usury in favor of economic brotherhood, an attack providing ideological arguments for the combat of the humbler classes against entrepreneurs (just before the age when the gilds made their appearance) and for the hostility of the older toward the newer rich.[17] The count, in short, seems to have profited from the religious problem in Toulouse, and, indeed, although seemingly well aware of the social divisions within the town and able to exploit them for a time, won his first success in the counter-attack on Toulouse in the sphere of religion and the repression of heresy.

On arriving in Toulouse, the clergy began work energetically.[18] They asked for voluntary confessions and required and received depositions against the heretics by the local populace and clergy. In the case of Peter Maurand, a true-blue member of the patriciate of Toulouse, the clergy won a great victory. Although Peter at first denied heresy, his answers to the questions he was asked were found to be heretical by the clergy assembled in the basilica of the canons regular of Saint-Sernin in the Bourg. Condemned, he was sentenced to lose all his property, and his towers and fortifications were ordered demolished. After negotiation, Peter settled for the penitence of going to the Holy Land for three years, the destruction of his towers, and a fine of 500 pounds of Toulouse (1000 pounds of Tours) to be paid to the count of Toulouse.[19]

[17] See my *Toulouse*, pp. 59-66.

[18] See the recitation of these events in my "Une famille Cathare: Les Maurand," *Annales: ESC* (1974) 1211-1223.

[19] Other than the materials contained in the Maurand family history in Part 3 below, our source for these events are the letters of Cardinal Peter and of Henry of Clairvaux recorded in the *Gesta regis Henrici secundi Benedicti abbatis*, Rolls Series 49, 1: 203ff and also in PL 199: 1119ff. The *Gesta* itself was copied by Roger of Hoveden in his *Chronica*, Rolls Series 51, 2: 150-166. The *Gesta*, pp. 217-218, asserts that Peter, at first "in multitudine divitiarum suarum et parentum numerositate confidens," would not talk, but that pressure by friends made him present himself. Then, confronted by the clerical and secular power, and wishing to escape "ab imminentis mortis periculis," he abjured.

Overconfident perhaps, the clerical group then went too far. Forgetting that persuasion has no place when men are arguing about insoluble mysteries, they tried an unfortunate experiment in free speech. They questioned two notable Cathar "perfecti," Raymond of Baimiac and Bernard Raymond. They got nowhere because the presumed heretics (who, of course, claimed they were orthodox) were protected by a safeguard rashly issued by Cardinal Peter, and refused to take an oath on it. As the cardinal recounted in a long letter, Raymond and Bernard retired from Toulouse, pursued only by excommunication. The clerical taskforce then repaired to Béziers somewhat shaken by what had happened at Toulouse. Cardinal Peter gave vent to his frustration in a letter notable for his annoyance at having had to discuss sacred matters in the vernacular, an annoyance perhaps natural in a man who appears to have believed that the sacred scriptures had been written in Latin! [20] Abbot Henry also wrote about their adventures, and there repeated a line already taken at the time of Bernard of Clairvaux' unsuccessful preaching mission in 1145: without their visit, he said, everybody at Toulouse would have become heretical within three years.[21]

These events show us that the church did not yet really comprehend Catharism, and that the clergy were somewhat at a loss as to how to handle these heretics. It is true that Henry of Clairvaux gives evidence that Peter was a Cathar. He speaks of two primordial principles or two gods, and, in a typically polemical passage, refers to the "noctuae" of Toulouse at night worshipping as a king this "laicus et idiota" all dressed up in robes! That a modern reader is tempted to ask whether Peter's "noctuae" were Minerva's stuffed birds or merely Toulousan night owls should not hide from him that Henry was clearly referring to the so-called "adoratio," evidencing how soon churchmen found a way of mocking the Cathar ritual of greeting their clergy.[22] But the clerical unfamiliarity with

---

[20] The pertinent passage is in the *Gesta*, p. 203, where Peter stated that the "evangelia et epistolae ... Latino eloquio noscuntur esse conscripta."

[21] *Gesta*, p. 220.

[22] *Gesta*, pp. 215-216 in which Henry reports that the devil had so blinded Peter "ut seipsum Johannem Evangelistam diceret; et Verbum Quod erat in principio apud Deum, ab alio quodam rerum principio, tanquam a Deo altero segregaret. Hic erat in urbe illa pereuntium caput et princeps haereticorum. Qui licet, tanquam laicus et idiota, nihil saperet, inter eos tamen velut quidam diabolicae sapientiae fons, perditionis et mortis felleos latices emanabat. Conveniebant ad eum noctibus noctuae tenebrosae, et ille indumento quodam ad instar tunicae dalmaticaeque vestitus, cum sederet inter eos, tanquam rex, circumstante exercitu, erat et inerat disipientium praedicator." Note the perceptive remarks on the orthodox polemical use of the "adoratio" in Kolmer, *Ad capiendas vulpes*, p. 126.

the sect is shown by the fact that Peter Maurandus was obliged to take an oath repudiating his heresy,[23] and that the best the clergy could find in their books was an old formula of abjuration, the celebrated oath Berengar of Tours took in 1059 concerning the real presence in the eucharist.[24] Given its overtones of "cannibalism," this oath was not highly considered by theologians of the time,[25] and, in fact, was already being toned down.[26]

On the other hand, not everything was old fashioned there in the minds of those in the basilica of Saint-Sernin where Peter Maurandus took oath. Two of the actions taken in 1178 were indicative of the future. The first was something that elicited popular support. Henry of Clairvaux tells us that not only was Peter ordered to dismantle his "castrum" (by which he presumably meant his "forcia" or fortified farm at Valségur or his towered town house) and return ecclesiastical property, especially tithes, he had "usurped," but also that he was to restore to the "poor" the usuries and illicit gains he had extorted from them.[27] Typical of the sadly partial fulfillment of man's hopes, we have no evidence of the restoration of ill-gotten gains to the poor, but know that the tithes were surrendered to Saint-Sernin.[28]

---

[23] The text is published on pp. 1222-1223 of my article cited in note 18 above from an original undated parchment in Saint-Sernin 688 (21 79 1), hence from the library of the basilica in which Peter read it to the assembled notables.

[24] Berengar's abjuration was carried in Gratian's *Decretum* (D. 2 de cons. 42). Friedberg's edition (*CIC* [Leipzig, 1897], 1: 1328-1329) compares his version with those of Ivo of Chartres and Alger of Liège in his notes. R. Somerville, "The Case against Berengar of Tours – A New Text," *Studi Gregoriani* 9 (1972), 68-69.

[25] This is rehearsed in Lubac, *Corpus mysticum*, pp. 165 and 169ff.

[26] Note especially that the second oath required of Berengar in the Roman Council of 1079 (Gregory VII's register 6, 17a, in Jaffé, *Bibliotheca rerum Germanicarum: Monumenta Gregoriana*, 2: 353) avoids the "grinding teeth." Also, although Peter Lombard *Libri IV sententiarum*, 4.12 in PL 192: 865 presents a truncated version of the oath of 1059 with its "sensualiter," "manibus tractari," "dentibus atteri," etc., he recommends gentler formulations of the same idea. Lastly, when the Berengarian oath finally entered the Roman pontifical books in the *Pontificale Guillelmi Durandi*, 3.9.10 of the late thirteenth century (published by Andrieu in *Le pontifical romain au moyen-âge*, vol. 3, Studi e testi 88 [Vatican City, 1940] p. 619), it was stripped of any reference to the eucharistic question and was adapted to be used to show the adhesion of a confessing heretic to the belief of the Roman church on any and every point.

[27] *Gesta*, p. 219: "... ecclesiarum bona quae abstulerat reddere; usuras omnes quas acceperat reddere; damna pauperum quos afflixerat resarcire; et castrum quoddam suum ... ab ipsis fundamentis evertere."

[28] For these see the Maurand family history in Part 3 below and especially the two original instruments of the "restoration" of the tithes at Launac, Castillon, and Valségur in Saint-Sernin 594 (10 32 4) and 599 (10 35 2) of which one is published in Douais, *Saint-Sernin*, No. 688, the "conscriptio" of both being dated January 1179.

The second action of 1178 indicative of the future was the employment of coercion against Peter Maurandus, and the linking of that use of force to an explosive mixture of ideas. Peter has the unhappy distinction of being the individual around whom clustered ideas that fused or confused the defense of the poor with the recuperation of tithes, linked the attack on heresy to that on usury, and joined these attacks to coercion by armed might, that is, to a "Roman war" or crusade.

Things moved rapidly after 1178. The third Lateran Council issued its well-known legislation against both heresy and usury in 1179. At the council, furthermore, Henry of Clairvaux, by then cardinal of Albano, was directed to lead a formally promulgated crusade against the heretics. This enterprise resulted in the capture of the town of Lavaur, not far from Toulouse, in 1181. There, Raymond of Baimiac and Bernard Raymond fell into Henry's hand, and, confronted by the lively persuasiveness of the sword, abjured their heresy and joined the ranks of the clergy, the former to be a canon of Saint-Sernin and the latter a canon at Saint-Étienne in Toulouse.[29]

In the meantime, local secular repressive law was also developing rapidly. In 1211, during the full flood of the Albigensian crusade, the consuls of Toulouse tried hard to show that they had always combated heresy. They referred to their enforcement of a law which they claimed had been promulgated by Raymond v, the count of Toulouse seen above.[30] It is probable, in fact, that, before his death in 1194, Raymond had issued a law ordering death and confiscation of property for heresy, and had therefore outpaced other fervid catholic princes in this matter.[31]

---

[29] Puylaurens, *Chronica*, pp. 28-30. Among others, Maisonneuve, *Origines de l'Inquisition*, pp. 132-135 has told us that the mixture of preaching and military action characteristic of 1181 was a stage in the transition from the preaching of Bernard to the warlike crusade of 1209.

[30] The consuls asserted in *HGL*, vol. 8, No. 161 "scientes preterito processu longi temporis dominum comitem patrem moderni comitis ab universo Tolose populo accepisse in mandatis, instrumento inde composito, quod si quis hereticus inventus esset in Tolosana urbe vel suburbio, cum receptatore suo pariter ad supplicium traderetur, publicatis possessionibus utriusque; unde multos combussimus, et adhuc cum invenimus idem facere non cessamus."

[31] Scholarship is inclined to doubt that the consuls or even the counts did anything in this direction, but such an action would fit with the evidence of the increasing severity of the law against heretics issued by the kings of Aragon whose richest domains were Catalonia, Roussillon, and Provence. There, in 1192, all punishments other than death and dismemberment were envisaged, and, in 1197, Peter ii added that of burning. The texts of the laws are available in G. Gonnet, *Enchiridion fontium Valdensium*, 1: 91-94. The reader will remember that this same Peter fought the crusaders, and died in the battle of Muret in 1213.

On the other hand, the consuls' claim is open to suspicion. The count meant much at Toulouse, it is true, but Raymond v's attempt to revive comital power had been transitory. He had regained his place in the early 1180s, but, in 1189, a renewed push by the leadership of Toulousan society severely weakened comital authority. The old county and town council or "capitulum" thereafter became the increasingly restive board of consuls, and, for two decades, Toulouse evolved in the manner of an Italian city republic. As was the case of its models, also, the town was beginning to move toward popular government. An example occurred in 1202 when new men pushed their way into the consulate, until then more or less dominated by a quasi-oligarchical group of families, some of which were of early twelfth century origins. This radical change, soon mitigated by compromises, may well have been initiated by the count, whose "populism" might have been inspired by his anger at the independence of the town's elite. If so, he was soon to be disabused, because, from 1202 to 1205, the popular consulate launched wars against twenty-three towns and villages of the Toulousain, clearly designing to conquer a "contado," the "patria Tolosana." [32] In short, Raymond v may have issued a law, but the free consulate would not have had to obey it.

Still, there must have been something in the statute books. In 1203, the consulate and a group of select worthies, possibly the consuls' small council, took oath against heresy to the legates Peter of Castelnau and Magister Radulf. In return for this, the legates agreed to uphold the laws and customs of the town. [33] Conflict was not slow to arise. Two years later, in 1205, the consuls defended what they called, probably correctly, a traditional town custom. It is well-known that one of the methods of pursuing heretics adopted by the church was to judge the dead for heresy, and then to disinter and burn the bodies of those who were adjudged to have died in the divergent faith. [34] Responding to this rather gruesome practice, the consuls ordered that, unless the individual suspect had been accused or given himself over to the heretics before his death, no deceased

---

[32] For these events, see my *Toulouse*, pp. 66-73.

[33] PAN, JJ 21, fol. 77r. The oath was taken in December 1203, and the act was written in March 1204. Other than the consuls, 16 other notables took the oath. After the oath of the citizens and consuls, the "prefati legati sua sponte concesserunt atque in perpetuum propter illud posse quod summus pontifex eis dederat confirmaverunt omnes illas libertates et omnia usatica et omnes illos mores qui in Tholosa erant vel constituti habebantur ullomodo antequam illa eis essent facta sacramenta et ne propter hec sacramenta libertates vel consuetudines sive usatiqua Tholose in aliquo ullo tempore lederentur vel minuerentur."

[34] Kolmer, *Ad capiendas vulpes*, pp. 129-130.

person could be accused.[35] It is obvious, therefore, that papal and other law was being received in the town,[36] but equally obvious that it was either not being enforced or actively prosecuted. In fact, until the largely ecclesiastical repression began in the 1230s, there is not a scrap of evidence to show that any heretic, dead or alive, had been burned at Toulouse.

Force, indeed, was not being applied, or not being applied sufficiently. Our familiar Peter Maurandus, we recall, was threatened and hastened to capitulate in order to save his life, but he was not thereafter pursued or watched. It is likely that the clergy assembled at Saint-Sernin in 1178 shed their "tears of joy" at his conversion in vain. It is all but certain that he returned to Toulouse after performing his penance – if, indeed, he ever went to the Holy Land – and resumed his normal life without grave harm. And since, as is clearly shown in the history of the Maurand family, his posterity was shot through with Catharism, it seems altogether improbable that he was converted from his gratifying status of being a Cathar "perfectus."

C. The Crusade against the Albigensians

The Cistercians had nevertheless come a long way from Bernard of Clairvaux's inconclusive preaching mission. A first step was the election of a Cistercian abbot, Fulk of Marseille, to the see of Toulouse in 1205.[37] Once at Toulouse, Fulk looked about for stronger medicine than that provided by the white monks from whose tradition he had derived. He fostered Dominic Guzmàn's mission there and thus prepared the ground for the largely Dominican-led Inquisition of the 1230s. The new bishop was also in close touch with the northern French church. He was a friend of James of Vitry, and an admirer of the early Beguines in the Low Countries.[38] He was influenced by the movement for the renewal of the

---

[35] TAM, AA 1 52 (March 1205): "... quod aliquis vel aliqua non possit accusari post mortem de heresi, nisi in vita accusatus esset aut infirmitate positus dedisset seipsum vel seipsam hereticis aut nisi moreretur in manibus hereticorum."

[36] The consuls certainly could not refuse to admit ecclesiastical law on this point (canon 27 of the third Lateran Council, Lucius III's *Ad abolendam* of 1184, and especially Innocent III's *Vergentis in senium* of 1197 carried in *Compilatio III* 5 4 1, and all in *X*. 5 7 8-10), but they could try to limit its effect because of the agreement of the legates on the custom of the town the year before.

[37] For Fulk's background, see Stronski, *Le troubadour Folquet de Marseille* (1910), and for the events in Toulouse my *Toulouse*, pp. 59-92. He had been abbot of the Cistercian house of Le Thoronet.

[38] The information about Fulk's connections with Vitry and the Beguines is outlined in R. Lejeune "L'évêque de Toulouse Foulques de Marseille et la principauté de

crusades and the polemic against the "violence" of the martial aristocracy and against the usury of businessmen published by the circle of Robert of Curzon, the Parisian master and papal legate.[39]

Soon after his election, Bishop Fulk saw to it that Toulouse "received" the canons against usury and put them into practice.[40] The only extant decision of the bishop's court against a usurer, Pons David, or against his heirs, the Hospitalers, was dated 1215, but there were other prosecutions, and charters containing promises by debtors not to sue their creditors before ecclesiastical courts tell us that usurers had been threatened with prosecution from at least 1211.[41] This information and much else, including a rent strike against the heir of the dead Pons David, tells us that Fulk had wedded the popular issue of usury to the attack on heresy. He was so successful at this, indeed, that Toulouse was much divided at the start of the crusade. Fulk had created an association called the White Confraternity to combat both heresy and usury. Headed by scions of the town's older aristocracy, two of whom were from one of the town's most seigniorial families, the Castronovo (Castelnau-d'Estretefons), this confraternity elicited much popular support in the most populous and industrial part of the town, the City. The organization set the two parts of the town against each other, and, in response to it, another confraternity, called the

---

Liège," in *Mélanges Félix Rousseau*, pp. 433-448, and the text *De B. Maria Oigniacensi* in the *Acta sanctorum* June vol. 5 [23 June], pp. 542-572.

[39] The principal persons in this matter were Curzon, Vitry, and, according to some, Stephen Langton. Matthew Paris, *Vita sancti Stephani archiepiscopi Cantuariensis*, in Liebermann, ed., *Ungedruckte Anglo-Normannische Geschichtsquellen*, pp. 327-328 tells how his hero Stephen cleansed Arras and Saint-Omer and parts of Flanders "iuvante eum [Stephanum] ... Roberto de Curcun, ... adeo usura eliminando usurarios persequebatur ... usum radicitum extirparet et regnum Francorum ab illa eluvie mirabiliter emundaret. Cuius sermones ... quas Dominus pro eodem archiepiscopo et magistro Roberto memorato necnon Iacobo de Vitriolo [*lege* Vitriaco!] ... qui legere desiderat, Librum additamentorum annalium que apud Sanctum Albanum sunt, adeat inspecturus."

[40] A celebrated papal letter of 11 November 1209 was addressed to the archbishop of Narbonne and his suffragans, who included Toulouse. The letter was against both heresy and usury, the second part dealing with the latter subject, recommending restitution as a cure. An original is reproduced and transcribed in Galabert, *Album*, fasc. 1, Plate I, 5, pp. xiii and 6, and publications are in *Layettes du Trésor*, No. 899 and PL. 216: 158 (Potthast 3828).

[41] For Pons David, see the David family history in Part 3 below. The text of the judgment of the episcopal court is published in my *Toulouse*, No. 15, pp. 208-209, but is marred by typographic errors: "Villamurensi" should read "Vilamurensis," and "apponentes quod" "apponentes et mandates quod." There is also evidence of another case before the episcopal tribunal, a case directed by Mascaronus, provost of the cathedral chapter and episcopal vicar, sometime between 1211 and 1221. For this, see my "Un usurier malheureux," in *Hommage à M. François Galabert*, pp. 123-125.

Blacks, arose to support the count and attack the bishop.[42] In an age when the corporate structure of the gilds was just about to make its appearance, this appeal to the older rich and to the mass of the humbler artisans and shopkeepers was bound to lead to popular support.[43] The linking of these themes, usury and heresy, were to be seen in the propaganda for the Albigensian crusade, a war that, launched in 1209, only affected the Toulousain two years later.[44]

The second step taken by the Cistercians was to wed their cause, and therefore, in effect, to lose control of it, to the crusade. Their final manifestation was another Cistercian abbot, Arnold Amalric, papal legate and ecclesiastical commander of the Albigensian crusade, soon to be elected archbishop of Narbonne. Proof of the fact that the campaign against heresy was becoming ever hotter is a celebrated, if unreliable, report about what this prelate is supposed to have said. When asked by the crusading soldiers to distinguish between the heretics and the Catholics after the capture of Béziers in 1209, he proposed killing them all lest the sources of infection escape. "God," he said, "will know his own." Save for Arnold, it matters little whether he really spoke those words; what counts is that our sole source, Caesarius of Heisterbach, was a Cistercian writing for Cistercians and obviously expected his anecdote to ring a clangorous bell.[45] And so it has, although not quite in the way the white monk hoped for.

Once launched, war and force took control. In the start, and somewhat persistently, there was strong support for the crusaders within Toulouse.

---

[42] According to Puylaurens, *Chronica*, p. 64, Bishop Fulk, in order "quod omnes ejus cives Tholosani ista que extraneis [crucesignatis] concedebatur indulgentia non carerent, utque per hanc devotionem eos ecclesie aggregaret, atque facilius per eos expugnaret hereticam pravitatem et fervorem extingueret usurarum ..., optinuit Tholose magnam fieri confratriam, confratres omnes consignans Domino signo crucis ...." Two of the leaders of Fulk's confraternity were the knights Almeric de Castronovo "iuvenis" and his brother Arnold, for whom, see the Castronovo family history in Part 3 below.

[43] Mary Ambrose [Mulholland], BVM, "Statutes on Clothmaking: Toulouse 1227," in *Essays in Medieval Life and Thought*, pp. 167-180 published the first extant statutes of a Toulousan industry. The document is marked by its solicitude for the entrepreneur's interests, but begins a tradition that will build gild corporatism during the thirteenth century.

[44] The references in Latin are too numerous to quote, but see a statement in the vernacular in the part of the *Canso* by William of Tudela that favored the crusader side: *Canso*, ed. Martin-Chabot, 1: 150 stating

> "e tuit li renoier le renou laicharan
> E si gazanh an pres tot primer lo rendran."

[45] *Dialogus miraculorum*, 5.21, ed. Strange, 1: 302. Arnold Amalric had been abbot of Cîteau.

Simon of Montfort's siege of Lavaur in 1211 provoked real division in the town. Fulk's White Confraternity actively supported the crusaders over there just to the east of Toulouse, sending both supplies and men. Count Raymond vi pleaded in vain against this aid, and despatched a force under his seneschal Raymond de Recaut to help the defense.[46] Later in the year, reinforced by his victory at Lavaur and perhaps hoping for aid from his supporters within the walls, Simon tried to take Toulouse itself by a coup-de-main. The townsmen fought. Fulk ordered his clergy to leave the town, and, with that act, Raymond's cause became the cause of Toulouse.[47]

Even after that, however, there were citizens who did not favour the count's or the southern side. We know that, when, in 1217, the southern side retook or "liberated" the town from the crusaders, not a few inhabitants joined the French in the Château Narbonnais, and others took refuge with the clergy in the episcopal palace and the Closes of Saint-Étienne and Saint-Sernin.[48] We hear of gentlefolk from the Toulousain serving on the crusader side, presumably because they were bound by their feudal service to Simon of Montfort once he had been legitimized as count of Toulouse at the fourth Lateran Council in 1215.[49] Later, during the siege of Toulouse in 1218, an heretical rural gentleman who rented a house in town at the Croix Baragnon, Estolt (Stultus) de Rocovilla, captured three footmen serving among the crusaders. Estolt sold his prisoners to the consuls, and, curiously, one of them later became a Cathar.[50] A public notary named Bernard de Podiosiurano (Pexiora) was forced to flee because of "collaboration" with the crusaders, but was

---

[46] For these events see Puylaurens, *Chronica*, pp. 64-70, and Vaux-de-Cernay, *Historia Albigensis*, 1: 216-220, 233, and 239-240.

[47] Vaux-de-Cernay, *Historia albigensis*, 1: 233, and referred to in a letter written by the provost Mascaron in September 1213, a letter published in an appendix to this history in ibid., 3: 200-205.

[48] Puylaurens, *Chronica*, p. 100: "cum Gallicis."

[49] See the case of Sicard de Montealto, lord of Montaut, who, having fought on Simon's side gallantly from 1216, was finally captured by the southerners at Baziège in 1219, and thereafter went with them. For him see note 57 below. Another is William Capelli (Capel) de Vesseriis (Bessières) who is seen below in the Gamevilla family history in Part 3 as a co-seignior of Bessières. When an aged man, he gave testimony in PAN J 305 32, fol. 8v (circa 1274) and there reported that he was "in dicta guerra cum Ricardo de Cornados, domino tunc de Ruppe Cesarea" (Roqueserière not far from Bessières to the northeast of Toulouse). According to the *Canso* 2: 273, Richard was a Norman from Tournedos. He was killed at La Salvetat-Saint-Gilles to the west of Toulouse trying to arrest the advance guard of the army of Raymond vi when that prince was coming to lead the town's revolt in September 1217.

[50] TBM MS 609, fol. 66v.

"reintegrated" after the signing of the Peace of Paris.[51] There is even the strange case of the two Pons Palmatas, one junior and one senior, one of whom was early condemned as a Cathar, and the other (or perhaps the same one?), for having failed to contribute to the taxes raised for the town's defense, whose property was consequently confiscated and sold.[52]

The violence of the struggle was such that force took precedence over persuasion. The great preachers of the age, the utopian papal legate Robert of Curzon and the unusually generous minded James of Vitry, whose encouragement of popular devotion had inspired Bishop Fulk of Toulouse with such hope, certainly enlisted some crusaders, but their intervention in the Midi won few souls. Not is this to be wondered at. If we are to believe the exemplars attributed to him, James was capable of believing that a man who claimed to be orthodox was heretical because he was physically unable to cross himself, and that heretical dualism could be simply confuted by saying that the orthodox clergy could summon forth the Holy Ghost![53] His colleague Robert likewise took time out from his arduous preaching and legatine schedule to burn a few Waldensians at Morlhon in 1214, a tactical victory, perhaps, but, given the fact that the Cathars were the main enemy and the Waldensians almost allies, a strategic error.[54]

Propaganda intensified the violence of the fighting. War crime stories were concocted, not a few being seen in the magnificent and polemical *Historia Albigensis* of Peter of Vaux-de-Cernay. One of these was the story about the "martyrs" of Montgey, a place not far from Castelnaudary on the way to Lavaur, where, in 1211, a force of crusaders was surprised unharnessed and massacred by the count of Foix. This may not have been chivalrous, but it was perfectly legal warfare, involving surprise, that is, "dolus bonus" as the jurists said. What is interesting about the tale is that

[51] Malta 1 116 contains an act of September 1213 which was in Bernard's materials, and which was written up by another notary on order of the consuls who remarked that Bernard had fled and was recognized "pro inimico domini ... comitis et totius ville Tolose." The terms of the Peace of Paris and the decrees of the papal legate Cardinal Roman "reinstituted" him as a citizen. See an act drawn by him in Malta 5 345 (June 1233).

[52] E 579 (published in *HGL*, vol. 8, No. 210), (December 1220). The taxes were raised "ad communem deffensionem." See the Palmatas under No. **15** in the amnesty in Chapter 5 below.

[53] For the occasional appearances of these two personages in the Midi during the crusade, see the index of Vaux-de-Cernay, *Historia Albigensis*. The "exempla" derive from Jacques de Vitry, *Exempla from the Sermones Vulgares*, ed. Crane, No. 26.

[54] See Peter of Vaux-de-Cernay, *Historia Albigensis*, 2: 208 where the crusaders burned seven Waldensians "cum ingenti gaudio."

it spread everywhere. Mary of Oignies, the noted Beguine near Liège, was outraged by this "crime," having probably heard of it from her friend James of Vitry, the famous preacher who later habitually carried one of her finger bones as a relic.[55] Nevertheless, there were examples of legality and justice in the midst of fighting. During the time of the crusaders' defeat before the intervention of the French monarchy, for example, a man who broke the truce and murdered a Frenchman was executed by public authority in the Lauragais just south of Toulouse.[56] Another example was that of Sicard, lord of Montaut, who was captured on the field of Baziège in 1219. In spite of having served Montfort since 1216, Sicard was preserved unhurt by his southern captors, an action that has much to do with the solidarity of the nobility, because one of his enemies at that engagement was William Unald, lord of Lanta, his brother-in-law.[57]

In spite of such moments of practical toleration, things were so bitter at Toulouse that, save for the few months of Montfort's occupation, Dominic Guzmàn's mission wavered. During the long years of conflict, although Dominic and his Toulousan disciple Peter Seilanus tried to carry on the work of persuasion right within the walls of Toulouse, the "dominus" and his brethren were clearly on the crusaders' side.[58] Dominic joined the crusaders at the first siege of Toulouse in June 1211

[55] Vaux-de-Cernay, *Historia albigensis*, 1: 217-218: "o rabies iniquorum ... o preciosa in conspectu Domini mors sanctorum !" For Mary of Oignies, see Lejeune's article cited in note 38 above.

[56] In Puybusque, *Généalogie Puybusque*, p. 18 and especially p. 26 we hear of a suit in 1244 over the inheritance of one Stephen Casals at Saint-Martin-de-Mauremont between Raymond de Podiobuscano and Arnold de Falgario (Le Fauga). Stephen had "murdered" a pilgrim, a crusader, that is, "quan le coms de Montfort era en treva ab le conte de Tolosa ... et dis hom que Carcasona fo desamparada per franceses ...."

[57] Puylaurens, *Chronica*, pp. 104-105 says that, in the rout of the host commanded by the notable Frenchmen, the brothers Fulk and John of Berzy, "dominus Sicardus ..., relevatus de campo ab amicis quos ibi habebat, in hostibus est eductus." And this, in spite of the fact that the Berzy brothers were considered to be war criminals by the southerners, and were eventually executed. In PAN J 323 70 (November 1222) the notable William Unaldus, lord of Lanta, made Sicard the principal executor of his testament, a fact of some interest when one realizes that the Unaud family was shot through with Catharism.

[58] Vicaire, *Dominique et ses prêcheurs*, p. 45, note 51, notes the conversion of Raymond William de Altaripa "pelleganterio" sometime before June 1215. As an example, see TBM MS 609 where a witness records a debate between Cellanus, a Toulousan himself, and some "perfecti" in Raymond Rotgerius "maior's" house in the parish of Saint-Sernin about 1215. Raymond was No. 17 in the amnesty in Chapter 5 below, and was known to be a "perfectus." Although Dominic was usually called a canon, as in Vicaire's text and that cited in the note below, he is termed "dominus frater" in the act of PAN, J 321 60 (partially published in *Layettes du Trésor*, No. 1118) in April 1215 in which Peter Seilanus' house, now known as the House of the Inquisition, near the Château Narbonnais constituted the "domus quam idem dominus Dominicus constituerat."

which must have vitiated his cause with many Toulousans. His brethren were with Simon at the siege in December 1217.[59] According to the depositions taken by the inquisitors from the small town and villages of the Lauragais in 1245/46, not a few of those converted by Dominic had relapsed into heresy or indifference.[60] It is true, of course, that, as we have seen, some Toulousans sided with the crusaders, and we may be sure that these had a bad time of it. Their cult was surely mocked, indeed, we are told that one heretic even voided his bowels next to the altar of a Toulousan parish church, and wiped himself with the altar cloth.[61] In spite of the Cathar aversion to physical violence, it seems likely that the "collaborators" were physically attacked and probably even suffered the loss of, or gained, one "martyr." [62] But, after 1211, the resistance of those who favoured "the party of the church" as against "the party of the count" – as a gaggle of aged Toulousans called them around 1274 [63] – was modest indeed. Even before that date about the only miracle recorded was in 1210 when the parish priest of the Dalbade saw crosses on the wall of his whitewashed church.[64] Given the fact that Béziers and Carcassonne had both fallen and the crusaders were about to begin the campaign that led them to Lavaur and Toulouse itself, one wonders why every citizen was not seeing crosses on walls.

Bishop Fulk, whose mission had begun at Toulouse with a real measure of popular support became an exile from much of his diocese, wandering about with armies and given to bitter stories and angry rejoinders,

---

[59] *HGL*, vol. 8, No. 611. During the siege of 1217 Count Simon, soon to die, took the "domos et res karissimi nostri fratris Dominici canonici" under his protection in a letter published in an appendix of the edition of Vaux-de-Cernay, *Historia Albigensis*, 3: 205.

[60] TBM, MS 609, fols. 5v and 20r-v where, of three women converted from heresy by the saint at Mas-Saintes-Puelles, two lapsed altogether, and one never bothered to wear her crosses; fol. 251r where a man from Castelnaudary reported that his parents were converted by Dominic around 1214, but that the mother subsequently relapsed and was burned; and fol. 252r where Pons Jaule of the same town stated that he was an heretic even before 1200, was later converted by Dominic, but lost his letter of remission. On Dominic's female religious house of Prouille, note that, on fol. 151v, a witness claims to have seen at Fanjeaux around 1220 "perfecti" being adored by two clerks and also by "Gausbertus capellanus comitis Montisfortis et Petrus Rotgerii de Pruliano conversus" !

[61] Vaux-de-Cernay, *Historia Albigensis*, 1: 37 tells us "quod [Hugo Faber] juxta altare cujusdam ecclesie purgavit ventrem et in contemptum Dei cum pallia altaris tersit posteriora sua. O scelus inauditum !"

[62] Ibid., 2: 308 says that this took place during the great siege that began late in 1217, and that an acolyte named Bernard Scriptor was slain by the mob. The story is possibly true, because, if "perfecti" never shed blood, "credentes" could and did. There was also a family named Scriptor (Scriba or Escrivan) at Toulouse.

[63] PAN, J 305 32.

[64] Vaux-de-Cernay, *Historia Albigensis*, 2: 163-165.

sometimes not without wit. Late in the war in 1227, when accompanying a royal force besieging Labécède in the Lauragais Fulk was told that the defenders were shouting that he was not their bishop, but rather the "bishop of devils." He replied "Right enough: they are the devils, and I am their bishop." [65] Earlier on, after the battle of Muret, the count's advisor and seneschal Raymond de Recaut wished to retire into the hospital called the Mainaderie, and, being a gentleman, to head it up, the bishop likened him to a murderer who came to collect some of the charity distributed by the executors of the victim's testament. When passed over, the fellow is supposed to have said: "Nothing for me? Me, who made it possible?" And, in many ways, Raymond was what Fulk most detested: the kind of tolerant "politique" so common in the Midi. The seneschal would have agreed with another southern gentleman who told Fulk that the local people could not crush the heretics "because we have been raised with them, have relatives among them, and see them live honestly." [66] Even those who are not known to have had any interest in heresy, but who refused to accept the decision of the Lateran Council that gave Toulouse to Simon of Montfort could themselves easily be embittered by the harshness of the struggle. William Raymond and his brother Aycard de Claustro (the Close of Saint-Sernin) suffered the destruction of their family home in the Bourg because they were "faiditi" or rebels when Simon of Montfort held the town. They also lost half the family farm of Fontanas, to the north of town, because, while the brothers waged the guerrilla against the crusaders, a sick cousin was forced by the war to become an oblate at Saint-Sernin at the cost of his half of the farm. In their lawsuit before the consuls, the brothers deliberately implied that the abbot of Saint-Sernin was a "collaborator." "Business is business," however, and the consuls favored the monastery's claim to the property.[67]

---

[65] Puylaurens, *Chronica*, pp. 125-126: "Utique, respondit ipse, et verum dicunt. Ipsi enim sunt diaboli, et ego episcopus sum illorum."

[66] Anent the bishop's story, see Puylaurens, *Chronica*, p. 93: "Annon, inquit, michi qui totum feceram erogabis?" The same source p. 48 tells the story of Ademar of Roudeille answering Fulk's complaint: "Non possumus [eos expellere]; sumus enim nutriti cum eis, et habemus de nostris consanguineis inter ipsos et eos honeste vivere contemplamur." The reader will note that many of the family histories seen in Part 3 below clearly illustrate this "tolerance," even those that involve a person noted for orthodoxy, such as Pons de Capitedenario.

[67] Together with a long document concerning the litigation between the brothers and the canons of Saint-Sernin over the farm, a piece describing life in Toulouse during the war, the history of this severely weakened family is to be read in my "The Farm of Fontanas at Toulouse," *BMCL* n.s. 11 (1981) 29-40.

I have remarked above that, once well begun, the war took over control. After their initial great defeats, especially that of Muret in 1213, and the momentary loss of the whole of western Languedoc to Simon of Montfort, what was, in effect, a conquest largely by northern French soldiers was stopped dead in its tracks by southern resistance. Toulouse rose against the crusaders in 1216, but failed. In the next year, however, the Rhone valley broke out against the French, and precipitated a new war, especially because of the successful weathering of a siege by Beaucaire. In September 1217, Toulouse rose again, thus beginning the siege of Toulouse by Simon of Montfort, the engagement in which this great soldier was slain. As the crusader position crumbled, losing Carcassonne and almost all of maritime Languedoc, Rome summoned again not only further pilgrims or crusaders from the north, but also offered advantageous terms to the French monarchy. Their other great feudatories, the Angevins of England and Atlantic France and the princes of the Champagne and Flanders, having weakened or been defeated, the Capetians were happy to intervene against the Toulousan house of Saint-Gilles. In spite of strong resistance, the Rhone valley speedily capitulated, and, after a long siege, Avignon also fell in 1226, causing the loss of all the domains of the house of Saint-Gilles except Toulouse and its immediate region. After two great sieges and a ruinous war that gutted the Toulousain, the French and their monarchy won the war, and the victory was recorded in the Peace of Paris of 1229. Although not alone enough to effect the end desired by the orthodox, the war was the essential foundation on which the rest of the structure of coercion was to be built. Direct persuasion of active Cathars having failed, force was successfully employed.

2

The Royal Amnesty of August 1279

A. From 1229 to the Amnesty of 1279

Although the business of this book is the repression of heresy, the reader is perceptive enough to recognize that this action was merely one aspect of manifold and many great social changes in this period. One of these was the slow but sure absorption of this region into an expanding France. At the Peace of Paris in 1229, maritime Languedoc had been organized into the royal seneschalsy of Beaucaire, and that of Béziers and Carcassonne, once ruled by the viscounts of the Trencavel house, into the seneschalsy of Carcassonne. A final attempt in arms by the Trencavels to regain their lost territories was easily snuffed out in 1240. In the meantime, a declining measure of the traditional southern autonomy was retained under the last prince of the local dynasty, Raymond VII, count of Toulouse. Stripped of much territory and of his ducal title of Narbonne, the turbulent life of this short-lived prince was filled with attempts to reverse the results of the lost war. His final defeat and humiliation at the hands of the Capetians in 1242-1243 was the death knell of southern independence, and his death in 1249 caused the provision of the Peace of Paris, which he had done so much to avoid, to come to pass. His county passed through his daughter to her husband, the Capetian brother of Louis IX, Alphonse, count of Poitiers and Toulouse. Except briefly in May 1251 at the beginning of his reign, Alphonse never visited Toulouse, but instead ruled it from the neighborhood of Paris, where he preferred to live. On his death in 1271, Languedoc and Toulouse fell to Philip III, king of France. Thereafter, with what consequences we shall touch on, Toulouse and the Toulousain were gradually subjected by the weightier power of northern France, and also invited to participate in what seemed to be the most successful monarchy of the age.

Along with this gradual movement went basic changes within southern France, in part everywhere, but especially marked in Toulouse. I have noted in the first chapter that from 1189 until 1229, the town seemed to be evolving in the manner of an Italian city republic. This similarity is especially noticeable when the somewhat aristocratic and oligarchical near monopoly of the board of consuls was broken by a "popular" party in 1202, and when an expansionist program began that would surely have led to the creation of a "contado" in the familiar Italian style, had not the great twenty-year war called the Albigensian crusade intervened. By 1229, however, the "republican" tradition had much to boast. Enlarging on traditional ambitions, the town government had in effect won the free election of the consulate, the appointment of the vicar (the count's officer in Toulouse and the vicarage around it) and his staff, the right to try all cases involving the physical and economic harm done to a Toulousan citizen, and freedom from all tolls on commerce in the domains of its count and those of several allied princes. As I long ago remarked, by 1229, the count of Toulouse might conceivably have won the war, but he would surely have lost Toulouse and most of the Toulousain to the inhabitants of his capital.[1]

This quasi-republican constitution fell apart, beginning to crumble right after the Peace of Paris. Motivated by a desire to rule his reduced territories efficiently in order to recover his power in Provence and maritime Languedoc, Raymond vii, "lo jove," the beloved hero of war-time Toulouse, attacked the old free consulate, reduced the size of that body by half, appointed its members not for the traditional yearly term, but for terms at his will, and created new courts to reinsert his authority between the town and the countryside. He also began to regain control of the mint of Toulouse, and to renew the power of the vicar, by seeing to it that the traditional appointment of vicars from among the citizenry of Toulouse itself was replaced by the appointment of foreigners. Under this active, if unhappy prince, the social policy that was to be carried forward under Alphonse of Poitiers was sketched. Raymond clearly favored the town's artisans over its patricians, and also tried to protect the rural seigniors and their communities from the power of his capital. It is true that, in the period from 1245 through 1248, Toulouse rose to invade at least one rural seigniory again, and reasserted with dying brilliance the freedom of consular elections.[2]

---

[1] For these events, see my *Toulouse*, p. 89.

[2] A few general observations on the general setting of the thirteenth century are to be seen in Wolff et al., *Nouvelle histoire de Toulouse*, pp. 119-181: "Reconversion et Maturation." Badly needing revision, there is a sketch history of the constitutional history up to the death of Raymond vii in my *Toulouse*, pp. 159-169.

Under his Capetian successor, surely one of the more successful absentee rulers known to history, all of these policies came to fruition. In the 1250s and 1260s a series of great conflicts between the prince and the consulate resulted in the nearly total defeat of the latter body. The count was wise enough not to fight the battle alone, but instead sought and found allies. One such ally was the rural interest, the seigniories and small towns of the countryside. The countryfolk gained protection from the greater economic power of the capital by being equipped with legal defenses. The mid-century saw the articulation of a system of rural "baillages" and judgeships, all sponsored by the prince.[3] A growingly widespread rural public notariate accompanied this advance.[4] The judges insisted that town citizens must answer before their jurisdictions, and that a local notary's act was to be as valid in a town court as that written by a public scribe of Toulouse. This was also complemented by the appearance and growth of local government, especially the rural consulates. Although most village consulates were not free from seignorial domination, there were some in small towns, such as l'Isle-Jourdain, that bear comparison with the institutions of Toulouse herself.[5]

The other useful ally of the prince was the popular party, the "populares" or "communitas popullarium Tholose," the urban plebeian element in short, together with its frequently non-plebeian leaders. The favor of the urban plebs was won by changes in the consulate. Half of that board was to be attributed to the "mediocres," and half to the "maiores." More consequential was the institution of a regular hearth tax based on a sworn and public evaluation of the means of each citizen.[6] Along with this, the prince's government favored legal professionalism over the informal jurisprudence that had characterized the older partly arbitrative system of the consuls and their appointed sworn judges. Among the few advantages of this multiplication of lawyers and judges was the teaching of Roman and canon jurisprudence at the newly founded university of Toulouse,[7] and the requirement, following the precepts of Roman law,

---

[3] The basic work still remains Boutaric, "Organisation judiciaire du Languedoc," *BEC* 16 (1855) 200-230 and 532-560, and 17 (1856) 97-122. See also the excellent introduction of Fournier and Guébin, eds., *Enquêtes d'Alphonse de Poitiers*.

[4] On the yet to be studied rural notariate, see my "Village, Town, and City," in *Pathways to Medieval Peasants*, ed. Raftis, pp. 162-163. For the public notary of a large village or small town such as Bessières on the Tarn river, see note 13 in the Gamevilla family history in Part 3 below.

[5] See pp. 163-166 in my "Village, Town, and City."

[6] An initial statement of the development of a tax system is to be found in Wolff, "*Estimes*," pp. 23-42.

[7] See especially H. Gilles, "L'enseignement du droit en Languedoc au xiiie siècle," *CdeF* 5 (1970) 204-229.

that the poor and disadvantaged were to be provided with legal representation.

The results of these changes are almost self-evident. As a witness at an inquiry in the 1270s remarked, Alphonse of Poitiers' consuls were merely his officers ("officiales"). The number of the old board was halved, the consuls themselves being appointed by the prince. During this time, also, the power of the vicar and of his newly constituted court as well as that of the seneschal (the provincial governor, a office revived in Alphonse's time) and his tribunal grew by leaps and bounds, both bodies offering an appellate jurisdiction at the expense of the ever weaker consular board. Paralleling the emergence of a renewed princely or monarchical government was the splitting up of the once unified social fabric of the town into three sharply demarcated social groups, a true nobility, a class of bourgeois notables, and the plebs. "Divide et impera" was as good a rule then as it is now. Accompanying this weakening of Toulousan "republicanism" was an age of great economic growth and expansion, marked not only by growing trade, but also by the multiplication of gild and artisan organizations.

This introductory sketch is not yet complete. It was noted above that Count Raymond VII appointed the "first" non-Toulousan vicar. Under Alphonse, things were even darker from the Toulousan point of view. Although he had a southern party composed of persons such as Sicard Alaman who stood in for him in these parts at the beginning of his reign and was also the "locum tenens" for an absent seneschal in 1268-1270, almost all of Alphonse's appointments to the grades of vicar and seneschal, and most of his clerks or emissaries were northern Frenchmen, appropriately enough, largely from the region around Paris where he himself lived. With one exception, all of his vicars were from that area, and, save the "locumtenens" Sicard mentioned above, all of his seneschals. The French had come to rule the Midi.[8]

A not dissimilar picture is seen in regard to the repression of heresy. Here I shall not review the institutional history, partly because others have already done so, and partly because the same events will be remarked on later in this monograph.[9] It is known that serious repression

---

[8] The history of the vicar has yet to be elucidated, but that of the clerks and seneschals is studied in Fournier and Guébin, eds., *Enquêtes d'Alphonse de Poitiers*, pp. xxxiv-xlv and lxxvii-lxxxvii.

[9] The useful general survey of the repression is Thouzellier "La répression de l'hérésie et les débuts de l'Inquisition," in *Histoire de l'église*, 10: 291-340. The specialists of the Inquisition itself are Dossat, *Inquisition*, Wakefield, *Heresy, Crusade and Inquisition*, and Kolmer, *Ad capiendas vulpes*.

began with the Council of Toulouse convoked in November 1229 by the papal legate, Roman, cardinal deacon of Sant'Angelo.[10] Appointed by a papal letter of April 1233, inquisitors chosen from the Dominicans joined and partly took over the prosecution of heretics in Toulouse. Although these specialists often shared this field with the local clergy, the abbot of Saint-Sernin, for example, a parish priest, the ordinary, and sometimes with papal legates, they were the ones who elicited the greatest fear and detestation on the part of their "victims." This enmity led, in Toulouse, to the ejection of the Dominicans and the inquisitors from the town in 1235. At that time, there is some evidence of a division of minds in Toulouse, and one suspects that plebeian elements of the population were not as exercised against them as were the middle and upper classes that governed the town. The defeat of this effort of the town government, and the return of the Dominicans in April 1236 set the stage for a renewal of the inquisitorial effort which continued vigorously into 1237.

Thereafter came a break in the activity of the inquisitors from 1238 to 1241. Clearly ordered by the pope, Gregory IX, the reason for this hiatus is complex, involving the conflict between the pope and the Emperor Frederick II and the role of Raymond VII in that rivalry.[11] Since the count was involved here on the side of the pope, his opposition and that of the well-to-do of his principal city to the Dominican Inquisition meant much. The new legate had already been moved to ease the severity of the punishments, and, since the Dominicans were especially feared because of their rigidity, a Franciscan, Stephen of Saint-Thibéry, was added to the inquisitorial corps.[12] And there is little doubt that the Dominican Peter

---

[10] The history of this legislation is: the legate's arrival was announced to the count of Toulouse in a papal letter of January 1224 published in *HGL*, vol. 8, No. 228 iv. After summoning a council at Bourges and arranging for the clerical tithe to go to the crown, the cardinal accompanied Louis VIII on his victorious campaign against the southern French. Following the army, he was present at the siege and capture of Avignon in 1226 and then went over into Languedoc. He was in Paris in April 1229 when Raymond VII made his submission and signed, so to speak, the Peace of Paris. In November 1229 the cardinal convoked the council of Toulouse, and was at Avignon on his way back to Italy in December of that year (*HGL*, vol. 8, No. 314). In PBN, Doat 21, fol. 737r (around 1234), Peter Major, the archdeacon of Narbonne, dated an event as happening "eo tempore, quo fiebat inquisitio generalis apud Tholosam de mandato domini Romani apostolice sedis legati inter barones qui suspecti erant de haeresi."

[11] See Kolmer, *Ad capiendas vulpes*, pp. 145ff. on this period, and note the pertinent passage in Puylaurens, *Chronica*, p. 159 stating that "per litteram quocumque modo extractam de curia [Romana] mansit diu inquisitio in suspenso."

[12] Puylaurens, *Chronica*, pp. 152-154. The legate was the archbishop of Vienne, John of Bernin, who began in July 1233. His idea was to assign "penitencie tolorabiles" to those who came in on time, so to speak. "Adhuc quia predicatores magis ut rigidiores timebant, de fratrum minorum ordine collega additur qui videretur rigorem mansuetudine temperare."

Seillanus, a Toulousan citizen and the son and grandson of persons who had served as vicars of Toulouse, was a hard and driving inquisitor.[13]

The break was soon over, however, and the hunt was renewed in 1241. In the next year, the inquisitors had apparantly got so close to the jugular that they, including the unlucky Franciscan Stephen, were massacred at Avignonet to the south of Toulouse. This event helped stir the orthodox to raise an army that, in 1244, captured the last stronghold inhabited by Cathars, the fortress of Montségur in the foothills of the Pyrénées. Success led to excess. In 1248 the inquisitors condemned 156 inhabitants of Limoux to wear the cross. This judgement provoked the intervention of Innocent IV who annulled their action. Piqued, the inquisitors set everybody free, so that the pope placed the matter in the hands of the archbishop of Narbonne, and, in 1249, reorganized the inquisitorial institution by placing the inquisitors directly under the general of the order. The final change came with Alphonse of Poitiers' rule in Toulouse. In 1255 it was arranged that the inquisitors were no longer to be appointed from the Dominican mother house in Toulouse, but instead from Paris. The French became the inquisitors.[14]

This final event gives us an opportunity of examining the widely held southern French view that it was Alphonse and his northerners who were responsible for their sorrows. There is some truth here. The Albigensian war installed the northern French in the seneschalsies of Beaucaire (maritime Languedoc) and Carcassonne. The northerners also dictated the Peace of Paris whose terms, in spite of every effort on the part of Raymond VII, resulted in the unification of the county of Toulouse to France. Nor is that all. The threatening presence of the French in the southland was one of the reasons why, after 1229, Raymond VII and his supporters tried so hard to create a more coherent and centralized state than that which had existed before the war. In spite of these facts, it is evident that the basic changes in the social and political constitution of Toulouse had begun before the extinction of the line of Saint-Gilles, and must, therefore, be regarded as initiatives of largely southern French

---

[13] Pelisson, *Chronicon*, p. 100 reports that, in the late 1230s when Peter was chosen as an inquisitor, the count went to the legate, the archbishop of Vienne, and complained, "dicens etiam quod frater Petrus Cellani, qui fuerat de curia patrum suorum et civis Tholosanus modo, erat inimicus eius, et impetravit a legato, quod de cetero non esset dictus frater Petrus inquisitor in dyocesi Tholosana, sed tantum in Caturcinio," that is, in that of Cahors to the north. The most recent discussion of this quiescent period is in Kolmer, *Ad capiendas vulpes*, p. 145.

[14] Dossat, *Inquisition*, pp. 184-185, after protracted negotiations, including a papal attempt to give the burden to the Franciscans.

origin. The same may be said, and even more forthrightly, in regard to the repression of Catharism. The names of Peter Seillanus and William Pelisson, both Toulousans, are antonomastic of the great repression.

B. THE AMNESTY OF 1279

In view of this, it is curious to report that the persons who eventually issued the document that signalled the end − for a time − of the pursuit of heresy were "Gallici" who had spent their lives in the chase, as well as in other governmental activities. The model of this type of officer is Giles Camelini, the principal intermediary between Toulouse and the crown in 1279.

Giles began his career under Alphonse of Poitiers and continued in the service of his royal successor.[15] This clerk busied himself with the properties of heretics, dead or alive. In entries ranging from 1268 to 1270, Alphonse of Poitiers' correspondence shows him carrying money to Paris from the sale of confiscated properties, investigations as to whether the heirs of heretics had circumvented the law under Raymond VII, repurchases by individuals of property confiscated from their heretical forbears, complaints by individuals and by the citizens of Toulouse about Giles' heavy hand, and orders to him to assist the Genoese financier William Boccanegra recoup from the property of heretics what he was owed by the count.[16] Alphonse was also kind enough to assign Giles the property of the heretic Raymond of Lavaur.[17] From 1271 to 1274 he was "procurator regis" in suits against the heirs of heretics at Toulouse.[18] By the time of the amnesty of 1279 he was titled master and canon of Meaux, serving again as a royal proctor. His later career was distinguished. From 1281 to 1291 he was a judge in the king's court of "parlement," alternating between Toulouse and Paris, and was once gratified by having a southern French notable, the count of Astarac, fined for having maligned him.[19]

At the time of the commencement of direct royal government at Toulouse, a period when the consuls tried to reassert again the ancient

---

[15] Giles first appears in June 1267 as a clerk in the service of Alphonse in Molinier, *Correspondance ... d'Alphonse de Poitiers*, Nos. 159 and 162.

[16] For these references, see the index under Aegidius Camelini in Molinier, *Correspondance ... d'Alphonse de Poitiers*, and also *Layettes du Trésor*, vol. 4, No. 5600 (November 1269).

[17] PBN, Doat 22, fol. 57-59 (January 1269).

[18] PAN, KK 1228.

[19] For these stages in his career, see *HGL*, vol. 10, Nos. 53 and 69; Boutaric, ed., *Olim*, vol. 1, No. 507; and Roschach, *Inventaire*, 1: 28 for TAM, AA 3 154.

liberties and privileges of the town that had been eroded under Raymond vii and Alphonse of Poitiers, royal policy seems to have offset the town's claims by threatening to exploit the possibilities of old royal legislation to the fullest. The law involved was called "Cupientes," a constitution of Louis ix, which, it may be recalled, had been addressed to the royal domain, especially the seneschalsies of Beaucaire and Carcassonne, and had not been applied in the county of Toulouse, then, in 1229, under Raymond vii.[20] Nor did it apply there under his successors Alphonse of Poitiers. When the crown's government took over in 1271, the idea of enforcing this law in the Toulousain must have seemed to the royal officers a God-given opportunity to wring the tails of the Toulousan fat cats to the profit of the fisc. The necessary orders came from Paris. A royal letter of November 1273 instructed the judges Thomas of Paris and Fulk of Laon to enforce "Cupientes," and these judges straightway initiated a series of lawsuits against those who detained the property of onetime heretics.[21] A partially destroyed register contains the record of thirteen cases prosecuted by Giles, pleading before Master Thomas and Fulk of Laon from April 1272 to January 1274. In this litigation, the right to possess property once owned by heretics was attacked in the cases of eight non-Toulousans, the bishop of Toulouse, and four citizens.[22]

This policy excited great resistance, partly because it ruined the attempt of Toulouse's consuls to reassert the town's liberties at the start of the new royal administration, thus reminding historians how princely government could use two very different policies, the rejection of the town's freedoms and the prosecution of heresy, to distract the aim of those often quite different groups and persons who favored either heresy or urban self-government. Anent heresy, the consuls militated against Giles' attempt to revive condemnations stemming from the days of Cardinal Roman, forty-

---

[20] The royal edict or constitution "Cupientes" was issued on 13 or 14 April 1229 according to *HGL*, 7: 73-74. It was issued for the kingdom, and is not the first secular legislation ordering confiscation for heresy. Note, for example, the case of Peter Maurandus and the subsequent law in Toulouse and Catalonia-Aragon mentioned in Chapter 1 above.

[21] Roschach, *Inventaire*, vol. 1 on TAM, AA 3 120. Master Thomas of Paris, once a canon of Paris in *Layettes du Trésor*, No. 5393 (dated 1268), was then a canon of Rouen, and Fulk of Laon (Lauduno) was the archdeacon of Ponthieu in the diocese of Amiens.

[22] PAN, KK 1228. The suits against layfolk in Toulouse involved the inheritances of Peter de Esquivo, Comdors, the wife of a Rouaix, Hugh de Roaxio, Bernard Signarius, Arnold de Villanova, Alaman de Roaxio, Raymond Johannes, and Peter Ramundus "maior." All of these persons were mentioned in the amnesty of 1279. For these and all those who follow, see Chapters 5 and 6 below, the latter providing an alphabetical index for the former. Chapter 5 will direct the reader to the appropriate family history in Part 3.

four years before, and their representatives reminded the crown that many of those condemned had long since made their peace with the church and local secular authority.[23] They also tried to seem more orthodox than the inquisitors themselves, and even had the brass to request that persons who could be shown to be heretics should not be imprisoned or sent on pilgrimage, but instead burned.[24] Since both of the consuls who presented the petition came from families notable for their commitment to Catharism in the past, one suspects that the consuls were so forthcoming probably because there were no heretics to speak of anymore.[25]

Because there were no heretics, also, we may be sure that "Cupientes" seemed like confiscatory taxation to Toulousans. We may likewise remember that these prosecutions occurred at a moment when the whole relationship of this town and province with the crown was being negotiated, and not merely in the sense of the initial consular demands of 1271. The negotiations involved the basic customs of the town (finally issued in 1286), relations with the clergy and rural nobility especially in regard to the taxation of citizen nobles and the acquisition of so-called noble fiefs by townsmen, Toulouse's trade privileges, and the liberties of the town government and consulate. It is also certain that, probably for reasons having to do with the crown's Pyrenean ambitions and the necessary security of its base at Toulouse in the past wars with Navarre and Foix and the future ones with Castile and Catalonia-Aragon, the need for a general settlement of issues dividing the town from the royal government was keenly felt even at Paris. Toulouse was never really to regain its onetime freedom, but it was to become a privileged town in the monarchy.

The result, to speak here only about heresy, was that on 20 March 1279, in a document drawn up at Toulouse, a group of 120 male and

---

[23] See, as an example, Raymond Rogerius "minor," No. **81** in the list published in Chapter 5 below. The same must certainly have been true of the Castronovo (Castelnau-d'Estretefons) family whose members are Nos. **2**, **3**, **134**, and **135**.

[24] TAM, II 61 (undated), but specifically mentioning Giles and the judges Master Thomas and Fulk of Laon: "Item petunt quod heretici et illis creditores et adherentes postquam illos tales esse constiterit quod, omni occasione postposita et absque immuracione vel crucis importacione, ipso facto comburantur ubique invenientur in comitatu Tholose."

[25] The two consuls who presented the petition were Arnold de Castronovo (Castelnau-d'Estretefons), a knight standing for the City, and Raymond de Castronovo (Curtasolea) for the Bourg who were in office in 1273-1275. I exaggerate in relation to Arnold because only four of the Castronovo (Castelnau-d'Estretefons) family were condemned, but the Curtasolea have at least five, Nos. **12**, **13**, **92**, and **140-143**. For these clans, see Part 3 below.

female citizens, either representing absent members of their own families or acting as tutors and guardians of other persons, met together with Giles Camelini, clerk of Meaux and proctor of the king in the seneschalsy of Agen and Toulouse, before William, abbot of Belleperche, Peter, dean of Saint-Martin of Tours, and Master John of Puiseux, canon of Chartres, clerks of the king in the same seneschalsy charged with protecting the rights of the crown.[26] It was there agreed that the matter should be submitted to the crown, and, to effect that end, twenty-six proctors were appointed by the citizens to petition the king.[27] The importance of this document is shown by the fact that it was sealed by Giles Camelini, the consuls of Toulouse, and the royal seal used in the seneschalsy and vicarage of Toulouse.

Further information about these negotiations is scanty and derives from the first three instruments copied in a large roll containing copies of many documents designed to show the ancient liberties of the town of Toulouse.[28] We there learn that the consuls petitioned the royal government to cease prosecuting the citizens and the university of the town because of heresy and other crimes or because of the acquisition of military fiefs by citizens. Dated sometime after 20 March and before the amnesty of 1279, this petition was read to the king at Paris. The prince acceded to the request of his loyal subjects and ordered the publication of a "litera compositionis" between the crown and its citizens of Toulouse. The third and final act dealing with the business at Paris in 1279 is a patent letter wherein the king confirmed Toulousan citizens in their

---

[26] PAN, J 313 95 (20 March 1279). William Gaufredi of Belleperche had been earlier called to administrative duty as we see in Molinier, *Correspondance ... d'Alphonse de Poitiers*, No. 1598, January 1273. The dean, Peter, had served as a judge and investigator in southern and central France in 1277 and 1280, for which see *HGL*, vol. 10, Nos. 21, 29, 29 vii, 141, 168, and 170, and he was a judge in the "parlement" of Paris in Boutaric, ed., *Les Olim*, No. 1284 in March 1283. John of Puiseux [Puteolis] had been in the service of Alphonse of Poitiers before entering that of the king. A "mestre Jehan de Puiseux prestre" had been a witness at Alphonse's testament in *Layettes du Trésor*, No. 5712 in June 1270. According to Fournier and Guébin, eds., *Enquêtes d'Alphonse de Poitiers*, p. xli, John was in Toulouse in 1279.

[27] Of the original 26 proctors, only one, Raymond Johannes "major," was not listed among the petitioners. This may have been by inadvertence because Raymond Johannes was mentioned as having property in the hands of the bishop in a lawsuit with the crown in PAN, KK 1228, ff. 58rff. (dated October 1273 to January 1274), the suit being directed against the bishop. On the other hand, there was nothing very formal about the naming or even about the powers of the proctors. Two of the 15 present at Paris, for example, although among the original petitioners, were not among the original 26 proctors. For the proctors and petitioners, see Chapter 6 below.

[28] For the dating and diplomatic of TAM II 63 i see the introduction to Chapter 5 below. See the same for the other copy of the amnesty in TAM, AA 34 3.

possession of military fiefs if legitimately acquired, and specified that those who had acquired property prior to the past twenty years were to be protected from molestation and injury by prelates and other ecclesiastics as well as by the local royal officers, namely the seneschals, vicars, and justiciars. The king also promised to review the privileges of the consulate.

Interlarded in this roll between the consuls' petition and the act of enforcement with its promises described at the end of the last paragraph stands Philip III's diploma of amnesty. It tells us that, the petitioners having thrown themselves on the king's grace, the prince had seen fit to act of his mercy. The amnesty removed all threats to the inheritances or successions of Toulousan citizens who were under investigation by Giles Camelini before the royal clerks and judges named above. Starting with those whose penances had been enjoined by Cardinal Roman, legate of the Holy See, right at the end of the Albigensian crusade in 1229, these citizens were those guilty of heresy or other kinds of crime entailing confiscation up to the time the county had fallen to the crown.[29] The document then went on to specify the condemnations and confiscations promulgated by the inquisitors of heretical pravity and other judges between the early days of Cardinal Roman and those of the 1270s mentioned above.[30] It then proceeded to refer to sentences promulgated by the royal clerks Master Fulk of Laon and the onetime Thomas of Paris, and promised that there would be no further pursuits based on the constitution of Louis IX called "Cupientes." [31] Those persons who, or whose predecessors, had suffered the punishment of having their houses torn down were granted the license to rebuild. Lastly, since other royal French legislation than "Cupientes" may have been involved here, Toulousan citizens were exempted from surrendering the military fiefs they had acquired twenty or more years previously.

The amnesty then turned to designate what its compilers thought was a complete list of those guilty of heresy and other crimes. After a brief

[29] TAM, II 63 ii and TAM, AA 34 3: confiscations made "occasione penitentie dicti legati aut heresi, homicidio, falso, furto aliove crimine seu ex quacumque causa alia vel occasione propter que et quas dicte hereditates, res, et bona dictorum civium venerit vel venisse potuerint in comissum usque ad tempus quo possessio comitatus Tholose post mortem clare memorie Alfonsi patrui nostri, quondam comitis Pictavie et Tholose, ad nos noscitur pervenisse ...." For the general context of this and the following passages, see the full text published in Chapter 5 below.

[30] Ibid.: a reference involving the property "civium predictorum qui penitentiam a dicto legato dicuntur habuisse seu condempnatorum per inquisitores heretice pravitatis vel alios quoscumque judices vel fugitivorum per causis seu criminibus supradictis ...."

[31] Ibid.: "pretextu illius constitutionis que incipit 'Cupientes'."

reference to the thirteen representatives of the town who had appeared at Paris, the document listed approximately 278 names.[32]

It has been remarked above that the act of 1279 was part of a general settlement between the crown and town, and it may be added that what applied to Toulousan citizens individually also applied to Toulousan ecclesiastical institutions. In August of the same year, an agreement was reached between our familiar Giles Camelini and the abbot of the monastery of the canons-regular of Saint-Sernin before the royal auditors William of Belleperche, Peter of Tours, and Master John of Puiseux, and was confirmed by a royal diploma.[33] In September a similar diploma settled the controversies between Giles and the bishop of Toulouse.[34] Curiously, it was the episcopal act that came to be known to later Toulousan historians as "La Philippine" instead of the great diploma of August described above. Perhaps persons of the generation of La Faille, having the experience of crushing Protestantism and the "dragonnades," did not like to be reminded that their forbears had also been heretics.

C. The Contents of the Diploma

As noted above, the diploma of 1279 was intended to give a complete enumeration of those whose property was confiscated because of involvement in heresy or other crimes. It has also been seen above that Toulousans were interested in protecting their past acquisitions of military or noble fiefs. Are, in short, some of the persons mentioned in our diploma those who had been condemned because of the acquisition of knightly fiefs? Master John Dominici, one of the proctors sent by Toulouse to Paris in 1279 to arrange the final settlement was in fact a person interested in protecting recently acquired rural property. A notary, jurisconsult, wine merchant, and purveyor or creditor of the lords of l'Isle-Jourdain, John is seen from 1251, especially in regard to his acquisition of a substantial part, if not the whole of, the fief of Gémil not

---

[32] See Chapter 5 below, and also the alphabetical index in Chapter 6. As the reader will see when consulting the numbered list, there are various unnamed siblings included in it, and such unnamed and unnumbered persons consequently prevent one from giving an assured total.

[33] Saint-Sernin 600 (10, 42, 2) (August 1279), in a vidimus of October 1280.

[34] Published in La Faille, *Annales*, vol. 2 in the part of the book entitled "Recueil de plusieurs pièces concernant les fiefs ...," pp. iii-iv. La Faille skipped a line which has been transcribed by Roschach in his *Inventaire*, 1: 58 where he reports on an original of the act in TAM, AA 4 18.

far from Montastruc-la-Conseillère to the northeast of Toulouse.[35] This inhabitant of the Bourg was therefore vitally interested in laws prohibiting town dwellers from acquiring rural property or penalizing them for having done so.[36] Our evidence about this point is complicated, however, by the fact that John was the child of a Peter Dominicus who lived in the early thirteenth century and was dead by 1259.[37] This Peter may well have been related to a heretic named Pons Dominicus mentioned in the amnesty of 1279 and known to have been condemned in 1246.[38]

Whatever John Dominicus' motives, the issue of the acquisition of noble land by commoners had no significance for the 278-odd persons at the time they were condemned. This is proved by the introduction to the amnesty itself. The inheritances relieved of the threat of confiscation have a prescription period of twenty years. No person there enumerated, therefore, was condemned for any action after 1259. What is more, the acquisition of military and noble fiefs was hardly an issue until after the death of the last count of the line of Saint-Gilles, Raymond vii, in 1249. It was only during the reign of his successor, Alphonse of Poitiers, that a system of fines or taxes levied by the government on those who had recently acquired noble property, especially ecclesiastics, began to be structured.[39] In brief, noble land was mentioned in the amnesty simply because some of the condemned persons had acquired what was later so considered.

[35] E 286 (May 1251), as a notary. *Calendar of the Patent Rolls*, April 1269, describes a John Domingi of Toulouse as busy in the wine trade with Bordeaux and England. Most of the information about John derives from PAN, J 328 1, a roll concerning John's acquisitions of the fief of Gémil. John's first acquisition is No. xix of June 1256, in which, incidently, he was called "Magister" for the first time. Actions favoring John's acquisition and possession of the fief of Gémil taken by the ordinary judge of Toulouse, the seneschal of that county, and the vicar and subvicar of that city from November 1253 to June 1261 are found in Nos. xx, xxiv, xxvi, xxvii, and xxviii of the Gémil roll. One may doubt, however, that John had gained complete possession of Gémil by 1279. Dossat, *Saisimentum*, under November 1271 shows that this place was still or again in the possession of the crown.

[36] In MADTG, A 297, ff. 549v and 552r (respectively dated December 1287 and January 1288), we learn that Helis, widow of Magister John Dominici "jurisperitus," living on the "carraria maior prope ecclesia Sancti Saturnini" and her son William Dominici, still in tutelage, were collecting debts owed by the lords of l'Isle-Jourdain. That John had more than one heir is seen in Saint-Bernard 38 (August 1293) where property at Lalande owned by his heirs is mentioned, and we also see the above mentioned son William described as the son of the dead Jehan Dominici, in E 436 (October 1296).

[37] Malta 1 19 (July 1211) for Peter Dominicus as a witness, and Grandselve 9 (October 1259), in a charter written by our notary and jurisconsult John, where we see John's brother William Dominicus, son of the deceased Peter Dominicus. PAN, J 328 1 xxii (May 1254) describes John as the son of Peter Dominicus.

[38] See No. **233** in Chapter 5 below.

[39] See the long article on this subject by Guébin, "Les amortissements d'Alphonse de Poitiers."

It also seems probable that all the 278-odd deceased persons listed in 1279 were onetime heretics. Of those listed there, as we shall see, some 157 were condemned by February 1237. This is our earliest group, and the one for which we have the least reliable evidence. Of this group, we know that approximately 40 percent were either condemned heretics (13 percent), or were known or probable heretics, leaving, as is evident, the majority unidentified. It is worth recording, however, that of the 157 persons, there are heretics and condemned heretics running from the first to the 153rd in the list. There is, moreover, no visible pattern among those whose heresy cannot be ascertained, the largest bloc of which contains thirteen persons in sequence.[40] The next group is 38 in number, of which about 87 percent are identified as involved in heresy and condemned for it in 1237.[41] Of the third group totalling fifty-seven individuals, the majority of whom were condemned in 1246-1248, approximately 86 percent were heretical.[42] In the final portion of the diploma, 26 persons are listed. Among these, the percentage of those either condemned (15 percent) or heretical sank to about 35 percent. Here again, as in the earliest group discussed above, however, there are heretics and condemned heretics listed in the start of the group up to No. 276 of the whole sample of 278. In fine, the composition of the list makes it seem likely that all the persons therein listed were involved in heresy.

Other arguments support this case. We saw above that about 60 percent of the first 157-odd persons cannot be shown to have been interested in divergent thought, and it may therefore be conjectured that a substantial number of them were individuals who resisted the occupation of Toulouse by the crusaders and the subsequent Peace of Paris in 1229. There is, however, no evidence that anybody rebelled against the Peace except when the count of Toulouse himself contested it in the 1240s, in which action, it may be remembered, the town was not involved. On the other hand, those who resisted Simon of Montfort's earlier occupation of the county and town of Toulouse have left records showing that, as "faiditi" or rebels, their property was confiscated and their houses destroyed, just as were those of condemned heretics. The two who can be shown to have suffered this penalty, William Raymond de Claustro and his brother Aycard whom we have seen above, are not listed in the

---

[40] The list is contained in Chapter 5 below, and the largest unidentified group of persons is numbered **70** through **80**.

[41] Nos. **158-195** of the list, all but the last four of whom were surely condemned, as will be seen below, from February to September 1237.

[42] Nos. **196-252** of the list.

diploma of 1279, however, and hence it seems unlikely that "faiditi" were included in it.[43]

Another serious question is whether the diploma of 1279 amnestied individuals guilty of grave criminal offenses not linked to heresy. This seems most unlikely. As we have seen, 120 citizens petitioned the crown in the act of 20 March 1279. Their supplication was buttressed by a corresponding petition of the consuls of Toulouse sometime after that month. Finally, 23 notables appeared at Paris to receive the gracious response of the sovereign in August of that year. It is hardly likely that these worthies were supplicating for common criminals. Some may perhaps opine that heresy, a crime against God, was considered by men of this period to be far worse than any crime against man, however violent. This opinion not only seems inherently unlikely, but also contradicts the available evidence about contemporary attitudes. In the 1270s, we see a Toulousan woman, the wife of a carpenter from Limoux, whose father had been burned for heresy. According to the witness, the man had been condemned because he refused to kill a chicken when ordered to by the Dominicans. Whatever the truth, the family clearly blamed the church for an "unjust" death, and protected the memory of its deceased member against the charge of heresy.[44] In brief, it seems sure that, although doubts may have been lodged in their minds, the heirs and successors of heretics would not confess in public that their ancestors had been guilty of a crime so great that it not only involved death but also the loss of all family property.

A final question is whether the diploma gives a fairly complete enumeration of those whose property was confiscated because of involvement in heresy. That it was intended to be complete, there is no doubt. Proof of this is the inclusion in the diploma of Raymond Rogerius "minor" in spite of the fact that he had been forgiven by the pope as early as 1238.[45] Still, any long list of this kind, medieval or modern, is likely to be imperfect, and it is sure that this one was. There may be, for example,

---

[43] For their history, see page 25 of Chapter 1 above.

[44] PBN, Doat 25, ff. 42r-44v in April 1274, containing testimony by the wife of a carpenter about Fabrissa and her daughter Philippa, the latter also married to a carpenter, and touching the husband, unfortunately not named, of Fabrissa's mother Ramunda. When the witness was asked why he was burned, she said that the inquisitors thought him an heretic "quia noluit ad mandatum eorum occidere quondam gallum sed dixit quod nullam culpam habebat gallus propter quod deberet eum occidere." Another part of this testimony about and from Fabrissa, the child of the slain carpenter, has been adduced earlier in this chapter.

[45] See No. **81** in the list published in Chapter 5.

several duplications of persons or names.[46] We may likewise infer that the reverse of that error, namely the omission of names, occurred in spite of the solemnity of the document and the care of those making the "vidimus." [47] Besides, there were occasional simple errors in the compilation.[48] We may go beyond surmise, moreover, by surveying earlier lists of heretics in chronicles and the records of condemned heretics in the registers of the Inquisition.

The major narrative source for the period from 1229 to 1237 is the chronicle of the Dominican William Pelisson, himself a working inquisitor with the mind of a ferret and nearly "total recall," as we say nowadays. Of the 61-odd persons in his book identifiable as citizens of the town, all but fourteen are to be found in the diploma of 1279. Of the fourteen, eight may be discounted as being delating heretics (therefore unpunished, indeed rewarded), a deceased mother, a dead Waldensian, or other special persons.[49] The remaining six can probably be accounted for by slips of the pen.[50] Pelisson, after all, recorded times when the earliest trials were hurried, almost like lynchings, and when many of the condemned were already deceased. In spite of that, as can be seen, all but every name in Pelisson is repeated in the diploma of 1279. Presumably deliberately, Pelisson also omitted a few onetime heretics. An example is the Raymond William de Altarippa "pelegantarius" converted by Dominic Guzmàn before June 1215.[51]

---

[46] In Chapter 5 below, see Nos. **64** and **70, 77** and **192**, and **165** and **278**.

[47] According to Pelisson, *Chronicon*, pp. 93-94 a John Textor was burned, and he tells the story with enough detail to make it almost a certain case. Besides, if my conjecture is correct, his wife is listed as No. **205** below.

[48] For slips or errors, see Nos. **49** and **205**.

[49] These were the delator Arnold Dominicus, Peter Donatus who was a deceased clerk or oblate of Saint-Sernin, the Waldensian Galvanus already deceased, Raymond Grossus the noted "perfectus" and delator, Peter Jacmars of the City who was dead when burned, Vital Medicus de Cassamilh who was probably not a Toulousan citizen, and Oliva, mother of Embrinus and Peter Embrin who was dead when condemned (but her sons are mentioned in 1279, for which see No. **59** below), and the delator William de Solerio.

[50] Bartholomew Boerius (an error for No. **180** below?), William Peter Durandus (the same as the Peter Durandus "sartor," No. **42** below?), Bernard de Solerio "fibularius" (not mentioned in 1279, but see No. **156** below), Bernard Ramundus "teulerius" (perhaps the same as the Bernard Ramundus "cellarius," No. **31** in 1279? – the crafts are very different, a "cellarius" being a saddlemaker and a "teulerius" a tilemaker, but, if we assume that one scribe was reading aloud to another when concocting the amnesty, very easy to misunderstand), Michael de Pinu (a William de Pinu No. **52** in 1279), and John Textor (no. **205** in 1279 where his name is given as William).

[51] Vicaire, *Dominique et ses prêcheurs*, p. 45 tells us that Dominic had handled the case in the absence of the bishop.

Because they did not depend on the memory of an historian, the figures derived from the records of later inquisitors are somewhat more accurate. In the period from 1237 to 1241 inclusive, seventy-three Toulousan citizens are listed in the materials left us by the inquisitors William Arnaldus and Stephen of Saint-Thibéry.[52] Of the twenty-four not to be found in 1279, fourteen are known to have been assigned the penance of pilgrimage or other service not entailing confiscation of property.[53] Of the remaining ten, six were women, three being dead at time of sentencing, and almost all closely connected with persons on the list of 1279.[54] The relatively large number of women absent from the list of 1279 is surely to be accounted for by the fact that many condemned women did not have "hereditates" to leave, which is all the amnesty was interested in recording. In brief, all but three of the seventy-three penitents are either found in 1279 or their absence is easily explained.[55] To turn now to the fifty-seven condemnations echeloned from 1246 to 1248 inclusive, almost all of which are listed in materials derived from the inquisitors Bernard of

[52] These are the condemnations in PBN, Doat 21. The persons involved are Nos. **156** to **192** inclusive. As the reader will see, this leaves Nos. **193-195** unaccounted for. Since, however, No. **193** is the brother of **192** who is listed in PBN, Doat 21, the list certainly included him. Nos. **194-195**, the Affusorii husband and wife, have been assimilated to this list purely for the sake of convenience.

[53] I enumerate here the citizens together with the folios in PBN, Doat 21 and the date of their sentences: Arnold Raymond Boumont, fol. 173v – July 1241; Raymond Capel, fol. 170r – June 1241; Arnold de Cuc, fol. 171v – April 1238; Arnold Estiu, fol. 176r – October 1241; Arnold de Lugan, fol. 176v – June 1238; Mantelina, wife of Raymond de Capitedenario, fol. 175r – September 1241; Maurannus, son of Maurannus "senior," fol. 177v – March 1237; Bonmacip Maurandus, son of Peter Maurandus, fol. 178r – September 1241; Raymond Maurandus "luscus," son of Maurandus "senior," fol. 178r – April 1237; Raymond de Montesquivo, fol. 169r – April 1238; William Pictavini, fol. 167v – August 1241; Stephana, wife of Arnold de Lugan, fol. 177r – June 1238; Bernard de Villanova knight, fol. 178v – August 1241; and Raymond Arnold de Villanova knight, fol. 172v – May 1241.

[54] Alesta, wife of Embrinus, dead at condemnation, fol. 179v – September 1237; Bernarda, widow of William Vitalis "campsor," converted by Bishop Fulk but relapsed and sentenced to life imprisonment, fol. 151r – February 1237; Esclarmunda, mother of Ondrada, condemned when deceased, fol. 179v – September 1237; Geralda Medica sentenced to life imprisonment, fol. 151r – April 1237; Oliva, sister of Raymond Rogerius, and conjectural wife of Hugh de Murello (see No. **17** in Chapter 5 below), fol. 149v – February 1237; Philippa condemned to life imprisonment, fol. 150r – February 1237; and Ramunda, wife of Peter de Roaxio, fol. 179v – dead when condemned – September 1237.

[55] The three absent persons were men. Two were dead when condemned and the remaining one was absent: Peter Chammar (Pelisson, *Chronicon*, p. 111 spells it Jacmar) deceased when sentenced, fol. 179v – September 1237; Raymond Embrini excommunicated when absent, fol. 145r-July 1237; and Raymond de Turre dead when condemned, fol. 179v – September 1237.

Caux and John of Saint-Pierre, all without exception are to be found in 1279.[56] One may therefore conclude that the diploma of 1279 truthfully represented reality, and that the total number of citizens condemned to death, imprisonment, or excommunicated as contumacious, all of which penalties entailed confiscation of property, was around 278.

[56] These records are published by Douais in his *Inquisition* and are Nos. **196-252** in Chapter 5 below. Nos. **206-213** are not listed in the manuscript used by Douais, but, since they are in the same series, were surely condemned at the same time.

3

The Inquisitors and the Heretics

A. The Depth and Rapidity of the Repression

Studied together with the inquisitors' records and the contemporary historians, the amnesty enables us to take some further, if tentative, steps toward estimating the number of heretics condemned by the inquisitors. Owing to the fact that the amnesty is concerned only with confiscations of "hereditates" and not with condemnations for heresy, the number of women contained in it is well below the approximate half of the population one might expect. Since, in the amnesty of 1279, there are 205 men and only 73 women, one estimates that a full enumeration would give about 410 persons.[1] Even this larger number, moreover, does not include the many heretics or sympathizers put through the ecclesiastical and secular Dispose-All, who emerged shredded only with smaller penances that did not include confiscation.[2] It is certain that there were many individuals sentenced to punishment of whom we have no record. An anonymous and undated charter, for example, informs us, as it was intended to inform others, that "dominus" Aimeric de Roaxio and Peter Raymond Descalquencs were illegally serving as consuls because both had been "crucesignati" in the past.[3] The fact that this informer told the truth is attested in my family histories of these clans, and both of these persons were consuls in the term of 1270-1271.[4] Looking at the sparse and fragmentary evidence of the condemnations of 1237-1241, one calculates that 30 percent of those there listed suffered penalties that did

---

[1] The reason why many women lacked "heriditates" is discussed below.

[2] Our only figures for alternative punishments derive from the list of sentences of 1237-1241 preserved in PBN, Doat 21 described above in Chapter 2 note 53.

[3] PAN, J 317 107.

[4] TAM, BB 189, fol. 64r-v, lists of April, September, etc. 1270, and TAM, II 9 (March 1271). Consular lists will not be referred to in the rest of the book because the practice would enlarge the notes enormously.

not involve confiscation.[5] Were we to add that percentage to the number of 410 in 1279, our total would rise to about 533 persons. A correction must, however, be applied here. Some 15 of the 278 persons listed in the amnesty, 5 percent of the whole, are known to have been dead at the time of their condemnations. When this percentage is removed, we have approximately 506 condemnations.[6]

Until new documents are found, one can go no further with numbers. We may conjecture, however, that what is seen in 1279 was the tip of an iceberg. The vast majority of those who both dabbled with divergent belief, for example, and also voluntarily avoided severe penalties by means of timely confessions are not represented in our recorded sentences. Although the majority of Toulouse's inhabitants were presumably normal Christians, this category must have been very large. This may be illustrated from the history of the Maurand family. We have seen that Peter, the grandfather, who was forced to abjure in 1178, was probably a "perfectus." We know nothing about the convictions of his four sons, except that his youngest, Maurandus "vetus" (as Pelisson calls him in the 1230s) was also a "perfectus." Peter's male grandchildren were nine in number, and, although one, Maurand de Bellopodio, seems to have been orthodox, four others were condemned and their property confiscated, and two underwent pilgrimage, thus inducing the conviction that the majority of the sons of the Peter of 1178 were believers in heresy. "Vetus"' three older brothers had merely been lucky enough to die before the serious hunt for Cathars began. To add to this, there were also two wives and possibly two sisters of the same clan whose "hereditates" had been seized.[7] The sparseness of such material naturally prohibits one from making any firm estimate as to how large a part of the population was claimed by this alternate religion, but it undoubtedly shows that Cathars constituted a solid and entrenched minority of the population.

To return to those punished, however, when the extant sentences to pilgrimage and other penances that did not entail confiscation are examined, moreover, one perceives that our records contain only relatively severe punishments. Few of the pilgrimages imposed were easy. Several of the early penitents were obliged to go to the Holy Land, and,

---

[5] This rough estimate is derived from the fact that there were 44 men sentenced in 1237-1241 of whom 13 were assigned lesser punishments.

[6] In Chapter 5, see Nos. **59, 88, 95, 131, 163, 169**, and **181-188**, of which no less than eight are women.

[7] For the Maurandi, see the materials in Chapter 1 above, Nos. **89, 128, 147, 153** of the list in Chapter 5, below, the women Nos. **92, 179, 220**, and **253** in the same, Raymond and Bonmacip above in Chapter 2 note 53, and the family history in Part 3.

since this punishment was exceptionally heavy, they were either given upwards of seven years to settle their affairs, or it took them that long to run out of appeals to Rome or elsewhere, before departing as crusaders.[8] Among other duties, a man (whose wife was also condemned) was ordered to go to Valencia in Spain and there serve in the medieval equivalent of a penal battalion for seven years against the Muslims.[9] Naturally on foot and sometimes requiring parts of two years, voyages to places as far away as Rome, Canterbury in England, and Saint-Denis in northern France were not infrequent.[10] Sickness sometimes excused our onetime Cathars. Because of illness, one penitent had his trip to Rome commuted to a voyage to Saint James of Compostella, and a woman initially ordered to visit that Spanish center was instructed to give instead 100 shillings of Tours to the poor because of her indisposition.[11] Visits to Saint James of Compostella in Leon and places in southern France and Provence were common.[12] Naked and barefoot, such penitents also were obliged to visit the parish churches of Toulouse once a month and accept at each "una disciplina," a formal, one hopes, lashing. Some of them had to provide not inconsiderable quantities of bricks, lime, and sand to help the Inquisition build its prisons, and others were to feed the poor or contribute to the church for the same and other purposes.[13] All were required to attend a mass and sermon every Sunday and feast day.

[8] For the Holy Land, see Chapter 5, No. **16** (and the family history in Part 3) for Arnold Guido "maior," and for Peter Sobaccus, No. **107** in Chapter 5. We have testaments drawn by both men before departing in March of 1237, documents that refer to the cardinal who condemned them.

[9] The inadvertent crusader was Arnold de Lugan whose wife Stephana will be seen below. The names of the various persons mentioned in the notes to the rest of this paragraph are mentioned above in Chapter 2 note 53, in the discussion of the sentences imposed by the inquisitors William Arnaldus and Stephen of Saint-Thibéry.

[10] For those involving Rome, see Arnold de Cuc and Raymond Maurand. Arnold Raymond Boumont, Raymond Capel, William Pictavinus, Bernard de Villanova, and Raymond Arnold de Villanova were obliged to visit Canterbury, and Mantelina, wife of Raymond de Capitedenario, and Bonmacip Maurandus were ordered to Saint-Denis.

[11] Raymond Maurandus was the penitent initially ordered to Rome, and Stephana, the wife of Arnold of Lugan mentioned above, offered the shillings.

[12] Other than Compostella and Valencia, the only Spanish locality was San Salvador in Asturias. Those in southern France are Saint-Pé-de-Génères, the Benedictine monastery of Saints Peter and Paul in the diocese of Tarbes near Angelès, Le Puy, Saint-Martial in Limoges, Saint-Léger-de-Malzieu, a Benedictine priory in the diocese of Mende, Rocamadour, Saint-Gilles on the Rhone, Souillac, N.-D.-de-Verdelay, a Benedictine priory in the diocese of Vence near Grasse in Provence, Saint-Antoine-de-Viennois, a Benedictine priory in the diocese of Vienne near Saint-Marcellin.

[13] Arnold Raymond Boumont, Arnold de Lugan, Raymond de Montesquivo, William Pictavinus, and Raymond Arnold de Villanova were in this category.

In fine, our 506 penitents probably constitute a small part of those condemned to repent their association with Catharism, and a much smaller percentage of those who had tasted it. By itself, however, the number 506 is impressive. Since the population of Toulouse could hardly have topped 25000 of all sexes and ages in this period – one following hard on a war that had lasted twenty years with a battlefield massacre and two major sieges – and since only those who had reached majority were pursued, the scythe of the inquisitors must have cut a rather wide swathe in town society, wounding or nicking a substantial number of the adult population.[14] One therefore presumes that the repression of Catharism was successful in part because it was severe.

It was also extremely rapid. Exceptions apart (although I know of none), the list of names published in 1270 runs in chronological order, and is divisible into four groups. The first group contains slightly over half of the total, the first 157 persons, most of whom, as we have seen, appear in the Dominican Pelisson's chronicle and in the later retrospective testimony of 1245-1246 about this early period collected by the inquisitors Bernard of Caux and John of Saint-Pierre.[15] This group poses problems derived from its size and complexity. Of the 157 persons, some had been dealt with very early indeed. One was sentenced by Cardinal Conrad sometime during his legation in 1221-1223, an example that brings us all the way back to repressive attempts during the Albigensian war itself.[16] Three others are known to have been condemned by Cardinal Roman in 1229.[17] Since the last person known to have been penitenced at that time is Peter Sobaccus (No. 107), it is possible that most or all of the

---

[14] The difficulty is the lack of any statistics. Wolff, *Estimes*, pp. 54-55 estimates the population in 1335 at about 32,000. Basing himself on the same figures but with different statistical methods, Biraben, "La population de Toulouse," *Journal des Savants* (1964), p. 300 reached 45 to 50,000 inhabitants. If the growth of Toulouse followed the normal pattern of increasing until the famine and plague years of the fourteenth century, the estimate given above seems not unreasonable. Furthermore, as to the age group on which the punishments were levied is concerned, one must presume that, in any given year in a modern post-industrial society (I am using statistics from the United States), the age group 15 years old and below would be at least 24 percent of the whole population, or that of 21 years and below, 34 percent. In the medieval pre-industrial community, the percentage of the young would surely be much higher. The ages of majority at Toulouse in this period range from 15 to 25, but canon law used the lowest.

[15] See the Bibliography, p. 310, for a description of the register TBM, MS 609 containing this testimony.

[16] Raymond Rogerius "minor" No. **81**. Conrad of Urach, abbot of Cîteaux and, cardinal bishop of Porto, was appointed legate in 1219, was briefly back in Rome in July 1223, and was again in France in 1224.

[17] Nos. **16**, **42**, and **107**. For Cardinal Roman see above, Chapter 2 note 10.

condemnations up to or around the number 107 date from the Council of Toulouse or immediately thereafter.[18] In short, perhaps just over 100 condemnations really constitute the first of five groups. To deal with the whole group of the first 157 persons again, however, a minimum of 27 were either themselves sentenced anew in 1237-1241 or 1246-1248, or, if still alive, saw their spouses condemned in these periods.[19] Not counting these, about 36 other persons or their spouses are mentioned either in Pelisson's chronicle or are described in the inquisitorial investigation of the period 1245-1246 as having been active in Catharism in this early time.[20] Lastly, not a few of these persons can be identified in the family histories of Toulouse I have compiled as being active in the town during this period.[21] In short, it is all but absolutely certain that the first group of 157 individuals were all sentenced in the period up to February 1237, the date at which the condemnations of the next group begins, and it is also very likely that the cases of over 100 of these had been heard around 1229.

The history of the remaining groups is less complicated. The second group contains 38 persons of whom all but two can be shown to have been condemned from February to September 1237.[22] Containing 57 persons, the third group was sentenced in the period from 1246 to 1248 by the inquisitors Bernard of Caux and John of Saint-Pierre.[23] When the

---

[18] The cases of Peter Sobaccus and No. **16**, Arnold Guido "maior," are perfectly clear. For the former see the list in Chapter 5, and for the latter the family history in Part 3 as well. Peter Durandus "sartor" (No. **42**) had relapsed by 1234 and was therefore condemned at that time, although he was sentenced again in 1241, at which date we learn of his connection with the cardinal. Raymond Rogerius "minor" may also have relapsed, although there is no reference to it in the papal letter described in No. **81** in the list below (Chapter 5).

[19] See the following Nos. in Chapter 5: **4, 6, 17, 22, 34, 42, 45, 50, 51, 61, 89, 94, 95, 97, 108, 112, 130, 131, 136, 153, 167, 179** and **244**. The principals are both male and female, and their attached relatives are usually wives but also some siblings and mothers.

[20] Nos. **2, 3, 5, 10, 11, 13, 16, 17, 19, 23, 25, 29, 32, 34, 38, 39, 42, 44, 49, 50, 60, 69, 80, 81, 85, 86, 88, 89, 95, 96, 120, 126, 133, 134,** and **156,** the vast majority being mentioned in Pelisson and in TBM, MS 609.

[21] For these, see the entries in Chapter 5 and the family histories in Part 3 below.

[22] Nos. **158** to **195** inclusive, of which only the latter two cannot be shown to have been condemned at the same time. Except for Nos. **168, 186, 190, 191**, possibly **193, 194,** and **195**, three women and four men, most of whom are to be seen in Pelisson and TBM, MS 609, all of the persons listed in 1279 are published in PBN, Doat 21. This volume, however, contains about 73 sentences, as has been seen above. Of these, 17 are attached to the first 157 persons, and two others to individuals coming after the section of the enumeration presently being discussed.

[23] Nos. **196** to **252** inclusive, these names are found in PBN, MS lat. 9992 published in Douais' *Inquisition*. About seven of the persons numbered from **1** to **195** in the amnesty were also listed in Douais, as well as three listed after No. **253**. The only individuals in

remaining 26 were sentenced is not known, but it may be surmised that some of these persons were condemned in the same period, that is, from 1246 to 1248, one for which we have only very spotty and sparse records. Although very unlikely, others may have been later, sometime in the fifties, but, as noted above in regard to the prescription period, all were certainly condemned prior to 1259.

B. The Inquisitors' Objective

A social analysis of the names given in the diploma of 1279 reinforces the evidence of the rapidity of the repression recorded in the preceding paragraphs. The inquisitors seem to have aimed high. In his laconic way, the contemporary historian William of Puylaurens informs his readers that the first serious inquisition was instituted by the legate Cardinal Roman during and immediately after the council held at Toulouse in November 1229. The onetime "perfectus" William of Solerio appears to have provided a basic list of names. Citizens reputed to be orthodox were then summoned to name other names, after which those who were suspect were called in, all being interviewed and investigated rather awkwardly by the bishop of Toulouse and the other prelates assembled at the council. Beginning in 1232-1233, the Dominican inquisitors, Peter Seilanus of Toulouse and William Arnold of Montpellier, were assigned this task and were consequently able to devote full time to the "chasse aux hommes" in a way that the conciliar fathers could not. They first tracked those who could be condemned easily, and then, bit by bit, moved toward the important Cathars, the "maiores." [24] Although William was a polemist, a partisan of the vehement Bishop Fulk of Toulouse, he was an unusually level-headed man for an historian of contemporary events. His account is amply confirmed by other sources, notably by William Pelisson, the Dominican inquisitor who sometimes shocks today's readers by his lack of what moderns imagine the Christian spirit to have been. Pelisson also tells us about William de Solario, and then goes on to revel in the delation of Raymond Gros, recording for us the fact that Ray-

---

that set not listed in Douais are Nos. **206** to **213** inclusive, a fact that tells us, as does much else, that the compilers of the amnesty did not use a list similar to that of the manuscript in the Bibliothèque National.

[24] Puylaurens, *Chronica*, pp. 136-138 for the legate and the bishops, and 150 for the later inquisitors. The historian describes their actions in these terms: "qui ... quosdam quos facilius convinci posse presumebant citaverunt, et convictos hereticos iudicaverunt. Sicque paulatim cepit maiores quosdam inquisitio pervenire ...."

mond's information enabled the delighted Dominicans to go after the town's patricians and knights.[25]

Pelisson's "magni burgenses" and Puylaurens' "maiores" both echo reality. Churchmen were out to decapitate Catharism. One may argue that their aim was "religious," that, namely, they were shooting only at the leaders of the Cathar sect, and that they had no conscious social policy whatsoever. That may be so, but it is worth noting that both the count and the aristocracy of Toulouse believed that the inquisitor Peter Seilanus, the native Toulousan Dominican who directed the persecution of the Cathars in those early days, was conducting a vendetta specifically against them.[26] It is certain, in fact, that the investigators' initial cone of fire was especially, although possibly inadvertently, directed at the rich and powerful who supported this divergent belief. Patrician Toulousans constituted a substantial 20 percent of the males listed in 1279.[27]

The intensity of the attack on the middle range of the population is harder to discern, partly because a relative lack of family histories makes it hard to see the dimension of the group. Over 15 percent of the names of those enumerated in 1279 were of this class, and that is probably a minimal figure.[28] It is also noticeable that a number of the heretics of 1279

---

[25] On p. 94 he records that, "erant enim in illis diebus [1229] multi crucesignati ad transfretandum propter illa que commiserant contra fidem, et quidam alii in aliis penitentiis a domino Romano, apostolice sedis legato, damnati, quia eos Guillelmus de Consolario, conversus ab heresi, discohoperuerat, et isti cum aliis quampluribus semper contra ecclesiam et catholicos repugnabant." In April 1236, he reports (pp. 109-110) that Raymond Grossus of Toulouse came to the Dominicans and eructed a mass of names, as a result of which "multi tunc confessi sunt veritatem, et inde inquisitio fuit elucidata. Quo viso et intellecto, gavisi sunt fratres valde, et credentes hereticorum supra modum fuerunt perterriti." The inquisitors then "vocaverunt multos et magnos ad confessionem." Pelisson first listed the dead heretics then condemned and afterward proceeded to the living, introducing his remarks by reporting that Raymond Gros had reported heretications of dead persons "... et inquisitio hereticorum per ipsum totaliter, Deo dante et jubente, directa, in tantum quod magni burgenses et nobiles et quidam alii [I have favored the reading given by Molinier in his edition of this text, p. 44] per sententiam condempnati sunt ...." Raymond Grossus is reported to have entered the Franciscan order after the delation. See also the conjecture about him in the conclusion below.

[26] See the text from Pelisson, *Chronicon*, p. 100 above in Chapter 2 note 13, and the discussion of Peter there.

[27] As stated here, this includes males only. Females are not registered because that would exaggerate the representation of the upper social elements since rich women were more likely than poor ones to have "hereditates." For the limitation on the representation of women in the diploma, see the discussion below. The ones listed here are Nos. 2-5, 12-14, 22-23, 32, 56, 66, 77, 81, 89, 95-96, 100, 111, 114, 116, 128, 130, 132-133, 145, 147, 152-153, 157-158, 190, 192-193, 199, 214-215, 225, 241, and 265.

[28] For the reason mentioned in the note above, only males are counted here and in this whole section. The names of the families are mentioned in the next note.

bore the names of new families that had entered the consulate between 1202 and the war years ending in 1229, or were individuals of similar quality such as merchants, money changers, minters, notaries, etc.[29] A comparison with the persons mentioned in 1279 and the consular lists also shows that many of the consuls during and immediately after the war inclined to Catharism.[30] What this rather high rate of adhesion to this faith may well reflect is not so much the desire of this group to experiment with alternate religions, but instead the anger provoked by the crusade and the need for mental reinforcement during wartime.

The pressure on the members of the lower classes is equally or more difficult to weigh. About a quarter of the sentenced persons bear the names of a craft or trade. This figure is not as trustworthy as it seems because, at this time, it was not usual to define a man by his profession or business when he was acting in a private, religious, or political capacity.[31] The amnesty of 1279, for example, describes only two men as public notaries, but there were probably four others.[32] Furthermore, the employment of a craft, trade, or professional designation as a last name does not mean that the person carrying it was actually in the business described. This is obvious in the case of a common name like Faber, but it is a far more general problem than that.[33] To exemplify the difficulty, one reads the name of Peter Feltrerius both in the oath to uphold the Peace of Paris of February 1243 and among the proctors of the petitioners in March and August 1279. If, as is possible, these were two different persons, neither was a felter. The first was a notary and the second a minter.[34]

[29] Names like Centullus, Chivus, Gaitapodium, Grillus, Signarius, Siollio, Sobaccus, Surdus, Unde, etc. shown in the list below were more or less monopolized by the families holding them, and most appear during the time mentioned in the text above. In marking this statistic, I added the professional people: one "Magister," the notaries, "medici" (either a family name or a profession), minters, money-changers, and merchants although they were often different from the average artisan or tradesman.

[30] The wartime lists of consuls may be seen in my *Toulouse*, pp. 181-188. Two rough samples shall be taken. Individuals bearing the same names of those later condemned for heresy and who were consuls in the terms running from 1217 to 1228 make up about 21 percent of the total number of consuls; in the post-war terms from 1229 to 1238 around 36 percent.

[31] For this, see my *Toulouse*, pp. 67-68, 157-158, 162-163, and 226 note 29.

[32] The notaries described as such were Nos. **71** and **277**, and the others in this profession are **149**, **151**, **207**, and **267**. As I discovered when writing family histories, notaries are especially difficult to trace because they scarcely ever used their notarial title when doing private business in this period.

[33] See No. **94**, Bernard Faber "specierius" (druggist) below.

[34] Alternately, if the two were one and the same, Peter was both a notary and a minter, a normal duplication of functions or businesses. For the oath, see the note immediately below, and for March 1279, Chapter 6.

In spite of such insufficiencies, to reject the available information is to throw the baby out with the bathwater. Although a name does not mean that the one who used it necessarily practised the specified occupation, it does reflect social origins. Exceptions apart, persons with such names probably derived relatively recently from the lower and middle elements of the population. With this in mind, it may be useful to compare the numbers or percentages of patricians, artisans, and tradesmen listed in the diploma of 1279 and similar figures derived from the 1028 Toulousans who swore to uphold the Peace of Paris in 1243.[35] In 1279, we have seen, about 20 percent were from notable families, and about 25 percent bore the names of crafts and trades. In 1243, the former category did not reach 10 percent, and the latter was 16 percent of the sample. One concludes that, by accident or design, the "maiores" in heresy were also very often the more worthy persons in a social sense.

Lastly, there is evidence that, however inadvertently, the upper elements of the social scale were chronologically the first to be hit. In the first 195 persons listed in the amnesty of 1279 all of whom were condemned by the end of 1237, just above 23 percent were demonstrably gentlefolk and patricians, and only about 15 percent crafts- and tradespersons. In the remaining 83 individuals enumerated, those penitenced, as we know, after 1237, the percentage of the well-to-do dropped to about 10 percent and that of the artisans and tradesfolk rose to 17.

The same picture is to be seen, moreover, when we turn our attention to the women listed in 1279. Women constituted just over 26 percent of our whole sample, and it may also be noted that those there listed were principally cited as wives, sisters, and mothers of males, and were often not even named. Of the 73 women listed there, about 20 percent were not named, but merely referred to in terms of their relationship to men and their siblings; of the 205 men, only two were so treated. This palpable underestimation is because few women had "hereditates." Some did, of course. Some had paraphernal goods (those, that is, independent of marriage), and others were named as heirs by parents (presumably in the absence of male issue), or were widows granted shares of the family property by their deceased spouses. On the whole, however, a woman's property mainly consisted of her marriage settlement, and one therefore does not expect women to be as heavily represented in the amnesty as were men. On the other hand, it is obvious that, since wealthy women are

---

[35] PAN, J 305 (dated 29 February 1243). The reader will have to take my figures on faith. The list is too long to publish for the moment.

more likely to have "hereditates" than poor men, our women are of better class than our men.[36] In spite of this, it is clear that the inquisitors went after the males first. To examine the chronology of our evidence, of the first 195 persons, only about a quarter were women, and, of the remaining 83, about 30 percent. As was true of the males, then, the way in which women were listed in the amnesty shows that the inquisitors first hunted what they thought to be the bigger game.

This evidence explains much about the early history of the Inquisition in Toulouse. The famous attack on, and expulsion of, the Dominicans from the town in 1235 by the consuls, Raymond VII's attack on the inquisitor and Dominican Peter Seilanus, and the nagging doubts that eventually disturbed the Dominican order itself are made explicable by the ferocity of the attack on the society of this community. Strains and later regrets aside, this rapid and deep surgery was successful. Although mopping up operations continued, the back of Toulousan Catharism had been broken by the end of September 1237. In March 1222 the consuls met with the notables of their council, the two bodies totalling 153 persons. In February 1248, as we have seen above, 1028 adult male Toulousans took oath to maintain the Peace of Paris.[37] These lists cannot be compared in terms of the names of specific heretics known in other sources. All that can be done is to list families known to have been involved in divergent thought. In 1222 about 21 percent were of such families; in 1243 just above six. This impressionistic statistic helps to confirm what I think has been proved above, namely that, serious repression having begun late in 1229, the Cathar cult had been all but extirpated in the capital of western Languedoc in the course of eight years.

C. Class and Catharism

The amnesty, as we see, shows us the depth and speed of the surgery on the Toulousan body social, but one wonders if it can tell us anything about the social adhesion to heresy. It does. The fact that, as we have seen above, patrician Toulousans were 20 percent of the males listed in 1279, shows us that, whatever the case of any other group, this class was deeply moved by Cathar thought or liked the idea of an alternate religion. What

---

[36] About 31 of the 73 women were notables as against 13 in the arts and crafts, 42 percent, in short, against 17.

[37] For the council, see TAM, AA 1 75 (March 1222). The reference for the oath of February 1243 is given in note 35 above.

has been stated above about the direction of the inquisitors' cone of fire may seem to contradict this position, but the reader is invited to see the following arguments in its favor.

Of the five most conspicuous knightly families of the town, the Castronovo (Castelnau d'Estretefons), Gamevilla, Tolosa, Turribus (Las Tours), and Villanova, members of all but the Turribus are listed among the heretics of 1279, in which group, in fact, were some of their most distinguished scions.[38] Taking one small step down, we see the substantial burgher families of the patriciate. These are here defined as those whose members served as consuls before 1202, were rich, and often held significant landed properties in the countryside around Toulouse. Some of these clans were also related to knightly or seignorial lines in the countryside, several had members who were knighted or entered the nobility, and not a few normally wore the sword.[39] Of this group, a very considerable number, if not quite so many as among the knights, joined their betters in tasting the alternate belief of Catharism. If some, such as the Astro, Cossano, Prinhaco, etc. seem to have no members who adhered to heresy, the Baranhoni, Caraborda, Curtasolea, Descalquencs, Maurandi, Roaxio, and others were far more experimental and paid dearly for it.[40] The strong adherence to Catharism of the aristocracy, both noble and commoner, is reinforced by the fact that the rural nobility was also much taken by this religion.[41]

A variety of reasons have been given for this. One is that, in a growingly commercial world, the landed interest was suffering severely. The materials from Toulouse do not support this assertion. Two of our families assuredly suffered severe economic losses in the Albigensian period, the Maurandi and the Villanova. Prior to their difficulties with the inquisitors, both lines lost a major farm (in 1225 and 1228) because of

[38] See the family histories in Part 3 below.

[39] It will be noted that three of the grand burgher families whose histories are recorded in Part 3 below were partly noble and knightly by the end of the thirteenth century, and some had been so before. These are the Barravi, Maurandi, and Roaxio clans. There were others of this kind, such as a part of the Prinhaco, whose history is not written here, that moved in the same direction, not to speak of quite a few individual burghers.

[40] To give the reader a somewhat loose statistic, I have composed or published nearly 60 family histories (of which 26 are published in Part 3 below). Of the 60-odd, approximately 36 are knightly, patrician, or solid burghers. Of this group 18 families had persons involved in Catharism.

[41] Douais, "Les hérétiques du comté de Toulouse dans la première moitié du xiiie siècle d'après l'enquête de 1245," *Bulletin théologique, scientifique et littéraire de l'Institut catholique de Toulouse*, n.s. 2 (1892) 160-173 and 206-209. This view is also repeated in J. Guiraud's *Cartulaire de Notre-Dame de Prouille* of 1907 and in his *Histoire de l'Inquisition* of 1235.

debt.[42] These difficulties, however, seem to have been caused by the war rather than by an economic crisis. Furthermore, in this age when the wine trade was beginning to flourish (although the vineyards around the town of Toulouse were damaged by the war, especially during the last siege), there is little or no evidence that the landed interest was being harmed in this expanding economy, and much to prove that it was doing well. Proof of this assertion may be seen repeatedly in the family histories appended to this monograph. It is therefore unlikely that an anger provoked by economic hardship prompted this group to turn to divergent thought.

Nor is there much evidence that conflicts over tithes between landlords and the church caused widespread bitterness. There were conflicts, surely, and consequent losses borne by lay families. We have already seen the surrender of tithes required of Peter Maurandus in 1178. A court of elected arbiters also decided in favor of the canons of Saint-Sernin against the Curtasolea family over tithes in 1191.[43] Far more dramatic was the resistance to paying tithes by a member of the great baronial family of Lanta, Gerald Unald. In 1258 "decimatores" or collectors reported that the tithing in Venaldric and Saint-Anatholy traditionally belonged to Saint-Sernin, but that Gerald and the "knights" had made it impossible to collect them during and right after the crusade.[44] Gerald was an undoubted Cathar, the son of a "perfectus" burned at Toulouse after the war, and the brother of Jordan de Lantario, one of the heroes of the southern armies during the crusade.[45] But, during the crusade, the southerners naturally used everything they could lay their hands on.[46] Besides the major problem about tithes was not the resistance to paying them half so much as the loss of tithes to creditors of the church, not a few of whom were "decimatores" or tithe collectors. The historian William of

[42] Valségur for the Maurandi lost in 1228, and Castanet for the Villanova in 1225, both to pay debts for which see Part 3 below.

[43] See Part 3 below.

[44] Saint-Sernin 594 (9 33 4) a roll of testimony in the episcopal court of August 1259 recorded the testimony of these collectors given in April 1258. It was there reported that "dominus" Gerald and "milites erant mali et impediebant ne possint [decimatores] percipere et auferebant monachis."

[45] Pelisson, *Chronicon*, p. 112: "Condemnaverunt etiam Ramundum Hunaldi, dominum de Lantario. Guillelmus Bernardi Hunaldi, pater Jordani, qui erat perfectus haereticus, combustus fuit Tolosae. Abbas enim Sancti Saturnini ... cepit eum apud Bousquet ...." Gerald's brother Jordan de Lanta is often seen in the *Canso*, for which see the index to the edition, and he even made the prose version in *HGL*, 8: 192 where, as in the original version, he is described as commanding the Saint-Étienne Gate at Toulouse during the great siege of 1218.

[46] See my *Toulouse*, p. 206 for Saint-Bernard 32 (September 1215) listing the seizure of food and timber from the hospice of Grandselve by the consuls of Toulouse.

Puylaurens remarked that one of the reasons the bishopric of Toulouse was so poor before it was reestablished during the Albigensian war was because the "decimator" got three-quarters of the tithe, the parish-priest a quarter, and the bishop nothing.[47] As faithful a Christian as the "patronus" of the Dominican order, Pons de Capitedenario, dealt extensively in the tithes of Saint-Sernin.[48] All the evidence demonstrates is that, in an expanding economy, some make profits and some, a slightly lesser percentage, do not. And, on either side, it is likely that, in the absence of repression, some would enjoy the liberty of playing with an alternate faith.

Among the well-to-do on the level of the Curtasolea and the Maurandi, there were merchants. Many have thought that, given their opportunities for travel and their "practicality," merchants would be more "broadminded" than most, and therefore more inclined to play with divergent thought.[49] In fact, as the family histories show, not a few families showing signs of heresy counted traveling merchants among their members. But what can be done with that rather banal fact? Although merchants were not necessarily rich, a well-to-do urban family was likely to have one or two, especially in an area that specialized in the exportation of wine and other goods. Things are never simple, however. One of the biggest Toulousan wine merchants in the thirteenth century was Bertrand de Palacio, a person of undoubted orthodoxy, although his assistant or apprentice was Arnold Unde, one of whose earlier relatives was a condemned Cathar.[50]

Similar to merchants in the "liberal" imagination is the professional. Although we see a few "medici" in the amnesty list published below, we have no evidence to speak of about the leaning of the medical profession in spite of much talk in the secondary literature. We do have some knowledge, however, about jurists and notaries. A minimum of about thirty-eight public notaries were instrumenting circa 1230, and the putative number of six mentioned in the amnesty says little. One of them,

[47] Puylaurens, *Chronica*, p. 40.

[48] See the Capitedenario family history below, especially the material in note 19.

[49] See, for example, Evans, "Social Aspects of Medieval Heresy," in *Persecution and Liberty*, published in 1931. Borst, *Die Katharer*, p. 49 refers to Evans "socialistic thesis," meaning by that curious phrase, perhaps, that one who thinks of heresy as having something to do with society and the economy is a Marxist or socialist. Mr Evans had the soul of a liberal Protestant with mildly "capitalist" leanings, whatever they are.

[50] See the family histories of the Baranoni (one was a Waldensian merchant), Barravi, Caraborda (one a Cathar), Curtasolea, Guido, Maurandi, Ponte, Roaxio, and Unde. For Bertrand de Palatio, see the Unde family history.

it is true, was Peter Raymond de Samatano, one of three scribes of his family who instrumented prolifically in the period from 1200 to 1256.[51] On the other hand, we have reviewed the history of Bernard de Podio-siurano, who "collaborated" with the crusade. Again, in regard to the lawyers and judges described in the family histories published below, one, the clan named Cossano, was orthodox, and the other, the Descalquencs, heavily heretical.

Nor does it seem that, in spite of the success of clerical propaganda against usury among families of old wealth or among craftsmen (both often in need of capital and/or credit), individuals who invested in usurious or "leonine" partnerships with artisans, lent money at interest, or who mortgaged property were especially prone to Catharism. It is surely true that the undemanding morality required of the ordinary "credentes" did not pinch a man's conscience if he broke a law which, in the view of the Cathars, could claim no obedience whatsoever. Catharism could therefore have been part of the climate in which moneylending, indispensable in human commerce, could flourish, but that does not mean that usurers themselves necessarily shared that faith. Not only do our family histories prove that most of the successful families in the latter half of the twelfth century used the usurious "pignus" (mortgage) and lent money, but also that, if there are some usurers like Peter Sobaccus and some Curtasolea and Roaxio who leaned toward heresy, we also have our Dominican "patronus" Pons de Capitedenario, at once a veritable Croesus and fount of orthodox charity.

The fact that our list contains a minter, the wife of a "cambiator," a male of that profession, as well as several merchants, notaries, and lawyers is little indication of a special interest in Catharism by the mercantile or professional classes. But yet another test may be made. Were the persons of the old "popular" party that entered the consulate in the period from 1202 to the beginning of the war, the first consulates in which the consular lists mentioned individuals as merchants, moneychangers, or notaries especially interested in Catharism ? Altough one can say little about individuals, family names had a measure of stability, and may roughly indicate how many families of this group were leaning toward divergent thought. Of the about forty names of the older aristocracy seen in consular (or, earlier, capitular) office, anywhere from 44 to 46 percent produced heretics named in 1279. Of the thirty-eight names first seen

---

[51] My card catalogue of notaries tells me that 32 were busy around 1210 and 38 around 1230. See No. **151** in the amnesty below. The other two notaries of the Samatano family are mentioned there.

from 1202 to 1207, only about 37 percent were reflected in the list.[52] In short, since the sample of the middle and upper middle classes contained in the amnesty is too small to do much with, one can say little about the attraction to heresy of the middle to upper middle range of the population.

As we have seen, only about a quarter of the persons sentenced listed in the amnesty bore craft titles or names derived from them. This seems strange, and it may well be, therefore, that this deformation of the possible social reality derived from the needs of the police to hunt the "maiores" first, as stated above. After all, humbler people are more exploited than others, and this fact has inspired some to view them as facing the nearly monolithic upper classes and the political and religious institutions these groups are said to have created.[53] Furthermore, that the poor are rarely happy makes it probable that they will question the institutions of the world.[54] These facts make it seem not unlikely that the poor or the humbler classes were more important in Catharism than is indicated by the amnesty.

That there were craftsfolk and workers in Catharism, no one can doubt. As early as 1215, Dominic Guzmàn was said to have converted a leather worker named Raymond William de Altarippa. He did, and we know about Altarippa's family, one specialized in furs and skins.[55] We also hear of a wight from Les Cassés in the Lauragais who came to Toulouse to learn leather work circa 1230, and learned Catharism as well.[56] As is so

[52] A tabulation of the family names in the lists published in my *Toulouse*, pp. 180-181.

[53] Recent "Marxist" analysis may be exemplified by Ernst Werner, *Pauperes Christi* (Leipzig, 1956) and T. Manteuffel, *Naissance d'une hérésie* (Paris, 1970), from a Polish original.

[54] A widely held view, "Marxist," "Capitalist," or what-not. The notion expressed by Norman Cohn, *The Pursuit of the Millennium*, 2nd. edn. (New York, 1961) that the humble are often hurt by rapid economic growth seems not without meaning for Toulouse in this period.

[55] Vicaire, *Dominique et ses prêcheurs*, p. 45 tells us that Dominic had handled the case in the absence of the bishop. Raymond William de Altarippa derived from a family some of whom were in the leather industries, and may himself have appeared in TAM, II 44 (February 1239), where the leather workers addressing the count included a Bernard Vital de Altarippa and a Raymond William de Altarippa. The one "pelliparius" of this family who can be traced somewhat is Bernard. Bernard's contract of marriage with Esclarmunda in Malta 4 206 v (April 1219, copied in 1243), notes that his wife, now marrying her second husband, brought a dowry of a house, a half arpent "malol" (a new vineyard), and another of arable. In return for this, she was to receive as her marriage portion her dowry plus 20 shillings "pro consolamento." Bernard was among the several "pelliparii" serving as "sponderii" to the testament of Raymond Peter "pelliparius" in Malta 3 158 ii (April 1230, copied in the same year). Malta 20 53 (May 1245) notes a Bernard de Altarippa "pelegantarius," son of the deceased Bernard, and his wife selling the half arpent "malol" mentioned above.

[56] TBM, MS 609, fol. 226r "ad addiscendum artem pellicerie."

often the case in histories written by professional people, the real workers are portrayed as being a bit comic or foolish. One even suspects that the anti-Cathars found that stories about them were especially memorable, perhaps because of their value as propaganda. Pelisson tells of John Textor of the Bourg who, as he was being haled off to be burned, won a brief stay in prison by shouting out that the inquisitors were out to ruin the town and the count, and that he was no Cathar, but instead a good, faithful Catholic because he slept with his wife, had children, ate meat, and lied and swore.[57] Another case involved a fight between two citizens in which a Bernard Pictavinus called a Bernard de Solario "fibularius" (buckle-maker) a heretic. Solario took the case to the consuls on the grounds of criminal libel, and they fined Pictavinus. The latter hastened to the Dominicans, who brought the matter before the bishop, where the town's representatives fought it out with the Dominican inquisitors, notably Peter Seilanus and William Arnaldi. Solario eventually fled the town and went to Lombardy, as did so many of the town's Cathars.[58]

It is naturally possible, also, that the under-representation of the humble may have been caused by the nature of the inquisitorial action in another sense. We have seen that the decapitation of the movement was very rapid. This speedy action may have inclined the modest and humble citizens to duck out quickly, leaving their betters to hold the bag. If such is the case, it shows that their commitment was as modest as their social level. This unkind remark, however, says little because the devotion of the wealthier elements may have merely reflected the fact that they had been caught before they had time to drop their divergence.

On the other hand, perhaps the most satisfactory argument for the case that Catharism attracted a disproportionate adhesion on the part of the wealthier classes is the simple fact that the religion was crushed so rapidly. Had there been an even distribution of adhesion to Catharism among the rich, the middling, and the lower classes and, consequently, a measure of solidarity between these groups, it seems likely that Catharism would have resisted longer before succumbing to repression. Even in the earliest days when the lynch-like tactics of the vicar Durand de Sancto Barcio and the early inquisitors provoked widespread indignation, there were no mass movements to protect heretics from extirpation. In fact, the only

---

[57] Pelisson, *Chronicon*, p. 93. He hereticated in prison and was burned. For him, see No. **205** in Chapter 5 below.

[58] Pelisson, *Chronicon*, p. 92: the inquisitors "qui eum [Pictavinum] viriliter defende-runt, in tantum quod succubuit ille miser [Solario] et fugit in Lombardiam, et adjutores ejus remanserunt confusi."

evidence one has of a popular and spontaneous movement occurred in
1235. At that time, as we know, the Dominicans were sent to Coventry by
the vicar Peter de Tolosa and a relatively aristocratic consulate. According
to Pelisson, the religious were fed by the people, and, when their cloister
was actually blockaded, food was thrown over the walls.[59] There is,
furthermore, some evidence that churchmen consciously exacerbated the
difference between the classes to gain support. In the case against the
"fibularius" before the bishop's court cited above, Pelisson is careful to
say that his inquisitorial colleagues simply presented "faithful witnesses"
in their confrontation with "not a few burghers, and important people of
the town, and the lawyers," who, when their champion ran away to
Lombardy, were confounded.[60]

I will argue elsewhere, moreover, that the generally strong support of
new orthodox initiatives such as the spread of the mendicant mission and
new agancies for public charity and education seems to show that
plebeian adhesion to heresy was relatively weak. But, for the moment, the
matter had better be left here. It is obvious that the amnesty does not give
adequate information on classes other than the highest.

D. WOMEN, FAMILY, AND CATHARISM

It is obvious, furthermore, that far too few women are listed in the
diploma of 1279. The reason is simplicity itself. Because it does not deal
with persons, but rather with "hereditates" which relatively few women
had, our diploma is a somewhat empty vessel. Even comparative figures
are of no service. When we compare, for example, the figures of the
amnesty with those derived from three tax roles, one from the Bourg of
Toulouse in 1335, and two others from neighboring Albi in 1343 and
1357, we perceive that women are better represented in the diploma of
1279 than in these later documents, 26 percent of the whole sample of
1279 as against anywhere from 9 to 19 percent.[61] This is to compare,
however, apples and oranges. The tax roles listed the heads of households,
and there were many more women who had "hereditates" than there
were persons of their sex heading households.

[59] Pelisson, *Chronicon*, p. 103 reports that, in spite of the orders of the consuls and the
vicar, the people fed them, and, when the building was guarded, threw food over the
walls.

[60] Pelisson, *Chronicon*, p. 92: "quamplurimi burgenses et majores de villa et advocati"
against the "testes fideles."

[61] The figures from Toulouse derive from Wolff, *Estimes*, pp. 128ff., and Geneviève
Prat, "Albi et la peste noire," *AduM* 64 (1952) 17ff.

Of itself, for reasons both repeated and obvious, none of this proves a lack of female interest in Catharism, and it may well be that many individuals of this sex were drawn to divergent thought. Historians have often advanced this argument, and have even gone so far as to state that Catharism was essentially propagated by the women of the upper classes.[62] The root of the modern argument, moreover, seems to be a notion that women were more inclined than were men to question the values of the world in which they lived because the orb was ruled by the latter sex. To this has been added a "class" conception, namely the argument that women, like the poor, were a naturally rebellious or even revolutionary element in society, as being among the "exploited." [63]

These positions may be veracious. There is evidence to show that the heretics offered a women a somewhat more elevated role in their religions than did the orthodox. That they were preponderant among the Cathars, however, is doubtful. Evidence in a recent study shows that, although somewhat more so than Catholic female religious, Cathar "perfectae" were not as active as were the male "perfecti." [64] In addition, women were not included in the Cathar hierarchy rising to the grade of bishop. In short, if women were looking for institutional equality, some of the Waldensian sects would have come far closer to fulfilling their ideal. Indeed, it seems not unlikely that women, who were a substantial part of the "poor in spirit," acted in much the same way as did the poor in material goods. Although active in heresy, they also constituted one of the strongest popular constituencies for the new movements of Catholic devotion and especially charitable work.

The reader is also asked to consider the fact that there may have been disadvantages inherent in the relative equality gained by women through heresy. Given the circumstances (especially the lack of meaningful birth control, for example), one wonders if the achievement of an institutionalized religious equality between men and women, especially between a husband and wife, would have made up for the loss of the protection given women against their men by the church. Although, just as did men, it "exploited" women, the church protected them by insisting on the equality of husband and wife, a fictional equality in terms of the realities of power and property in this period. It is also possible that this fiction

---

[62] A view recently reiterated by Lambert *Medieval Heresy*, and shared by both Douais and Guiraud cited in note 41 above.

[63] See, for example, G. Koch, *Frauenfrage und Ketzertum im Mittelalter* (Berlin, 1962).

[64] R. Abels and E. Harrison, "The Participation of Women in Languedocian Catharism," MS 41 (1979) 215-251.

was maintained in place principally because of the sacerdotal presidency over the laity the heretics were so bent on destroying. Faced by the laity, "divide et impera" was a good rule for churchmen, and perhaps, if accidentally, for women also.

Because women in past times were seen in terms of their families, we might look briefly at the relationship of families to heresy. This is well exemplified when we link the amnesty of 1279 to the family histories published in this study. That the need for security made it necessary for man, wife, and children to cleave together in heresy is obvious. But that does not mean that they always did. Even within the central cell of the small family group, there were grave divisions of opinion, ones that may be likened to divorce. When her knightly husband, Peter de Resengas, was seriously sick, his wife Austorga, a Toulousan citizen, had the heretics brought to the bedside to hereticate him. Out of fear or a genuine wish not to participate, he angrily said that he wanted none of that! [65] Usually, however, we see the other side of the coin, as in the Maurand family history, for example, or that of the line of the Rouaix derived from Alaman, and not a few others. The loyal wife also appears. Mabelia, wife of Maurandus "vetus," the condemned perfect, was a Cossano woman who came from a family none of whose males were Cathars. She suffered life immurement for her belief. Another example is Dias Astro, all of whose brothers and male relatives were orthodox, but who was married to the Cathar Vasco de Turre. One child could therefore be of one religion, and his or her siblings of another.

The family histories tell us much. The Toulousan family was small, consisting, even among the rich, largely of a man and wife, an occasional older parent, and children. One branch of a family could therefore be of one religion, and another of another. Look at the Capitedenario. Pons we know to have been the very symbol of Catholic fidelity. Not long after his death, we find his widow Aurimunda interested in the fate of a rural branch of the family, two of whose members were sentenced for heresy. And when we look at the seignorial and knightly line of the Castronovo (Castelnau-d'Estretefons), we see an uncle, the distinguished Aimeric "probushomo," condemned for Catharism, and his nephew Aimeric "junior," heading Bishop Fulk's White Confraternity against heresy and

---

[65] Called Resenquis, Austorga is No. **216** in the amnesty. This event is recorded in TBM, MS 609, fol. 238r in testimony taken in November 1245 about events two years previous: "et tunc ... Petrus ... respondit iratus quod nolebat eos [hereticos]." This Toulousan woman was married to a lord of Cambiac near Caraman in the Lauragais.

usury. The junior Aimeric finally changed sides, and even dabbled with Catharism, but was never touched by ecclesiastical authority.

A final example. The family history will tell the reader that Pons de Capitedenario left 10,000 shillings of Toulouse in charity. A near contemporary was Bernard de Miramonte of the Portaria (now the Place du Capitole).[66] When Bernard dictated his testament in 1237, some years after Pons, he proposed distributing 25,000 shillings (1250 pounds of Toulouse, 3500 of Tours) as well as much property, especially to relatives. His wife's marriage jointure of 4000 shillings and his daughter's dowry of 3000/4000 shillings were on the level of those of grand seigniors.[67] Indicative – could it be? – of the state of mind at Toulouse during the high point of the attack on heresy, Bernard, although clearly Catholic, arranged for his only child, a daughter named Francisca, to marry Stephen de Castronovo, a young man of the Curtasolea family, whose father and uncles, all of them without exception, were to be condemned Cathars. This story is not repeated here to prove that love conquers all. It does not, alas, if only because Francisca was dead by 1254, and Stephen remarried. It merely proves that life is complex.

[66] PAN, J 328 24 (August 1237). See the Curtasolea family history.

[67] A modest artisan, such as the Altarippa seen above in note 55 above, would have a jointure (dowry and marriage gift) of about 60 shillings. When still a modest man, Pons de Capitedenario's wife brought a dowry of 200 shillings (a jointure, then, of about 300 shillings). A patrician, such as the young Astro woman who married into the Cossano, brought a dowry of 1000 shillings, a Castronovo daughter named Castellana brought one of 2600 shillings, and a natural daughter of the count of Toulouse who married the lord of l'Isle-Jourdain had a jointure that may have equalled 10,000 shillings, but she herself only brought 5000.

4

Conclusion

This monograph has examined the history of the gradual conquest of the Midi by the greater power of northern France, and has viewed the rapid crushing of Catharism, the divergent and alternate religion characteristic of this region, as a manifestation of this apparently slow movement of northern might. This extirpation was not unlike a brief and violent storm that precedes a lasting change of weather.

The abatement of the storm after the 1230s does not mean, however, that the people of the time forgot what had happened. Their memories were jogged not only by their own histories, but even by what they saw in their town. An ancient punishment for great crime was to have the home of the criminal torn down. An example may be seen in the case of the Claustro brothers, whose fate has been described earlier. The destruction of their town house in the Close of Saint-Sernin by Montfort's bailiff was among the punishments visited on them for being "faiditi." The rebels' mother persuaded the abbot of Saint-Sernin to have the house torn down brick by brick or beam by beam so that the building materials could be sold by the family.[1] The "destructio domorum" was also visited on condemned heretics. The reader will recall that, in the case of Peter Maurandus, the fathers assembled in Saint-Sernin proposed to destroy his towers in 1178, but the punishment was presumably not carried out. The practice came into its own during the later attack on Catharism. We learn from the register of Gregory IX that, in 1236, the count of Toulouse petitioned the pope in vain to obviate this practice. The count pleaded that such destruction not only hurt the landlord's interest, but also and more appealingly that "so noble a city should not be deformed by ruins, especially because it is men who sin and not property." [2] This curious medieval punishment had social meaning as well. Like many southern

---

[1] See my "Farm of Fontanas at Toulouse," pp. 30 and 36.

[2] *Register*, 2: 1245, No. 4758 (June 1236). The count's arguments were resumed in item 6. The landlords are the "domini," and the phrase translated above reads "cum ... tam nobilem civitatem ruinis non deceat deformari, maxime cum non res sed homines peccaverunt ...."

French and Italian cities, Toulouse was a towered town. Quite deliberately, Montfort did as much harm to its towers as did Louis VIII to those of
Avignon when that city was taken in 1226. Patricians were those who
owned towered houses.

When rehearsing the history of Giles Camelini, the royal officer
intimately involved in the publication of the amnesty of 1279, furthermore, we have seen that, although their incidence was rare in Toulouse
after the 1230s, confiscation and other punishments continued to lower
like threatening clouds. More, not a few comital and later royal officers
like Giles were gratified and perhaps, to use too modern a word, even
salaried by confiscated heretical properties.[3] Even if the back of the town's
Catharism had been broken in the 1230s, the Inquisition was nevertheless
omnipresent. That, to speak of its legal procedures, it was more careful,
no one can doubt. The mid-century northern French inquisitors even
wrote to Alphonse of Poitiers complaining about past illegalities
connected with the Inquisition, asserting that secular authorities had torn
relapsed persons convicted to life imprisonment from the prisons, burning
them forthwith. What was worse, this action had been done with the
complicity of past inquisitors.[4] This legalism does not mean, however, that
the Inquisition had become gentle. We have seen that it was not. It is true
that the great papal codification "Ad extirpanda" of 1252 did not apply at
Toulouse, but the practices of judicial torture, forced delation as a
penitential mechanism, etc. were to appear in the future among the
inquisitors in the Midi.[5]

And if things were undoubtedly easing somewhat within Toulouse's
walls, the rural folk were suffering in the forties and fifties. Curiously,
but, in fact, typically, they were being investigated by a much more
deadly and efficient, and, at the same time, "law-abiding" group of
inquisitors. Gone were the days of the almost lynch-like repression of the
1230s. One may conjecture, in fact, that the ultimate fulfillment of this
institutional evolution awaited the twenties of the fourteenth century
when Jacques Fournier and the inquisitor of Carcassonne conducted their
meticulous investigation into the religious beliefs and private lives of a few
farmers or shepherds, a gentlewoman, a homosexual, a "seduced" priest,

---

[3] Another – of many – example being the southern French notable and officer of
Alphonse of Poitiers named Pons Grimoardi who in Grandselve 9 (October 1253) is seen
holding property once of Bernard Curtasolea, clearly confiscated for heresy.

[4] *HGL*, vol. 8, No. 465 (dated January 1255) written by Reginald of Chartres and John
of Saint-Pierre. Dossat, *Inquisition*, p. 191 has emended this date to January 1257.

[5] P. Fiorelli, *La tortura giudiziaria* (1953) 1:80. Issued in 1252, "Ad extirpanda" was
confirmed and expanded to all of Italy in 1259 and 1265.

a leper, and a passing Jew. Then, so to speak, not a few "policemen" with more than enough time on their hands pursued a few marginal "criminals." [6] Heresy had been driven not only from the capital city, but also from the plains, up into the foothills of the mountains.

I do not wish to leave the reader with the impression that coercion alone destroyed Catharism in Toulouse and its region. Although indispensable, force was not enough, and indeed tended to create its own antidote. There were therefore other ways by which the base of divergent thought was undermined and its appeal dispelled. The growth of preaching helped to destroy this divergent belief.[7] Education, symbolized by the University of Toulouse, was producing its first trained jurists by mid-century, and, even before that, the rude monks of the countryside were flooding into town to study letters and create a more instructed clergy.[8] As or more appealing to the people was the expansion of charitable agencies and of social policies by the clergy and laity of the time,[9] with which should be associated the development of the monarchical principle and the social and economic corporatism sketched above earlier in this book. Two caveats ought to be introduced at this point. The first and most important one will not be argued or proved in this monograph. It is this: that we do not witness here a case of a people simply responding to the initiatives of

---

[6] One of the happy results of this strange event is that the record about the deviants of 1325 recorded in the register of Jacques Fournier, bishop of Pamiers, gives far richer information about the persons being investigated than the record of the investigations of 1245-1246 recorded in TBM, MS 609 and discussed in my "Village, Town, and City," pp. 141-190, and often in these pages. In spite of the contemporary chronicles by William of Puylaurens and William Pelisson mentioned below, we have still less information about the persons investigated or condemned at Toulouse before the 1240s. TBM, MS 609 has yet to be published, but the text of the depositions of 1325 has. See J. Duvernoy ed., *Le registre d'inquisition de Jacques Fournier*, and, for some observations about its rich contents, Le Roy Ladurie, *Montaillou* (1975).

[7] On preaching and reconversion, see the recent study of 1977 by Father Vicaire about the first generations of the Dominican order called *Dominique et ses prêcheurs*.

[8] See my "Village, Town, and City," p. 177 especially note 33. There we see that a prior of Saint-Pierre-des-Cuisines had become a "magister in decretis" before October 1253, and how a Thomas de Dalbs, who had been among the clergy from Moissac "in Tholosa studentes et sequentes studium litterarum" as a "clericus" in December 1241, was described as a "magister" in October 1253.

[9] For hospitals, etc., see my "Charity and Social Work in Toulouse 1100-1250," *Traditio* 22 (1966) 203-288, a lengthy article now being expanded and revised. It mentioned, but failed to understand, the prime importance to the poor of the popular confraternities such as that associated with the Hospital of Saint-Jacques, and it failed to record the new and specialized function of housing fallen women shown in the Dominican seizure of the old town hospital of the Arnaud Bernard Gate, a point picked up by Father Vicaire in his *Dominique et ses prêcheurs*, p. 248.

their princes and prelates. The initiatives were instead ones that were generated by the people as well as by their "leaders." [10]

The second caveat is that persuasion may not be divorced from coercion. Preaching is great, but we must remember that, when the mendicants preached against heresy, attendance was obligatory. [11] Education is great, but Roland of Cremona, the first Dominican to hold a chair of theology at Paris did not only teach. Come to Toulouse to help found the university, this "divinus" was among the leaders of a mob on Christmas day in 1231 who rushed to the house where the Waldensian Galvannus had died, tore it down, made it into a latrine, disinterred the body, and dragged it off to be burned in the dump. [12] Still, education was winning out over repression by the mid-century. In 1250 Bishop William of Agen, papal inquisitor, granted the monastery of Saint-Sernin a house across the street from the monastery's Hospital of Saint-Raymond, in which poor students were already being housed. Confirmed by the Dominican inquisitors six years later, this building had been a prison of the Inquisition. Now, housing students, it helped create the College of Saint-Raymond. [13]

In conclusion, it cannot be doubted that the violence of the Albigensian crusade and the subsequent violence of the trials, the obligatory attendance at public preaching, indeed the whole structure of repression created by the inquisitors and their supporters among the people left deep and angry memories. This does not, however, mean that the families on whom the heaviest measure of the oppression fell lost more than the minds and bodies of those members who were killed or imprisoned, together with a certain amount of property. Although it stands to reason that the immediate families of those whose goods were confiscated must have suffered, what the family histories appended here nevertheless clearly prove is that hard hit clans could not only survive, but flourish

[10] For the main lines of this argument, see the introductory sketch to the history of Toulousan political institutions at the beginning of Chapter 2 above, which forms the central argument of a forthcoming study, and my proposal to deal seriously with the confraternities mentioned in the note above.

[11] PBN, Doat 24, fol. 85 (January 1247) where the count repeated orders to the people of the castles and villages to cease work and listen to the preaching of the Dominicans and Franciscans not merely on Sundays and feast days, but whenever they arrived.

[12] Pelisson, *Chronicon*, pp. 86-88: "Legebat ibi tunc temporis theologiam magister Rotlandus, qui venerat de Parisius, ubi fuerat factus magister in theologia cathedralis." A large mob or procession went to the house "et eam funditus destruxerunt, et fecerunt eam locum sterquilinii ...." The body having been dug up, it was dragged "per villam" and burned "in loco communi extra villam ...."

[13] See my "origins of the College of Saint-Raymond," in *Philosophy and Humanism*, ed. E. P. Mahoney (Leiden, 1976), pp. 454-461.

greatly. What is more, this is shown not only by large and broadly based clans, such as the Castronovo (Castelnau-d'Estretefons), Maurandi, and Roaxio, but also by small families, such as Curtasolea and Unde. What the families that managed to survive and even flower lost was simply the liberty of choosing which religion suited their bent best. Gone were the days when a gravely sick woman lying at Beaupuy outside of Toulouse had a friend of the lordly Unaud family of Lanta who thoughtfully brought out "perfecti" from town to hereticate her. She allowed, however, "that she did not want to be hereticated, but instead to enter an order, as indeed she did." [14] A later Brialhas de Bellomonte would no longer have the choice.

The feeling of Toulousans about what had transpired varied widely. In part there was bitterness. The reader may remember Raymond Gros who delated on the Cathars early in the days of the Inquisition, and who entered the Franciscan order. Could this possibly have been the Franciscan friar of the same name who is recorded in the testimony of a fantast named Raymond Garsias in 1247 as having been hereticated at death by a Cathar "perfectus"? Whether or not this is so, Raymond Garsias is himself fascinating because he shows that Catharism was becoming syncretist, picking up conceptions derived from the developing radicalism of the "left" Franciscan sects then largely seen in Italy and Provence, and soon to flourish in maritime Languedoc. Apart from his compulsive boldness in speaking his mind, what is remarkable is this dualist's hostility to property generally and specifically to Pope Sylvester who had "corrupted" the church. He added that, including those of Francis of Assisi, visible or non-mental miracles were pure nonsense, and that crusaders, whether against the Saracens, the Hohenstaufen, or the defenders of Montségur, were mere murderers. [15]

Raymond's testimony is intriguing because ideas similar to his had taken root in the minds of people whose bitterness persisted. In 1274, a group of "heretics" was rounded up. Living here and there in the town, their world was one composed largely of turners, carpenters, needle-makers, humble smiths, an occasional Crutched Friar, and a Franciscan. These workers had not forgotten or forgiven the repression, and used

[14] TBM, MS 609, fol. 201v testimony of July 1246 about an event 15 years prior. Raymond Unaldus brought the heretics who were living in the house "dels Rochovilas" in town near the Croix Baragnon, and "ipsa infirma mandavit eis quod nolebat hereticari sed monachari, et ita fiat monachata."

[15] C. Douais, *Documents pour servir à l'histoire de l'inquisition*, 2: 90ff. For this, see also No. **201** in Chapter 5 below, namely Raymond Peter de Planis who is said to have been a "perfectus" when called to the deathbed of the Franciscan Raymond Gros.

views like Raymond's to justify their anger. Some were convinced that the mendicants were the false prophets foretold in the gospel; others had heard an odd idea from the Franciscan who asserted that the faith did not come from Rome, but instead from nature itself.[16] Having had her father "unjustly" condemned to the fire, the wife of a carpenter named Fabrissa recalled that a condemned heretic on the run said that Languedoc was under the French heel, and that the French and the clergy had combined to crush the people of the region.[17]

By this time, around 1270, persons of higher social status were either more careful or more resigned to the rule of the French monarchy. A response to the vain attempt of Toulouse to restore its old political liberties, an investigation into the government of the town at the time of Raymond VII was mounted around 1274. Thirty-two aged witnesses, the majority, perhaps all, being citizens and town dwellers, were brought forward. Our sample is biased: all of our witnesses are those who spoke for the crown. All the same, what we are dealing with here does not concern the burden of the testimony by these old men. Those on the opposing side would merely have argued that, in the days of Raymond VII, the town elected its own consuls, and would scarcely have had different opinions about the fact of the conquest by the northern French.

Of these worthies, ten had fought, only two being absent during wartime, one comfortably ensconced in Marseille. Five of the ten had been wounded, two specifying that they had been hit by quarrels, one adding that he had lost his horse.[18] Another was happy to report that, if he was twice wounded, he had also wounded enemy soldiers.[19] Oddly enough, in view of the importance of the battle of Muret in September 1213, only one witness spoke of that disastrous field, and then indirectly.[20]

---

[16] PBN, Doat 25, ff. 15v-16r and 25r-v (June and July 1273). The Crutched friar was Gerald Bonuspanis from the house in the City of Toulouse who was met on the route from Rome.

[17] Ibid., ff. 41v-44r (February 1274): "dicens idem Poncius quod multum sibi displicebat dominium Gallicorum et quia clerici et Gallici convenerant pro eo quia pro hoc ... gentes destruunt et confundunt." Doat's dating is confused, the transcriber having sometimes written 1273 and sometimes 1274. It could therefore be a year later. The person who made these observations was a Pons de Gomervilla, for whom see the family of farmers mentioned in the Gamevilla family history below.

[18] PAN, J 305 32 (circa 1274) ff. 3r, 6v, and 8r.

[19] Ibid., fol. 2r-v where John de Morlas (Morlanis) said he was "in dicta guerra vulneratus et ipse vulneravit aliquos de Theutonicis."

[20] Ibid., fol. 6v where Peter Bernard "boaterius" said that "fuit vulneratus in dicta guerra [Simonis Montisfortis] cum carrello per tibiam et plures alii de Tholosa cum ipso usque ad .xxx. homines de Tholose qui erant de parte comitis Ramundi." The "boaterius" was presumably speaking of his company, because many more Toulousans died at Muret than 30.

The absence of the name of this great engagement in this testimony tells us that these oldsters were not just old soldiers reminiscing about "their" war, they were also expressing the ideas of the southern side, those of the defeated party. Only one person stated unequivocally that he had served in Simon's army.[21] Only two referred to the fact that Toulouse had been under the interdict during the war, and the war itself was never termed a crusade, but instead a "guerra" between the party of the counts of Touluse "et inter ecclesia et sibi adherentes." Royal France, with which Toulouse was bound up by 1274, was treated carefully. Louis VIII was always called a king and the grandfather of the present king, and he always moved "cum suo exercitu." The witnesses' venom was reserved for Simon and his son Amaury. When Amaury was with his army, he was always "cum suis complicibus." Simon was treated even more harshly. His victories at Castelnaudary and Muret went unrecorded, and his death in harness before Toulouse was passed over without comment. In fact, these often quite intelligent old men did not like to say that they had been beaten by the French from the north. Until the Capetian monarch intervened, they describe – quite inaccurately, in fact – the enemy as the "Theutonici seu Alemanni." [22] This desire to escape the reality of the defeat at the hands of the northern French, shows the bitter memory hidden in the minds of the Toulousans of the generations of the war, but it also shows resignation, a wish to call it a day.

Others paraded pro-French sentiments. In 1269 an individual named Garnier was charged with having incited a riot against public authority because of the local tolls on Toulousan trade. During the riot, one of the vicar's policemen had been assaulted, and our man had addressed a mob estimated at 4000 men, crying out that "we [citizens] are as oppressed as any Jew from Jews Street!" [23] Exculpating himself during his trial,

---

[21] See the brief history of William Capel in Chapter 1 note 49 above, and also the Gamevilla family history in Part 3 below.

[22] PAN, J 305 32, fol. 2r typically: "Item dixit quod vidit quod Theutonici seu Alemanni dicto tempore obsederunt civitatem et villam Tholosam et fecerunt guerram generalem seu universalem in terra ista seu comitatu Tholose." Naturally, an "Alemannus" was a person from the border overlapping the French and German speaking frontier. Furthermore, troops other than French played a role in the crusade, but a rather small one. Most of the troops from imperial territories were French-speaking. At Montgey (for which see the discussion of purported war crimes in Chapter 1 above), the defeated force of "Teutonici vel Alemanni" were crusaders under the command of Nicholas of Basoches, up near Reims. The southern side, moreover, itself employed troops raised in the Empire, notably Brabantese.

[23] PAN, J 192b 21, partially published in *Layettes du Trésor*, No. 5487 pp. 324b-325b: "... quod sumus plus sosmes que nulh Juzios de Juzaigas" – Jew's water, or Joutzaigues, a modern street in the City.

Garnier argued that he had always been loyal to the crown, and notably so. He was, he said, especially close to the French ("Gallici") and their officers. This was because, when Montfort was making war on Toulouse, his father and brother sided "with the church," and hence had become exiles taking refuge in Carcassonne. His brother, indeed, had been killed in the war, and his father, a "royal archer," had died in the king's service.[24]

Motivated love, surely. But is there any other here on earth?

---

[24] Ibid.: "Item quod est et esse consuevit familiaris curialium et Gallicorum. Item quod tam frater quam pater suus se tenebant cum ecclesia, tempore quo comes Montisfortis garrificabat contra Tholosam. Item quod propter illud fuerunt facti exules et amiserunt quicquid Tolose habebant. Item quod ipsi secuti fuerunt comitem Montisfortis Carcassonam. Item quod ibi frater suus fuit interfectus in bello per inimicos dicti comitis. Item quod pater suus, arquerius regis, decessit in suo servicio."

Part Two

The Petition and Amnesty of 1279

5

The Royal Amnesty of August 1279

The amnesty was recorded in a lengthy instrument dated, as was the custom of the royal chancery, only by the month and the regnal and calendrical years. I found two copies of this act. The first is in a large roll housed in the town archives of Toulouse containing copies of past privileges by the counts of Toulouse, designed to persuade Philippe vi, king of France, of the validity of Toulouse's traditional privileges. Catalogued as TAM II 63, the roll is entitled "Requête presentée au Roy Philippe iv par les consuls de Toulouse pour la confirmation des privilèges de la ville," and was composed sometime during or after 9 January 1309, the latest document there included. This dating derives from Saint-Blanquat's entry in his *Inventaire*, 2:2. The text of the amnesty follows immediately after the initial act contained in the roll. Badly damaged, this act records the petition by the consuls of Toulouse to the king described on pp. 35-36 above. The prologue introducing the copy of the amnesty describes it as "litera compositionis." A second copy is also to be found in the town archives of Toulouse in AA 34 3. This is a vidimus dated 1 February 1313 made by the vicar of the "judex ordinarius" of the town. In the roll of around 1309 (TAM II 63 iii) cited above, the amnesty is immediately followed by a royal letter confirming the possession of knight's fees acquired by Toulousan citizens and ecclesiastics within a prescription period of twenty years, a letter that unfortunately contains no date of the year, but is merely dated by the phrase: "Datum Parisius in vigilia nativitatis beati Joannis Baptiste." Although the Nativity of John the Baptist was 24 June, it seems sure that the date was 25 August, the feast of his Decollation or "Dies Natalis," so named in honor of his birth into eternal bliss. This date, together with the fact that the diploma containing the amnesty of 1279 included the regnal year – the ninth year of Philippe iii – enables us to date it as having been issued sometime between August 1 and 24.

The spelling of the names of these persons reflects the style of the time when the amnesty and its copies were written. The older custom of Toulouse's notaries whereby a person was known by the nominative forms of his Christian names, for example, Bernardus Ramundus de Tolosa, had slowly given way to the use of the genitive for the second Christian name. A striking example of this is an individual named "Bernardus Ramundi Baranhoni filius quondam Bernardi Ramundi Baranhoni" seen as a proctor in the petition of March 1279 in PAN, J 313 95. If, furthermore, the second name was a family name, as Raymond Centullus, the style had come to be to use the genitive in this case also, Raymond Centulli, for example. This was purely a matter of style. Elsewhere, as in Italy, for example, the use of the genitive in the case of a second name meant that the person was the son of the individual whose name was in the genitive. It had no such meaning in Toulouse at this period. If, however, the surname or second name was a craft or professional designation, that name sometimes remained in the nominative, Bertrand Petrarius, for example, or Bernard Medicus. This retention of the nominative for a craft or professional title seems to imply that the person so designated was in that craft or profession, but such was not necessarily the case. Lastly, the scribes of the copies, or perhaps of the original or originals, were not consistent because they were adapting to the new style texts that had been written in the older one. A result of this is that I have changed the names back to what they were when the individuals were condemned. If there is a family sketch or history in Part Three dealing with the person mentioned, it is signalled at the end of the entry by the appropriate name of the family in capitals, thus ROAXIO, etc.

The text is printed in its actual sequence with the list of the names inserted in its original order, but each name will have attached to it the available archival information. To avoid repetition, however, certain documents are not explicitly cited in this section. These include TAM, AA 1 75 (a list of the consuls of Toulouse and their councillors in March 1222), PAN, J 310 45 (the hostages sent to Paris in April 1229), and PAN, J 305 29 (those who took oath in February 1243 to uphold the Peace of Paris of 1229).

IN NOMINE SANCTE ET INDIVIDUE TRINITATIS, AMEN.

Philippus dei gratia Francorum rex notum facimus universis tam presentibus quam futuris quod, cum inter magistrum Egidium Camelini, canonicum Meldensem, clericum et procuratorem positum pro nobis et nomine nostro ex una parte, et omnes quamplurimos Tholosanos tam pro se quam pro concivibus suis et aliis quorum intererat vel interesse poterat ex altera, super hereditatibus, bonis et rebus quibusdam quas et que iidem cives, et qui ab ipsis vel aliquibus civibus tamen Tholose, de quorum bonis habitus est tractatus inferius, ipsi causas habent possidendi, habebant, tenebant seu possidebant vel quasi, quas et que idem procurator noster asserebat vel asserere poterat ad nos pertinere de jure, scilicet tam occasione penitentie que dicebatur fuisse iniuncta per bone memorie Romanum tituli Sancti Angeli dyaconum cardinalem tunc apostolice sedis legatum aut occasione heresis, homicidii, furti, falsi quam occasione etiam alterius cuiuscumque criminis a civibus Tholose vel antecessoribus eorum civium Tholose dudum comissi vel qui poterat dici comissum, propter quod bona eorum tanquam comissa vel fiscalia vaccantia peti posset et que petere intendebat vel poterat ex causis et rationibus antedictis coram dilectis fidelibus nostris G. abbate Belleperitice, P. decano ecclesie beati Martini Turonensis, et Magistro Johanne de Puteolis canonico Carnotensi, clericis nostris ad Tholosanam et Agenensem senescallias pro requirendis juribus nostris destinatis, esset vel esse posset vel posse speraretur materia questionis, tandem memorati cives pro se et aliis universis et singulis rerum seu bonorum predictorum possessoribus tam civibus quam aliis a quibus ipsi vel qui ab ipsis civibus causam seu causas habuerunt possidendi que tamen bona fuerunt civium Tholose et quorum interest vel intererat et interesse poterat, nostre super predictis se supposuerunt omnimode voluntati.

Hinc est quod nos, consideratis devotis desideriis omnium predictorum, et volentes agere misericorditer cum eisdem, de gratia speciali quam nos eisdem civibus facimus et facere intendimus per nos, heredes et successores nostros, donamus, concedimus, cedimus, absolvimus et quitamus et ex certa sciencia confirmamus civibus memoratis, heredibus et successoribus suis, et etiam aliis qui ab ipsis causas habent et habuerunt possidendi vel quasi, hereditates, res et bona predicta que dudum fuerunt civium Tholose pro quorum delictis vel penitentiis hereditates predicte et bona venerunt in comissum seu venisse dicuntur ex causis predictis, et quorum hereditates et bona dumtaxat per presentes litteras intendimus confirmare, ab eisdem civibus et antecessoribus eorumdem civium Tholose dudum vel in presenti adquisita, habita et possessa vel quasi, et quicquid juris vel actionis habemus vel habere debemus vel possumus in hereditatibus, bonis vel rebus eorumdem quoad proprietatem et possessionem ex quocunque comisso, quacunque forefactura, scilicet occasione penitentie dicti legati aut heresi, homicidio, falso, furto aliove crimine seu ex quacunque causa alia vel occasione propter que et quas dicte hereditates, res et bona dictorum civium venerint vel venisse potuerint in comissum usque ad tempus quo possessio comitatus Tholose post mortem clare memorie Alfonsi patrui nostri, quondam comitis Pictavie et Tholose, ad nos noscitur pervenisse, habenda, tenenda, possidenda pacifice et quiete per eosdem cives et alios possessores, heredes et successores eorum, et quod voluerint titulo iusto concessionis presentis et suo jure perpetuo libere quecumque sint et ubicumque sint dum tamen fuerint civium predictorum qui penitentiam a dicto legato dicuntur habuisse seu condempnatorum per inquisitores heretice pravitatis vel alios quoscumque judices vel fugitivorum pro causis seu criminibus supradictis vel antecessorum eorum civium tamen Tholosanorum aut ab eis fuerint habita vel possessa seu in quibus de predictis jus aliquod habebant prout melius actenus ipsi vel antecessores eorum ea habuerunt et tenuerunt vel etiam ipsi cives et alii possessores habent et possident in presenti de dictis bonis, et que de dictis bonis possidebant tempore motelitis seu controversie seu usque ad tempus orte questionis per procuratorem et gerentem nostram coram predictis decano et eius collegis et etiam coram magistris Fulcone de Lauduno et quondam Thoma de Parisius clericis nostris pro predictis ad partes illas destinatis a nobis vel quocunque alio tempore predicta bona possidebant vel possiderant vel quasi, et ad utilitatem ipsorum possessorum melius dici vel intelligi possit pro sua voluntate tanquam de rebus propriis perpetuo facienda; donationes insuper venditiones, absolutiones, compositiones, confirmationes, infeudationes, et quaslibet concessiones factas de predictis bonis in toto vel in parte predictis possessoribus vel eorum antecessoribus vel illis a quibus habent causam per dudum comites Tholosanos, senescallos, vicarios et ministros eorum de hereditatibus, bonis et rebus supradictis de gratia speciali approbamus, laudamus et certa scientia confirmamus, nolentes quod predicti cives, heredes et successores eorum quoad predicta bona decetero molestentur pretextu illius constitutionis que incipit "cupientes" aliove statuto vel jure aliquo, insuper processus et sententias pro nobis vel pro dudum comitibus Tholosanis super predictis rebus et bonis universis et singulis habitis nullum volumus in posterum nocumentum afferre civibus antedictis.

Item volumus quod de predictis bonis ratione feudi militaris nulla de cetero questio moveatur eisdem.

Predictas autem concessiones et confirmationes facimus, salvis nobis, heredibus et successoribus nostris redevanciis nostris quas inde debebant et debent nobis facere vel predecessoribus nostris facere consueverunt veteres possessores, et salvo iure nostro super superprisiis rerum et jurium nostrorum si quas contra predictas hereditates seu bona dicti cives fecerunt, et salvo jure quolibet alieno. Rursus

[TAM, AA 34 3]	[TAM, II 63]
domos que per sententiam, preceptionem vel ordinationem dicti legati vel cuiuslibet judicis vel persone ecclesiastice occasione criminis heresis vel alterius cuiuscumque [criminis] dirute fuerunt seu condempnatione que ne dirutioni sed condempnationi istas commoda subjacet, reffici seu rehedificari et redificatas et integras remanere perpetuo concedimus et restitudendas et quitandas duximus	pro nobis et successoribus nostris nolumus aliquod impedimentum affer[r]i civibus Tholosanis quorum interest sub pretextu sententie, precepti, ordinationis cuiuslibet judicis que proponi possent pro nobis super dirutione domorum, quominus liceat ipsis domos que dirutioni subiacent in statu in quo nunc sunt vel meliori tenere, destructas refficere, rehedificare, vel rehedificatas et integras retinere. Nos etiam ipsas quantum ad nos attinet perpetuo restituendas sibi duximus et quitandas, scilicet

possessoribus earundem pro omnibus suis voluntatibus inde perpetuo faciendis, exceptis illis que a viginti annis citra fuerint condempnate.

Nomina vero civium qui pro seipsis et concivibus suis et aliis quorum interest et interesse potest absentibus omnibus et singulis presentem munificenciam literalitatem nostram et gratiam receperunt hec sunt, scilicet

[See the list of proctors below in Chapter 6]

Ad maioris sane gratie cumulum concedimus filiis et nepotibus omnium predictorum qui de predictis criminibus dicebantur teneri et aliis de genere eorundem quod possint et eis liceat juste tamen et justis titulis acquirere et acquisita tenere, heredes et successores quos voluerint facere et habere et testari valeant de eisdem vendere, alienare, distrahere et donare et facere suas ex omnes inde perpetuo voluntates. Verum si a predicto tempore quo adepti fuimus possessionem predicti comitatus, aliqui ex ipsis comiserint propter quod bona eorum venire debeant in comissum, ipsos ab eodem comisso non intendimus liberare.

Nomina vero illorum civium quorum hereditates et bona dumtaxat confirmamus et intendimus per presentem litteram confirmare sunt hec:

1 Raymond Centullus. For Raymond's wife, see No. **166** below. Raymond was presumably the member of the count's court seen in 1200/1 and a consul in 1202-1203. He is seen as a creditor for 90 shillings in E 501, iii (August 1230, copied in 1238). Pelisson remarks (pp. 101 and 111) that he was a "credens" when condemned. PBN, Doat 21, fols. 145v-146v tells us that he was one of those protected by the consuls in July 1237.

2 Aimeric de Castronovo. According to my family history, Aimeric, the youngest son of Peter William Pilistortus, was usually entitled "maior" to distinguish him from his nephew of the same name. A knight, he was also a lord of Castelnau-d'Estretefons and a frequent consul. He often appeared in the testimony about heresy, as did his wife, for whom see below No. **134**. CASTRONOVO

3 Castellusnovus, his son. This knight is seen from 1222 to 1249, and we know that he was dead by 1258, when he left two sons, Aimeric and Castellusnovus. Like his father, he is seen in most of the sources recording evidence about heresy. For his wife, see No. **135** below. The petitioners and proctors of March 1279 are listed below in chapter 6. They were Castellusnovus, the son of the Castellusnovus mentioned in this entry. This younger Castellusnovus is seen in the charters from 1258 to 1279. In addition to him were the petitioners Aimeric de Castronovo "domicellus" or squire, and his brother Raymond, the former of whom was seen from 1271 to 1279, and both of whom were the sons of Castellusnovus' brother Aimeric, who was dead by 1271. CASTRONOVO

4 Raymond Carabordas. The son of William Carabordas, Raymond was described as a merchant in 1230, and was among the creditors of Maurand "vetus" in 1233. According to my family sketch, he was dead by 1254, leaving sons named Raymond and William. Active in heresy, he was sentenced to life imprisonment in February 1237. For his wife, see No. **138** below. The above named sons, Raymond and William, were presumably the two who were petitioners in 1279, and are seen from 1254 until 1283. CARABORDAS

5 Carabordas. My family sketch is unable to identify this member of the family more specifically. The use of a family name as a complete appellation was frequent in Toulousan families, but does not exclude the possibility that such a person carried an ordinary Christian name also. An individual named Carabordas was a consul in 1231-1232. He and his wife

Elis are mentioned as heretics around 1226 and 1227, and for her, see No. **69** below. CARABORDAS

6 Bernard Signarius. Bernard was a consul in 1217-1218, 1222-1223, 1231-1232, and 1235-1238, and, as we also see in PAN, J 330 9 (July 1222), he was close to the count. We learn in Saint-Sernin 674 (19 63 6) (July 1200) that he had a brother named Pelegrinus or Peregrinus. He may have been the Peregrin mentioned below as No. **266**. Bernard is mentioned by Pelisson, pp. 101 and 106 and in vernacular spellings of his names, Seneier, for example, in PBN, Doat 23, fols. 293r and 924v. He was condemned to perpetual immurement as relapsed in PBN, Doat 21, fols. 149v-150r in March 1237. There is reference to his confiscated property in a lawsuit against the bishop of Toulouse in PAN, KK 1228, fol. 58v in October 1273-January 1274, and also in "La Philippine" of September 1279 published in La Faille, *Annales de la ville de Toulouse*, vol. 1, "Recueil de plusieurs pièces," pp. iii-iv.

7 Raymond Signarius. He was a relative of the above Signarius and possibly a brother of the Peregrin Signarius seen as No. **266** below. Raymond is seen with Peregrin in G. A. Puybusque, *Généalogie Puybusque*, pp. 16-17 (September 1219), and was a councilor for the consuls together with Peregrin and Bernard in March 1222. The last charters mentioning Raymond are several in Garidech terminating with Malta Garidech (1 2) 1 ii (June 1235, copied in 1238). He was surely deceased when we see a reference to his son John Signarius in Clares 24, 2nd act of 2 tied together (May 1268, copied in 1292).

8 Arnold Onda. My family sketch notes that Arnold was a consul in 1218-1220, and that he was seen in 1224. In 1262 his sons, called those of the quondam Arnold Unde "de Cruce Baranhoni," are seen. Presumably one of these sons, an Arnold Unde served as petitioner and proctor in 1279. UNDE

9 Peter Onda, his brother. Peter is seen as a consul in 1226-1227, and also in 1228. For his wife, see No. **137** below. UNDE

10 Raymond de Mirapisce. Pelisson, p. 101, describes him as a "credens." For his wife, see No. **140** below.

11 Arnold Rogerius. According to Pelisson, p. 101, he was sentenced in 1236, and later became a bishop of the Cathars. MS 609, fols. 65r and 197v (respectively dated around 1230 and 1220) has reference to his house in town and his son Raymond. Arnold was seen in the following charters: E 538 (October 1218) as holding a mortgage, and Malta 116 24 (August 1222) where we see him and his son Raymond. He also served as a consul in 1222-1223. See also Nos. **17** and **81** below. A William Rogerius "apotecarius" was a petitioner in 1279 which may mean little.

12 John Curtasolea. My family sketch notes that this was a brother of Stephen, Peter Raymond, and Bernard. Several times a consul during the war, John was active from 1204 to the oath to uphold the Peace of Paris of February 1243. For his relatives and wife, see Nos. **92**, **132**, and **141-144** below. CURTASOLEA

13 Stephen Curtasolea. Stephen was also seen in the house of Maurand "vetus," together with his wife Bermunda, circa 1232. The relationship of the Curtasolea and the Maurandi was always close, and helps to explain how both families were so given to Catharism. For Maurand "vetus" or senior, see No. **89** below. Stephen was once a consul during the war years, and had three sons Stephen, John, and Raymond who respectively appeared in 1237, 1243, and 1232. These sons were very successful and changed the name of the family, or of part of it, to (de) Castronovo. The petitioner and proctor of this family was Raymond de Castronovo de Burgo acting for himself and for the heirs of John de Castronovo. In my family sketch, Raymond was presumably the aged son of the heretic Stephen Curtasolea and was first seen in the charters in 1232. The heirs of his brother John (seen from 1243 to around 1274 and possibly to 1276) were represented only by a Stephen seen in 1257 and perhaps again in 1283. Note also the William de Garrigiis who acted for his wife domina Johanna de Castronovo, clearly a Curtasolea woman. CURTASOLEA

14 Arnold de Roaxio. My family history records several contemporary Arnolds of this family, one of whom was the brother of the notable Alaman senior, for whom see No. **130** below. Judging from the petitioner of 1279, however, this Arnold is presumably the one seen in charters of 1224 and 1231, and whose son named William is mentioned in 1230, or, alternatively, he is the brother of Alaman seen first in 1200 and deceased by 1236 whose son William is seen in 1236 and 1249, and who was possibly dead by 1273. Spoken for by Berengar Barravus, the petitioners were the heirs of the deceased Doat de Roaxio, seen in the charters from 1272 to 1277. Doat was the son of William, and grandson of Arnold, and left two sons, a Peter and Sicard, seen in 1294. Note also the petitioner Aimeric who descends from a Bernard, a cousin of Alaman and Arnold. The final petitioner is a Bernard who can be found nowhere in my family sketch. ROAXIO

15 Pons Palmata. It is not known which of the two Pons Palmatas this is. There was a Pons junior, the son of an older Pons who was consul in 1204-1205. The junior was consul in 1207-1208 and again in 1218-1220, and was, as we see in E 509 (July 1205), an associate of Arnold and Pons Puer (or Mancipius, for whom seen No. **40** below), and a creditor of Maurand "vetus" (No. **89** below) in Saint-Sernin 599 (10 35 15), 6th of 9 charters tied together (November 1233). One of these Pons Palmatas' property was confiscated and sold by the consuls of the Bourg, the quarter in which he lived, in E 579 (December 1220) published in *HGL*, vol. 8, No. 210 for non-payment of taxes.

16 Arnold Guido "maior." Pelisson records the name of this "credens" condemned to pilgrimage by Cardinal Roman. In 1237 we see the testament of this man "volens ire in partibus transmarinis ratione penitentie sibi iniuncte a domino Romano apostolice sedis legato ...." My family sketch records that his father's name was William, and that he was called "maior" when consul in 1218-1220 in order to distinguish him from his cousin Arnold who was his heir in the testament mentioned above. His mother was Rica (for whom, see No. **182** below). His cousin Arnold, who had been called "iuvenis" when listed as a consul in 1217-1218 and 1225-1226, must have effectually replaced him when he went to the Holy Land, but the older Arnold may have returned. We have a family charter in which a witness is Arnold de naRica in June 1250. Just as a father's, a mother's name could be used in lieu of a surname at Toulouse. The proctor of 1279 was a Bernard Guido de Burgueto Novo (Borguet-Nau) whose relationship to the heretic is not known, but who is seen in the charters from 1268 to 1279. GUIDO

17 Raymond Rogerius. Pelisson, pp. 99, 101 and 111 records that Raymond was called major (for his son of the same name called minor, see No. **81** below), lived in the Bourg, and was a "perfectus." MS 609, fol. 197v shows him active in Catharism around 1220, and Bernard Oth, lord of Niort, testified the same in Doat 24, fol. 88v. Doat 23, fol. 301v gives us the impression that he died at Montségur. He was excommunicated in July 1237 and, together with his sister Oliva, sentenced to perpetual imprisonment as relapsed in February 1237, for which see Doat 21, fols. 145v and 149v. Unusually, Oliva is not listed here, but she may have been the wife of Hugh of Murello mentioned below as No. **150**.

18 Raymond de Ulmo. This person was surely a consul in 1221-1222, and may have been so before in 1204-1205 and 1207-1208. Belonging to an artisan family or one of that milieu, a person of this name is seen in Douais, *Saint-Sernin*, No. 67 (September 1181), a sale of property to Raymond and his wife Vitalia. In E 2 (December 1201, copied in 1211) we see the brothers Peter and Raymond, and in Malta 2 168 iv and v (respectively dated February 1205 and March 1236, both copied in 1236) the brothers Raymond and Bernard de Ulmo. In TAM, II 45 (October 1215) we confirm what was in the consular list, namely that our man is a Raymond de Ulmo de Burgo. For a possible relative, see No. **102** below. A Raymond de Ulmo was a petitioner in 1279.

19 Bernard Faber. A consul of that name in 1203-1204, 1220-1221, 1224-1225, and 1231-1232. A Bernard Faber appeared in Doat 23, fol. 295r-v, but, since the name means Smith, little can be done with it. The same is true of the Bernard Faber who took the oath of 1243 to the Peace of Paris. See the other "fabri" below in Nos. **94** and **263**.

20-21 Bernard Faber's unnamed brothers. There is no information on these people.

22 Jordan de Villanova. At least three times a consul, this knight is heard of in the charters used in the Villanova family history from 1183 until 1230. Together with his wife Magna, he is mentioned prominently in Pelisson. Jordan was given a life sentence as being relapsed in February 1238. See also No. **25** below. The petitioner for this family was Arnold de Villanova, whose relationship to Jordan and his son cannot now be traced. VILLANOVA

23 Arnold de Villanova his son. The family sketch shows him as active from 1207 to 1222. Several times a consul, he had a son named Pons seen from 1243 to 1250. This knight is often referred to in MS 609, where, among other things, we see him "adoring" some "perfecti" in the house of the knight Estult de Rocovilla near the Croix Baragnon during the Albigensian war (for the Rocovilla family, see Nos. **121** and **130** below). One reference of 1245 also describes him as defunct. We learn in a suit of the crown against the bishop of Toulouse of October 1273 that the bishop had obtained his property near Verfeil. VILLANOVA

24 Ramunda, wife of Arnold de Villanova. See the next person listed. VILLANOVA

25 Magna, wife of Jordan de Villanova. The amnesty's text reads: "Jordanus de Villanova, Arnaldus ejus filius, et eorum uxores Ramunda et Magna." My family history and all other available sources, however, prove that Magna was Jordan's wife. VILLANOVA

26 Raymond de Moysiaco.

27 Bernard Clavellus.

28 Peter Lavanderius.

29 Terrenus Cassanellus. A consul Terrenus Martin de Cassanello in

1227-1228 is clearly the same person, and he was seen in MS 609, fol. 197r (circa 1223), together with his brother.

30 William Ramundus his brother.

31 Bernard Ramundus "cellarius."

32 Sicard de Tholosa. Described as a knight by Pelisson, he is also there named both Sicard de Gamevilla and Sicard de Tolosa. Sicard of Gamevilla is listed as No. **190** below. Pelisson may well have been correct, but one cannot tell. The Sicard de Tolosa we know of is a shadowy figure. That he was a knight is indubitable. He was also closely related to the principal Tolosa family. One of the most important scions of that line was Toset de Tolosa, active from 1152 to 1189, when he was one of the arbiters set to police the peace between the count and the town in the settlement of that year. One of Toset's brothers was a William, whose son, also named William, was under Sicard's tutelage in 1215 and 1221. Until condemned, Sicard was doing very well in the count's service where we see him until June 1235. There were several petitioners for the Tolosa family, either claiming Sicard's inheritance or, more likely, that of some woman of another family they had married. One was Oldric de Prinhaco, tutor of the children of the deceased dominus William de Tholosa, and the other was Peter, son of the deceased knight Peter de Tholosa, the latter being seen from 1232 to 1251, and recorded as dead in 1255, and the former active from 1255 to 1282, and perhaps even later. TOLOSA and GAMEVILLA

33 Arnold de Trageto. A consular councilor in 1222 and consul in 1227-1228. According to my family sketch, there are several "cultellarii" or cutlers in this family. The petitioner was a minor named Bernard Arnold de Trageto, spoken for by Bernard Hugo de Dealbata in 1279. TRAGETO

34 Pictavinus. Pelisson, pp. 97-98 and 111 mentions two Pictavini, one Pictavinus Borsier or Bursarius and the other Pictavinus Laurentiae, the latter being what he calls a "nuncius hereticorum." No. **167** below is Laurentia Pictavina. The amnesty may have confused the two male Pictavini. A Pictavinus senior is mentioned in MS 609, fol. 58v living on a City Street called Olm Sec, which is where Pelisson said the "borsier" lived, and was sentenced to an indeterminate sentence in Douais, *Inquisition*, 2: 5 (March 1246). The property of a Pictavinus is mentioned in Saint-Bernard 138, fol. 181v (May 1218), a Pictavinus "ganterius" is seen in PAN, J 330 12 iii (April 1225), and a Pictavinus "fivelerius" in Grandselve 6 (March 1229). A simple Pictavinus swore the oath of 1243 to the Peace of Paris.

35 Terrenus Calcaterra. There was a consul of this name in 1248-1249, and a Terrenus and Peregrin Calcaterra swore the oath of 1243 to the Peace of Paris. The petitioner of 1279 was the notary Arnold Bernard Calacaterra.

36 William de Cuneo.

37 Peter de Vendinis. A person of this name was a consular councilor in March 1222 and a consul in 1226-1227. See also No. **264** below. A Peter Raymond de Vendinis was the petitioner in 1279.

38 Raymond Laurentius. Mentioned in MS 609, fol. 110r, where we see him in his own house around 1217. He is also seen in PAN, J 330 5 ii (May 1238). A person of this name took the oath to the Peace of Paris of 1243. See his brother immediately below, and his sister in No. **236** below.

39 Peter Laurentius, his brother. Sometimes called "de Petra," thereby showing that he lived on the Place de la Pierre (eastern segment of the present Place Esquirol), Peter is seen in Malta 3 155 ii (January 1228, copied in 1229), Malta 3 170 ii (June 1230, copied in 1238), together with his wife Blancha, and the same pair again on the same parchment vi (January 1235), and lastly as a bailiff for the count in PAN, J 320 43 (January 1232). MS 609, fol. 197v shows him at Toulouse in Carabordas' house approximately 1233. A person of this name swore the oath to the Peace of Paris of 1243. The petitioner of 1279 was William Laurentius, the son of another William Laurentius.

40 Pons Mancipius. The alternate version of this name is Puer. A consul of 1202-1203 and again in 1213-1214, Pons first appears in Grandselve 58, 12th act on the reverse of a roll (May 1171) where we see his father John. He is seen for the first time with his brother Arnold in E 538 (December 1198). The brother was a minter and had a nephew named Bernard as we learn in E 501 (March 1194), and TAM, II 61 (June 1202), and PBN, MS lat. 9189, fol. 230va-b, where Arnold is also called "de Portaria" (area of the present Place du Capitole) in September 1203. We also know the name of Pons' wife. She was a Ricsenda, who shared the inheritance of her father Amalvinus with Bernard Raymond de Vetera Tolosa. Both consular councilors, the two brothers Arnold and Pons are seen together for the last time in 1222.

41 Peter de Quinto. A person of this name took the oath of 1243 to the Peace of Paris.

42 Peter Durandus "sartor." Pelisson mentions a "perfectus" named William Peter Durandus. The testimony of Austorga de Resenga (for whom see No. **216** below) dated January 1245 reported that a Peter

Durandus "de Tolosa" was active in town around 1227 in Doat 24, fol. 1v. Our man is also seen in Doat 23, fol. 295v (around 1234), and was condemned in absentia as having failed to perform the penance assigned by Cardinal Roman and being relapsed in Doat 21, fol. 153r (October 1241). His wife is No. **62** below.

43 Pons Umbertus. The name is frequently spelled Y- or Imbertus. There were several Imberti named Pons. One of these had died in 1213, and I therefore presume that this Pons is the "iuvenis" seen in E 510 (November 1201), and as a lender of money in TAM, AA 6 131 (March 1228, copied in 1232 and 1256). This Pons may have been the one whose contract of marriage with Willelma de Furno was recorded in E 509 ii (January 1231, copied in 1232 and 1256). The new menage was not rich, because the marriage settlement on Willelma was set at 100 shillings and her bed. Pons was dead when, in the same parchment iii (October 1235) his widow, described as the relict of Pons Umbertus "magister," married Peter Rixendi "recuperator." This was a family of craftsfolk, and it is therefore suitable that the next person to bear the name Pons Umbertus was a notary in E 501 i (September 1235, copied in 1247). For another Imbertus or Umbertus, see No. **149** below.

44 Arnold Petrarius. It seems probable that the compilers of the amnesty skipped Arnold's father whose name was Arnold William. Pelisson 111 tells us that Arnold William Peyrer and his wife Ondrada, her mother, and her mother's mother, were alive and sentenced in 1237, and that Arnold William was the father of Arnold Peyrer. Other sources inform us that the manuscripts of Pelisson contain an error because Arnold Peyrer was the father of Arnold William Peyrer and his brother Bertrand. See Nos. **49** and **50** below.

45 Ondrada, wife of Arnold Petrarius. As above, and she was ex-communicated in Doat 21, fols. 145v-148v (March 1237). Her mother Esclarmunda was condemned in Doat 21, fol. 179v (September 1237) when already deceased.

46 Peter Rogaterius. A consul in 1220-1221, and, for his wife, see No. **67** below.

47 Peter de Turre "sartor." A consul in 1231-1232, this Turre was probably not of the richer families bearing this name mentioned below. See No. **56** below. TURRE

48 Bernard Arnaldus "lanacerius."

49 Bertrand Petrarius, his son. It seems sure that the compilers of the amnesty of 1279 erroneously inserted Nos. **46**, **47**, and **48** into the middle of the Petrarii, and that **49**, **50**, and **51**, should have followed on No. **45**. At any rate, Pelisson, pp. 99 and 111, tells us that Bertrand Peyrer was disintered and burned in 1236 or 1237. Bertrand was also often seen by the witnesses in Doat 23, fols. 292v, 293v, 295r-v, and 298r, where we are also told that his mother's name was Ondrada. He was the son of Arnold Peyrer mentioned in No. **44** above, and the brother of Arnold William.

50 Arnold Guillelmus "petrarius," brother of Bertrand Petrarius. Like his brother, he was mentioned in Doat 23, fols. 292r-293v and 295r-v. He and his wife Beatrice were sentenced to perpetual immurement as relapsed heretics in Doat 21, fols. 149v-150r in February 1237. They had fled and are mentioned as being in Cremona in the early 1250s in TADHG, MS 124, fol. 201r, along with their son Peter Raymond.

51 Beatrix, wife of Arnold Guillelmus "petrarius." See the note above.

52 William de Pinu. A consul in 1224-1225, and his wife is No. **72** below. The relationship, if any, of this Pinu to the Ponte family (Nos. **57** and **58** below) which also carried the name Pinu is not known. PONTE

53 William Auriolus. A William Auriollus is seen in C. Douais, *Travaux pratiques d'une conférence de paléographie* (Toulouse, 1900), No. 19 (March 1225) as a creditor of Arnold de Villanova (see No. **23** above). His connections were excellent as is shown by the fact that he was the husband of India, daughter of Bernard Raymond de Tolosa, the son of the celebrated Toset de Tolosa in Malta 1 128 (June 1232). There were Aurioli in Toulouse and also at Castelsarrasin to the north of town, and the family from the latter place seems to have been the richer one in this period. TOLOSA

54 Raymond Gamicius. The name is usually spelled Gamiscius. A person of this name was consul in 1203-1204, 1220-1221, and 1224-1225 from the Bourg.

55 Raymond Borrellus. A Raymond Borrellus was a consul in 1226-1227 and again in 1235-1238. A person with this name swore the oath of 1243 to the Peace of Paris.

56 Gasco de Turre. As my family sketch shows, there were two major Turre families in Toulouse, one in the Bourg and the other in the City. This is the family of the Bourg, one that was closely connected with the Astro family of the same quarter. Gasco, in fact, was married to Dias Astro, and he and his brother William were frequently consuls during the years of the war. Gasco appears last in a private charter of August 1229.

His brother William is probably No. **100** below. The petitioners for the Turre family of the Bourg were a proctor named John de Turre, the grandson of Vasco, and son of a John who was active from 1237 to 1248, and a William de Turre de Burgo "legista" who was a proctor at Paris and is seen in the charters from 1270 to 1285. TURRE

57 Peter de Ponte. This was the son of a Peter de Ponte who died between March and November 1237, a brother of Hugh de Pinu who was deceased by 1225, and of Raymond mentioned below. Peter de Ponte "iuvenis" was a consul in 1221-1222 for the Bourg, and again in 1225-1226. He had a son named Raymond. PONTE

58 Raymond de Ponte, his brother. Raymond was probably the hostage of this name sent to Paris in April 1229 (PAN, J 310 45 – this instrument will not hereafter be cited in this appendix). The petitioner of the family in 1279 was Bernard de Ponte, son of the deceased Raymond de Ponte. PONTE

59 Peter Embrinus. Pelisson tells us that the brothers Embrinus "maior" and Peter Embrinus, their mother Oliva, and Embry's wife Alesta were all deceased when condemned in 1237. The father of these brothers and the husband of Oliva is a Peter Embrinus senior who is seen in the charters from 1183 until 1207, but who is not mentioned in this amnesty. His son Peter was a consul in 1212-1213, a consular councilor in March 1222, and very briefly a consul again in 1235. For his brother Embrinus or Embry, see No. **112** below, and my family history tells me that, over and above Embry and the Peter condemned here, Peter Embrinus senior also had a son named Arnold (see No. **108** below) and another named William. For the petitioner of Peter's inheritance, see No. **112** below. EMBRINUS

60 Bernard Embrinus. Pelisson describes him as alive at the time of his condemnation. The family sketch records him as dead by 1266, and his son William petitioned for his inheritance in 1279. The relationship of this Embrinus to the members of the family mentioned in the previous reference is not presently known. EMBRINUS

61 Bernard Medicus de Sancto Paulo. This is probably the Bernard Medicus we see in E 538 (May 1206), the consul of that name in 1215-1216, and the Bernard who appeared in PAN, JJ 19 38 (April 1235). Note also a Geralda Medica (wives usually took their husband's names or designations) sentenced to life imprisonment in Doat 21, fol. 151r (February 1237). She is not to be found in this list. After this condemnation, the line continued. A Bernard Medicus de Sancto Paulo was seen at the oath of 1243, and was a consul in 1272-1273.

62 wife of Peter Durandus "sartor." See No. **42** above.

63 Arnold Soel. See Nos. **148** and **222** below. This name is spelled with many variations – Suelh, Siollio, Suollio, etc.

64 Bernard Pellicerius. A Bernard Pelliparius (the trades are the same) was consul in 1227-1228. See also No. **70** below.

65 Peter Guillelmi Ramassa.

66 Bertrand Descalquenc. Bertrand and his relative Arnold de Escalquenchis (the spelling of the name varies considerably) appear during the war years. Arnold, a distinguished "jurisperitus," is seen from 1218 to 1258. Bertrand appeared in 1222 as a consular councilor, and, after the beginnings of a busy public and private career, vanished after 1225. He reappears again in 1243, served as a consul in 1246-1247, and my family history records his testament of 1252. In that document, we learn that his wife was Aymengarda, and that they had had five sons, all of whom were alive. Because this family had relations with the Centulli, it is not inconceivable that the Aymegarda Centulla mentioned below (No. **166**) was Bertrand's sister, married into the Centullus family. Bertrand's own petitioner was his son Raymond who is to be seen in the documents from 1252 to 1281. Two other family petitioners of 1279 were Bernard and Stephen Descalquencis, the latter of whom was a proctor at Paris. Stephen represented the deceased brothers Arnold and William, respectively seen in the charters from 1248 to 1277 and the oath of 1243 to 1274, and Comdors, William's widow. These brothers were the sons of Arnold, the relative of the Bertrand mentioned as the heretic in our list. The petitioner for Aymengarda Centulla was Bertrand, the son of Bertrand's son Peter Raymond Descalquencs. This Bertrand was seen from 1277 to 1281. DESCALQUENCS

67 wife of Peter Rogaterius. See above No. **46**.

68 Arnold de Garanhaga.

69 wife of Caraborda. See No. **5** above, where a reference to MS 609 tells us that her name was Elis.

70 Bernard Pellicerius. See No. **64** above.

71 Bernard Vitalis "scriptor." A Bernard Vitalis was a public notary who has left quite a number of extant acts. The first is Saint-Bernard 35 viii (October 1200, copied in 1229), and the last Saint-Sernin 678 (20 9 7) (January 1158), a copy attested by Bernard in August 1228. The petitioner for this inheritance in 1279 could have been either Bernard Escrivanus or Pons Vitalis "notarius" who served as a proctor at Paris. Used more or less as a surname, the name Vitalis was that of an important scribe in the twelfth century, Pons Vitalis, and may have persisted in a notarial family. Since, however, it is a common Christian name, nothing can be done with it.

72 wife of William de Pinu. See No. **52** above.

73 Raymond de Terrasona. A consul with this name in 1227-1228.

74 Tholosanus Cortada.

75 Pons de Armanhaco. William de Armanhaco was a petitioner in 1279.

76 Bernard de Armanhaco, his brother.

77 Raymond Ysarnus. See No. **192** below.

78 Arnold de Sayssos. The name in Latin is Saxonibus.

79 Bertrand David. My family sketch records that his father's name was Bernard, and that his successful brother was the minter Pons who mentioned Bertrand in his will of 1208. Bertrand is seen in the charters from 1180 to 1235, and was at one time married to a Brus Martina. Curiously, for a person whose brother left his property to the Hospitalers, Bertrand appears to have become an heretic, and also a person of more lasting repute in the town. DAVID

80 Hugh de Murello. A consul in the Bourg in 1224-1225, and seen in E 501 (November 1232), as having the guardianship of the children of Calvet Danceanis or de Anceanis. Ms 609, fol. 43r says that he had a house in town circa 1220. For his wife, see No. **150** below.

81 Raymond Rogerius minor. For his father, Raymond senior, see No. **17** above. Raymond minor was not the Raymond Roger among the consuls who played so active a role in the expulsion of the Dominicans according to Pelisson, pp. 102 and 106. That was a relative who also dabbled in heresy, but who was a son of Arnold Rogerius. Ms 609, fol. 197v records Arnold and his sons Arnold and Raymond dealing with the famous "perfectus" No. **17** above. Malta 116 24 of August 1222 also shows Raymond together with his father Arnold. It is probable that this group of Rogerii were City people, whereas the two Raymonds major and minor were from the Bourg. Anyway, Raymond minor is seen in MS 609, fols. 58v and 197v (respectively around 1215 and 1227) where we seen him in his father's house and also find a reference to his condemnation by Cardinal Conrad. He appears to have accepted this penance around 1222 or 1223, and was subsequently forgiven his sentence by Gregory IX in a letter published in his register as No. 4295 (p. 988) dated April 1238, on the grounds that his father had corrupted him in his youth. A Raymond

Roger appeared in the oath of 1243. Fournier and Guébin, *Enquêtes d'Alphonse de Poitiers*, p. 330, No. 128 (dated 1270) inform us that there was still a claim outstanding against him because of a debt he owed when condemned.

82 Bernard Martinus. A consul of the City with this name seen in 1223-1224. Note also the unnamed brother of Raymond Martinus in Nos. **90** and **91** below.

83 Pons Gayrardus. A Pons Geraldus was consul in 1226-1227. A William Geraldus "parator" was a petitioner in 1279.

84 John Centullus. A John Centullus who was a relative of William Berengar is seen in PAN, J 317 24 (November 1237).

85 Raymond Vasco. Ms 609, fol. 197v notes a person of this name (Gasco, etc.) as having a house in town in the 1220s. Someone with this common name was also at the oath of 1243.

86 "Magister" Peter Guillelmus de Orto. Pelisson, p. 99, remarks that Delort lived in the Bourg. The same source tells us that he was captured by the abbot of Saint-Sernin and the town vicar Durand de Sancto Barcio but speedily saved from them by Raymond Rogerius (No. **81** above) and Peter Esquivatus (No. **242** below). He is mentioned in Doat 23, fol. 293r as active in heresy in the late twenties. A person with the name of Peter William de Orto was consul in 1207-1208, 1217-1218, and 1231-1232. We see this person as a creditor in E 573 (March 1225), as a witness in Malta 116 25 (January 1227), and in Grandselve 8 i (March 1243), where William de Orto, his brothers Peter William and Gerald, and their sister Alamanda, children of the deceased Peter William de Orto, together with their mother Ricardis and Arnold Puer (see No. **40** above for this worthy), sold some property. In 1279, the petitioners were a Peter William for himself and for his brothers Gerald and Raymond de Orto, the latter a notary.

87 Arnold de Sancto Felice. A consul of this name is seen in 1218-1220 and 1224-1225. An Ainard de Terra Sancti Felicii was in refuge in Italy during the 1250s according to TADHG, MS 124, fol. 201r.

88 Stephen de Yspania. In 1245, Austorga de Resengas (for whom see No. **216** below) reported that Stephen de Hispania "frenerius" had been with her in Toulouse around 1227 in Doat 24, fol. 1v. Pelisson, p. 111, records that he was dead when burned in 1236.

89 Maurandus senior. My family history records him as the youngest son of the Peter Maurandus who was sentenced and penanced in 1178. Maurand first appears in the charters in 1200, although we know he was alive in 1179, and is seen until 1244. Pelisson informs us that he was a "perfectus" and conjectures that he was among the Cathars slain at Montségur. He is called "vetus" by this Dominican, but was also known as "de Vallesecura" (from the family property at Valségur). His sons Raymond "luscus" and Maurand were penanced to pilgrimage for heresy in, respectively, March 1237 and April 1238. For his wife, see No. **179** below. The petitioners were the sons of Maurand "vetus" son Maurand (seen from 1235 to 1263), and were named Maurand (seen from 1263 to 1295 when he was deceased) and Raymond (seen from 1279 to 1282). MAURANDUS

90 Raymond Martinus. A person with this common name swore the oath of 1243 to the Peace of Paris.

91 the brother of Raymond Martinus.

92 Johanna Mauranda, sister of the Curtasolea. The Curtasolea brothers are Nos. **12** and **13** above, and this may be one of the sisters mentioned below but not named as Nos. **141** and **142**, although one cannot be sure because she may have been the one married sister of the batch. Her surname Mauranda shows that she was married to a member of that family, and we have seen above that the family sketch of the Curtasolea proves the close links of the two families. CURTASOLEA and MAURANDI

93 William Auriolus de Burgo. Note No. **53** above, and recall that the "carraria de frenariis" was in the Bourg.

94 Bernard Faber "spetierius." A consul in 1222-1223, and condemned to an indeterminate sentence in Douais, *Inquisition*, 2: 5 (March 1246).

95 Ademar de Turre. He was active in Catharism in the late twenties and early thirties along with his brother, No. **96** below. He was sentenced when deceased in September 1237. The family history shows us that Ademar was a member of the City family named Turre. He first appeared in the charters in 1205, a year in which he was consul, and was still alive in November 1230. The petitioners of the Turre family of the City were Aimeric and his brother Bernard, sons of the deceased Bertrand (active from 1235 to 1253, and dead by 1269), Bernard Raymond de Turre, son of William (in the charters from 1250-1272), a cousin of the above brothers, Bernard Raymond's brother William who served as a proctor at Paris, and possibly their own father called "olierius" who is seen in the charters from 1250 to 1273, and who may well have been alive in 1279. TURRE

96 Bernard de Turre, his brother. The copy of the amnesty in TAM, II 63 gives the name Bertrand, but this is surely a mistake as may be seen in the family sketch, and also in the condemnation of his widow Johanna, No. **97** below. TURRE

97 Johanna, widow of Bernard de Turre. Douais, *Inquisition*, 2: 31 (June 1246) notes that she was already a nun at Lespinasse, and was condemned to solitary immurement in the monastery. TURRE

98 Bernard de Borrigiis.

99 Sancius de Borrigiis, his brother.

100 William de Turre. A wartime consul, William was the older brother of Gasco, No. **56** above, of the Turre of the Bourg. William was last seen in August 1229, according to my family sketch. TURRE

101 William Peter de Casalibus. A consul of this name in 1218-1220 and 1222-1223. The petitioner of 1279 was Pons de Casalibus, acting for his father William de Casalibus.

102 William Peter de Ulmo. In E 501 (June 1226), a William Peter de Ulmo, his wife Arnalda, and their son-in-law Peter Johannis sold six houses near the wall of the Bourg.

103 William Bosquetus. A consul in 1218-1220, a creditor in PAN J 317 24 (November 1237), William del Bosquet is mentioned in MS 609, fol. 203r (approximately 1225). A person bearing this name is seen in the oath of 1243.

104 Aimeric Golmarius.

105 Peter Soquerius.

106 William Peter his brother.

107 Peter Sobaquus. Peter was a consul in 1220-1221. He appears in the charters from 1213 until he drew his testament in E 505 (March 1237), before leaving for the Holy Land according to the penance enjoined on him by Cardinal Roman. His widow Matheva was alive in 1279 and petitioned for the amnesty, and was still to be seen in her sister's testament of 1282. Our heretic Peter had had two sons. One, named Peter after his father, was a notary who instrumented from 1243 to 1260 and may have become a monk at Grandselve in 1265. The second was William, a shadowy figure seen after 1272. A family history of this line has been prepared but not included in this monograph.

108 Arnold Embrinus. My family sketch shows that this was the brother of the Peter Embrinus mentioned above No. **59**. He is seen in the charters from 1222 to late in 1237, and was active in heresy in the late twenties. EMBRINUS

109 Raymond Tapicerius. A consul named Tapierius (upholsterer or tapestry maker) is seen in 1217-1218 and 1224-1225.

110 Bernard Arnold Peregrinus. This person was a councilor for the consuls in 1222, and a consul for the Bourg in 1223-1224. In Malta 15 181 (June 1225), he sold a house near the Comminges Gate. He was a judge delegate for the consuls in TAM, II 45 (February 1228). In TAM, II 75 iii (March 1223), we learn that he bought a house. In the same parchment iv (October 1234), the house was sold by his widow Alamanda, his mother Ramunda Peregrina, and his brother Peter.

111 Oldric de Gamevilla. A wartime consul, Oldric was an important man who left a record in the family sketch extending from 1205 to 1241. For others of this family, see Nos. **169**, **186**, **215**, and **226** below. The only petitioner of this family in 1279 was a Sicard de Gamevilla. GAMEVILLA

112 Embrinus. Eldest son of Peter Embrinus, and brother of Arnold (No. **108** above), Peter (No. **59** above), and William Embrinus, Embrinus was a consul in 1217-1218, and alive in 1221. Called the son of Peter Embrinus senior, this person was condemned to life imprisonment in September 1237 as relapsed. His wife Alesta was deceased when sentenced in September 1237. She is not listed in the amnesty. In 1279 the petitioners were William Embrinus and Embry (the latter a proctor at Paris), son of the deceased Peter Embrinus, the latter being seen in the charters from the oath of 1243 until we hear in 1260 of his death. Embry was therefore the grandson of our heretic. We do not know whose child the petitioner William was. EMBRINUS

113 Carruga Barberius. This barber was presumably named "The Cart."

114 Raymond Baranhonus. This is either Raymond, the son of Raymond, seen from 1198 to 1254, or his nephew Raymond William Baranhonus, sometimes simply called Raymond, who was seen from 1237 to 1257. According to my family history, the heretic was either the brother or the nephew of the Alamanda mentioned below in No. **116**. There was a consul of this name in 1218-1220 and again in 1231-1232. The petitioner and proctor of 1279 was Bernard Raymond Baranonus, son of the deceased Bernard Raymond, who was probably the brother of the heretic Raymond. BARANHONUS

115 Raymond de Capite Denario. Although the family sketch is not altogether clear, this is probably Raymond, brother of Martin de Capite-denario (see No. **152** below), who is seen in the charters from 1231 to 1257, and derived from the rural branch living near Capdenier to the north of the town. A Raymond de Capitedenario is seen in the oath of 1243. Raymond had a wife named Mantelina who was condemned to pilgrimage in July 1241. The petitioner and proctor at Paris in 1279 was Martin de Capitedenario. CAPITEDENARIO

116 Raymond William Atadilis. The Atadils must have been a family of consequence. In Grandselve 3 iv and v (May 1198), we learn that Raymond William and Ispanus de Portaria were the husbands of the sisters of Bruno Baranonus and his brothers, the sons of Raymond Baranonus. Raymond William is seen again in Grandselve 4 (April 1201 and December 1202), where we learn that his wife's name is Alamanda. He was also a consul in 1225-1226 for the City. In the oath to maintain the Peace of Paris in 1243, we see two people with this name, a simple Raymond William and a Raymond William junior, and a Bernard Atadillis of whom nothing more is known. The petitioner of 1279 was Raymond Atadils.

117 Raymond Pellicerius. A Raymond Pellicerius was consul in 1207-1208.

118 Raymond Aymericus "sutor."

119 Bernard de Martris.

120 William de Cavaldos. In Latin, the name is Equodorso, and as such we see William as a consul in 1221-1222. He appears in MS 609, fol. 68r as having a house in Toulouse around 1233, and we see him acting in Malta 4 203 ii (August 1233, copied in 1241).

121 Bernard de Rocovilla. This citizen is not to be confused with the Rocovillas from Les Cassès in the Lauragais. Like many rural notables, the knights of the Lauragais Rocovillas lived in Toulouse during the war, but do not appear to have been citizens. Sometimes called Bernard Peter de Rocovilla, Bernard is seen in E 501 v (July 1201), where we read his father's testament. Peter left his son Bernard only 50 shillings, and gave his house to Bernard's brother Peter to share with his widowed mother Alamanda. In the same membrane vi and vii (both dated August 1206), Peter surrendered his interest in the house to his brother Bernard. A Bernard de Rocovilla was a consul in 1227-1228. Bernard is probably the one of this name who, in TADHG, MS 124, fol. 201r, is recorded as having fled to Pavia where he was living circa 1253. A petitioner in 1279 was a Peter Vital de Rocovilla.

122 William Boerius. For his wife Na Thomas, see No. **180** below.

123 Arnold de Bosco Mediano. As Arnold de Nemore Mediano, this person was a consul in 1226-1227 and 1230-1231. In 1279 the petitioners were Peregrin and Raymond de Bosco Mediano.

124 William de Fonte "barberius." A Raymond de Fonte was a petitioner in 1279.

125 Martror. Curiously named "All Saints," this person was surely a man.

126 Arnold Sancius. Pelisson, pp. 96-97 (Molinier's manuscript, pp. 21-22, called him Sancerius, but Douais' had Sancius) describes him as "faber de Cruce Baranhonis" who was burned after a kind of drumhead courtmartial while protesting his innocence in 1234. This is surely not the Arnold Sancius listed below as No. **261**. A person with this very common name was in the oath of 1243.

127 Vital Bonushomo. Although Bonushomo is a relatively common name, this may have been the one who sold property at the Pont-des-Clèdes in Malta 116 25 (January 1227), and who was a judge delegate for the consuls in Saint-Sernin 599 (10 35 4) (February 1228), and is last seen in E 501 ii (October 1232, copied in 1233).

128 Oldric Maurandus "qui aliter vocabatur Pedas." My family history has several Oldric Maurandi, but this is probably the third son of Maurandus "vetus" brother Raymond. This Oldric is seen from 1218 to 1255, and is known to have been dead by 1266. MAURANDUS

129 Raymond William de Samatano. What this person's relationship is to the Peter Raymond who is No. **151** below is not known. There was also a family in town named Samarano.

130 Alaman de Roaxio. My family sketch shows that there were two Alaman de Roaxio, father and son, involved in Catharism. The key charter is of November 1222 wherein Alaman senior appears as does his son Alaman then in training to become a knight with William Unald, a lord of Lanta. The two Alaman are conflated in the royal diploma, although it is equally possible that only Alaman junior was meant here. Alaman senior is seen from 1200, and received much at Villèle from his wife Lombarda in 1217. Last seen in a charter in 1222, the evidence listed below shows that both died late in the 1220s. Ms 609 put Alaman and Lombarda at home in Toulouse around 1226/8, and, around that time, speak of Lombarda as "quondam uxor Alamanni." At about the same time, other inquisitorial reports have them associating with the Lauragais Rocovillas (see No. **120** above). Seen from 1222, the junior Alaman is described by Pelisson as sentenced, and, in May 1237, we learn that he had reneged on the penance promised to Cardinal Roman and was therefore condemned to perpetual imprisonment. He escaped the hands of the Inquisition, however, and we know, for example, that he collected grain for the defense of Montségur according to Bernard Oth, the lord of

Niort, testifying in 1242. In January 1248, he was again given a life sentence to which was added a sum of 50 shillings to be paid annually to a servant of a onetime "officialis" or episcopal judge of Toulouse. He and his wife Johanna (see No. **244** below) had four children. We see them together with Hugh called Bego or Bec, Austorga, and Blancha in MS 609 and also around Avignonet, Gameville, Lanta, and Toulouse. In December 1272 suits were levied by the crown against Hugh de Roaxio and his wife Tholosa and against his brother Raymond de Roaxio, both sons of Alaman. Lastly, the record of a suit against the bishop by the crown begun in October 1273, mentions a house near Saint-Étienne once owned by Alaman de Roaxio and now in the bishop's possession. The proctor of this family at Paris in 1279 was Hugh who spoke for himself and his brother Raymond. Both seen from 1273 to 1279, these were the sons of the Alaman who appeared in charters from the 1230s and 1241 and was deceased by 1273, himself the son of the Alaman (and his wife Johanna) seen from 1232 to 1248, the latter the son of the Alaman (and his wife Lombarda) of 1200 to 1222, himself the son of Arnold active from 1173 to 1196, and was surely dead by 1200, and the latter, in turn, being the son of the Peter de Roaxio known of in 1150 to 1164. ROAXIO

131 wife of Alaman de Roaxio. Surely the Lombarda mentioned above. This "uxor quondam Alamanni de Roaxio" who had died "statim post pacem" was sentenced when deceased in September 1237. ROAXIO

132 Bernard Curtasolea. According to my family sketch of the Curtasolea-Castronovo, Bernard was the youngest brother of John and Stephen and was seen from 1204 onward. He was a consul in 1223-1224, and probably appears into the 1230s. For his other relatives, see Nos. **12**, **13**, and **92** above. Indeed, this Bernard may conceivably have lived until 1279 because a petitioner at that time was a Bernard Curtasolea. CURTASOLEA

133 Bertrand de Montibus. This was probably the Bertrand of this distinguished family who is seen in my family sketch from 1202 to 1237, and was a consul in 1214-1215, 1222-1223, and 1225-1226. He is mentioned in MS 609 around 1230 at Toulouse. MONTIBUS

134 wife of Aimeric de Castronovo "maior." Her name was Constantia. For her husband, see No. **2** above. CASTRONOVO

135 wife of Castellusnovus. Her name was Esclarmunda. For her husband, see No. **3** above. CASTRONOVO

136 wife of Arnold Onda. Named Ramunda, she was condemned to perpetual immurement in May 1246. For her husband, see No. **8** above. UNDE

137 wife of Peter Onda. For her husband, see No. **9** above. UNDE

138 wife of Raymond Caraborda. For her husband, see No. **4** above. CARABORDA

139 wife of Caraborda. In the reference about her husband in No. **5** above, she was named Elis. CARABORDA

140 wife of Raymond de Mirapisce. For her husband, see No. **10** above.

141-142 "sorores et uxores" of John and his brother Stephen Curtasolea. For their brothers and possibly sister, see Nos. **12**, **13**, **92**, and **132** above. CURTASOLEA

143 wife of John Curtasolea, No. **12** above. CURTASOLEA

144 wife of Stephen Curtasolea, No. **13** above. Her name, as we saw there, was Bermunda. CURTASOLEA

145 Arnold Barravus. Few families were as difficult to trace as the Barravi. Still, although there were several contemporary Arnold Barravus, this was probably the Arnold, son of Bernard, first seen in 1174 with his brothers, especially the important Bernard Raymond. This Arnold was certainly alive to 1227 when he acted with Bernard Raymond. His wife was named Dias (see No. **181** below), and he had at least one son, Roger, and maybe two others, a Peter perhaps and another Arnold. The older Arnold was probably the consul of this name in 1192-1193, 1199-1200, 1214-1215, and possibly in 1222-1223 and 1225-1226, and could also have been the town hostage sent to Paris in 1229. The petitioners for this family were three in number. Arnold, Bernard, and Raymond Bernard, of which two were proctors and one went to Paris. The family history has three brothers by these names, but what their relationship to the Arnold Barravus who was condemned for heresy was is not known. Note also the Raymond de Roaxio who petitioned for himself and for a Do Barravus, son of a dead Peter Barravus. Raymond served as a proctor at Paris. BARRAVUS and ROAXIO

146 Pons de Ulmo. A Pons of this name was seen taking oath to maintain the Peace of Paris in 1243.

147 Bertrand Maurandus. Following my family sketch, this Bertrand was probably the eldest son of Maurand "vetus" brother Peter, and is seen from 1229 to 1255. MAURANDUS

148 Pons de Suollio. There is a consul of this name in 1221-1222, 1227-1228, 1231-1232, and 1239. A Pons de Siol owed the Daurade a rent in Daurade 189 dated 1227. A Pons appears in PAN, J 330 5 ii (May 1238), and again in H Daurade 117 (March 1239). In MADTG, A 297, fol. 202r (August 1250), we see a Pons and his nephew of the same name, and on fol. 822v (January 1260), a Pons nephew of the deceased Pons de Siolio. For another of the same name, see No. **222** below. The petitioners of this name in 1279 were a Peter and Aimeric whose relationship to our Pons or Raymond below is not known.

149 Peter Imbertus. A Peter Umbertus was a public notary of Toulouse who instrumented from Grandselve 6 i (December 1204, copied in September 1223 with Peter in attendance), to Grandselve 9 (December 1249 written by Peter and copied in 1255). The notary of the latter act was probably a relative.

150 Oliva, wife of Hugh de Murello. See the sister of Raymond Rogerius mentioned in No. **17** above.

151 Peter Raymond de Samatano. This person was a distinguished and prolific public notary. He was active from TAM, AA 1 33 (December 1200) to E 257 (July 1206, copied by Peter Raymond in September 1234 and copied again in 1246 by another notary. He worked together with and was obviously closely related to Bernard de Samatano who instrumented from 1221 to 1256 and Peter de Samatano who drew acts from 1220 to 1256.

152 Martin de Capite Denario. Following my family sketch, this was a member of the rural line of the Capdenier who was seen only once in a charter of 1231. CAPITEDENARIO

153 Bonus Mancipius Maurandus. Seen in the charters from 1241 to 1265, this Bonmacip or Bonuspuer was probably the third son of Peter, an older brother of Maurand "vetus." Ms 609 mentions Bonmacip, his father Peter, his brother Maurand de Bellopodio, and his sisters Magna and Condors, wife of Bertrand, one of the lords of Baziège during the war years and the early thirties. On the other hand, there were two other Bonmacips. The first was the older brother of Peter and Maurand "vetus" who is seen from 1179 to 1200/19, but who is a most unlikely candidate for this slot. The second was the eldest son of the Raymond who was another brother of Peter and Maurand "vetus." The heretic was sentenced to pilgrimage in September 1241. In their later lives, it is hard to distinguish the third son of Peter from the first son of Raymond. One of these Bonmacips was still alive around 1274, and gave testimony to the crown about the government of the town during the war years and just after. For the wife of the heretic, see No. **220** below. The identification of our Bonmacip is not helped by the petitioners and proctors of 1279. Active from 1247 to 1279, and dying in 1283, one of these was Ademar Maurandus, probably the son of Maurand de Bellopodio, son of the

Peter who was the brother of Maurand "vetus." Another petitioner was Bertrand, a son of the deceased Bonmacip Maurandus, himself presumably the son of Bonmacip, a son of the same Peter and who was active from 1265 to 1269, and dead by 1283, leaving issue. The last representative of 1279 was the proctor Raymond, son of Peter, presumably the son of the Peter who was the son of Maurand "vetus" brother Raymond, and who was seen from 1266 to 1279, and was surely alive around 1274. MAURANDUS

154 Magna wife of Peter William de Ardinhano. For what it is worth, note the Magna in the entry above.

155 Centulla. A domina Centulla is seen with property near the Pont-des-Clèdes in Malta 118 179 (June 1184).

156 Sibilia de Solerio. This may have been the wife of a Bernard de Solerio "fibularius" mentioned in Pelisson, p. 92, as having been called a heretic by Bernard Pictavinus. Solerio had appealed to the consuls on the grounds of libel, and had been supported by them against Pictavinus, but Bishop Raymond of Toulouse and the Dominicans drove him so hard that he fled to Italy.

157 Raymond William Atadillis junior. See above No. **116**. A Raymond William Atadillis was seen at the oath of 1243.

158 Bertrand de Roaxio. According to Pelisson, a Ramunda, wife of Bertrand de Roaxio, was the sister of Raymond Isarnus and of Dias, wife of Arnold Barravus (see above No. **77** and No. **181** below), and was burned when deceased in 1237. My family history is not clear enough to find out which of the possible two Bertrands this is. We hear of a Bertrand and his brother Toset in 1230. I feel happier and know more about a Bertrand who was the son of Arnold, and grandson of the Peter and Alamanda of the major family line. This Bertrand is seen in 1221 with his brother Peter. At any rate, a Bertrand was condemned as relapsed in February 1237, and, as we see below in No.**183**, his deceased wife Petrona was sentenced in September 1237. A source tells us that a Cathar named Raymond, son of a Bertrand, was in Cremona and Piacenza around 1253/4. In May 1270 the count returned the family property of Bertrand who had been freed by Innocent IV (d.1254) to his heirs, his widow Alamanda, his son Raymond, and daughter Sibilia, wife of Bernard Garinus. When imprisoned, Bertrand was a hero to the Cathars as we learn from the testimony of Peter Garcias of the Borguet-Nau in August 1247. ROAXIO

159 Pons de Arzenquis. Described as Arzencs, he was condemned to perpetual imprisonment as relapsed in Doat 21, fol. 149v (March 1237).

160 Vital Sicredus. Vital Sicre, his wife Aicelina, and sister Esquiva were active in heresy in Doat 23, fol. 297r during the late war years. Vital was given life in Doat 21, fol. 149v (March 1237), as was his wife, for whom see No. **172** below.

161 Raymond Stephanus "mercerius." Sentenced to life immurement as relapsed in Doat 21, fol. 149v (February 1237), it was probably he who, around 1234, was active in Catharism in Doat 23, fol. 295v. A Raymond Mercer is seen at Pavia in TADHG, MS 124, fol. 201r (July 1257).

162 Arnold de Monteliis. Condemned to perpetual imprisonment as relapsed in Doat 21, fols. 149v-150r (March 1237). His wife Auriola had died as a Cathar circa 1229/31 according to Doat 23, fol. 300v.

163 Raymond Bernardus "Magister." Sentenced when deceased in Doat 21, fol. 150r (March 1237). His nephew was William John "cultellarius" mentioned below as No. **165** (possibly also No. **278**).

164 Guillelma, widow of Raymond Bernardus "Magister." Although the name is variously given as Arnalda and Guillelma in Doat 21, fols. 149v-150r, the woman was given life immurement as relapsed in March 1237.

165 William Johannes "cultellarius." Nephew of No. **163**, the cutler (perhaps the same as No. **171** below) was condemned to perpetual imprisonment in Doat 21, fol. 150v (March 1237), as was his sister Frezata, for whom see No. **171** below.

166 Aymengarda Centulla. Wife of Raymond Centullus (No. **1** above), she was sentenced as relapsed to life immurement in Doat 21, fol. 149v (February 1237). The petitioner who stood for her in 1279 is described in the major family entry of the Descalquencis at No. **66** above.

167 Pictavina Laurentia. She was condemned to perpetual imprisonment in Doat 21, fol. 150r (February 1237). Her son (for whom see No. **34** above) was possibly the Pictavinus Laurentie seen at Piacenza and Pavia in TADHG, MS 124, fol. 201r-v in the 1250s. Note also for what it is worth, the condemnation of a Laurentia, the widow of a Gerald Pictavinus, who was sentenced to life immurement in Doat 21, fol. 149v (February 1238).

168 Arnalda widow of Pons Umbertus. For her husband's condemnation, see No. **43** above.

169 Fais de Gamevilla. Pelisson and a condemnation of March 1237 describe her as sentenced when deceased. See her mother Blanca, No. **186** below. GAMEVILLA

170 Philippa widow of Hugh Grassa. An undescribed Philippa was condemned as relapsed to perpetual imprisonment in Doat 21, fol. 150v (March 1237).

171 Frezata sister of William Johannes "cultellarius." Sentenced to life immurement in Doat 21, fol. 150r (March 1237). See her brother above in No. **165**.

172 Aycelina wife of Vital Sicredus. Condemned to perpetual imprisonment in Doat 21, fol. 149v (March 1237). For her husband, see No. **160** above.

173 Angelesia widow of Stephen de Yspania. Sentenced as widow of Stephen de Yspania (see No. **88** above) and to life immurement as relapsed in Doat 21, fol. 150r (March 1237).

174 Esclarmunda wife of Bernard Tornerius. Variously called de Reula and Torneria (the latter after her husband), she was mentioned in Doat 23, fol. 296r as involved in heresy around 1233, and condemned to perpetual imprisonment in Doat 21, fol. 150r (March 1237).

175 Laurentia wife of Raymond Pelliparius. Sentenced to life immurement as Laura in Doat 21, fol. 151r (February 1237), and see Raymond Pellicerius, No. **117** above.

176 Aycelina de Roaxio. Condemned to perpetual imprisonment as relapsed in March 1237. She was the wife of William de Roaxio, the son of David, and cousin of the senior Alaman de Roaxio (for whom, see No. **130** above). Her husband is seen in the charters from 1218 to 1223. ROAXIO

177 Bernardis Dominica wife of Julianus. Sentenced to life immurement as Dominica, wife of Julian, Doat 21, fol. 150v (March 1237).

178 Bernard Rosaudus. Condemned to perpetual imprisonment as relapsed in Doat 21, fol. 150v (March 1237).

179 Mabelia, wife of Maurandus de Vallesecura. The wife of Maurand "vetus" mentioned in No. **89** above, Mabelia was sentenced in February 1237 to life immurement. She was a rich woman of the Cossano family (her marriage portion being 3000 shillings), and the sister of Raymond Aimeric listed below as No. **197**. MAURANDUS and COSSANO

180 Na Thoma wife of William Boerius. Condemned to perpetual imprisonment as relapsed in Doat 21, fol. 150v (February 1237). For her husband, see No. **122** above.

181 Dias wife of Arnold Barravus (No. **145** above). Pelisson and her condemnation report that she was disinterred and burned in September

1237. She was the sister of Raymond Isarnus for whom see either No. **77** above or No. **192** below. BARRAVUS

182 Rica wife (or mother) of Arnold Guido. Although our two copies of the amnesty disagree, she was surely the mother of Arnold Guido. According to my family sketch, she was the wife of Arnold's father William. For her son Arnold, see No. **16** above. She was deceased when condemned in September 1237. GUIDO

183 Petrona wife of Bertrand de Roaxio. Sentenced when dead in September 1237. For her husband, see No. **158** above. ROAXIO

184 Carabordas "mater Grivi." Clearly a woman of the Caraborda family, Caraborda was the wife of the Peter Grivus who appears in my family history from 1180 to 1203. Her son Peter Grivus de Roaxio is seen from 1210 to 1251. The nickname Grivus was used to distinguish this set of Peters from the many other Peters of this family. When deceased, she was condemned in September 1237. CARABORDA and ROAXIO

185 Mabriana wife of deceased Raymond Bertrand de Sancto Luppo (Saint-Loup-Cammas, just northeast of Toulouse). Pelisson, p. 99, tells us that a daugther of Jordan de Villanova (No. **22** above) was the wife of the knight Raymond de Sancto Luppo, and that she was dead when sentenced. The condemnation is in Doat 21, fol. 179v (September 1237), and we there learn her name and that she was a widow at the time of her death. According to MS 609, fol. 60r, she had been active in Catharism around 1216 in the Toulouse house of the Gameville family together with her husband. A William Hugh de Sancto Luppo was a proctor at Paris in 1279 and petitioned for himself and for Helia Arnold de Villamuro. VILLANOVA

186 Blanca (Blancha) de Gamevilla. MS 609 tells us that she, her daughter Fais, and daughter-in-law Johanna were busy in Catharism at Toulouse approximately 1225. According to Pelisson, Blanca was burned when dead in 1237. GAMEVILLA

187 John Saladinus. Calling him Saladis, Pelisson, p. 111, describes him as dead, and Doat 21, fol. 180r (September 1237) says the same about this City dweller at the time of his condemnation.

188 Natalis de Salvitate. A simple Natalis was condemned when deceased in Doat 21, fol. 180r (September 1237). This is presumably the servitor of the count who is called "mercator de Salvitate" in Saint-Étienne 227 (26 DA 2 47) (November 1230, copied in 1249 and 1256). Note also PAN, JJ 19, fols. 173v-174r (December 1236) where Arnold Natalis, son of the deceased Natalis "mercator," confessed that he and his father and their ancestors were serfs of the count.

189 Stephen Massa. Mentioned as sentenced in Pelisson, p. 111, and given life immurement as relapsed in Doat 21, fol. 139v (March 1237).

190 Sicard de Gamevilla. Pelisson calls him a "credens" and, as we have seen in No. **32** above, names him Sicard "de Gamevilla vel de Tholosa." Another source has Austorga de Resengas (see No. **216** below) noting that the knight Sicard de Gamevilla was "adoring" heretics in Toulouse around 1227, and MS 609 has him active in heresy at Toulouse and elsewhere from around 1215 on. In my family sketch this knight was in the retinue of the count in 1215. GAMEVILLA and TOLOSA

191 Raymond Ademar de Montetotino. A Raymond de Montetotino was an active Cathar in the late twenties and very early thirties in MS 609, fol. 66r and in Doat 23, fols. 293v and 295r-v. TADGH, MS 124, fol. 201v shows the same Raymond together with his sister Beatrix as adherents of Catharism in the late thirties. A Raymond variously called de Fide or de Montetotino was a consul in 1220-1221.

192 Raymond Isarnus brother of William. See above No. **77**. He was described as dead when condemned in Doat 21, fol. 179v (September 1237). A consul in the Bourg in 1225-1226, Raymond was important enough to be a hostage sent to Paris in April 1229.

193 William Isarnus brother of Raymond. A person with this name was a consul presumably from the Bourg in 1194-1195, 1197-1198, 1201-1202 and 1212-1213. Although one can only rarely write a family history of persons bearing common names, it seems likely that the William Isarnus in E 575 (June 1191) was a person of wealth and good family. In Malta 135 41 (January 1213, copied in 1229) we see the property at Larramet of William Isarn de Suburbio.

194 Arnold Affusorius.

195 wife of Arnold Affusorius.

196 Berengaria wife of Assalitus de Montibus. This widow was condemned to perpetual imprisonment in August 1247. MONTIBUS

197 Lombarda widow of Raymond Aimeric de Cossanis. This woman was sentenced to life immurement in August 1247. The sketch of the Cossano family tells us that her husband was the oldest son of Bernard Peter de Cossano, a notable jurist and more or less the founder of the family fortune. Raymond Aimeric's sister was also the Mabelia who was the wife of Maurand "vetus," for whom see Nos. **89** and **179** above. He was consul in 1211-1212 and again in 1217-1218. He was dead by 1247, and his son, also named Raymond Aimeric, is seen in the charters from 1261 to 1287, and was the petitioner for the family in 1279. COSSANO and MAURANDI

198 Maria wife of William Hugo. This widow was condemned to life imprisonment in Douais, *Inquisition*, 2: 44 (August 1247). Her husband was probably the William Hugh who was consul in 1226-1227, and a person of the same name was consul and described as a "pelliparius" in 1246-1247.

199 Bertrand de Turre. Sentenced to perpetual immurement in August 1247. This Bertrand was probably of the Turre family of the City, and, if so, my family sketch makes him out to be the son of Johanna and Bernard de Turre, Nos. **96** and **97** above. TURRE

200 Arnold de Planis. Condemned to life imprisonment in Douais, *Inquisition*, 2: 49 (August 1247). An Arnold de Planis "medicus" is seen in Malta 17 34 (June 1224) and, not described as a doctor, an Arnold of this name took oath to maintain the Peace of Paris in 1243.

201 Raymond Peter de Planis. Sentenced to perpetual immurement in Douais, *Inquisition*, 2: 49 (August 1247). In testimony of August-November 1247 in the same volume by Douais (p. 90), he is said to have been a "perfectus" when called to the deathbed of the Franciscan Raymond Gros.

202 Pons de Planis. Condemned to life imprisonment in Douais, *Inquisition*, 2: 49 (August 1247). A Peter de Planis "espazerius" (armorer?) was a petitioner in 1279.

203 William Donatus. Sentenced to perpetual immurement in Douais, *Inquisition*, 2: 53 (September 1247).

204 Ramunda, mother of William Donatus. Condemned to life imprisonment in Douais, *Inquisition*, 2: 53 (September 1247).

205 Juliana wife of William Textor. Douais, *Inquisition*, 2: 62 (October 1247) records the condemnation to life immurement of a Juliana, widow of John Textor. This fits the account in Pelisson, pp. 93-94, who records the history of a John Textor who was almost lynched, momentarily remanded to jail but finally burned as a Cathar. See the anecdote in Chapter 3 above.

206 William John de Sauzeto.

207 Peter Borellus. A Peter Borrellus was a public notary whose first extant act is TAM, II 46 (October 1215) when serving as a consular notary, his last in Grandselve 7 (January 1234), and we know he was deceased in Saint-Étienne 230 (27 2 unnumbered) v (an act recording an "actio" dated September 1230), when the consuls assigned his materials to another notary in June 1235.

208 Arnold de Morovilla.

209 Raymond de Villamuro. See No. **185** above for the petitioner acting in 1279 for Helia Arnold de Villamuro.

210 Peter Sutor. Although it means little because the craftname is common, a Peter Sutor is seen in the oath of 1243 for the Peace of Paris.

211 Rixendis, wife of Peter Dauzetus.

212 Raymond de Narbona "faber." When absent, sentenced to confiscation in Doat 21, fol. 154r (November 1241) as Raymond de Narbona de Besseta (Labécède north of Castelnaudary, quite far south in the Lauragais).

213 Ramunda, wife of Raymond de Narbona.

214 Peter de Roaxio. According to my family sketch, this Peter de Roaxio was the grandson of Bertrand and his wife Ramunda. Bertrand was active from the 1170s until 1203, and possibly into the 1220s. His wife, Ramunda, is described as such in Pelisson, but the Dominican may have been mistaken because the wife of Bertrand's son Peter was certainly named Ramunda. Peter is possibly seen as early as 1217, and surely in 1221 and 1227, and was dead by 1230 leaving as relict Ramunda who, as deceased, was condemned in September 1237. Their son Peter may have been the one who "adored" some "perfecti" circa 1222, and who brought liturgical dishes to others in MS 609. According to Pelisson, he was sentenced in 1237, and, if so, he was again condemned as relapsed and in flight in March 1246. As is obvious, some of these actions may have been done by, or have been visited on, either the father or the son, although the amnesty mentions only one Peter de Roaxio. At any rate, a charter dated February 1248 records an action by the count of Toulouse giving the inheritance of Peter, son of Peter de Roaxio, to one of his supporters. From my family history, it seems sure that this Peter de Roaxio was not the celebrated Peter Grivus de Roaxio seen above in No. **184**. ROAXIO

215 Pons de Gamevilla. Ms 609 shows Pons around 1215 with his wife Aurimunda together with the wives of Bertrand de Sancto Luppo (see No. **185** above), Castellusnovus (see No. **135** above), and Sicard de Gamevilla (see No. **190** above). Pelisson describes him as a "credens" in 1236, and, as absent and relapsed, he was sentenced to confiscation in March 1246. He may have been in circulation slightly before because a person of this name swore the oath of 1243 to the Peace of Paris. Pons may also have been twice married. See No. **226** below. GAMEVILLA

216 Austorga de Resenquis. Mentioned in MS 609, fols. 5v, 84r, 174r and 200r, from around 1230 into the early 1240s, Austorga is seen together with her daughters Alamanda and Orbria, the latter the wife of the rural notable William Saisses, and her son Peter de Resengas. In Doat 24, fols. 1v-8r (January 1244) we are given her own testimony in which she tells us that, in about 1227, she was living near Falgarde, to the west of Castanet south of Toulouse. She also mentioned her son Peter in 1240. As the widow of Peter de Resengas, she was condemned to perpetual imprisonment in Douais, *Inquisition*, 2: 4 (March 1246).

217 Raymond Gaubertus de Tauro. Raymond Gausbertus of Toulouse was sentenced to life immurement in Douais, *Inquisition*, 2: 4 (March 1246). A person of this name took the oath of 1243.

218 Arnold Gairerius. With his name variously given as Guerrer and Guerrerius, Arnold was condemned to perpetual imprisonment in March 1246, but, having escaped the prison, was sentenced anew when absent in March 1248. This information is in Douais, *Inquisition*, 2: 4 and 76.

219 Austorga de Vadegia. Widow of Vasega or Vaseia, the lord of Baziège, Austorga was condemned to an indeterminate immurement in Douais, *Inquisition*, 2: 5 (March 1246). Before that time, as we see in MS 609, fols. 43v, 58r and 60r, she had lived in her houses in Gardouch, Baziège, and at Montaygon (Place Saint-Georges) in Toulouse.

220 Bernarda de Massos. Sentenced to life imprisonment as the wife of Bonmacip Maurandus (see above No. **153**) in July 1246, Bernarda was first, according to MS 609, the wife of William de Massos around 1230 and "nunc" in 1245 the wife of Bonmacip. MAURANDUS

221 Aycelina, sister of William Mercaderius. William is No. **249** below. She is also the sister of Cortesia (see No. **250** below) and of Ramunda Barrava (No. **257** below) with whom she was condemned to an indeterminate immurement in Douais, *Inquisition*, 2: 5 (March 1245).

222 Raymond de Suollio. As Suelh and Syolh, sentenced to an indeterminate imprisonment in March 1246. He escaped and was condemned again when absent in March 1248. This information is in Douais, *Inquisition*, 2: 5 and 76. Doat 23, fol. 292v tells us that he was an associate of the famous Raymond Gros. Raymond de Sioil appears also in PAN, J 329 39 (December 1235).

223 Bernard de Lantari. Bernard de Lantario de Tholosa was sentenced to an indeterminate immurement in Douais, *Inquisition*, 2: 5 (March 1246). A Bernard de Lantario was a petitioner in 1279.

224 Petrona Escudeira. Doat 23, fol. 297r shows her active in Catharism just before the Peace of 1229. She was condemned to an indeterminate imprisonment in Douais, *Inquisition*, 2: 5 (March 1246).

225 Raymond de Villanova. Sentenced to an indeterminate immurement in March 1246. According to my family sketch of the Villanova, this person does not seem to have been in the major town family of this name unless he could have been a Raymond Arnold de Villanova, sometimes called Arnold Raymond, a knight and citizen condemned to pilgrimage and taxed to equip the prison of Saint-Étienne for the Inquisition in May 1241. But this is extremely unlikely because Raymond Arnold was soon back in business and remained an important personage in town. My family history points out, moreover, that the name Villanova, being that of innumerable places around town and of a quarter of the town itself, was not monopolized by any family, however great. VILLANOVA

226 Titburgis, wife of Pons de Gamevilla. Sentenced to fifteen years imprisonment in March 1246. For her husband, see No. **215** above. GAMEVILLA

227 Vital de Sala. As Salas, given ten years immurement in Douais, *Inquisition*, 2: 6 (March 1246).

228 Fabrissa, wife of Peter Maquesius. As Marchesii, given ten years imprisonment in Douais, *Inquisition*, 2: 6 (March 1246). In PAN, J 318 78, dated around 1251 (No. 2428 in *Trésor*), we learn that Peter Marquesius had had trouble with the parish rector of Saint-Étienne in Toulouse over the burial of his mother.

229 William Arcmannus. As Arcmandi, given ten years immurement in Douais, *Inquisition*, 2: 6 (March 1246).

230 Pons Bladerius. Life imprisonment in Douais, *Inquisition*, 2: 8 (May 1246).

231 Peter de Albegesio. Perpetual immurement in Douais, *Inquisition*, 2: 8 (May 1246). A person with this name swore the oath of February 1243.

232 Raymond Sabaterius. Life imprisonment in Douais, *Inquisition*, 2: 8 (May 1246), but he was allowed to live with his poor father to support him in his old age.

233 Pons Dominicus. He was seen in Doat 23, fol. 296r (circa 1233), and again in MS 609, fol. 203v around 1240 with his wife Esclarmunda. Condemned to perpetual immurement in Douais, *Inquisition*, 2: 8 (May 1246). Esclarmunda is not mentioned in the amnesty. As noted above, it is possible that "Magister" John Dominicus, notary and merchant, was the proctor for this interest at Paris in 1279.

234 Raymond Maurinus. Sentenced to life imprisonment together with his wife Arnalda (No. **235**) in Douais, *Inquisition*, 2: 9 (May 1246). In

Grandselve 2 (December 1191 or 1195), a Raymond and his brother Arnold were creditors.

235 Arnalda, wife of Raymond Maurinus. For her condemnation, see No. **234** above.

236 Aldriga Laurentia. Sister of Peter Laurencius (No. **39** above) and wife of Bernard Raymond "cambiator" (see the "cellarius" No. **31** above), she was condemned to perpetual immurement in Douais, *Inquisition*, 2: 11 (May 1246).

237 Bernard de Prato, father of Stephen. Sentenced to life imprisonment in Douais, *Inquisition*, 2: 11 (May 1246).

238 Stephen de Prato, son of Bernard. The son is not mentioned in the Douais reference given in the note above. A Stephen de Pratu is seen in the oath of 1243, and, in 1279, a "Magister" Bernard de Arpis acted for himself and for Bigordana, daughter of the deceased Stephen de Pratu, and a Peter Raymond Bardi spoke as the tutor of a Bernarda, daughter of the dead Stephen.

239 Johanna, wife of William de Solerio. Condemned to perpetual immurement in Douais, *Inquisition*, 2: 11 (May 1246), this woman could possibly have been the wife of the delator who, according to the chronicler Puylaurens, *Chronica*, and the inquisitor Pelisson, p. 94, tripped off the great attack on Toulousan Catharism in the mid-1230s. Although both extant manuscripts of Pelisson call him Consolario, it is pretty sure that his name was simply Sola- or Solerio. Puylaurens says so, and so do several charters in which we see a person of this name in Malta 1 76 (September 1183), Malta 3 96 (February 1187), and Malta 17 49 (May 1203, copied in 1237), in which final reference the name is given in the vernacular as William del Sol. As is known from the historians mentioned above, William was rewarded for his evidence against Toulousan Catharism by being made a canon of the cathedral at Toulouse and it is as such that we see him in Doat 21, fol. 42r (around 1235 – according to Wakefield, "The Family of Niort," p. 111, the earliest possible date was 1234 and Kolmer, *Ad capiendas vulpes*, p. 106 puts the date of the trial at January 1236).

240 Guillelma de Manso. Known in the early 1220s as a Cathar in MS 609, fol. 197v, she was sentenced to perpetual imprisonment in Douais, *Inquisition*, 2: 11 (May 1246).

241 Stephen de Roaxio. Stephen is seen acting as a Cathar circa 1232, and was condemned to life immurement in May 1246. Although my family sketch of the Rouaix cannot place Stephen in a specific filiation, he was assuredly a member of this patrician group. His name was embedded among those who can be shown to be of the family in the oathtaking to defend the Peace of Paris in 1243. ROAXIO

242 Peter Esquivatus. Pelisson, p. 99, records him as actively opposing the Inquisition in the Bourg during the 1230s. He was sentenced to perpetual imprisonment in Douais, *Inquisition*, 2: 16 (May 1246). A Peter Esquivatus took the oath of 1243.

243 Domina Assaut. Ms 609 tells us that she was the wife of Raymond Unald of the family of Lanta around 1233, and that, around 1245, she was the wife of Raymond de Castronovo. The testimony of Austorga de Resengas (No. **216** above) recalls that, circa 1240, Assaut was still the wife of the knight of Lanta (the first seigniory to the south of Toulouse in the Lauragais). She was condemned to life immurement in May 1246. CASTRONOVO

244 Johanna, wife of Alaman de Roaxio. In June 1246 a life sentence assigned to the wife of the younger Alaman de Roaxio, for whom see above No. **130**. ROAXIO

245 William Dauri. As "de Auri," sentenced to life immurement in Douais, *Inquisition*, 2: 27 (June 1246).

246 Rica, wife of William Dauri. Sentenced to the same punishment at the same time as her husband above.

247 Arnold de Johanne minor, brother of Jacob. As "den Joan" (son of John), condemned to perpetual immurement in Douais, *Inquisition*, 2: 26 (June 1246). This person is seen in PAN, J 305 49 (February 1242).

248 Jacob de Johanne, brother of Arnold. Sentenced to the same punishment at the same time as his brother above.

249 William Mercaderius, brother of Cortesia. Pelisson, p. 111, remarks that Mercadier and his sister Cortesia were sentenced in 1236/7. Perhaps they were then let off with a warning because the two were condemned to indeterminate imprisonment (William now being called "mercator") in Douais, *Inquisition*, 2: 5 (March 1246). The two fled and were excommunicated as being absent in ibid., 2: 37 (July 1246), and appear in TADHG, MS 124, fol. 201r in Cremona in Lombardy around 1254.

250 Cortesia, sister of William Mercaderius. See the note above.

251 Ramunda, widow of Raymond Johannes. Sentenced to life immurement in Douais, *Inquisition*, 2: 44 (August 1247). According to my family sketch (not recorded in this monograph), her husband was assuredly not the Raymond Johannes "jurisperitus," son of the famous

Hugh Johannes of wartime years. There are two other possibilities. The first is a public notary whose first instrument in my collection is Saint-Sernin 502 (1 1 57) (March 1191, copied in 1209 and 1224). This notary was dead in E 510 (July 1201) because the consuls assigned his materials to a successor at that time. The other is a Raymond Joan "mercader" mentioned in the rent roll of 1227 in Daurade 189.

252 Peter Garcias. Called a "cambiator," and elected to serve as a consul in the term 1247-1248, Peter Garcias de Bourguet-Nau was crushed by testimony collected in August-December 1247. This extraordinary material, along with his excommunication of February 1248 when he had fled, is in Douais, *Inquisition*, 2: 74 and 91 ff. Doat 22, fol. 51r (December 1268) records a gift to the Inquisition by Alphonse of Poitiers and Toulouse of 100 shillings confiscated from Peter. In the same year, also, we hear of a claim on his "hereditas" in Molinier, *Correspondance*, 1: 504 and 2: 46.

253 Mauranda, widow of Arnold de Brantalo. From her name, this was surely a Maurand woman. Which of the possible Arnolds de Brantalo or Brantalone this was is not known. PBN, MS lat. 9189, fol. 221va (December 1190) notes an Arnold "qui manet apud crucem Baranhonis," and in Malta 17 79 i (October 1203, copied in November 1254) we see an Arnold called junior. One of these Arnolds was a public notary. My first example of his instruments is in Douais, *Paléographie*, No. 7, an original written in July 1181 with a copy attested by Arnold in November 1204, and the last is E 501 i (1157 or 1158, copied in August 1207 by Arnold). MAURANDUS

254 Peter de Bovilla. Pelisson, p. 111, described a man with this name as a "perfectus," and implies that he may have died at Montségur. TADHG, MS 124, fol. 201r, however, has a person of this name (Beuvilla) at Piacenza and Cremona in the early 1250s.

255 William Ferraterius. William Ferrater of Toulouse is seen around 1230 in Doat 23, fol. 30v.

256 Godus de Fanoiovis.

257 Ramunda Barrava. The wife of Barravus de Corrunsaco. A somewhat shadowy personage mentioned in my family history of the Barravus family, Barravus appears as busy in Catharism in the late 1220s. Ramunda was condemned to indeterminate imprisonment together with her sister Aycelina (see No. **221** above for this sibling and the rest of the family). BARRAVUS

258 Arnold Petrus de Sancto Saturnino.

259 Raymond Corregerius. Although there must have been a number of strap makers in Toulouse, I was able to write a brief history of a family in this craft. There, a Raymond was a son of a Peter Corregerius, and appears in the charters in 1215 and 1218. He was dead by 1242 when his widow Orbria and his nephew Peter Corregerius sold his house. There is no way of showing that the Raymond described below in the family sketch is the person sentenced for Catharism. Raymond was perhaps the most common Christian name in Toulouse, and there were plenty of strap-makers in that town of leather industries. CORREGERIUS

260 Raymond Sancius. See his brother immediately below.

261 Arnold Sancius, brother of Raymond Sancius. Ms 609, fol. 207 (June 1246) records the testimony of a Raymond Dominicus who, living as a boy in Arnold Sancius' house in Toulouse, led "two perfecti" out of town on Arnold's request.

262 Raymond Barta. Because that person was not a citizen of Toulouse, this could not be the Cathar knight Raymond Barta, a close relative of the lord of Montmaur, a person who, among other notable actions, once lived with his concubine in hiding in the leperhouse of Laurac, the woman being herself sick. See MS 609, fol. 75v, and much else.

263 Bernard Faber de Villasicle. Surely not the smith called Bernard Faber de Sancto Romano mentioned with his wife Esclarmunda in testimony of 1274 in Doat 25, fol. 49.

264 Aimeric de Vendinis. Note No. **37** above for the family name.

265 Arnold de Montibus. Possibly a member of the notable Toulousan family bearing this name. The only mention of an Arnold de Montibus is as a councilor of the consuls in 1222. Basing himself on PAN, JJ 24 B, fol. 6r, No. 49, Dossat, *Inquisition*, p. 305 notes that his inheritance was given to one of Alphonse of Poitiers' officers. MONTIBUS

266 Peregrinus Signarius. As will appear in this note, there were two Peregrins, one older than the other. When one ceases and the other begins to appear in the charters is not known. See the probable brother of the older one in No. **7** above, as well as another member of the family in No. **6**. The older Peregrin is first seen in Malta 123 9 (December 1196), as a witness, together with Raymond Signarius in a reference cited in No. **7** above. He was also a consul in 1214-1215 and a "curialis vir" for Simon de Montfort's government in 1217. A Peregrin is seen in E 501 ii (October 1232, copied in 1233). A Signarius of this name was among those attesting to the Peace of Paris in 1243. In MADTG, A 297, fol. 38v (June 1256) a Peregrin, son of a deceased Peregrin, is to be seen.

267 Isarn Grillus. Isarn Grillus was probably the notary of this name who appears in 35 acts in my collection beginning with Saint-Bernard 138, fol. 63v (January 1200) and ending with Grandselve 8 (July 1243). He was called a notary when listed among the consuls in 1222-1223, and he also appeared in the oath to maintain the Peace of Paris in 1243. In Saint-Sernin Canonesses 34 (October 1254) we see Isarn's widow Bernarda as the possessor of a quarter of the "curia" or farm called "des Leusis" in Lalande north of Toulouse.

268 Arnold Molinus. A consul in 1220-1221, and a person with this name at the oath of 1243.

269 Arnold Martellus. An Arnold Martellus swore the oath to uphold the Peace of Paris in 1243.

270 Raymond de Pomareda. Henri Gilles, ed., *Coutùmes de Toulouse (1286) et leur premier commentaire (1296)* (Toulouse, 1969), pp. 128-129, records a claim by Raymond's widow to her marriage portion on the property of her husband confiscated for heresy by the vicar of Toulouse. This claim is in article 120a of the customs, and was not allowed by the crown.

271 Bernard Grandis "parator." This is possibly a mistake (in which source?) for the Peter Grandis, son of Jacob Dodarz, seen approximately 1243 by a witness in MS 609, fol. 203v at the house of Willelma Calveira near the "Peira" (Place de la Pierre, modern Esquirol) along with Esclarmunda, the wife of Pons Dominicus (No. **233** above). A Peter Grandis took oath to maintain the Peace of Paris in 1243.

272 John Pagesius. A proctor in 1279 was William Peter Pagesia.

273 Benechus Arnaldus. Molinier, *Correspondance ... d'Alphonse de Poitiers*, No. 1237 (dated 1269), records Arnold Benedictus asking for the return of his deceased father Benedict Arnaldus' property at Grisolles, arguing that it had been given away before he was sentenced. Arnold Benedictus may have lost his case because property at Grisolles described as having been that of Benedict Arnaldus was mentioned in the settlement between the crown and Saint-Sernin in Saint-Sernin 600 (10 442 2) (August 1279).

274 John Tosetus.

275 Arnold de Bracavilla.

276 John de Manso. This person is mentioned along with Raymond de Pomareda (for whom see No. **270** above) in the refused article 120a of the customs of Toulouse. John de Manso "mercator" was a petitioner in 1279.

277 Arnold Guillelmus "notarius."

278 William Johannes "cultellarius." Possibly the same as No. **165** above.

Ut autem premissa omnia et singula perpetue stabilitatis robur obtineant presentem paginam sigilli nostri auctoritate et regii nominis caractere inferius annotato fecimus communiri. Actum Parisius, anno domino millesimo ducentesimo septuagesimo nono, mense Augusto, regni vero nostri anno nono; astantibus in palacio nostro quorum nomina supposita sunt et signa: dapifero nullo, signum Roberti ducis Burgundie camerarii, signum Johannis buticularii, signum Imberti constabularii.

DATA VACANTE [monogram] CANCELLARIA

Anent the final protocol of the diploma, note that the offices of the seneschal and chancellor were vacant, the latter more or less since 1185 and the former from 1191. As was customary, the subscribers were the constable, Imbert of Beaujeu, the butler, John of Acre, and the chamberlain, Robert ii, duke of Burgundy.

6

Alphabetical Lists

A. The Amnestied

Affusorius, Arnold **194**
Affusorius, wife of Arnold **195**
Aimericus, Raymond, sutor **118**
Albegesio, Peter de **231**
Angelesia, *see* Ispania, Stephen de
Arcmannus, William **229**
Ardinhano, Magna, wife of Peter William **154**
Armanhaco, Bernard de, brother of Pons de Armanhaco **76**
Armanhaco, Pons de **75**
Arnalda, *see* Maurinus, Raymond
Arnalda, *see* Umbertus, Pons
Arnaldus, Benechus **273**
Arnaldus, Bernard, lanacerius **48**
Arzenquis, Pons de **159**
Assaut, domina **243**
Atadilis, Raymond William **116**
Atadillis, Raymond William, junior **157**
Auriolus, William **53**
Auriolus, William, de Burgo **93**
Aycelina, *see* Mercaderius, William
Aycelina, *see* Sicredus, Vital

Baranhonus, Raymond **114**
Barberius, Carruga **113**
barberius, *see* Fonte, William de
Barrava, Ramunda **257**
Barravus, Arnold **145**

Barravus, Dias, wife of Arnold **181**
Barta, Raymond **262**
Beatrix, *see* Petrarius, Arnold William
Berengaria, *see* Montibus, Assalitus de
Bernardis, *see* Dominica
Bladerius, Pons **230**
Boerius, Na Thoma, wife of William **180**
Boerius, William **122**
Bonushomo, Vital **127**
Bor(r)ellus, Peter **207**
Borrellus, Raymond **55**
Borrigiis, Bernard de **98**
Borrigiis, Sancius, brother of Bernard Borrigiis **99**
Bosco Mediano, Arnold de **123**
Bosquetus, William **103**
Bovilla, Peter de **254**
Bracavilla, Arnold de **275**
Brantalo, Mauranda, widow of Arnold de **253**
Brantalone, *see* Brantalo
brother, *see* Martinus, Raymond
brothers, *see* Faber, Bernard

Calcaterra, Terrenus **35**
Capite Denario, Martin de **152**
Capite Denario, Raymond de **115**
Carabordas **5**
Carabordas, mother of Grivus **184**

Grassa, Philippa, widow of Hugh **170**

Grillus, Isarn **267**

Guido, Arnold, maior **16**

Guido, Rica, wife or mother of Arnold **182**

Guilelma, *see* Magister

Guillelma, *see* Magister, Raymond Bernard

Guillelmus, Arnaldus, notarius **277**

Hugo, Maria, widow of William **198**

Imbertus, Peter **149**

Isarnus, Raymond **77**

Isarnus, Raymond, brother of William **192**

Isarnus, William, brother of Raymond **193**

Ispania, Angelesia, widow of Stephen de **173**

Ispania, Stephen de **88**

Johanna, *see* Mauranda

Johanna, *see* Roaxio, Alaman de

Johanna, *see* Solerio, William de

Johanna, *see* Turre, Bernard de

Johanne, Arnold de, minor, brother of Jacob **247**

Johanne, Jacob de, brother of Arnold **248**

Johannes, Ramunda, widow of Raymond **251**

Johannes, *see* Cultellerius, William Johannes

Johannes, William, cultellerius **278**

Juliana, *see* Textor, William

Julianus, Bernardis Dominica, wife of **177**

Ianacerius, *see* Bernard Arnaldus

Lantari, Bernard de **223**

Laurentia, Aldriga **236**

Laurentia, *see* Pelliparius, Raymond

Laurentius, Peter, brother of Raymond Laurentius **39**

Laurentius, Raymond **38**

Lavanderius, Peter **28**

Lombarda, *see* Cossanis, Raymond Aimeric de

Mabelia, *see* Maurandus de Vallesecura

Mabriana, *see* Sancto Luppo, Raymond Bertrand de

Magister, Guillelma, wife of Raymond Bernard **164**

Magister, Raymond Bernard **163**

magister, *see* Peter William de Orto

Magna, *see* Ardinhano

Magna, *see* Villanova, Jordan de

Mancipius, Pons **40**

Manso, Guillelma de **240**

Manso, John de **276**

Maria, *see* Hugo, William

Marquesius, Fabrissa, wife of Peter **228**

Martellus, Arnold **269**

Martinus, Bernard **82**

Martinus, Raymond **90**

Martinus, brother of Raymond **91**

Matris, Bernard de **119**

Martror **125**

Massa, Stephen **189**

Massos, Bernarda de **220**

Mauranda, Johanna, sister of the Curtasolea **92**; *see also* Johanna

Mauranda, *see* Brantalo, Arnold de

Maurandus de Vallesecura, Mabelia, wife of **179**

Maurandus senior **89**

Maurandus, Bertrand **147**

Maurandus, Bonus Mancipius **153**

Maurandus, Oldric otherwise called Pedas **128**

Maurinus, Raymond **234**

Maurinus, Arnalda, wife of Raymond **235**

Medicus de Sancto Paulo, Bernard **61**

Mercaderius, Aycelina sister of William **221**

Mercaderius, William, brother of Cortesia **249**

Mercaderius, Cortesia sister of William **250**

Mercerius, Raymond Stephen **161**

mercerius, *see* Mercerius, Raymond Stephen

Mirapisce, Raymond de **10**

Mirapisce, wife of Raymond de **140**

Moissiaco, Raymond de **26**

Molinus, Arnold **268**

Monteliis, Arnold de **162**

Montetotino, Raymond Ademar de **191**

Montibus, Arnold de **265**

Montibus, Berengaria, wife of Assalitus de **196**

Montibus, Bertrand de **133**

Morovilla, Arnold de **208**

Murello, Hugh de **80**

Murello, Oliva, wife of Hugo de **150**

Narbona, Raymond de, faber **212**

Narbona, Ramunda, wife of Raymond de, faber **213**

notarius, *see* Arnold Guillelmus

Oliva, *see* Murello, Hugh de

Onde, Arnold **8**

Onde, wife of Arnold **136**

Onde, Peter, brother of Arnold **9**

Onde, wife of Peter **137**

Ondrada, *see* Petrarius, Ondrada

Orto, Peter William, magister **86**

Pagesius, John **272**

Palmata, Pons **15**

parator, *see* Grandis

Pedas, *see* Maurandus, Oldric

Pellicerius, Bernard **64**

Pellicerius, Bernard **70**

Pellicerius, Raymond **117**

Pelliparius, Laurentia, widow of Raymond **175**

Peregrinus, Bernard Arnold **110**

Petrarius, Arnold **44**

Petrarius, Arnold Guillelmus, brother of Bertrand **50**

Petrarius, Beatrix, wife of Arnold Guillelmus **51**

Petrarius, Bertrand, son of Bernard Arnaldus lanacerius **49**

Petrarius, Ondrada, wife of Arnold Petrarius **45**

Petrona, *see* Roaxio, Bertrand de

Petrus, Arnold, *see* Sancto Saturnino

Philippa, *see* Grassa, Hugh

Pictavina, Laurentia **167**

Pictavinus **34**

Pinu, William de **52**

Pinu, wife of William de **72**

Planis, Arnold de **200**

Planis, Pons de **202**

Planis, Raymond Peter de **201**

Pomareda, Raymond de **270**

Ponte, Peter de **57**

Ponte, Raymond de, brother of Peter de Ponte **58**

Prato, Bernard de, father of Stephen **237**

Prato, Stephen de, son of Bernard **238**

Puer, *see* Mancipius

Quinto, Peter de **41**

Ramassa, Peter William **65**

Ramunda, *see* Donatus, William

Ramunda, *see* Johannes, Raymond

Ramunda, *see* Narbona, Raymond de, faber

Ramunda, *see* Villanova, Arnold de

Resenquis, Austorga de **216**

Rica, *see* Daurus, William

Rica, *see* Guido, Arnold

Rixendis, *see* Dauzetus, Peter

Roaxio, Alaman de **130**

Roaxio, Johanna, wife of Alaman de **244**

Roaxio, wife of Alaman de **131**

Roaxio, Arnold de **14**

Roaxio, Aycelina de **176**

Vadegia, Austorga de **219**

Vallesecura, *see* Maurandus de Vallesecura

Vasco, Raymond **85**

Vendinis, Aimeric de **264**

Vendinis, Peter de **37**

Villamuro, Raymond de **209**

Villanova, Ramunda, wife of Arnold
de **24**

Villanova, Arnold de, son of Jordan de
Villanova **23**

Villanova, Jordan de **22**

Villanova, Magna, wife of Jordan de
25

Villanova, Raymond de **225**

Villasicle, Bernard Faber de **263**

Vindemiis, *see* Vendinis

Vitalis, *see* Bernard Vitalis Scriptor

wives (unnamed), *see* Arnold Affusorius, Caraborda, Raymond Carabordas, Castellusnovus, Aimeric de
Castronovo maior, and John and
Stephen Curtasolea

Ysarnus, *see* Isarnus

Yspania, *see* Ispania

B. The Petitioners and Proctors of March 1279

This is the list of petitioners and proctors in the charter PAN, J 313 95,
dated the Monday before the Annunciation (20 March) 1279. There were
120 petitioners – male and female citizens – of whom 25 were also named
proctors (noted as "Proctor" in the list).[1] A twenty-sixth proctor,
Raymond Johannes "major," was not a petitioner. Thirteen of these
original proctors actually went to Paris for the amnesty of August 1279
and are noted as such in the list ("Paris"); two more of the original 120
petitioners, not among the original 26 proctors, acted as proctors in Paris
("Proctor only at Paris").

The individuals are listed alphabetically and the actual spelling of the
names, especially the use of the genitive for the second name, is retained.
Some family or second names were not in the diploma of August 1279;
these are signalled by the phrase, "Name not in August 1279."

Alacer, Bernard; Name not in August
1279

Armanhaco, William de

Arpis, Magister Bernard de, for self and
domina Bigordana daughter of deceased Stephen de Pratu

Atadils, Raymond

Baranhoni, Bernard Ramundi, son of
the deceased Bernard Raymond Baranhoni; Proctor

Barbarani, *see* Beloti

Bardi, Peter Raymond, as tutor for
Bernarda daughter of said Stephen
de Pratu

---

[1] See above, pp. 35-36.

Barravi, Arnold; Proctor

Barravi, Berengar, for the heirs of Doat de Roaxio

Barravi, Bernard, son of deceased Bernard Barravus; Proctor, Paris

Barravi, Raymond Bernard

Becs, Peter, son of deceased Peter Ciramelator; Name not in August 1279

Belis, William, notarius; Name not in August 1279

Beloti, Peter, de Palacio mercator, as tutor for the children of the deceased Raymond Barbarani; Name not in August 1279

Beneiti, William, faber, for self and his daughter Sazia; Name not in August 1279

Bequini, Matthew, mercator; Name not in August 1279

Berengarii, William, campsor; Name not in August 1279

Bosco Mediano, Peregrinus de

Bosco Mediano, Raymond de

Buxi, Raymond; Name not in August 1279

Calcaterra, Arnold Bernard, notarius

Capellerius, Bernard; Name not in August 1279

Capitedenario, Martin de; Proctor, Paris

Carabordas, Raymond

Carabordas, William; Proctor

Casalibus, Pons de, for William de Casalibus his father

Castellusnovus

Castronovo, Aimeric de, domicellus; Proctor Paris

Castronovo, Raymond de, de Burgo, for self and heirs of John de Castronovo; Proctor

Castronovo, Raymond de, brother of Aimeric; Proctor

Castronovo, see Castellusnovus

Causiti appotecarius; Name not in August 1279

Cerneria, Stephen de, pelliparius; Name not in August 1279

Cossanis, Raymond Aimeric de, son of the deceased Raymond Aimeric de Cossanis

Curtasolea, Bernard

Descalquenchis, Raymond de

Descalquenchis, Stephen, as spondarius and for heirs of deceased brothers William and Arnold Descalquenchis and for domina Comdors, widow of the said William; Proctor, Paris

Descalquencs, Bertrand

Dominici, Magister John; Proctor, Paris

Embrini, Peter

Embrini, William

Embrinus, son of deceased Peter Embrini; Proctor, Paris

Escalquenchis, see Descalquenchis

Escrivani, Bernard

Faber, Raymond, de Petra; Name not in August 1279

Faber, Vital, de Borgueto Novo; Name not in August 1279

Falgario, dominus Arnold de, miles; Proctor; Name not in August 1279

Feltrerii, Peter, monetarius; Proctor, Paris; Name not in August 1279

Fonte, Raymond de

Furnerii, Bernard; Name not in August 1279

Galterii, Stephen, notarius; Name not in August 1279

Gamevilla, Sicard de

Garrigia, William Raymond de; Proctor

Garrigiis, William de, iuvenis, for his wife domina Johanna de Castronovo

Gaure, Peter de, mercator; Name not in August 1279

Grimoardi, dominus Peter, and Pons Grimoardi his brother; Name not in August 1279

Guido, Bernard, de Borgueto Novo; Proctor

Guiraldi, William, parator

Hugo, Bernard, de Dealbata, curator for Bernard Arnold de Trageto

Lager, Bernard de; Name not in August 1279

Lantari, Peter Raymond de

Laurentii, William, son of deceased William Laurentii

Lauzino, William Raymond de, notarius; Name not in August 1279

Levis, Peter de; Name not in August 1279

Mancii, Raymond; Name not in August 1279

Manso, John de, mercator

Maurand, Ademar

Maurand, Raymond, son of Peter Maurand; Proctor

Maurandi, Bertrand, son of deceased Bonmacip Maurand

Maurandi, Maurand and Raymond Maurandi, son of deceased Maurandi

Molini, Raymond, for self, and his brother William Molini; Proctor, Paris

Nigreti, Raymond, macellerius; Name not in August 1279

Odo, Oldric; Name not in August 1279

Odo, Vital Faber; Name not in August 1279

Orto, Peter William de, for self and Gerald his brother

Orto, Raymond de, notarius; Proctor

Pagesia, William Peter; Proctor

Palacio, Hugh de; Name not in August 1279

Parator, William Vital, notarius; Name not in August 1279

Petri, Bernard, pelliparius, for himself and his brothers; Name not in August 1279

Planibus, Peter de, espazerius

Ponte, Bernard de, son of the deceased Raymond de Ponte

Portali, Berengar de; Name not in August 1279

Porterii, Bonet and his brother Aimeric for all property except for the village of Rebigue; Name not in August 1279

Pratu, see Arpis

Pratu, see Bardi

Prinhaco, Oldric de, as tutor of the children of the deceased dominus William de Tholosa and for the rents of Monteaygone

Prinhaco, Peter Raymond de; Name not in August 1279

Pryshaco, William de; Name not in August 1279

Radulph appotecarius; Name not in August 1279

Ranavilla, Arnold de; Name not in August 1279

Raymundi, Bernard, de Monteaygone; Name not in August 1279

Recaldo, Raymond de; Name not in August 1279

Roaxio, Aimeric de

Roaxio, Bernard de

Roaxio, Hugh de for self and Raymond his brother; Proctor, Paris

Roaxio, Raymond de, son of deceased dominus William de Roaxio for self and for Do Barravi, son of deceased Peter Barravus; Proctor only at Paris

Roberti, *see* Rotberti

Rocovilla, Peter Vital de

Rogerii, William, appotecarius

Rotberti, William, de Matabove; Name not in August 1279

Rotberti, William, son of the deceased Peter Rotbertus, for self and for Aladaicia his mother; Name not in August 1279

Salvaros, Bernard; Name not in August 1279

Sancto Amantio, Bernard Raymond de; Name not in August 1279

Sancto Luppo, William Hugh de, for self and for Helia Arnold de Villamuro; Proctor, Paris

Secorioni, William, ferraterius

Sobac, domina Mateva, widow of Peter Sobac

Sobaccus, *see* Sobac

Suollio, Peter de

Syolio, Aimeric de

Tholosa, Peter de, son of deceased dominus Peter de Tholosa miles

Tholosa, *see* Prinhaco

Trageto, *see* Hugo, Bernard

Turre, Aimeric de, and his brother Bernard, sons of the deceased Bertrand de Turre

Turre, Arnold de

Turre, Bernard Raymond de

Turre, John de; Proctor

Turre, William de; Proctor, Paris

Turre, William de, de Burgo; Proctor legista, Paris jurisperitus

Turre, William de, olierius

Ulmo, Raymond de

Unde, Arnold; Proctor

Valle, William de; Name not in August 1279

Vendinis, Peter Raymond

Vesceriis, William de, notarius; Name not in August 1279

Villamuro, *see* Sancto Luppo

Villanova, Arnold de

Vindemiis, *see* Vendinis

Vitalis, Pons, notarius; Proctor only at Paris

Ysalguerii, Raymond; Name not in August 1279

Part Three

The Family Histories

Introduction

There are a total of twenty-two family histories in this section. As could be expected from the nature of our sources, principally instruments housed in ecclesiastical archives, the average social class is pretty high. Five (Castronovo, Gamevilla, Montibus, Tolosa, and Villanova) were knightly and even seigniorial lines. Of the fifteen rich families traced here, three (Barravus, Maurandus, and Roaxio) were great patricians of early twelfth-century origins, of which some scions were counted as nobles by the end of the thirteenth century. Two others, perhaps three (Cossano, Descalquencs, and one of the Turre lines), won wealth and distinction by their specialization in law, especially by their service as arbitral judges. One (David) was a rich minter, and three others (Capitedenario, Curtasolea, and Unde) were clearly self-made lineages of recent origins. There are only two working class families included here (the Corregerii and Trageto). Although references to such activities are rare, there were traveling merchants in at least six lines (Baranonus, Barravus, Curtasolea, Ponte, Roaxio, and Unde). Lastly, one notes that some families were split into branches, and also that some of the names here were merely surnames carried in common by different families. The Capitedenario, for example, consisted of three more or less independent lines. There were two large families named Barravus, Caraborda, and Turre, one family in the City and one in the Bourg. Common names like Tolosa and Villanova were so ordinary that I have included examples to show that the great clans bearing those names could not hope to monopolize such common designations. It is worth noting, however, that, although this same is true of the huge Barravus family of the City, whose common name of Barrau was spread everywhere, the Barravi constituted an unusually homogeneous clan.

Mixed up together, "pell-mell like rats in the straw," as Zwingli said of the Anabaptists, these families are listed alphabetically simply in order to ease consultation. Most of the histories are accompanied by genealogical trees and by maps showing the principal possessions of the families involved. The attentive reader will note that there are two concentric frontier lines sketched on the maps. The inner ring is an approximation of the frontiers of the "gardiage" of the town, the part of the countryside that was always directly administered by the consuls. The outer ring is that of the vicarage, an area administered by the vicar, the count's principal officer in town. During the time when the vicar's office was weakening from 1189 to 1229, this was also a region that increasingly fell under the town government. After 1229, the vicarage was to become independent of the town once again.

Baranonus

Three branches of the Baranoni (Baranho, Baragnon, etc.) can be traced in our period, and it is evident that all three were closely related.[1] Further evidence of the relationship is that their homes were in the parishes of the Daurade and Saint-Étienne, in and adjacent to the Portaria, on the streets called Pujolibus and Cervuneriis (present rue des Gestes and the northern end of the rue Saint-Rome). Curiously, although they presumably derived their name from, or gave it to, the Croix Baragnon, none can be shown to have lived there at this time.[2]

The first of the three lines is that of Bruno Baranonus, who, heard of from 1157, was deceased by 1196, and who, by 1190, had founded the leperhouse named after him in Saint-Cyprien.[3] His son, William Bruno, inherited the sponsorship of this foundation, and is seen in the charters until 1227.[4] The relationship of this father and son to the persons mentioned below is not known, but notice the rare Christian name Bruno in the line below.

The second line is that of a Raymond Baranonus who, appearing in 1173, was dead by 1198, when we momentarily see all of his children

---

[1] Members of each of these lines served as witnesses to important acts of, or testamentary councilors to, the other lines, thus permitting the conjecture that the original Bruno was a brother of the progenitor Raymond of the second line and of William John of the third line. See the document of April 1217 cited in note 21 below; that of July 1225 in note 4 below; and that of December-January 1275 in note 17 below. In Grandselve 4 (May 1208), there was also an Arnold Baranonus and his wife Ermengarda, whose relationship to the lines discussed here is not known.

[2] The locality was already called the Croix Baragnon. The earliest reference to it is in TAM, AA 1 19 (November 1190), but others, such as PBN, MS lat. 9189, fol. 221v (December 1190) and E 503 (June 1192, copied in 1198 and 1204), follow close on it.

[3] *Gallia Christiana*, vol. 13, Instrumenta No. 39, p. 26, a papal letter of September 1190 speaking of the "domus Baranhonis" with its chapel. Bruno is seen in Saint-Étienne 227 (26 DA 2 102) (January 1157); Douais, *Saint-Sernin*, Nos. 69 and 70 (September 1158) records an acquisition of property in the Close of Saint-Sernin; Saint Bernard 138, fol. 2r (May 1166); Grandselve 2 i (February 1174, copied in 1201); and Daurade 117 (July 1196), when his son William Bruno gave a servile family to work in his father's leperhouse, and stood by himself to act as advisor.

[4] PBN, MS lat. 9189, fol. 230va (September 1203); PAN, J 318 16 (October 1208); Malta 3 137 iii (July 1225) where he served as a witness to a charter dealing with the rights of Grauzida, wife of Bruno Baranonus; and Daurade 189 (December 1227) a rent role wherein he is called William Brus Baranho.

before they divided their inheritance (See Table 1). The sons were named Bruno, Raymond, Bernard Raymond, Berengar, William Bernard, and Arnold Raymond. There were also two sisters who were not named in the charter, but were spoken for by their husbands, Ispanus de Portaria and Raymond William Atadillis. We later, in 1201, learn that Raymond William's wife was named Alamanda.[5] Bruno is seen in the charters until 1225, and was married to Grauzida of the Dalbs family, one closely associated with the Daurade.[6] His brother Raymond was a consul in the terms of 1218-1220 and 1231-1232, and was active until 1254.[7] He may also have been a witness in defense of the memory of Raymond VI in 1247 and a consul again in 1248-1249, but this may have been his nephew Raymond Arnold, the son of his brother Bernard Raymond, who was sometimes simply called Raymond.[8] Furthermore, either he or his nephew, but presumably he, was condemned for Catharism sometime before February 1237.[9]

The next brother, Bernard Raymond, was one of the luminaries of the family, but, since his children are known, we shall treat him later, and instead turn now to his brother Berengar, sometimes called "de Portaria." Berengar was a consul in 1225-1226, and may have been the one of that name who swore to uphold the Peace of Paris in 1243.[10] On the other hand, this may have been his son Berengar of whom we hear briefly in 1272. At that date, the latter Berengar received a bequest from his father's brother William Bernard, a scion who was himself not otherwise seen in

[5] Grandselve 3 i (before 1173) where Raymond enfeoffed a property; ibid. ii (July 1173) where the same enfeoffed the same lot; ibid., iii (September 1187) where the use right of the property was sold or subinfeudated with the consent of Raymond the landlord; ibid., iv (May 1198) where Bruno and his brothers (all named) sold the same piece for themselves and their unnamed sisters; and ibid., v (May 1198) when this act was confirmed by Ispanus de Portaria and Raymond William Atadils, who stated that the daughters would give consent when they attain majority. See also Grandselve 4 (April 1201 and December 1202) where Atadils' wife Alamanda herself appears.

[6] E 273 (February 1224), and the document of July 1225 cited in note 4 above.

[7] TAM, II 39 (March 1254, copied in 1286) containing the division of the extensive properties of Bernard de Miramonte de Portaria, the son of Peter, among whose heirs were the heirs of Raymond Bernard Baranonus, his sons, that is, William Bernard and Raymond (usually called Raymond Arnold), who acted with the consent of Raymond Baranonus, who seems to have been exercising a typically avuncular function.

[8] J. H. Percin, *Monumenta conventus Tolosani ordinis fratrum praedicatorum* ... (Toulouse, 1693) Appendix: "Inquisitio de Raymundo Comite Tolosano" (August 1247), described as a "civis." For the name Raymond, see also the note above.

[9] He was No. **124** in the amnesty published above.

[10] PAN, J 305 29 (February 1243).

the charters.[11] The last brother, Arnold Raymond, was a consul in 1227-1228, and was probably also at the oath taking of 1243.[12] The fate of the two sisters is not known, but it is evident that the otherwise unknown father of the brothers had instructed them to maintain the property in community or "fratrisca" until the girls had received their dowries.

TABLE 1: BARANONUS – LINE OF RAYMOND BARANONUS

```
                              Raymond
                                1173
                                1187
                              db 1198
                                 |
  ┌────────┬────────┬─────────┬────────┬─────────┬────────┬──────────┬─────────┐
 Bruno    Raymond  Bernard  Berengar  William   Arnold   Alamanda   Unnamed
 1198      1198   Raymond     de      Bernard   Raymond    1198      female
(Grauzida  1254    1198    Portaria    1198      1198      1202       1198
 1225)             1239      1198    db 1271 ?   1243 ?   (Raymond   (Ispanus
                 db 1254     1226                          William      de
                (Lombarda                                  Atadil)   Portaria)
                 to 1254)
                    |                   |
  ┌─────────┬───────┴──────┐           |
Raymond   William     Bernard     Berengar
 Arnold   Bernard    Raymond         de
 1237      1237         jr        Portaria
 1254      1254        1254        1243 ?
db 1272   db 1272      1279         1272
                     (Lombarda
                      to 1273)
```

To turn back to the active Bernard Raymond, we know that he married Lombarda, the sister of the very rich Bernard de Miramonte de Portaria, and that he and two of his sons had been gratified in the will of that worthy in 1237.[13] Bernard Raymond served as a consul in 1214-1215, 1220-1221, 1223-1224, and possibly also in 1238-1239.[14] This history

[11] Grandselve 11 (December 1272) where Berengar Baranhonis, son of the quondam Berengar Baranhoni de Portaria, confessed that he had received 50 shillings from Grandselve for payment of the testamentary bequest left him by William Bernard Baranhoni.

[12] See the document cited in note 10 above.

[13] PAN, J 328 24 (August 1237) where, described as the testator's brother-in-law, Bernard Raymond was the principal counsellor for the will, and his sons Raymond Arnold and William Bernard were there called the testator's nephews. Bernard Raymond was not the brother of Miramonte's wife Ramunda; she was instead the daughter of Hugh Johannes, the well-known vicar of Toulouse. Bernard Raymond was therefore the husband of Miramonte's sister.

[14] He also appeared in Malta 4 203 (December 1220, copied in 1241); E 538 (June 1236); and in the testament of August 1237 cited in the previous note. He was dead by 1254, for which see the document of March 1254 discussed in note 7 above; and also

makes it seem probable that the family rose into prominence during the Albigensian war, and that it was initially associated with the popular party. Bernard Raymond was dead by 1254 and had three sons as heirs, Raymond Arnold, sometimes simply called Raymond, who was mentioned above,[15] William Bernard, who, like his brother Raymond Arnold, is heard of only in 1237 and 1254 and was deceased by 1272,[16] and the more important Bernard Raymond. Sometimes called "junior" to distinguish him from an older relative who shall be seen below,[17] Bernard Raymond's son Bernard Raymond was married to a Lombarda,[18] and was probably the one of this name who was consul in 1262-1263, 1270-1271, and 1275-1276. In 1267 he regained half of the third part of the secular justice of the seigniory of Bazus (northeast of Toulouse near Montastruc), of which his father had been "wrongfully" despoiled by Raymond VII, but, in 1273, was obliged to sell his portion of the tolls of the town to the crown.[19] It was he who petitioned the crown in 1279 in order to clear the inheritance of the once sentenced heretic Raymond Baranonus.[20]

The third Baranonus line takes its origin from a William Johannes "mercerius" or "mercator" who was dead by 1217 when his children's interests were being protected during their minority by two "procuratores et badlierii infancium et rerum," one of whom was the elder Bernard Raymond Baranonus mentioned above.[21] We later learn that two of these children were Bernard Raymond, sometimes called "de Burdegala" (Bordeaux) and sometimes "senior" to distinguish him from the younger Bernard Raymond seen above, and Burdegala's brother William Ray-

---

E 531 ii (April 1268) where a Bernard Raymond, son of the quondam Bernard Raymond Baranonus, is seen.

[15] See the testament of March 1254 discussed in note 7 above.

[16] For August 1237, see note 13 above where Raymond is called Raymond Arnold, and for March 1254, note 7, where Raymond Arnold was called Raymond.

[17] PAN, J 324 28 (December 1274-January 1275) where Bernard Raymond Baranonus "junior" attested an act of Bernard Raymond Baranhonus "senior" "qui dicitur de Burdegala," son of the deceased William Johannes "mercator" and "burgensis" of Toulouse, together with the latter's wife Ramunda.

[18] PAN, J 324 6 vi (November 1273) when, living on the street called "de Cervuneriis" (the part of the modern rue Saint-Rome between the Place du Capitole and the rue Du May), he, his wife Lumbarda, and his father's widow Lumbarda, sold their share of the tolls of the town for 140 pounds of Toulouse.

[19] The record is seen in several places: Fournier and Guébin, Enquétes d'Alphonse de Poitiers, No. 84 (November 1268), an act witnessed by Bernard Raymond Baranho "de Burdegalis, civis Tholose" and No. 100 (June 1267), with an original in PAN, J 312 30 (June 1267). For the sale of the tolls, see the note above.

[20] See the list in Chapter 6 above.

[21] Malta 15 112 (April 1217).

mond, the latter of whom was certainly dead by 1271.[22] Although a citizen of Toulouse, Bernard Raymond resided for a time at Bordeaux, and returned home sometime in the 1260s to suffer no mean difficulties there.[23] In 1274 he was called on by the Inquisition to testify concerning his long contact, dating from approximately 1224, with Waldensian circles in Toulouse and Bordeaux.[24] After that surely disturbing experience, he, together with his wife Ramunda, was obliged to sell his tolls in Toulouse to the crown in late 1274 and early 1275 in return for an annual rent of 65 shillings on the Bastide of Castillon near Cépet.[25] The Christmas of 1274 must have been a rather grim festival in his house on the street "de Pujolibus," but, to judge from his Waldensianism, the books he collected, and the polemical literature he knew, his must have been a mind well stocked with righteous indignation. According to his testimony of 1274, he had read the New Testament, knew by heart the famous anti-papal "D'un sirventès far" of Guillem Figuera, and owned copies of the life of Saint Brandon and of the "Bible" of Guyot of Provins.

[22] Dossat, "Les vaudois méridionaux" p. 221 refers to a document of 1248 referring to both brothers, and Grandselve 11 (March 1271) mentions that his house on the rue des Couteliers (in the City either in the Dalbade or Pont Vieux quarters) was sold first to John de Castronovo and then to Arnold de Falgario.

[23] Other than the date 1248 seen in the note above, we see him in town also in the act of November 1266 cited in note 19 above.

[24] The testimony is recorded in PBN, Doat 25, fol. 196ff. (December 1274), and discussed by Dossat, "Les vaudois méridionaux," p. 222.

[25] See the act of December 1274-January 1275 attested by Bernard Raymond Baran-honus "junior," in note 17 above.

Barravus

The history of the Barravus clan of Toulouse is complicated by the commonness of the name Barrau in the Midi. Apart from some early Barravi of the late eleventh and early twelfth centuries whose relationship to the later main line of the City carrying this name cannot be established,[1] there were always Barravi who were not part of the greater family.[2] A family appears in 1164/5 in the person of a Bernard Barravus Caput de Soca.[3] The Caput de Soca family ran for three generations into the early 1200s, but cannot be traced further.[4] Several of the Barravi of the Bourg had modestly distinguished careers. One was John Barravus who served as a consul for the Bourg in 1222-1223. A moneylender who acquired property near the Hers river at the Pont-des-Clèdes, John is reported to have been seen at Cathar conventicles around 1224.[5]

[1] Note a pair of brothers named Bruno and William seen in Douais, *Saint-Sernin*, Nos. 103, 129, and 188 (undated); ibid., Nos. 67 and 69 (1136 and September 1138); ibid., No. 102 (January 1144), by which date Bruno was dead; and possibly ibid., No. 446 (October 1158) mentioning a William Barravus de Blaniaco (Blagnac). Others of the same kind are a Barravus de Montebeo, Berald his brother, and his son Pons in ibid., No. 79 (January 1136).

[2] Saint-Bernard 36 ii (June 1200), a William Barravus "tegularius" (tyler), presumably in the Bourg; E 538 (October 1201) where Capdenier rented land for clearing to a William Barravus and Bernard Johannes "ortolanus" (gardener); PBN, MS lat. 9189, fol. 230va (sometime in 1209, copied in 1215), a witness Raymond Barravus "ortolanus"; and Malta 17 26 (either in 1221 or 1227) when Gerald Barravus sold Pons Barravus an arpent of vineyard, not, this time, in the Bourg.

[3] Saint-Sernin 688 (29 79 6) 3rd act tied to others (March 1164 or 1165), "de Coca." One notes that there were "souques" in not a few places in Toulouse. Jules Chalande, *Histoire des rues de Toulouse* ... (Toulouse, 1919), 1: 131-139 identified the Soca Albiges (now Nazareth in the City) and Wolff, *Estimes*, Map 3 located a "souque" of Lascrosses near the gate of that name in the Bourg. One also notes that there was a "souque" very near the Dalbade church in the City. See the "carraria de Cesqueriis qui vocatur de Soca" in Malta 12 87 (January 1279), also called the "carraria de Sesceriis" PBN, MS lat. 9189, fol. 240b (March 1217). Because all the documents deal with vineyards at Montvincent to the east of the Bourg, however, I slightly favor the "souque" in the Bourg.

[4] Grandselve 1 (January 1173) Peter Barravus, son of Barravus Caput de Soca; E 538 i (September 1174) Peter Barravus Caput de Zoca; Saint-Bernard 138, fol. 61r (January 1186) Peter Barravus; ibid., fol. 180r (September 1199) the same; ibid., fol. 67r (February 1205) Barravus Caput de Soca; and the same in ibid., fol. 70r (October 1211).

[5] PAN, J 1024 1 (May 1200) as a creditor at Belberaud near Montgiscard south of town; Saint-Bernard 32 (September 1210); ibid., 138, fol. 88v (February 1221); E 538 (December 1225); ibid. (November 1227) with his wife Ademaria; and TBM, MS 609, fol. 197v (approximately 1224).

Other Barravi who seem to have been domiciled in the Bourg were the brothers Arnold and Elias. Arnold, who was dead by 1230, was a distinguished public notary who both served the consuls and drew private acts principally for inhabitants and institutions of the Bourg. He instrumented from 1196 to 1211, and he was also a merchant because he composed an act for Toulousans when at Troyes in 1210.[6] Although we have instruments from Elias only from 1201 to 1209, we know that he was in business with his brother and that he outlived him.[7] In 1230 he collected restitution for usury for himself and his deceased brother from the heirs of Pons de Capitedenario.[8] Elias may have lasted until 1243 when a person bearing his rare first name is seen among the many Barravi taking oath to uphold the Peace of Paris.[9] A later William Barravus instrumented in 1255 and is therefore possibly a relative of these notaries. This may have been the one of this name who married Bertranda de Caturcio of the bourghal family in 1240.[10] There is no evidence that any of these Barravi were related to the family to which we shall now turn our attention. It is worth noting here that similar family names are often carried by separate families in the Bourg and the City.

The main Barravus family was domiciled in the Dalbade and Daurade parishes of the City. Members of this family owned a tower on the Saracen wall between the City and Bourg, as well as houses on an adjacent street variously called "de molinariis" or "Arnaldi Barravi" until this property was alienated to the Dominicans in the mid thirteenth century.[11] As shall be seen later in this history, the family owned mills in

[6] There are about 25 extant acts of which the first is Daurade 118 ii (October 1196, copied in 1204) and Grandselve 6 (January 1174, copied in April 1211 by Arnold). The charter from Troyes is in E 569 (May 1216) recording events some six years earlier. Most of Arnold's acts were drawn for the Astro, Capitedenario, Embrinus, Maurandus, and Rossellus families, and for Saint-Sernin. As a consular notary he took oath before the legates to maintain the faith in PAN, JJ 21, fol. 78r (December 1203).

[7] Elias' first and last acts are Saint-Bernard 138, fol. 181r (November 1201) and Grandselve 4 (original of January 1178, copied in January 1209 by Elias, further copied in 1214). The two brothers together authenticated copies in Grandselve 2 i-iii that start with an original of October 1176 and are all copied in March 1206, and E 510 of December 1152, copied in April 1206 by the brothers.

[8] E 538 i-iii (June 1230) a restitution in the guise of a sale, but in conformity with Pons' testament.

[9] The oath in PAN, J 305 29 (February 1243) lists the following Barravi: line 19: Peter, Aimeric, Roger, Bernard, William, Stephen, Bertrand, Arnold the brother of Peter, and Arnold; line 25: but separated one from the other, Durand and William; line 27: Vital; and line 31: Elias.

[10] Grandselve 8 (March 1255) is William's act. The marriage is in Malta 27 65 (January 1240). This is mere conjecture because, as the reader will see below, there are Williams of the main City line extant at the time.

[11] Bernard Guy, *De fundatione et prioribus conventuum provinciarum Tolosanae ...*, ed. P. A. Amargier, in *Monumenta ordinis fratrum praedicatorum historica*, 24, 1961,

the Daurade and Bazacle complex and had extensive holdings along all the waterfront of the Garonne from the town wall in the south of the City and the Ile-de-Tounis to the New or Daurade Bridge. These properties, together with their interests in Saint-Cyprien, Lardenne, and westward over to l'Isle-Jourdain, help establish the unity of this great burgher clan. So also did their close association with the monasteries of the Daurade, the Hospitalers, the Templars, and, later, the Dominicans.

After the original progenitors of the late eleventh and early twelfth centuries, if such they were, a Bernard Barravus appears as a witness in the late 1130s to acts concerning the foundation of the "salvetat" of Larramet near Lardenne to the west of Saint-Cyprien. These acts contained grants to the Templars by the bishop of Toulouse, local notables, and members of the Tolosa family of the City.[12] Significantly, many of the later Barravi shared waterfront rights with the Tolosa family and also had property at Lardenne. Shortly after this, in 1146, we see another Bernard Barravus (perhaps the same), a worthy who inhabited the City region then called the "capud de Ponte" (the head of either the Old or the New Bridge) who was among those who sponsored and protected the Daurade Hospital in Saint-Cyprien.[13] In 1150 we see yet another Bernard (perhaps again the same) who, together with his two sons, witnessed a grant by the Tolosa family of their rights in the Dalbade church to the Hospitalers.[14] The two sons bore curious names, one being Petrora and the other Ienorius. These persons are heard of again. A charter of 1195 informs us that property once owned by Petrora was in the hands of Bernard Barravus de Ponte, of whom more will be seen later.[15] Ienorius lived longer and seems to have been more important. He appears as a

---

pp. 32-37 (studied in Vicaire, *Dominique et ses prêcheurs*, pp. 307-339) where we learn that Roger Barravus sold the Dominicans a property in 1234, and that, in 1260 and 1263, he is heard of again as well as his property "in carreria dicti Arnaldi Barravi et in fundo illius carrerie erat turris rotunda in clausura civitatis, que turri erat predicti domini Arnaldi" and his brothers to whom all the houses on the street "ex utraque parte faciebat sibi censum obliarum" (p. 35). This tower is described as that of Bernard Raymond Barravus as we see in Dominicans 11 i (December 1198, copied in 1226), and we further know from TAM, AA 1 19 (November 1180) that waste and rainwater was to run from the "cornu turris Vitalis Barravi" by a path toward the Garonne, adjacent to properties of a William de Montetotino.

[12] Malta 133 1-3, a series of acts dated from June to September 1134, concerning the foundation of this "salvetat," the jurisdictions and rights of local landlords, and the church and tithing of the church of Sainte-Marie.

[13] Saint-Étienne 227 (26 DA 2 unnumbered) (March 1146 or 1147, copied in 1189).

[14] Malta 25 2 (December 1150).

[15] See note 19 below.

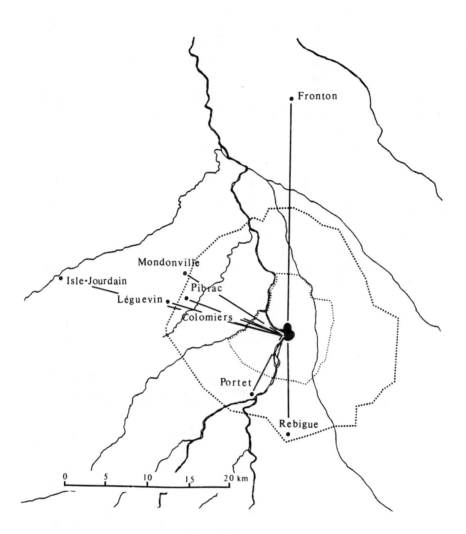

MAP 3. BARRAVUS

creditor acquiring property or rights to the west of Toulouse at Colomiers, Mondonville, and the region of the Touch river in the first half of the 1170s. The first of this family to show a connection with l'Isle-Jourdain, Ienorius appears in a charter of 1205 along with a Vital Barravus.[16] Vital is also interesting. Earlier in 1180, the Barravi tower on the Saracen wall was called that of Vital, who, in 1181-1182, was a member of the town chapter, the later consulate.[17] He also owned property in 1194 together with a Bernard Raymond and Raymond Bernard Barravus, two important scions of the main line who will be seen later on.[18] As is the case of Ienorius, Vital was clearly of the main family.

Another group of the City Barravi begins with a Peter, not in-conceivably the heir of the Petrora mentioned above. In 1192, with the consent of his wife Prima and his son Bernard, Peter Barravus entered the Hospital, reserving the usufruct of substantial properties donated to the order for his own life and for those of his wife and son.[19] This Peter may have been he who rose to become prior of the Hospital in the period 1207-1211.[20] His wife appears in the documents until 1196,[21] and his two daughters until 1202.[22] His active son Bernard, sometimes simply called

[16] MADTG, A 297, fol. 865r (March 1172 or 1173) about Mondonville; ibid., fol. 217r (March 1174/5) about Colomiers, the region of the Touch, and Toulouse; and Grandselve 4 (June 1205) together with Vital.

[17] See note 11 above.

[18] Malta 3 115, two acts dated August 1194 recording a sale by Vital to the Hospital of two properties, one with the consent of Bernard Raymond Barravus who had the lordship in pledge, and the other with that of Raymond Bernard Barravus, the lord. These are the brothers of 1174 who will be seen below.

[19] Malta 7 46 and 47 (May 1192), two copies of the same act. The properties are described more fully in Malta 1 89 and 58 iv (May 1195), and consisted of seven "operatoria" between the "ecclesiam novam" of Saint-Rémézy and the grand portal of the Hospital, an "honor" acquired at Puy from a Jacob, and a "casal," "curia," tithe, and dovecote adjacent to properties of the brothers William Peter and Bernard Barravus de Ponte, once owned by Petrora Barravus.

[20] Antoine du Bourg, *Ordre de Malte* (Toulouse, 1893), p. 24 lists him as prior in 1207-1209, but he appears to have had a second term in this office, one that changed almost yearly. He was prior again in Malta 58 unnumbered (January 1211).

[21] The evidence for this is in the two documents of May 1195 cited above in note 19, where Prima and her son Bernard give the Hospital the property, receiving it back in commendation for life, and are accepted as members of the house of Toulouse (to live nowhere else) when they wish, "et si eos in seculari abitu mori contigerit in cimiterio hospitalis sepoliri debent." In short, the mother and son had acquired a corrody at call by means of the gift they and Prima's husband had made the Hospital at the time of his entry into the order.

[22] Malta 7 56 ii (November 1201, copied in 1245) where Bernarda Barrava and her husband William Dominicus gave the Hospital a bakery with the consent of her mother Prima and brother Barravus. Ibid., 8 1 and 1[bis] (July 1202) in which the Hospital rented for life to Barravus de Hospitale houses and "honores" adjacent to houses of Willelma

Barravus de Hospitale, is seen until 1217. Although associated with the Hospital and presumably able to retire into it at will, Bernard both acquired property as far away as Fronton to the north of the town and fell into debt during his lifetime.[23] It is therefore not inconceivable that Bernard married and was the progenitor of some or one of the unidentified Barravi we shall see later.

What links this family to the Barravi generally is that some of its property was adjacent to land owned by another Bernard and his brother William Peter Barravus, the former brother sometimes being called "de Ponte" to distinguish him from "de Hospitale." Alive in 1192 and 1195, probably consul in 1194-1195, Bernard may have died by 1209, although it is altogether possible that he was one of the thirteenth-century Bernards seen below.[24] As significant for our family history is his brother William Peter. Seen with his brother in the 1190s, William Peter was intermittently in the charters until 1222, when he served as a councilor for the consuls.[25] Dead by 1230, we then learn that William Peter had married Fays, and that he had had a son named Bernard Raymond who served with him in 1222, and a daughter named Bernarda. What the relationship of these Barravi was to those who shall be seen below is not clear, but it was surely close. We know that a Bernard Barravus de Ponte held property once owned by Ienorius. His designation "de Ponte" relates him to all the other Barravi, both those mentioned above and those to come,

---

Barrava and Bernarda, Barravus' sisters, the "carraria que ducit apud Garonnam," property of Pons Rubeus, and the "communem clausuram huius ville," hence just on the southern edge of the City. To this the Hospital added "unum locarum quod est ibidem extra murum predicte clausure usque ad flumen Garonne" on which Bernard was to build a house at a cost of 60 shillings spread over time, and for all of which he was to pay 40 shillings "servicium" or rent yearly.

[23] Malta 1 107 (August 1206), with the consent of the Hospital, Bernard Barravus de Hospitale borrowed money from Peter Maurandus in a loan guaranteed by Bernard Raymond Tolose in order to buy three of the four parts of the "forcia" of Bersag on the Girou river near Fronton. Bernard gave the farm to the Hospital, and received it back in usufruct. In ibid., 108 (May 1209) we learn that this loan of 720 shillings "et de lucro" had been paid off by Bernard Raymond de Tolosa, and that the Hospital had taken it over and paid him 851 shillings, giving the creditor just about 18 percent in 31 months, an annual return of about 7 percent.

[24] See the acts dated May 1192 and May 1195 in note 19 above. The document of May 1209 cited in the previous note refers to properties mentioned in those earlier instruments, but described them as being simply of a William Peter Barravus. Bernard had therefore either sold them or died.

[25] William Peter as a witness in E 508 (April 1210) and E 501 (February 1215). In TAM, AA 1 75 (March 1222) the Barravi councilors of the consuls were Bernard, Vital, and Aimeric in one group, Durand alone, William Peter and his son Bernard Raymond, and an Arnold and John (the one from the Bourg) were consuls in that term.

who had interests in the Daurade and the New Bridge. Moreover, William Peter's daughter Bernarda married Raymond de Montetotino, and the Montetotino family held property adjacent to the Barravi tower on the Saracen wall.[26] Lastly, it is to be noted that William Peter's son was named Bernard Raymond Barravus, presumably after the distinguished Bernard Raymond whose history is to be found below.

The reader will remember that there were several Bernards of the Barravus family in the thirties and fifties of the twelfth century. One of these Bernards was dead by 1174, giving his inheritance to Bernard Raymond, the latter's siblings Raymond Bernard and Arnold, and to other sons not named in the charter and presumably minors (see Table 2).[27] Bernard Raymond was an important personage. He served five terms as a chapterman or consul, perhaps more.[28] The Bernard Raymond who was a consul in the terms of 1217-1218 and again in 1224-1225 may have been this man or his relative Bernard Raymond, the son of William Peter mentioned above. The Bernard Raymond of 1174 was a mill owner in the Daurade and Bazacle complex, a busy moneylender, and, together with his brothers, had interests everywhere to the west of Toulouse at Lardenne, Léguevin, and l'Isle-Jourdain.[29] Bernard Raymond and a

[26] For Bernard Raymond, see the document of March 1222 cited in the note above. Sales of property at Lespinet-Lesvignes (near Pouvourville) to the south of the town and in Saint-Cyprien by Raymond de Montetotino de Grepiaco (Grépiac near Auterive on the Ariège river) and Bernarda his wife to her brother Bernard Raymond Barravus in Malta 3 170 i (May 1230, copied in 1235); ii (June 1230) Bernard Raymond son of the deceased William Peter with the consent of his mother Fays; iii (July 1230) Bernard Raymond acting alone; iv (March 1232) Bernarda daughter of the deceased William Peter acting alone; and v (November 1232) Bernarda and her husband selling property.

[27] Grandselve 1 iv (February 1174, copied in 1200), referring to the "rachat" caused by the death of their father.

[28] 1183-1184, 1186-1187, 1194-1195, 1196-1197, and 1198-1199. He probably was the one of the name who took oath to maintain the faith in PAN, JJ 21, fol. 78r (December 1203).

[29] For the act of October 1180, see the note immediately below; Daurade 166 ii and iii (November 1183, copied in 1322) in which Bernard Hugh Barravus lent money in a charter witnessed by Bernard Raymond and his brother Arnold ; ibid., 171 (February 1187, copied in 1210, 1235, and 1303) wherein Bernard Raymond and his brother Arnold, the latter acting with the consent of his wife Pictavina, divided a house and "aula" in the Close of the Daurade; Bazacle 1 24, fol. 5v (September 1190) Bernard Raymond, Durand, and, as a witness, Raymond, possibly Bernard Raymond's son; ibid., 24, fol. 18r (June 1194) as a millowner; Malta 3 115 (August 1194) together with his brothers Raymond Bernard and Vital seen in note 18 above; Saint-Bernard 138, fol. 110r (April 1196) with his brother Arnold holding a mortgage of Sarracena de Noerio; MADTG, A 297, fol. 889r (April 1197) with his son Raymond as a witness; Malta 165 4 (September 1197) with his brother Arnold and son Raymond at a marriage between the families of the lords of Verfeil and Montaut; MADTG, A 297, fol. 410r (October 1198) a pledge of all property at Léguevin by the lord of l'Isle-Jourdain to Bernard Raymond, witnessed by the latter's

TABLE 2: BARRAVUS, OF THE CITY

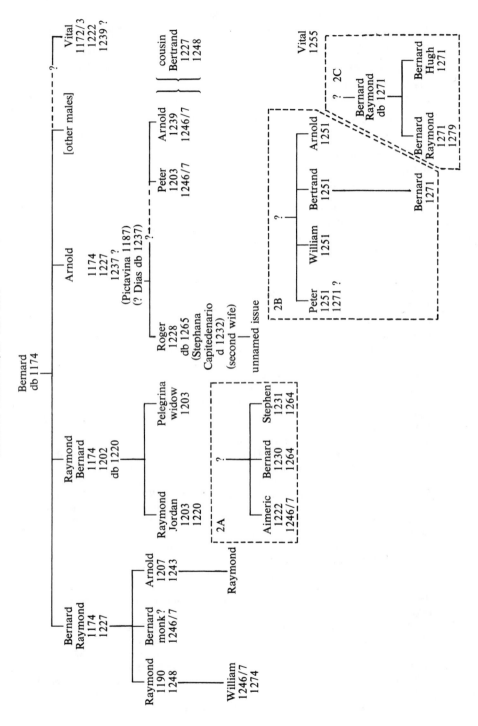

cousin had property in the Close of the Daurade, and he and his brother Arnold possessed the towered house once linked to the name of Vital Barravus.[30] The last time Bernard Raymond was surely seen was in a charter concerning l'Isle-Jourdain in 1227, where he acted together with his brother Arnold.[31]

The second brother of 1174 was Raymond Bernard. Twice a consul in 1197 and 1201-1202, he shared properties with his older brother in 1194 and 1201, and had died sometime before 1220, at which time we hear of his son Raymond Jordan (who had appeared in 1203), other sons who were not named, and a widowed daughter Pelegriva.[32] Attached to the familiar Raymond, the name Jordan was probably adopted in honor of the family connection with the lords of l'Isle-Jourdain who invariably carried this name.

The last of the three brothers was Arnold. Interested in the mills and possibly three or more times a consul,[33] it was probably this weighty man

---

brothers Arnold and Raymond Bernard; Dominicans 11 i (December 1198, copied in 1226) where he rented property on the street later called "Arnaldi Barravi" and next to his tower (see also ibid., ii [June 1203]); Saint-Bernard 138, fol. 44r (March 1201) where the three brothers Bernard Raymond, Arnold, and Raymond Bernard deal with their property at Frez Palers outside the Lascrosses gate in the Bourg; MADTG, A 297, fol. 443r (July 1201) a loan by Bernard Raymond to the lord of l'Isle-Jourdain at an annual rate of interest of 15 percent attested by his brother Raymond Bernard; Daurade 149 i (May 1203, copied in 1335) referring to property at Lardenne, that of his brother Arnold, that of Peter Barravus and his brothers, of Raymond Jordan, the son of his brother Arnold, and that of Peter Barravus and his brothers, and of Raymond Jordan, the son of his brother Raymond Bernard; TAM, AA 1 56 (September 1205) where he witnessed a consular act (as the cartulary shows, Bernard Raymond had in fact served as a councilor from 1203 until that date); and MADTG, A 297, fol. 414r (October 1206) where the debt owed Bernard Raymond in 1198 was paid off to Arnold Barravus, presumably his brother.

[30] Daurade 155 i (October 1180, copied in 1322) wherein Bernard Hugh Barravus lent 575 shillings arranging for repayment of the "cabalem" and "lucrum penalem" if needed. Witnesses were Bernard Raymond Barravus and his "cozinus" Heleazar, and mention is made of the property in the close. As to Vital's house, see the reference to the act of December 1198 above in note 11 above.

[31] MADTG, A 297, fol. 730r (December 1227) attested by the brothers Bernard Raymond, Arnold, and Bertrand Barravus.

[32] See the charters of August 1194, March 1201 and May 1203 in note 29 above. E 501 (November 1220) mentions Raymond Jordan, son of the deceased Raymond Bernard, as a mortgage holder on a property along with Pelegriva, the widow of Arnold Odo.

[33] See the instruments of November 1183, February 1187, August 1196, April 1196, September 1197, March 1201 and May 1203 in note 29 above. Arnold's interest in the Daurade-Bazacle mills is shown in Bazacle 3 1 July 1186, and in those of the Château Narbonnais in PAN, J 330 5 (December 1192) where the count granted the right to build mills there in an act drawn "in porticu Arnaldi Barravi." His consular terms are 1192-1193, 1199-1200, 1214-1215, 1222-1223, and 1225-1226, but one cannot be sure of the latter terms, there being so many Arnolds of the family by that time.

who was among the hostages sent to Paris in 1229.[34] Although the
candidacy of either one of two other Arnolds, one the son of Arnold's
brother Bernard Raymond and the other Arnold's own son named
Arnold, is almost as possible as that of Bernard Raymond's brother, he
may have been the one of this name who was listed in 1279 among those
condemned for heresy before February 1237.[35] What makes this open to
question is that our Arnold, the brother of Bernard Raymond, was
assuredly married to a Pictavina in 1187, whereas the Arnold who was
sentenced for heresy was married to a woman named Dias whose body
was dug up and burned in 1237.[36] Still, men occasionally have two
wives.[37] Perhaps also the street "Arnaldi Barravi" (or "de Molinariis")
next to the Barravi tower on the Saracen wall was named after him. At
any rate, the last certain reference to this Arnold is of 1227, when he acted
together with his brother Bernard Raymond about l'Isle-Jourdain. As we
shall see, Arnold probably had a son named Roger and possibly other
sons named Peter and Arnold.

It will be recalled that the brothers of 1174 had other siblings whose
names are not known. It is impossible to find out who these were. A
possible candidate is the Bernard Hugh Barravus who acted as a
moneylender in charters of 1180 and 1183 attested by the brothers
Bernard Raymond and Arnold, but, as is obvious, this might have been an
uncle or other relation.[38] Other possible candidates are the Bernard
Barravus de Ponte and his brother William Peter mentioned above. One
recalls that William Peter's son was named Bernard Raymond, clearly
after the more celebrated Bernard Raymond of 1174. Furthermore, we
know that an Arnold had a brother named Bernard with whom he acted
concerning the Daurade in 1207.[39] It may have been this Bernard
Barravus who was forced to make restitution for usury in 1211, although
this persom may equally easily have been the Bernard Barravus de Ponte
mentioned immediately above.[40] A second possible brother was a Vital

---

[34] PAN, J 310 45 (April 1229).

[35] Arnold is No. **145**. See the list in Chapter 5 above.

[36] Dias is No. **181** in the list of 1279 (Chapter 5), showing that the condemnation was
between February and September of 1237. Pelisson, *Chronicon*, p. 110 records the burning of Dias' body, and so does PBN, Doat 21, fol. 183v (September 1237).

[37] The other Arnolds are unsatisfactory candidates also. Both took oath to uphold the
Peace of Paris in February 1243 (cited in note 9 above), and had therefore not been
recently condemned for heresy.

[38] For October 1180, see note 30 above, and for November 1183, note 29 above.

[39] Daurade 177 (March 1207).

[40] E 508 (February 1211) wherein the usuries were forgiven by a debtor from Portet
in an illegal – from the point of view of canon law – form of restitution.

who may perhaps be distinguished from the earlier Vital seen above.[41] This Vital served as a councilor to the consuls in 1222 and witnessed a document about the management of the Daurade Bridge that involved most of the family in 1239.[42] Once as a usurer, Vital is seen in the charters until 1255.[43] A third possibility is a William Barravus. First seen in 1197, William had a house near the Château Narbonnais, and was deceased by 1218.[44] The only link between William and the other Barravi mentioned above is that his property close to the Château Narbonnais was near that of Bernard Barravus de Hospital and Bernard Barravus de Ponte and his brother William Peter. It is possible, therefore, that this William could have been the son of one of these Bernards.

A final possible brother is a Durand Barravus from whom springs a line that can be traced to the end of the thirteenth century (see Table 3). His relationship to the main line is shown by his participation in an act concerning the mills in 1190 along with the Bernard Raymond and Arnold of 1174 and in 1192 concerning the Close of the Daurade with Bernard Raymond's sons, of whom more anon.[45] Durand was mentioned in public instruments in 1202, 1221, and 1222,[46] and died sometime

---

[41] The argument against the two Vitals being one and the same is simply the fact that the earlier Vital would have lived a long time.

[42] The list of the councilors of March 1222 is in note 25 above. The compromise over the appointment of the "pontonarius" of the Daurade Bridge between the Daurade and the consuls is in Daurade 117 (May 1239). The arrangement was made with the consent of the following Barravi: Peter and his brother Arnold, Arnold son of Arnold, Roger, Bernard, and Peter, the son of the deceased Durand, and three other persons, namely Raymond de Montetotino, the husband of a Barravus woman (for whom see March 1230 in note 25 above), Arnold Guido, and Bertrand Balsanus. Vital Barravus was among the witnesses.

[43] MADTG, A 297, fol. 384r (October 1243); TAM, AA 1 101 (July 1247); and A. Blanc, Le livre de comptes de Jacme Olivier ... (Paris, 1899), vol. 2, pt. 2 – May 1255, witnesses Nos. 11 and 17, the later being Vital denying complicity.

[44] Grandselve 1 (January 1172) a property in the Bourg; ibid., 3 (February 1197) at Podium Sancti Germani outside the City toward Montaudran; see the tyler of this name in June 1200 in note 2 above; PAN, J 321 50 (April 1215) where we see that William's house was located next to that of the Seillani brothers, just to the west across the street from the Château Narbonnais, and not far from a "tegularium" – incidently there was a "tegularium" to the south of the Château Narbonnais called, at this time, the "tegularium Curvi [de Turribus]"; and Saint-Bernard 138, fol. 181v (May 1218) listing land once of William Barravus. As is obvious, there is no reason to think that these references refer to one individual.

[45] See the document of September 1190 in note 29 above. Daurade 173 (May 1192, copied in 1235) concerning property in the close enacted by Raymond and Arnold Barravus, brothers, and witnessed by Durand.

[46] TAM, AA 1 30 (August 1202); ibid., 90 (August 1221); and the act of March 1222 in note 25 above.

before 1239 when his son Peter is mentioned among the Barravi with rights on the New or Daurade Bridge.[47] Peter had a brother named Durand, and, in 1266, a document tells us that Durand and Peter, both by then deceased, had had their forest of Breuil at Rebique near Castanet unjustifiably confiscated by Raymond VII. In that year and the year after, when the family fell to litigation over the "nemus" they had just recovered, we learn that, typical of this family's indifference to the needs of future historians, the sons of the deceased Durand were named Peter and Durand, and their cousins, the sons of the quondam Peter, Peter, Arnold, and Durand.[48] It is furthermore possible that our original Durand or one of his sons was sometimes simply called Barravus de Corronsaco. This personage was clearly named after Corronsac near Castanet, and also owned property near the Hospital in Toulouse in 1230.[49] Other than the proximity of Castanet to Rebigue seen above, what makes this linkage possible is that Corronsaco's wife, Ramunda Barrava, was an active heretic in the late 1220s and was condemned in 1246.[50] And one of the later Durands of this family was a petitioner for the amnesty of heretical inheritances in 1279.[51]

To return now to the three brothers known in 1174 (see Table 2), their issue is hard to disentangle. Bernard Raymond's presumably eldest son Raymond appeared in charters from 1190 to 1197, and may have been the Raymond whom we shall see to have been active later on.[52] The history of Bernard Raymond's other sons is helped by two charters concerning the indebtedness of the lords of l'Isle-Jourdain to the Barravi. In the first of these, an act dated 1243, the two principal Barravi creditors of these great

[47] See May 1239 in note 42 above. Durand is also seen at the oath for the Peace of Paris in February 1243 in note 9 above.

[48] The restoration is in PAN, J 312 19 (a copy in PAN, J 190B, fol. 66ra) (November 1266), and the battle of the tutors of the heirs in Molinier, *Correspondance ... d'Alphonse de Poitiers*, No. 236 (May 1267).

[49] Malta 7 87 (November 1230) property near the Hospital.

[50] Douais, *Inquisition*, 2: 5 (March 1246). Ramunda was the sister of Aicelina and William Mercader, and was reported to have "adored" around 1228/9 in PBN, Doat 2, fol. 297r. Ramunda was listed as No. 257 in 1279 (see Chapter 5 above) which means she was sentenced either in the late 1240s or the early 1250s. Her sister and brother were also listed there.

[51] Chapter 6 above (March 1279) lists the following Barravi as petitioners for the amnesty: Arnold, Bernard son of the deceased Bernard, Do or Durand, son of the deceased Peter, who was represented by Raymond de Roaxio, Berengar Barravus speaking for the heir of Doat de Roaxio, and Raymond Bernard Barravus. The proctor who actually went to Paris for the amnesty of 1279 was Bernard.

[52] For the possible history of Raymond, see the material assembled three paragraphs below. These early references show him in September 1190 and April 1197 with his father in note 29 above, and in May 1192 with his brother Arnold in note 45 above.

magnates were Roger and Arnold.[53] Dated 1248, a settlement of these
debts negotiated between the debtor and the creditors shows us that the
debts ran back to the Bernard Raymond and Arnold of 1174. We also find
there that Roger was the son of the dead Arnold of 1174, and that
Raymond, brother of a deceased Arnold, shared with Roger the duty of
collecting or extending the debts of the lords. Among the creditors of 1248
were also other Barravi, Stephen, Bertrand, and, as a witness, Bernard, all
obviously close relatives, of whom more later.[54]

TABLE 3: BARRAVUS, OF THE CITY — LINE OF DURAND BARRAVUS

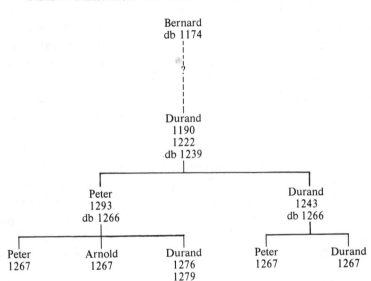

Roger's career is well known. A major by 1228, he was the husband of
Pons de Capitedenario's heiress Stephana.[55] Even after his wife's death
sometime in 1232, he served as an advisor for her widowed mother
Aurimunda until 1242.[56] Roger lived like a gentleman down by the

---

[53] MADTG, A 297, fol. 384r (October 1243).

[54] Ibid., fol. 403v (December 1248).

[55] Pons' testament is in Saint-Bernard 21 and 32 and PBN, Doat 40, fols. 216vff.
(March 1229).

[56] Stephana was last seen in E 575 (February 1232) and, in Saint-Bernard 21 (March
1233), the residual heir, the abbot of Grandselve, had requested an examination of the
documents concerning the inheritance that was to be his after Aurimunda's death. Roger
last served Aurimunda as a counsellor — a post in accordance with the terms of Pons'
will — in Grandselve 8 (October 1242).

Saracen wall, Capdenier having left him a "scutifer" (valet) in his testament of 1229. Other than his business at l'Isle-Jourdain, his properties adjacent to the Barravus tower and on the street "Arnaldi Barravi" are seen in 1234 and 1263.[57] He swore to uphold the Peace of Paris in 1243 and served as consul in 1246 and 1247.[58] He was involved in all the Barravi business in the City. He participated in the arrangements concerning the Daurade Bridge in 1239,[59] and gave testimony at the trial that resulted from the efforts of the Daurade priory to free itself from Moissac in 1246 and 1247, where he appeared for his close relative Bernard who claimed the office of prior.[60] Roger died sometime between 1263 and 1265, and we know that he had remarried after the premature death of Stephana de Capitedenario because he left issue, unfortunately not named in the charter.[61]

It is remotely possible that Roger had two brothers, ones who, how-ever, were never termed such in extant charters. This conjecture is based on a document of 1203 about property at Lardenne wherein we see the Bernard Raymond of 1174 and hear of property once owned by his brother Arnold adjacent to land of a Peter Barravus and his brothers. In 1251 the Daurade confirmed that the same property was owned by Peter, the son of the deceased Arnold, thus suggesting the filiation advanced above.[62] In the meantime, the brothers Arnold and Peter acted together in the settlement about the Daurade Bridge in 1239 and gave testimony in the suit over the Daurade priory in 1246 and 1247.[63] Although it could as easily have been the son of Durand mentioned above, it is possibly this Peter who married Sayssa de Tolosa in 1232.[64]

To turn now to the Raymond who acted with Roger in the charter of 1248 about the debts of l'Isle-Jourdain, we recall that he spoke for his

[57] See the materials cited from Vicaire in note 11 above.

[58] February 1243 in note 9 above.

[59] May 1239 in note 42 above.

[60] MADTG, G 713 containing testimony taken at various times in 1246 and 1247 includes the following Barravi in the order of their appearance: Raymond, brother of the prior named Bernard, Bertrand their cousin, Arnold "maior," Dominic, Roger, William, Arnold brother of Peter, Aimeric, William son of Raymond, and Bernard. MADTG, A 297, fol. 202r (August 1250) has Roger and Arnold attesting the will of a lord of l'Isle-Jourdain.

[61] Malta 140 (May 1265) wherein we learn that property at Cugnaux and Mauvers was owned by the children of the dead Roger.

[62] Daurade 149 iii (July 1251) where Peter, son of Arnold, possessed rights at Lardenne devolving from the brothers Bernard Raymond and Arnold of 1174, for which properties, see the act of May 1203 in note 29 above.

[63] For May 1239 see note 42 above, and for 1246 and 1247 note 60 above.

[64] Malta 1 128 (June 1232) with property near the Hospital toward the Garonne river.

dead brother Arnold, a person who was alive in 1243.[65] Both Raymond
and Arnold were involved in the settlement between the town and the
monastery in the matter of the Daurade Bridge in 1239, and both testified
at the trial of the prior Bernard Barravus of the Daurade, although Arnold
probably died during the course of that litigation sometime in 1246/7.[66] In
the testimony for that case, an Arnold (either this one or the one in the
previous paragraph) was termed "maior" to distinguish him from another
Arnold there present, and Raymond was identified as the brother of the
Prior Bernard who had usurped, according to the abbot of Moissac, the
priory of the Daurade, and who finally lost his appeal by the decision of a
judge delegated by the pope.[67] In all likelihood, there were, in short, three
brothers, one of whom had become a monk. Because of the involvement
at l'Isle-Jourdain in 1243 and 1248, furthermore, it seems not improbable
that these three brothers were the issue of Bernard Raymond Barravus of
1174, and that the Raymond mentioned above was Bernard Raymond's
son of that name who had appeared as early as 1190.[68] During the
lifetimes of their fathers, also, Raymond's son William appears as does
Arnold's son Raymond.[69]

Contemporaries of Roger and Raymond were the brothers Aimeric,
Bernard, and Stephen whose parents are not known (Table 2a). Identified
as brothers in 1236, [70] they had probably been active before. Aimeric was
a councilor for the consul in 1222 and witnessed a marriage in 1224.[71] He
and presumably both his brothers took oath to maintain the Peace of Paris
in 1243, and he and Bernard testified in the matter of the priory of the
Daurade in 1246 and 1247.[72] Bernard and Stephen were frequently active
together. They were seen at l'Isle-Jourdain and the Touch river region in

[65] See the information contained in the acts of October 1243 and December 1248 cited
in notes 53 and 54 above.
[66] For the bridge in May 1239, see note 42 above. MADTG, G 713 (register), fol. 31v
(late 1247): Raymond Barravus, brother of the claimant prior Bernard Barravus, reported
that his brother Arnold had been made a monk at the Daurade when dying. Since Arnold
gave testimony earlier on, one divines that Arnold died in this two year period.
[67] MADTG, G 713 (June 1248) recording the decision of Cardinal Hugh of Sancta
Sabina.
[68] See the acts of September 1190, May 1192, and April 1197 in note 52 above.
[69] TAM, AA 1 102 (January 1248) cites Arnold and Raymond his son, Roger, Peter,
and Aimeric Barravus. Raymond's son William is mentioned in 1246 and 1247 in note 60
above. William also attested a lawsuit in February 1274, for which see note 87 below.
[70] PAN, J 328 10 i and ii (May 1236), (also PAN, JJ 19, fol. 8v) where the three brothers
served as witnesses to an act by the count.
[71] For March 1222, see note 25 above. In MADTG, A 297, fol. 862r (September 1224)
Aimeric and Arnold Barravus at the marriage of a rich butcher.
[72] February 1243 in note 9 above, and 1246-1247 in note 60 above.

1231 and 1232,[73] again at l'Isle-Jourdain in 1248, where Bernard attested the charter and Stephen spoke for his brothers, recording in addition another debt owed to himself alone of a pourpoint sold to the lord. This charter also teaches us that Bernard and Stephen shared with Roger and Raymond the inheritance of the debts owed the brothers of 1174 by the lords of l'Isle.[74] It was probably this Bernard who was a consul in 1230-1231, an actor in the matter of the Daurade Bridge in 1239, a witness in the case of the Daurade priory in 1246 and 1247, and appeared at l'Isle-Jourdain in 1248 and 1255.[75] The two brothers, Bernard and Stephen, are seen together for the last time in 1264 when they attested a settlement about property adjacent to the Château Narbonnais.[76] Of the three brothers, Stephen appears to have been the most prestigious. He was twice a consul, in 1238-1239 and again in 1251-1252. He served as a "fideius-sor" in the great dynastic struggle over the inheritance of the barony of l'Isle-Jourdain in 1259-1260.[77] Bernard's compensation – if he needed one – was that he had a son named Bernard who, as a resident of the square of the Borguet-Nau, was among those who wanted to have the prostitutes who "infested" the town waterfront (the ends of the bridges in Saint-Cyprien and the City) driven out in 1271.[78] In the next year, we learn that this Bernard, together with his brothers Arnold and Raymond Bernard, had been paid all the debts owed to their father by the lord of l'Isle-Jourdain.[79] In 1279 Raymond Bernard served as a proctor and petitioner for the amnesty of deceased heretical inheritances, thus

---

[73] Malta 165 13 (August 1231) where they witnessed an act at l'Isle-Jourdain. E 436 (June 1232) records statements of Arnold de Tolosa and the brothers Bernard and Stephen Barravus about an assignment of lands on the Touch river toward Pibrac for reason of debt. The Barravi had won this assignment either in the consul's or the count's court. The lands had been pledged by the father or grandfather of Tolosa to the Barravi's debtor, the deceased Peter de Sancto Romano.

[74] December 1248 in note 54 above.

[75] See May 1239 in note 42 above and 1246 and 1247 in note 60 above. For 1248, see the note immediately preceding and MADTG, A 297, fol. 219v (April 1255) at l'Isle.

[76] TAM, DD 1 1 4 iv (June 1264, copied in 1270) on a property next the "abeurador" or the trough of the mills of the Château Narbonnais.

[77] PBN, MS nouv. acq. lat. 2046 (December 1259 and April 1260) where he stood for Isarn Jordan of the Laurac line against his cousin, the premier lord of the barony, Jordan IV de Insula.

[78] TAM, II 77 (April 1271, copied in 1299), published in G. Boyer, *Mélanges I: Mélanges d'histoire du droit occidental* (Paris, 1962), p. 199. The Barravi involved were Bernard, son of Bertrand, Arnold, Bernard Raymond and his brother Bernard Hugh, and Barravus and his brother Peter.

[79] MADTG, A 297, fol. 435v (November 1272). Less than 25 years old, the two minor brothers, Arnold and Raymond Bernard, had their attestation witnessed by the "officialis" of Toulouse and made the due renunciations of exceptions.

showing his relationship to the Cathar Arnold Barravus of so long before.[80]

Another contemporary of our Roger and Raymond was a Bertrand. He was described as the cousin of Raymond, the brother of the claimant for the priory of the Daurade in the testimony of 1246 and 1247, and he was among the Barravi creditors of the lords of l'Isle-Jourdain in the often cited charter of 1248. Bertrand had appeared in a document concerning l'Isle as early as 1227, together with the brothers of 1174, Arnold and Bernard Raymond.[81] He is last seen serving as a consul in the term 1247-1248 and in the charter of 1248 concerning l'Isle mentioned above.[82]

Hereafter only isolated individuals and groups of Barravi appear. Earliest among these are four brothers, Peter, William, Bertrand, and Arnold, who acted together in 1251 and 1253 (Table 2b).[83] One may reasonably conjecture that these were the sons of the Raymond seen above. There is no doubt that they were members of our City family because the properties of 1251 and 1253 were adjacent to the Temple, holdings of the Tolosa family, and the Garonne waterfront. One of the brothers was possibly later simply called Barravus because, in 1271, a Barravus and Peter Barravus, who lived on the square of the New or Daurade bridge, protested the prostitutes' use of the waterfront.[84] A Peter Barravus is seen in the Daurade mills in 1273.[85]

A further individual was Arnold, a son of one of the Arnolds described a page or so ago, and assuredly one of the true blue Barravi of the City. He liked to be styled the son of the quondam "dominus" Arnold Barravus "burgensis," and was a person of some distinction, being twice a consul in 1273-1273 and 1277-1278. His share in the ownership of the "leudae" or tolls of the City was investigated in 1269, and, together with his wife Magna, he sold them to the crown for 640 pounds of Toulouse in 1273.[86] He also protested the prostitutes in 1271, and he may have been, in 1274, a witness against the crown in a suit involving the properties of his

---

[80] March 1279 in Chapter 6 above; see note 51 above.

[81] December 1227 in note 31 above.

[82] December 1248 in note 54 above.

[83] Malta 2 147 iii (October 1251) about properties mentioned in Malta 4 215 (February 1253) wherein the brothers swapped property with the Temple. The lots in question bordered the Temple, the Garonne river, the City wall, and the street. It will be noted how similar these properties are to those of the Barravi de Hospitale and de Ponte seen so long ago in note 22 above.

[84] See April 1271 note 78 above.

[85] TAM, II 39 (March 1273).

[86] Molinier, Correspondance ... d'Alphonse de Poitiers, No. 1314 (July 1269), and PAN, J 324 6 iii (March 1274).

deceased mother Consors, daughter of Hugh de Roaxio, son of Alaman de Roaxio.[87] In 1279 he served as a proctor for the amnesty of heretical inheritances, thus showing his relation to the Cathar Arnold.[88]

The derivation of the last group of the Barravi to be treated here is not known, but there is no doubt that it was also of the main line (Table 2c). In 1271 we hear that a Bernard Raymond, the son of a dead Bernard Raymond, had interests in the Ile-de-Tounis, and that he and his brother Bernard Hugh lived on the waterfront somewhere near the Old Bridge.[89] Like so many of his family, Bernard Raymond was a creditor of the lord of l'Isle-Jourdain in 1274,[90] a millowner at the Château Narbonnais in 1278,[91] and a consul in 1278-1279. He was also a petitioner for the amnesty of 1279, and therefore related to the Cathar Arnold of so long ago.[92]

In fine, although a systematic genealogy of the Barravi cannot be composed (they had too many children who bore the name Arnold!), the vast majority of the persons carrying this surname in the documents were clearly derived from the Barravi of the City. Although there were one or more independent families, especially in the Bourg, the evidence testifies to the capacity of an important clan more or less to monopolize the use of a very common name in the area where it resided. Another characteristic of this family, and one that makes it difficult to trace, is that the successive generations of brothers, although obviously holding some properties in common, seem not to have lived together. They divided up their inherited property with remarkable alacrity. In their unicellular individualism, if that is the phrase to describe it, the Barravi seem altogether typical of the patrician burgher families among whom they lived and with whom they married.

The family also survived the Cathar crisis very well, perhaps because, being a large clan, it invested on both sides of the religious "market." In spite of the involvement of certain individuals with Catharism, the City Barravi had durable interests in the ecclesiastical institutions of their region, being especially closely connected to the Daurade and the

---

[87] PAN, KK 1228, fols. 53v and 56v (February 1274), and, for the waterfront, April 1271 note 78 above.

[88] See March 1279 in Chapter 6 above; see note 51 above.

[89] Malta 7 117 (March 1271) and April 1271 in note 78 above.

[90] MADTG, A 297, fol. 464r (March 1274) where a consortium of creditors relieved the lords of Lanta and l'Isle-Jourdain of a debt of 117 marks Sterling owed to Bernard Raymond Barravus.

[91] TAM, DD 4 unnumbered (June 1278).

[92] March 1279 in Chapter 6 above; see note 51 above.

Hospitalers, but also with the Templars and the Dominicans.[93] Economically we have seen that they were millowners on the Garonne, large scale moneylenders in town and outside, and owned property and had interests extending as far north as Fronton, west as l'Isle-Jourdain, and south as Castanet.

Politically, the family may be counted among the "old" patrician lines, having begun to serve on the board of chaptermen, later consuls, as early as 1181. Whatever their ancient relations to the counts, they were among those families that led the movement of urban liberty, serving in office almost every year during the 1190s and frequently throughout the war. Although one of the Arnolds was a count's creature in the long consulate of 1235-1238,[94] the family rallied strongly to the restoration of town freedom in the consulates of 1246-1248.[95] Thereafter, like most of its class, the family played a substantial but more modest role in the government of its native town.

---

[93] See the materials cited in note 11 above for the latter order. The relationship between the family and the order seems largely practical, a matter of business, but, according to Vicaire, *Dominique et ses prêcheurs*, p. 338, there was one donation. The brief appearance of the Christian name Dominic (see the materials about the litigation over the Daurade in 1246 and 1247 in note 60 above) in the family does not imply ideological adhesion. Dominic was a name known in the Midi before the arrival of Dominic Guzmàn.

[94] Percin, *Monumenta*, p. 81 where Arnold was also a witness for Raymond VII's attempt to restore his father's reputation in 1247.

[95] Quite apart from the consuls Roger in 1246-1247 and Bertrand in 1247-1248, all the City Barravi were exceedingly active in town government in the period 1246-1248, including, in TAM, AA 1 103 (January 1248) Aimeric, Arnold and Raymond his son, Peter, and Roger, and before in ibid., 101 (July 1247) the consul Bertrand, the ex-consul Roger, Arnold Peter, Stephen, and Vital.

Capitedenario

Having their origin in the hamlet of Capdenier to the north of the Bourg in the neighborhood of Castillon, Pechbonnieu, and Gratentour,[1] the most notable line of this family is that of Bernard and his son Pons de Capitedenario (see Table 4). Bernard was a modest person when he first appears in the charters in 1152.[2] By the time of his death between April and November of 1198, sometime in his early sixties, Bernard was well to do, and had prepared the way for his son Pons to become a very wealthy man indeed.[3] Pons, having already reached his majority, was a man of some

[1] Capdenier was in the hills overlooking the plain of the Hers river and the Garonne in the region mentioned in the text above. See two documents of the early twelfth century in the cartulary of Saint-Clar in Malta 360 1 xxix and xxx (dated from 1117 into the early 1120s) where a local notable gave the Hospital the church of Saint-Jean of Capdenier "ad salvetatem faciendam" and where the abbot Raymond William of Saint-Sernin contributed a wood called "de canalem" or "canilem" next to Capdenier "ad villam faciendam." The first act also mentions the Girou river, one of the confluents of the Hers in that region. This identification is not noted and would perhaps be contested by P. Ourliac, "Les sauvetés du Comminges," in his *Études d'histoire de droit médiéval* (Paris, n.d.) pp. 88-89, where the documents from Saint-Clar mentioned above are published. He may be right because one of the witnesses was the parish priest of the Salvetat-Saint-Gilles and because all the other acts in the roll concern places on the left bank of the Garonne. I think, however, that the mention of the Giron river, so near Capdenier, is enough to argue my case, and so is the participation of the canons of Saint-Sernin, so important in the same region. Douais, *Saint-Sernin*, No. 1 (p. 2) notes that Capdenier had a church, but its name is not mentioned in his text. See also an act of February 1167 in Douais, *Saint-Sernin*, No. 430 recording property between the Hers and Giron rivers "apud Castanearios." Saint-Sernin 600 (10 36 5) presents a group of 7 acts dated from 1135 to 1262. The first of these (dated November 1135) mentions Saint-Sauveur, Castillon, Castelginest, Launac, La Devèze, and both the Hers and Giron rivers, and a road from Capdenier to Toulouse via Castillon. Other acts mention property at Capdenier and Pechbonnieu, and a mill on the Giron river. The act of September 1231 cited in note 40 below shows that Capdenier had never grown beyond the level of a hamlet because the word "villa" is applied to Pechbonnieu and Launac (Launaguet), and the words "honor" or "locus" to Capdenier and Canet, all being close together. Lastly, Saint-Sernin 600 (10 42 3) (August 1279) describes the "castrum" of Vaquers as being bounded by Castelginest, Gratentour, Saint-Sauveur, and the Bastide-Saint-Sernin, with pertinences at Leus and Capdenier.

[2] Bernard's first appearances are as a witness in Grandselve 2, Roll iv xv (December 1152) and Douais, *Saint-Sernin*, No. 149 (November 1164). By the end of the 1160s, he had acquired two "casals" and an arpent and a half of a new vineyard or "malol" paying rents equaling 5s 2d, the property, in short, of a modest artisan.

[3] Of the about 163 acquisitions recorded for father and son, Bernard made 55 and Pons de rest. By his death Bernard had accumulated approximately a third of the rent roll to be

weight by 1194, and, two years later, shared with his father the "curia" of Saint-Quentin and its dependencies just outside the Bourg, one of the family's major acquisitions.[4] An inhabitant of the Bourg somewhere between the Pouzonville and Matabiau gates, Pons married Aurimunda, the daughter of Peter Surdus, a family well known in the Bourg. Their marriage settlement of about 200 shillings, dateable, probably, to the 1190s, was very modest indeed.[5] Aurimunda and Pons had one child, Stephana, who married the notable Roger de Barravus. Pons himself died sometime between October 1229 and March 1230. Unfortunately for his and his wife's hopes, the heiress Stephana died between February and July 1232.[6] On his widow's death sometime after December 1251, the monastery of Grandselve took over the estate.[7] Were Stephana to die without legitimate heirs, Pons had left his spacious home to the monks, proposing that it be turned into a hospice for the Cistercians, a foundation that later became the College of Saint-Bernard at the university.[8]

When he died, Pons was very rich, one of the richest men in Toulouse. In 1225 he acquired from Saint-Sernin, of which institution he was a

recorded in the Capdenier cartulary and the other documents. As further evidence of Bernard's means, see the substantial bequest left to the monastery of Pinel by his widow in April 1206 in note 5 below. The basis of this and the following analyses is the Capdenier cartulary (Saint Bernard 138) containing 144 acts, and about 129 to be found in other archival collections. This figure does not include about 33 other acts from the period after Pons' death in 1229 when the estate was managed by his widow. Bernard and Pons are also seen as witnesses in about 30 other charters, and Pons was several times a consul or a councilor for the consuls.

[4] E 509 (June 1194) Pons attested an act of his father-in-law Peter Surdus; E 510 v (December 1195, copied in 1197) Pons was a "sponderius" of the will of the humble Peter Raymond who left his property to his mother and gave 40 shillings to charity; and Grandselve 3 (May 1196) where Bernard and Pons rented out ("dare ad partem") the "curia" at Saint-Quentin with appendages at Castelariet and Columberium Beroardi for two years in return for half of the fruits, the maintenance of two pairs of oxen, two good "boerii," and provision for their sheep and an "ovelerius."

[5] Pons' testament is PBN, Doat 40, fols. 216v-231r and in transcriptions dated 1704 in Saint-Bernard 21 (March 1229) prepared for a lawsuit. This document mentions the marriage settlement, and also a paraphernal gift to Aurimunda by her father. As seen in the note above, Pons' first extant act had to do with the Surdi. Incidently, Pons' mother Ramunda is recorded as dead in Saint-Bernard 14 (April 1206) where Pons, acting as agent for the monks of Pinel not far from Fronton, bought property at Paisaucone (near Aurival on the Hers to the east of Toulouse), and gave them 200 shillings willed them by his mother in order to maintain a "bovem ad servicium domus et fratrum Pinelli."

[6] Stephana last appeared in E 575 (February 1232) and was no longer mentioned as being beside her mother in E 510 (July 1232). The contingent legatee, the monastery of Grandselve, asked for a showing of the will etc. in Grandselve 21 (March 1233).

[7] Her last act in my collection is E 579 (December 1251) where she acted as usual "nomine sponderagii dicti viri sui." Grandselve performed what used to be her role with one of Pons' properties in Grandselve 9 (March 1254).

[8] This history is discussed by Gérard "Le cartulaire des Capdeniers" 1-19.

major creditor, a towered house with a stone hall and chapel together with attached stores, all just across the irregularly shaped square from the choir of the basilica and its cemetery. This building was the one that was later converted into the College.[9] The style of life in this ample accommodation is shown by provision in Pons' will whereby his son-in-law, daughter, and wife were granted free residence for life in his "hospitium," and, furthermore, Roger Barravus was to be given a valet ("scutifer"), his daughter two personal maids, and his wife one, all other servants to be provided by the household. Earlier on, in 1205, a William Sanche de Capitedenario entered into personal servitude to Pons, a contract that may well indicate that he and his family served Pons as domestics.[10] Pons' feeling about family appears to have been conventional. According to his will, his wife would indeed have suffered a distinct loss of status had she moved out of his house or remarried, but, all the same, she and her daughtr were left in charge of the estate after his death, and both they and Pons' testament were protected against Roger Barravus, the son-in-law, who was, however, appointed an advisor in that document.

Pons was close to the church. He was a big donor, setting aside no less than 10,000 shillings and much property in his will to be distributed in charities, of which only a little over 1000 shillings went to specific lay beneficiaries. Grandselve was Pons' residual beneficiary, and, as was typical of his charity, he proposed that his house and inheritance, were they to go to the monks, would be a hospice for the religious of this house, an institution that already had a smaller installation in the town. His gifts not only gratified Grandselve and other outlying monasteries, but also the newer devotions of the time.[11] The Franciscans (called "menudelli" in his will) received 1000 shillings. Curiously, the Dominicans were not mentioned. This was probably because Pons had just bought the initial location for the later great church of the Jacobins for the price of 1200 shillings. This and probably other gifts of which we do not know resulted in Pons being described as the "patronus" of the mother house of the

[9] Saint-Bernard 138, fols. 91r, 93r, and 94v, containing the original sale by Saint-Sernin in October 1225 and attached properties acquired from the Astro family in May 1226. The house was bounded by possessions of the Claustro and Astro families and lay "inter carrariam maiorem [present rue du Taur] et carrariam de banquis." TAM, AA 1 100 (August 1240) tells that the attached stores Pons had acquired were hard against the "platea maior suburbii," and were located so close to Saint-Sernin that they impeded traffic.

[10] E 508 (June 1205). William Sancius was the son of a Guillelma de Capitedenario.

[11] The larger part of the gifts were to the infirmaries and hospitals of the various monasteries all over the region.

Dominican order.[12] He was therefore assuredly an acquaintance, perhaps even a friend of, Dominic Guzmàn.

Although one senses a relentless search for salvation, perhaps even a hope of bullying God as he probably bullied his neighbors, in Pons' testament, his extensive charities are partly explicable in terms of the time when he lived. Both father and son were obviously aggressive businessmen. Of the 163-odd acquisitions made by this pair, acquisitions that included a large farm, quantities of land and especially of vineyards on a wide arc running from Montvincent to the east of the Bourg northward to Saint-Geniès and southwest to Combe Salomon just outside of the Bourg, as well as much rental property in town, the vast majority took place in the periods from 1190 to 1205 and from 1210 to 1225. This neatly blocks out the period from 1205 to 1210, one in which the newly appointed Bishop Fulk of Toulouse was introducing the repression of usury with much popular support. This may possibly show that that sudden attack on economic individualism, if that is the term for it, impeded Pons' advance somewhat. On the other hand, the renewal of high rates of acquisition in the period from 1210 to 1225 clearly show that the assault on usury hardly slowed Pons' acquisitiveness. It also tells us that Pons did rather well during the troubled period of the war itself. After 1225, perhaps because of his increasing involvement in the political life of his town during the last five years of his life, his rate of acquisition suffered a real "rallentando." It is certain, moreover, that both Bernard and Pons were usurers, that is, moneylenders who collected interest on their loans. In fact, Pons' business was not only, as we have seen, slowed during the height of Fulk's attack on usury, but his favored contracts changed as a result of that pressure. He had begun by using contracts called "pignus" and "mutuum," but ended employing the preliminary forms of the "census" or "rente" contract.[13] Although moneylending was

---

[12] See the history of the origin of the Preachers in Toulouse in Bernard Guy, *De fundatione*, p. 32.

[13] The evidence is: E 538 i (September 1174) a "pignus" by Bernard for 400 shillings of two and a half arpents of arable; E 538 (May 1201) Pons lent 60 shillings at 12 pence "de lucro" monthly, i.e., 20 percent yearly not compounded; E 538 (December 1205) persons pledged to Pons 7 shillings less 3 pence rent annually for 146 shillings – 4.6 percent annually; E 501 iii (February 1206) where Saint-Sernin recognized that Pons had the tithe on an arpent and a half of new vineyard in pledge for 60 shillings; Saint-Bernard 138, fol. 133r (May 1206) a particular surrendered to Pons a "pignus" on a rent of 40 pence; E 503 (January 1207) a Villanova pledged to Pons and Arnold Aiscius the quarter, lordship, and tithe of 9 arpents of vineyard for 1500 shillings; E 508 ii (February 1212) where an individual pledged to pay Pons and Arnold Aiscius 60 shillings in three annual installments meanwhile granting a quarter of the fruits of a new vineyard as interest;

an essential part of business and altogether normal at the time, the period
of Pons' rise was one when men looked askance at such means of
economic domination, and it therefore seems reasonable to believe that
this prompted our Croesus to be unusually generous in his charities. In
accordance with the recommendation in his will, furthermore, his heirs
gave restitution for usury.[14]

Important though it was, moneylending or the provision of credit was
only part of a successful businessman's enterprise. As to other sources of
wealth, it seems unlikely that Pons was a long range merchant like, say,
the Bernard Raymond Baranonus de Burdegala, seen in the Baranonus
family history. In his thirty years of business activity, his name was absent
from the charters on an average of under four months a year. It is true that
there were three periods when his absences were more extensive. His
name does not appear in the charters for the whole year of 1208, and, in
fact, the period from 1208 to 1210 inclusive sees it absent for all but four
months. The second period was in 1225/6 with an absence of 10 months,
and the third extended from December 1227 to February 1229, Pons' will
having stated that he was planning to go to France. With the possible
exception of the period from 1208 to 1210, it seems unlikely that these
absences from the charters were caused by trade. It is more probable that
they were instead provoked by the attack on usury (and therefore on
foreclosing "pignora" or other means of acquisition by pressure on
debtors) and by the vicissitudes and needs of the town during the war.

E 508 (September 1213) wherein the Aiscii borrowed 200 shillings and promised to pay a
woman 2 pence daily as charity, thus 30 percent annually; E 43 (February 1218) an
individual borrowed six "sextarii" of grain, in which debt usury was expressly excluded,
but the borrower promised to return both the capital and the "gravamen"; E 538 and
Grandselve 5 (January 1219) where an individual gave Pons a half arpent new vineyard,
and, on the same day, received it back with an annual rent charge of sixpence – in short, a
"census" contract; and Saint-Bernard 138, fols. 9v and 169v (December 1219) where Pons
paid a debt of 40 shillings owed by an individual and thereby acquired a rent of 10d
1 obol, a safe investment returning 2.2 percent annually in perpetuity.

[14] Pons provided that his heirs, his wife and daughter, were to make restitution to the
"conquerentes" harmed by himself, his father, and his brothers. Some of the smaller
bequests to particular persons may also have been hidden restitutions, but one cannot tell
because all Pons' restitutions were "incerta." In E 538 i-iii (June 1230) Helyas Barravus
sold Pons' widow and daughter a half arpent of arable for an unspecified price, and, in a
separate contract, confessed himself satisfied "pro lucris nec pro usuris nec pro explectis
pignorum nec pro reditibus quicquid esset ullo modo" once paid by himself and his
brother Arnold. This is restitution disguised as a sale. It is also likely that Pons and his
"socius" Arnold Aiscius had made a hidden restitution during the full flood of the attack
on usury. In E 538 (June 1215) Maria, the wife of Peter Navarrus, reported that Pons and
Arnold had paid her 1000 shillings left her in her mother Vierna's will. Since testators
sometimes left claims for restitution to their heirs, this may have been a case of that kind.

What Pons did with his time is shown by his business charters. He was often absent from town in July, August, and even September, and most of his contracts and acquisitions were drawn up and made in December, February and May.[15] This pattern seems to reflect the tempo of business in Toulouse where the parties could assemble and the notaries write up the contracts most conveniently in the slow periods of the winter and spring. This obviously suited Pons who probably vacationed and/of busied himself during the summer and fall on his rural properties, all of which, as we have seen were near the Bourg, perhaps in the "curia" of Saint-Quentin near the chapel of the leprosery of the Arnaud Bernard gate or out at the "bovaria" of Estaquebiou, near Castillon and Saint Geniès. Doubtless the war, especially in its later years when Toulouse and its immediate environs became the battleground, worked changes here. Pons' will refers to sheep held at the monastery of Gimont, over to the west on the road to Auch.

TABLE 4: CAPITEDENARIA – URBAN

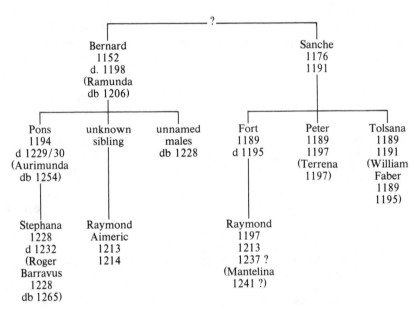

---

[15] Without citing the archival references for fear of drowning the reader, during Pons' 30 years in business from 1199 to 1229, there are, excluding receipts and other special acts, approximately 194 transactions in the charters. Of these 18 took place in January, 20 in February, 21 in March, 17 in April, 22 in May, 14 in June, 10 in July, 7 in August, 14 in September, 12 in October, 12 in November and 27 in December.

Pons' income from fixed rents in money in no way suffices to explain his wealth. It is nevertheless evident that, derived from the landlord's enfeoffement or subinfeudation of his holdings, the "feudal" rents, so to speak, or "oblie" were a convenient method of coupon clipping, assuring a modest but regular income with little work and less risk.[16] The value of such a "feudal" or "commoners'" fief was also enhanced by other lordly rights whose value was not inconsequential. The landlord gained what are traditionally known in northern France as "lods et ventes," fees, that is, paid at each mutation of the lordly and useful rights to the land, a penny on each shilling of the sale price, and halfpenny on each shilling of the mortgage value (that is, eight and a third percent of the value of the property being sold and slightly over four for that being mortgaged, i.e., put up as a "pignus"). There was also the "rachat," a fee owed on the death of the fiefholder and that of the landlord (or an officer, such as the abbot of Saint-Sernin) often fixed at twice the annual rent in "oblie."[17] Still Pons' principal income clearly came from an active exploitation or supervision of the means of production he owned or of which, in partnership with the Aiscii, Prulheco, and others, he owned a share. In town, for example, we never see the "real" rents he charged for his housing and stores. From other sources, however, we know that, if a landlord owned the use right of the property, the rent or "premium" he could charge was substantially higher than the fixed rent or "oblie" owed to him as "feudal" lord, if he happened to be that also.[18] In the countryside, moreover, Pons not only collected rents in money, but also, and especially, sharecropped his land, gaining a portion of the crop,

[16] At the time of his death, the roll of money rents was 222s 5d 1 obol annually.

[17] In E 538 (December 1226), for example, Pons collected 153 shillings on the "bovaria" of Estaquebiou (anciently Estacabiau) for the "rachats" of the deaths of the previous owner and of his son, several years rent, and the "pax" or "lods et ventes" of the sale to the new owners. The legal history of Toulousan property contracts has been explored in H. Richardot, "Le fief roturier à Toulouse," *RHDFE*, 4e sér., 14 (1935), 307-358, 495-569, and in Castaing-Sicard, *Contrats*. The question is one of subinfeudation, subleasing really.

[18] Examples of "premia" are not frequent among extant instruments because they were transitory contracts. That they were legal, however, is shown by the announcement by a consular "nuncius" to the renters of property once of Pons David (for whom see the appropriate family history below) and now of his heirs the Hospitalers in Malta 2 21 (June 1213) that they owed their various "premia." TAM, II 99 (July 1256) gives an example of an annual rent of an "operatorium" ("collocare ad NN") whose "collocatores" were to collect "pro premio dicti operatorii" a total of 60 shillings, 20 immediately, 20 the coming Christmas, and 20 on the feast of Saint John the Baptist. Naturally, so expensive a rental may have been hidden usury. Still, I use it to prove the point. One may estimate that the "oblie" on this property ran from 2 to 12 pence.

usually, in the case of fixed rents, a quarter of the fruits. Although it is difficult to penetrate beneath the formal or fixed rents in kind or money, one divines that Pons used his strong credit position to acquire lifetime exemptions from tithes owed churches, especially Saint-Sernin, and similar grants of extensive properties which he then subleased at a profit.[19] He also leased or subleased his properties for short terms, collecting up to half the crop, requiring the improvement of facilities, planting vineyards, and the like.[20] Although we know nothing about how he disposed of his considerable income in wine, we know that he dealt in grain,[21] and that he invested in animal husbandry, especially in sheep but also oxen.[22] To this we may add that our Croesus had acquired lumber workshops, and was therefore in the building business in town.[23]

Pons was equally active in political life. His first service as consul occurred in 1202-1203, the year of the victory of the popular party, and, as a consul of that year, he witnessed, and participated in, many of the treaties recording the subjection of rural communities and small towns to Toulouse. He was not again in office until 1213-1214 during the war, the year in which the town suffered the catastrophic defeat at Muret. Not altogether to be wondered at, he is next seen in 1217 as one of Simon de Montfort's "curiales viri," the small body that had replaced the consuls during the French occupation of the town. He had not forfeited the esteem of the citizenry, however, and avoided the fate of some collaborators because we see him active at Toulouse in December 1217 and thereafter. Surrounded by town knights who were not gratified by the mention of their titles, in fact, he was singled out to be called "monsieur" or

---

[19] Saint-Bernard 138 (March 1211) a lifetime grant by the monastery of all tithes owed by Pons, and Saint-Sernin 502 (1 1 45) (January 1223) in which Saint-Sernin granted him three "condamina" for life in exchange for 568 shillings.

[20] Examples are E 538 (July 1192) where Bernard rented ("dare ad partem") a "casal" at Castelmolt for two years, for half the crop and improvements; see the act of May 1196 in note 4 above; E 538 (November 1197) an act by Bernard and Arnold Aiscius similar to that of 1192 cited above; E 538 (October 1201) where Pons and Stephana Borselleria rented ("collocare") land for clearing and improvement for two "saxones" ("sazones") in return for the tithe and half the crop, the renters to get the gleaning ("palee et restollia"); and Grandselve 5 (November 1220) where Pons rented a new vineyard ("collocare") for 12 years, to be planted in four years, thereafter paying a quarter of the fruits.

[21] His testament mentions debts owed by various monasteries including one owed by Grandselve of 1020 shillings for grain. See also the act of February 1218 in note 13 above.

[22] The testament several times records Pons' sheep and once tells that the testator gave his wife a quarter "de omnibus animalibus meae cabane cujuscumque generis." Stephana got the other quarter, Pons keeping the other half for himself. See also the contract about the "curia" of Saint-Quentin in May 1196 in note 4 above. What Pons owned at Estaquebiou is to be seen in Malta 123 17 (April 1252).

[23] Called in his testament his "operatoria fuste."

"dominus" in a consular charter of 1222.[24] He was chosen consul again in 1225-1226. Lastly, it is not unlikely that he was among the hostages sent to France by the town at the time of the Peace of Paris in 1229.[25] It seems probable, in short, that his money helped provide the sinews of war for his native community.

The relationship of Bernard and Pons to the other Capitedenario seen in town may be reconstructed. A family line bearing the same surname derived from a Sanche who first appeared in 1176 (see Table 4).[26] This shadowy person may well have been Bernard's brother. Sanche, who is not seen alive after 1191 when he was in economic difficulties,[27] had three children, Fort, Peter, and Tolosana, who was married by 1189 to a William Faber, presumably a smith.[28] When dying in 1195, Fort confessed a debt of 87 shillings which he transferred along with his house to his creditors and to his brother Peter and his brother-in-law William Faber.[29] Peter and the creditors sold out their claim on this debt and on

---

[24] E 510 (December 1217). The "monsieur" appears in TAM, AA 1 81 (December 1222), and among the knights were the two estimable Aimerics de Castronovo. For these persons see the Castronovo family history below.

[25] Planning to go to France, he drew up his will on 2 March 1299. The Peace of Paris was completed 12 April of the same year. Pons was not listed among the Toulousan notables sent as hostages in PAN, J 310 45 (April 1229), but the extant list is garbled. It is, of course, possible that Pons never went north. Grandselve 6 i and ii (22 May 1229) mention him. He did not have to be there when those charters were being written, but four acts in E 538 all dated October 1229 clearly show that he was in town and busy not long before his death.

[26] E 538 iii (November 1176, copied in 1197).

[27] E 538 (December 1190) with the consent of his sons Fort and Peter, Sanche pledged some property just outside the Bourg to William Faber and Terrenus des Toron to pay a debt of 50 shillings he owed to Julian Faber; E 538 i (November 1191, copied in 1197) William Faber foreclosed on the debt Sanche owed Hugh de Pinu of 50 shillings for which William had stood as guarantor; and E 538 ii (September 1195) where Julian Faber records that William Faber and Terrenus de Torono had paid him the 50 shillings owed by Sanche and his sons.

[28] E 538 iii (December 1189, copied in 1197) where Sanche, with the consent of his sons, gave his daughter Tolsana and her children a lifetime grant of "illud nemus quod ipse habet ultra Yrcium apud Caputdenarium" to provide for "suo igni et ad domos constituendas, seu quolibet alio modo eis necessarium sit." Her husband, William Faber, is mentioned in the note below. Although Faber was often a mere family name by this time, one inclines toward the professional connotation here because of the sense of the act cited in this note and because several of the witnesses to the acts mentioned in the note above were "fabri."

[29] E 538 i (May 1195) where Fort admits that the brothers Raymond and Arnold Maurinus had covered a debt for him of 87 shillings, and pledges his house, next to that of his brother Peter, for payment. Ibid., ii (May 1195) in which Fort, described as being sick to death, gave his house in pledge to his brother Peter and "cognatus" William. Clearly he had pledged the property to two parties, and some arrangement had to be made. We see in the subsequent note that the creditors put the debt against more valuable rural property which they then sold to Bernard de Capitedenario.

another of his properties in 1197 to Bernard de Capitedenario.[30] In this act we also learn that Fort had a son named Raymond who was then about 16 years old, but considered to be a minor. Raymond had a difficult young adulthood. In 1201, his father's executor or the young man's guardian was obliged to pledge a piece of his ward's property to Stephen Astro. The latter promised that, when Raymond was 20 years old, the youth was to surrender the property and confirm the sale of 1197 to Bernard mentioned above. For this he was to be given 200 shillings, a modest inheritance indeed.[31] In 1213 Raymond, then 20 years old, was declared competent by his uncle Peter and others, and confirmed the alienation of his father's properties to Pons de Capitedenario.[32] Truth to tell, one cannot ascertain the true nature of these transactions. Bernard and Pons may have financed Raymond's youth, or, on the other hand, may have profited from the need of this unhappy branch of the family. But what the evidence clearly shows is that the two Capdenier branches were related.

Hereafter we are somewhat reduced to conjecture about the family. In 1213 a Raymond Aimeric de Capitedenario attested an act of our familiar Pons. It is not impossible that this is the Raymond seen above because he is described in the act as Pons' nephew.[33] More likely, however, the Raymond Aimeric seen in this one act and never again afterward may have been a child of another of Pons' brothers. Without naming them, Pons mentioned his brothers in his testament, and the mention implied that they were dead. One such brother may have been the Raymond Gerald de Capitedenario who witnessed charters in 1191 and 1193.[34] Raymond Gerald was surely associated with Bernard, Pons' father,

[30] Grandselve 2 records action taken in December and written in January either in 1197 or 1198, in which the creditors Maurini confessed to having been paid 100 shillings by Bernard de Capitedenario and surrendered their pledge on land paying a rent of 3s 4d (an annual profit of 33 percent). In Saint-Bernard 128, fol. 78r (November 1197) the Maurini and Peter de Capitedenario, with the consent of his wife Terrena, sold Bernard an adjacent place of property. Raymond Maurinus agreed to see that Raymond, Fort's son, would confirm this sale when "in perfecta etate constitutus" or he would himself pay the purchaser 75 shillings.

[31] E 538 (August 1201), the executor or guardian being Raymond de Saxonibus. Raymond was to be "in etate .xx. annorum constitutus."

[32] E 579 and E 896 (June 1213) two copies of the declaration of majority by Raymond de Saxonibus, Peter de Capitedenario, and another person. Saint-Bernard 138, f. 80r (June 1213) has Raymond confirming the sale of 1197 made by his uncle Peter and Raymond Maurinus, and shows him selling Pons the remaining half of the property.

[33] E 510 (December 1213).

[34] E 2 (October 1191), Malta 129 19 iii (February 1192, copied in 1260), and Grandselve 3 (November 1193).

because several of Bernard's "socii" of the Aiscii family attested a charter of 1190 in which Raymond Gerald lent 60 shillings payable in three years during which he was to collect the fruits deriving from two arpents of "malol." This usurious contract, moreover, resulted in Raymond Gerald's debtor selling the above mentioned two arpents to Bernard in 1193.[35] An Aimeric de Capitedenario is briefly seen in the 1250s, and may have been the successor of one of Pons' brothers. Here again, there is no knowledge of the degree of relationship, but also clear evidence of some kind of family linkage.[36]

TABLE 5: CAPITEDENARIO – RURAL

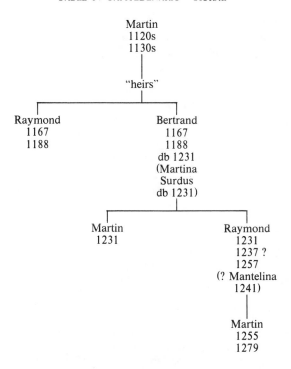

Martin
1120s
1130s

"heirs"

Raymond
1167
1188

Bertrand
1167
1188
db 1231
(Martina
Surdus
db 1231)

Martin
1231

Raymond
1231
1237 ?
1257
(? Mantelina
1241)

Martin
1255
1279

Another Capdenier line was of a quite different social level. Several charters of the 1120s and early thirties mention a Martin de Capitedenario (see Table 5) giving the church of Saint-Jean-de-Capdenier to the Hospital

---

[35] E 508 (July 1190) and E 43 (May 1193), Arnold Capatus being the debtor.
[36] Grandselve 9 (April 1252) as a witness, and ibid. (November 1258), a document that refers to properties once owned by Pons "in quadrivio seu iuxta plateam de Pozamilano" adjacent to property of this Aimeric de Capitedenario, thus showing the link between the two lines.

in order to create a "salvetat" (new village) at Capdenier and also witnessing the foundation of the "salvetat" of Saint-Sauveur by the convent of Saint-Sernin.[37] Subsequently in 1167 and 1188, a Raymond and Bertrand appear holding properties in the same region.[38] Bertrand was among the seigniors of Verfeil who capitulated to the consuls in 1203 as a result of the expansionist policy of the town in which Pons had played an important role.[39] In 1208 we see Bertrand again, who, married to Martina, presumably lived into the war years and was dead by 1231 (as was his wife), at which time we learn that he had had two sons Martin and Raymond, both obviously having reached their majority by 1231, if not quite some time before.[40]

Clearly rural knights, this family was in for a hard time after the Albigensian war. Perhaps preparing to avoid confiscation, Martin sold all of his property in the villages of Pechbonnieu and Launac (Launaguet) and the hamlets of Canet and Capdenier to his brother in 1231,[41] and was sentenced for Catharism before February 1237.[42] It is not impossible that this prevision failed because a Raymond de Capitedenario was also condemned for Catharism sometime before February 1237, and a Mantelina, the wife of a person of the same name who was described as a "civis," was sentenced to pilgrimage for the same belief in 1241.[43]

Whatever hardship afflicted this line of Capdenier, the family assuredly continued and flourished. We hear of a Raymond de Capitedenario from

---

[37] Martin is first seen in the acts dated 1117 and the 1120s in note 1 above. Martin appears again in Douais, *Saint-Sernin*, No. 256 undated but among the charters of the late 1120s at the time of the foundation of Saint-Sauveur.

[38] See the document of February 1167 cited in note 1 above. The act mentions property of Raymond de Capitedenario at Bovilla, specifically "apud Castanearios" between the Hers and Girou rivers. PBN, MS lat. 9994, fol. 237v (April 1188) records a grant to Grandselve by a William Salomon and the brothers Bertrand and Raymond.

[39] TAM, AA 1 64 (June 1203) being among 16 "milites et probihomines" of the community. Bertrand was surely a knight because his name follows hard on the first person listed, the celebrated heretic and lord Isarn de Viridifolio.

[40] PAN, J 318 15 (October 1208) Bertrand a witness. E 504 (September 1231, copied in 1234) with a dorsal note "domine Aurimunde," in which Martin sold his brother Raymond his share in all they had from their deceased relatives, their father Bertrand, their mother Martina, and their uncle Hugh Surdus.

[41] The grant in the sale of 1231 cited in the note above is of all "forcias, bovarias, ... homines et feminas et eorum infantes et tenencias, ... debita et barratas, ... pignora, penciones, lucrum et usurarum et aliarum rerum ...." It is notable that what distinguishes this family from that of Sanche is the fact that the witnesses to their charters are always local worthies.

[42] No. **152** in the amnesty of 1279. See the list in Chapter 5 above.

[43] Raymond is No. **115** of the list of 1279 (Chapter 5). There is, however, a Raymond of the same name connected to the urban branch seen above. Mantelina was condemned in PBN, Doat 21, fol. 175r (July 1241).

1240 to 1257, by which time we learn that he was a citizen, a knight, and that he had a son named Martin.[44] Lastly, this Martin, seen first in 1255, was of such presidency that he not only petitioned for the amnesty accorded heretical inheritance in 1279, but also served as a proctor at Paris as well.[45] The heretic, it will be remembered, was also named Martin, as was the original progenitor of this line.

What is especially intriguing about this family is that it seems to have been related to both the other lines described above. The charter of 1231 in which Martin sold his property to his brother Raymond has a dorsal note reading "domine Aurimunde." Lest one think that the gentlemanly and knightly branch bearing the surname Capdenier had merely hastened in its hour of need to discover a relationship that was purely fictitious, it may be noted that Martina, the wife of Bertrand mentioned above, was the sister of Hugh Surdus, and that Aurimunda, Pons de Capitedenario's wife , was a daughter of Peter Surdus. The two Surdi, furthermore, were closely related.[46] Hugh Surdus, moreover, attended the act declaring the majority of Raymond de Capitedenario, the member of the family of Sancius de Capitedenario seen above.[47]

If, as seems very probable, the bearers of this surname were all related, we learn a significant lesson about the families of the time. The surname covered persons who ranged from country knights to burgher millionaires, and to a family that rubbed shoulders with smiths and other artisans. In class terms, one line rose like a rocket, another, although probably tainted by heresy, held on successfully, but a third suffered loss, presumably economic, and faltered. In terms of religious adhesion, the family ran the gamut. Pons was exceptionally "orthodox," if his relationship with the church, and especially with the mendicants, is to be stressed, but, at the same time, his widow was close to family members who were Cathar believers.

---

[44] Saint-Sernin 600 (10 36 11) (month lost but in the year 1244) where the abbot of Saint-Sernin bought from Raymond a wood of the "bastide" Castillon and other lands near the woods of Capdenier and near Gratentour; PAN, J 305 29 (February 1243) taking oath for the Peace of Paris as a citizen; Douais, *Documents sur Languedoc*, 1: 15 where an inventory of September 1246 records the fact that a lawsuit had taken place between Raymond and Saint-Sernin over property in Valségur; TAM, AA 1 103 (October 1250, copied in 1257) where Raymond witnessed a consular act; Dominicans 11 (December 1255) where the knight and his son Martin dealt with property near Pechbonnieu; and Grandselve 9 (June 1257) where the knight was a witness.

[45] See the list in Chapter 6 (March 1279) above, and see the amnesty (Chapter 5) above.

[46] See the acts of June 1194 cited in note 4 above, September 1241 in note 40 above.

[47] See the acts dated June 1213 cited in note 32 above.

Caraborda

Spelled with or without a final "s" in Latin charters, this family makes its first appearance in the late eleventh century with an Oldric and Peter.[1] One branch of the family was domiciled in the Bourg, one of their homes being in the Portaria (the Porterie Basse, as they used to say before the Place du Capitole replaced the houses in the area). It may also be identified by the name or rather with the substantial farm later called the "curia Oldrici" at Bolencs near Estaquebiou and Saint-Geniès to the north of the town.

By the 1140s, we see three members named Stephen, Oldric, and Raymond, the first of whom is described as the son of Oldric, perhaps, then, the son of the Oldric of 1083 mentioned in the paragraph above (see Table 6).[2] Along with an Ademar to be described later on, Stephen was active in town government, and is seen witnessing an act whereby the town was granted freedom from tolls on salt and wine in 1141, and also subscribed the document announcing the foundation of the Daurade bridge.[3] Stephen, Oldric, and Raymond are described as brothers, and are visible in the charters until about 1183, where, among much else, we learn that Raymond's house was not far from the old Roman gate at the Portaria.[4]

[1] Douais, *Saint-Sernin*, Nos. 290 and 548 (July 1083 and the 1090s), the first, with Oldric as a witness, being the confession of a "wrongful" invasion of Saint-Sernin by William of Aquitaine, and the second the founding of the "salvetat" of Matapezoul, witnessd by Peter.

[2] Malta 123 3 and 4 (May 1141) concerning Bolencs and Estaquebiou and a Stephen, the son of Oldric. Stephen was also among the early "bonihomines" of the town between 1119 and 1130 and in 1147.

[3] Douais, *Saint-Sernin*, No. 143 (November 1141) freedom from tolls of salt and wine for the town of Toulouse witnessed by an Ademar and Stephen; Stephen and Ademar also witnessed the foundation of the Daurade or New Bridge recorded in Daurade 145. This act is an undated original written by the scribe Ricardus. It may be dated conjecturally by the mention of Raymond, prior of the Daurade, who was probably the Raymond II described in *Gallia Christiana*, 13: 104 as being prior circa 1135 between two other officers of this grade seen in 1130 and 1141.

[4] Grandselve 1 (January 1155, copied in 1191 or 1192) a "casal" of Raymond's on the "carraria maior de Frenariis" in the Bourg; Saint-Bernard 36 ii (December 1143, copied in 1227) Oldric; PAN J 307 57 (December 1146) Raymond; Douais, *Saint-Sernin*, No. 76 (August 1160) the brothers Oldric and Stephen as witnesses; E 575 (May 1162) Oldric and

TABLE 6: CARABORDA, OF THE BOURG

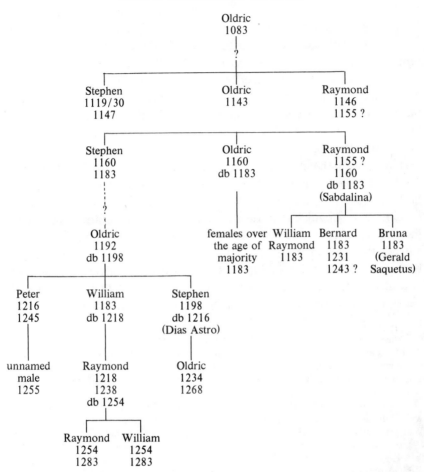

At that date, we learn that Oldric had left only daughters, and that his brother Raymond was married to a Sabdalina, from whom he had had two sons, a William Raymond and an unnamed brother, and a daughter Bruna who was married to Raymond Saquetus.[5] Later charters enable us

---

unnamed brothers garnering a "pignus"; Douais, *Saint-Sernin*, No. 447 (August 1163) Oldric and brother Stephen; and Grandselve 2 (September 1178) where we hear of a lane ("carrairola") leading to the house of Raymond Caraborda and his unnamed brothers and to the "castellum Portarie" (the old Roman gate) adjacent to the "carraria maior de Frenariis" (modern rue du Taur). For November 1183, see the note immediately below.

[5] E 506 (November 1183) containing a sale made by Oldric's executors one of whom was Gerald Saquetus, husband of Bruna, daughter of the dead Raymond Caraborda, with

to divine that Raymond's unnamed son was Bernard Caraborda de Portaria who last appears in 1231,[6] but whose succession is unclear.[7] Nothing more can be done with Oldric's son William Raymond either.

To turn back to the brother Stephen first seen in 1160, it will be remembered that his brother Oldric left only daughters, and that his brother had the family described above. Since the next generation mentioned an Oldric "iunior," it is probable that that was the name of Stephen's son. A peculiarity about Oldric "iunior" was that he was called "vicecomes Sancti Saturnini," something that was either a scribal error, or that meant that he was the "custos" or guardian of the Close of Saint-Sernin, or even that he had a remote relationship with the old viscounts of Toulouse.[8] Oldric "iunior" was dead by 1198 when we hear of his son Stephen holding property at Bolencs near Estaquebiou.[9] Also called "iunior" to distinguish him from a Stephen Caraborda of the family line of the City and Aussonne soon to be described, Stephen was a consul in 1201-1202, and charters of 1205 and 1216 reveal that he had two brothers, a William and a Peter, as well as other relatives, only some of whom can be identified.[10] Stephen himself appears to have died early because he is described in 1216 as the first or previous husband of Dias

---

the consent of his wife, Sabdalina her mother, and her male children, namely William Raymond and his unnamed brother. The two families had obviously divided the "casal" mentioned in the act of September 1178 cited in the note above, Oldric's daughters having half, next to the property of the Jew Ispaniolis, and Gerald sold Ispaniolis the "capud cornu de eorum casale."

[6] TAM, AA 1 35 (April 1203) Bernard Karaborda de Portaria, with the consent of his wife Ramunda, sold the town the tower and houses next the property of Raymond William Atadillis and the Saracen wall, and the "casaletum" or "curie" in the Bourg next to the same tower. This is the property mentioned in note 5 above. Saint-Bernard 138, fols. 153v and 156v (also E 510), (February 1205) records alienations to Pons de Capitedenario by Surdus with the consent of his wife Pagesia, presumably the daughter of Bernard Carabordas, with the consent of the latter's relatives, namely the brothers Stephen and William Carabordas, their nephew Stephen and Raymond William son of the deceased William Raymond. See also the Bernard de Portaria in Saint-Bernard 138, fol. 136v (July 1220); PAN, J 310 39 (December 1225); and Malta 3 168 (March 1231, copied in 1236) as a judge in a comital court. This Bernard was also a consul in 1213-1214.

[7] The problem is that there are two Bernards as we shall see in note 26 below.

[8] Douais, *Saint-Sernin*, Appendix No. 53 (October 1192) from Saint-Sernin 612 (12 42 2). Since the original act was lost by 1946, there is no way of checking this. As shall be shown later in the history of the Tolosa surname, the viscount of that time did not use the surname Caraborda. Anent the possibility of a scribal slip, it is to be noted that the name Vicecomes was a surname at Toulouse, for which see the Bernard Vicecomes who took oath to the Peace of Paris in the act cited in note 12 below.

[9] Malta 123 5 vii (February 1198, copied in 1234).

[10] For February 1205 see note 6 above; and AADML, Lespinasse (Register), fol. 5v (July 1216) along with Peter, son of the deceased Oldric.

Astro, daughter of William Pons Astro, by whom he left heirs.[11] The one heir we know about is his son Oldric, who appears in 1234 and is last seen in 1268.[12] The history of Stephen's brother Peter is easy to resume. First appearing in 1216, we know that he, like his brother, shared the "curia Oldrici" near Estaquebiou, and that he was dead by 1255, leaving a son whose first name has unfortunately been lost.[13]

The son of Oldric and brother of Stephen and Peter whose history may be followed in more detail is William. Probably in his majority as early as 1183 and a not infrequent consul in the 1190s, William was assuredly dead by 1218.[14] Described as a merchant in 1230, his son Raymond was a Maurandi creditor in 1233, but was already deeply involved in the heresy for which he was condemned before February 1237, possibly even during the war. His wife subsequently suffered the same fate. Raymond must have been penitenced and forgiven after his first condemnation. He was unable, however, to shake his devotion to the Cathar cause, because he relapsed and was again sentenced in 1238.[15] Whatever his fate (and the prognosis is not happy), he was certainly gone by 1254, and left children.[16] His son Raymond was several times a consul and served as a

[11] PBN, MS lat. 9189, fol. 241r (May 1216) the second husband being Vasco de Turre.

[12] Saint-Sernin 599 (10 35 17) 4th of 9 membranes tied together (July 1234); the oath to the Peace of Paris in PAN, J 305 29 (February 1243); consul in 1247-1248; and *HGL*, vol. 8, No. 522 v (February 1268) where we learn that he was a creditor of the deceased heretic Pons William de Turre.

[13] See the act of July 1216 cited in note 10 above; consul in 1229-1230; Malta 123 15 (January 1252) the property being called the "curia Oldrici qui fuit," and being owned by the sons of the deceased Stephen and by Peter who was still alive; and Grandselve 8 (March 1253) where the Christian name of the son has been washed off the document.

[14] Naturally, the earliest references here displayed may refer to another William whose history we do not know. E 575 (November 1183); Cresty, *Repertoire ... Saint-Étienne*, fol. 113r (reference to lost document in Cresty: 18 1 1), (dated 1184) a criminal action against a William de Quinto; a chapterman and consul of this name 1186-1187, 1194-1195, 1196-1197, and 1198-1199; Saint-Sernin 599 (10 35 16) 5th of 8 membranes tied together iii (January 1200, copied in 1220); February 1205 in note 6 above together with his brother and nephew; October 1208 at the base of note 26 below; and Saint-Bernard 138, fol. 31v (October/December 1218) where we see Raymond son of the dead William.

[15] See October/December 1218 in the note above; E 504 (November 1226) as a creditor in partnership with William Surdus and Peter de Prulheco; Lespinasse 28 ii (June 1230) called "mercator"; and Saint-Sernin 599 (10 35 17) 8th of 9 membranes tied together (November 1233) as son of deceased William. For heresy see the amnesty of 1279 (Chapter 5 above) where he was No. **4** and his wife (not named) was No. **138**, hence both before February 1237, but Raymond much earlier. His activities in Catharism are shown in TAM MS 609, fol. 197v (approximately 1226) and PBN, Doat 23, fol. 293v (about 1228). See also PBN, Doat 21, fol. 149r (February 1238) where he was sentenced as relapsed.

[16] Malta 17 74 ii (August 1254) where his son William is mentioned as well as his deceased father.

petitioner for the amnesty of 1279, as did his son William.[17] The latter served as a proctor at that time, and both are last seen in 1283.[18]

It is likely that the Raymond who was condemned for Catharism had a close relative, probably a brother, who was likewise sentenced. Because this person was simply named Carabordas, one may even guess that he was Raymond's younger brother, the use of a family name as a Christian name being more common for younger male children than for older ones. Carabordas and his wife Elis held heretical conventicles at their house in the Bourg and were both condemned, and Caraborda's condemnation must have occurred not long after his service as a consul in 1231-1232.[19] To round out the list of Caraborda Cathars, one notes that a Caraborda — the use of a family name for a daughter's Christian name was common — "mater Grivi," mother, that is, of Peter Grivus de Roaxio, was also damned.[20]

The second branch of the Caraborda, that of the City in the Daurade parish with property at Aussonne, began with an Ademar (see Table 7). Seen together with his brother William de Penna,[21] Ademar early represented the family tradition of intense involvement in town government.[22] He vanished from the charters after 1151, leaving a son Peter, who, in turn, is last heard of in 1171/2, when we first see his children.[23]

---

[17] Raymond and his brother William in E 296 (May 1251); Blanc, *Jacme Olivier*, has Raymond Carabordas as witness No. 31 in May 1255; E 531 ii (April 1268) both brothers along with Bernard Caraborda "probushomo"; and see the list in Chapter 6 above (March 1279) – the same pair of siblings.

[18] MADTG, A 297, fol. 784v (October 1283) William Caraborda "de Suburbio" was a creditor of the Berengar Caraborda of the City line described below.

[19] See the reference to TBM, MS 609 in note 15 above. In the amnesty of 1279 he was numbered **5**, and his wife, there not named, was twice listed as Nos. **69** and **139**. Naturally, Caraborda may have had two wives.

[20] See her history in that of the Rouaix family below.

[21] E 501 (late teens or early 1120s) Ademar; E 510 (November 1133, copied in 1207) the same; E 44 (January 1151) where William de Penna, brother of Ademar, ceded property in the Close of Saint-Sernin next to an "operatorium" Oldric de Portale acquired from Ademar's son Peter. The name "de Penna" vanishes save that we see the brothers William and Pons de Penna acquiring property near Belberaud to the south of the town in PAN, J 321 33 (January 1190).

[22] As one of the "bonihomines" in 1141. The Caraborda were so often in office during the twelfth century that I shall not bother to list their terms here.

[23] 1148 as a "bonushomo" in town government; Daurade 177 (April 1151); see the charter of January 1152 in note 21 above; Douais, *Saint-Sernin*, No. 91 (dated 1156) returning tithes to Saint-Sernin; and Grandselve 58 Roll I verso xviii (March 1171 or 1172) where his sons Bernard, Pons, Walter, and Stephen gave rights to the hospice of Grandselve in the Bourg for the souls of their parents. Note other Carabordas whose history are not known, notably the Stephen seen in November 1141 and approximately 1141 in note 21 above, and MADTG, A 297, fol. 217r (March 1174 or 1175) Vital Caraborda and his brother William Duran.

These were the brothers Bernard, Pons, Walter, and Stephen. If it is he who was the very active consul of that name,[24] Stephen may have lasted into the early years of the thirteenth century.[25] The brothers Bernard and Walter worked as a team, and it is through their properties at Frez Palers just outside the Bourg and especially through their acquisition of properties at and near Aussonne on the left bank of the Garonne that their succession may be followed. Although Bernard, who was also often among the consuls, was still alive in 1206, both were dead by 1208.[26] The brother named Pons is something of a mystery. In 1188/9, a Pons Caraborda gave the Cistercians of Grandselve pasture rights in return for the possibility of a corrody and death benefits when he wished to use them. Naturally, this provision may merely reflect Pons' prescience, but it may also represent the fact that he was on the point of retiring from the world.[27] One guesses, in fact, that this may have been the case. In 1201,

[24] 1190-1191, 1192-1193, 1193-1194, 1194-1195, 1196-1197, and 1199-1200, followed in 1201-1202 by a Stephen Caraborda "iunior" of the line of Oldric or the "curia Oldrici" to be seen below, our Stephen being called "probushomo" in Saint-Sernin 599 (10 35 16) 5th of 8 membranes tied together iii (January 1200, copied in 1220).

[25] Other than the references seen in the note above including the final one of January 1200, Stephen appears in Saint-Étienne 227 (26 DA 2 39) i (November 1180, copied in 1193) about Braqueville; Malta 1 24 xxix (published in Molinier, "Ensevelissement de Raimond VI," 84-85), (May 1183) where the count gave Peter Raymond and Bernard Carabordas an "honor" near Saint-Jory and Gorgairast, attested by Stephen; and PBN, MS lat. 9994, fols. 238r and 270v (both dated April 1188), the first witnessed by Peter Raymond Descalquencs and Stephen, brother of Bernard Caraborda, and the second by the same two Caraborda brothers.

[26] After the charter of March 1171/2 in note 23 above, we have Grandselve 3 (November 1176, copied in 1198) at Frez Palers with Bernard, Walter, and Bernard's wife Fais; ibid., 58, Roll I recto xvi (January 1177) Raymond and Bernard witnesses; the acts of May 1184 and April 1188 in note 25 above; MADTG, A 297, fol. 801v (November 1195) where the local family pledged a substantial part of the "villa" of Aussonne to Bernard and Walter for 1600 shillings, Pons Caraborda being a witness; fol. 797v (February 1197) where Walter sold for 1200 shillings all the income from the "honores" held by him in "pignus," but required that the local family pay him 156 shillings yearly at a stated term, and, if it failed, "lucrum de panalibus," Pons again witnessing; Saint-Bernard 128, fol. 43r (March 1201) Bernard and his brother Walter at Frez Palers; E 538 (May 1206) Bernard a witness; MADTG, A 297, fol. 795r (May 1208) where Pons Caraborda records that Maurinus de Levinhaco had pledged ("mittere in pignore") a sixth of Aussonne to Bernard, now deceased, and his brother Walter for 1600 shillings, so Pons, with the consent of hs wife Petrona and son Pons, released a part of the pledge made to Walter, a charter attested by William and William Peter Caraborda; and ibid., fol. 793v (October 1208) showing Peter, son of the deceased Bernard, confessing that Levinhac had paid the debts owed his father, but retains the "pignus," an action witnessed by William and William Peter Caraborda. Over and above this, Bernard was probably consul in 1196-1197 and again in 1199-1200.

[27] PBN, MS lat. 9994, fol. 238r (March 1188 or 1189), becoming a "particeps in omnibus spiritualibus bonis" whenever he wanted to receive the habit.

the above named Bernard and a Pons together acted as the bailiffs of the illumination of the Daurade church. Since the instrument does not call the two Caraborda brothers, it is possible that Pons was a nephew, whose history shall be related below.[28]

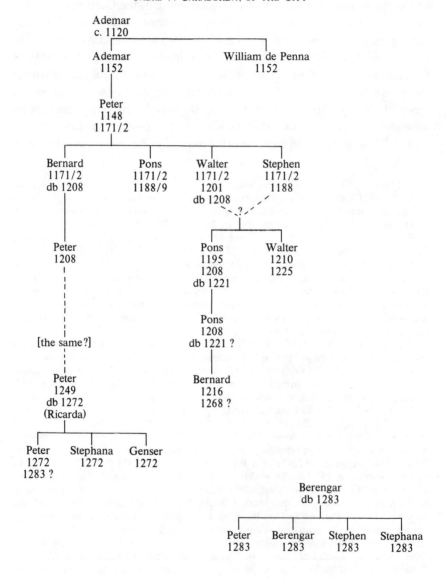

TABLE 7: CARABORDA, OF THE CITY

[28] E 510 (December 1201) where Bernard and Pons Caraborda rented property "pro badliam lampade ecclesie beate Marie" of the Daurade.

Bernard's line may be followed. His son was named Peter, a person who is easy to confuse with a contemporary Peter of the line of Oldric Caraborda or the "curia Oldrici," seen above. The Peter we are talking of here is the one who owned property at Aussonne and Frez Palers. First seen in 1208, he appears again with his wife Ricarda in 1249, holding property at Frez Palers. He was dead by 1272, when his son, also named Peter, sold for 3000 shillings his share of Aussonne to the lord of l'Isle-Jourdain with the consent of his widowed mother Ricarda and his two sisters, Stephana and Gensers, minors under 25 years of age.[29] This latter Peter may have been the merchant of this name who, as shall be seen below, served as an executor for another line of the City Caraborda in 1283.

Derived either from Walter or Stephen, the brothers of the Bernard mentioned in the last paragraph, or even being one and the same as the brother named Pons or his heirs, another Caraborda City line is represented by Pons and Walter, whose exact relationship is not disclosed by the documents. Pons was seen from 1195 to 1208, and his son Pons appears in that year.[30] Either the father or his son Pons died by 1221, when we see an heir named Bernard who probably served as one of Montfort's "curiales viri," and who presumably lived into the 1260s.[31] Walter was seen in 1210 and 1225, but thereafter disappears.[32] The charters subsequently skip a generation or two, and this line of the Carabordas is not seen again until 1283. We then learn of the deceased Berengar, one of whose executors was the merchant named Peter Caraborda, seen above, and whose children were named Peter, Berengar,

[29] See the reference to October 1208 in note 26 above. See also Peter and Ricarda in Grandselve 7 (May 1249), and Peter's heirs and widow in MADTG, A 297, fol. 871r (March 1272).

[30] See the charters of November 1195, February 1197, December 1201, and especially May 1208 cited in note 26 above. See also MADTG, A 297, fol. 796v (May 1210) a treaty between Maurinus de Levinhaco and Pons, both promising not to alienate their holdings at Aussonne save to each other's families, an act witnessed by Walter and William Peter Caraborda.

[31] PAN, J 330 24 ii (September 1221) Bernard son of the deceased Pons. A Bernard served as a consul in 1215-1216, as "curialis vir" in 1217, consul 1229-1230, and 1263-1264. Our Bernard was surely one of the two Bernard Carabordas who signed the oath of alliegance in 1243, and he and his property are seen in E 531 i (January 1249, copied in 1268) at Beauzelle, and again together with the property of a Raymond Carabordas and his unnamed brother in ibid. (April 1268). Bernard was there called "probushomo" to distinguish him from a young Bernard Caraborda extant at the time. In Grandselve 9 (March 1254) Bernard also shared property at Frez Palers with the Capdenier.

[32] See the act of May 1210 cited in note 30 above, and MADTG, A 297, fol. 810v (October 1225) where Walter was one of four arbiters settling the rights of the monastery of Lespinasse at Mondonville.

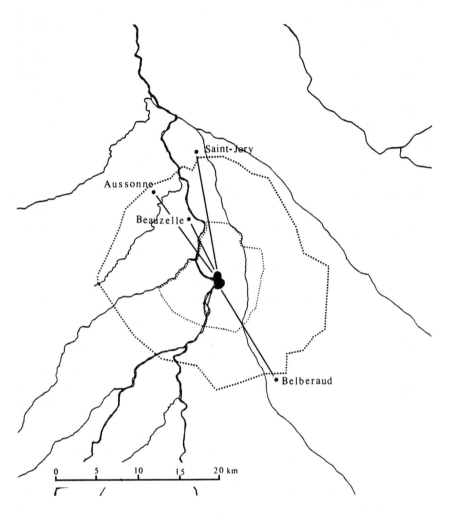

MAP 4. CARABORDA

Stephen and Stephana. Burdened with debts, the family was forced to sell its holding at Aussonne and Beauzelle to Arnold Maurandus.[33]

To summarize this history, one notes that the burghal branch of the Caraborda was heavily committed to the Cathar belief. This bears on the relationship of the two Caraborda lines, and clearly shows what other family histories also do, namely that there was no objection in the minds of contemporaries for the same name to be carried by major families in the City and the Bourg. Although it is naturally possible that the two branches were originally united, contemporaries thought of them as two families. Nepotism was surely rampant during the oligarchical period of the 1190s in the history of the consulate of Toulouse, but it would still be too much to expect that, for example, public opinion could stomach three members of the same clan among the twelve consuls in one term. The Bernard, William, and Stephen who served in 1196-1197 were undoubtedly from two families.[34]

A curious commentary on the nature of repression and the role of luck in family histories: the Caraborda of the City who had acquired the extensive property of Aussonne were untouched by Catharism, but obviously faced grave economic difficulties around 1283. The Cathar-ridden Caraborda of the Bourg seem to have been better off. In spite of everything, they retained the "curia" at Bolencs.

---

[33] MADTG, A 297, fol. 782r (August 1283). Berengar was clearly the heir of the Bernard and Walter whose twelfth-century history we have just reviewed. One of Berengar's executors was Peter Carabordas "mercator," and he and the others were busy in this act and in several subsequent ones of the same date alienating the family property to pay their father's debts. Other than Berengar's children, the act mentions Raymond Caraborda, son of the deceased Raymond, for whom see the Raymond mentioned in note 17 above. Another Caraborda of the "curia Oldrici" line involved in this history is William Caraborda "de Suburbio," for whom see note 18 above.

[34] An individual and a family have not been identified here. A William Peter Caraborda attested acts of the bourgal line in May and October 1208 in note 26 above and May 1210 in note 32 above, obviously, then, a close relative. This is probably the same person as the William Peter Caraborda de Viridifolio seen in Grandselve 4 (December 1201). The family was also from the Bourg, but nothing can be done with its history. Near the Pouzonville and Lascrosses gates in the Bourg, we hear of a Raymond "qui dicitur Tatavus" in E 575 (September 1175) and E 510 (February 1192), and of his son Raymond from Saint-Bernard 138, fol. 42v (January 1221), here as Raymond, son of the deceased Tatavi, E 538 (May 1225), and Grandselve 9 (November 1258) as deceased leaving property.

Castronovo

Two brothers named Pilistortus and Bernard Raymond were the "custodes et adjutores et defensores" of the old hospital and church of Saint-Rémézy when, between 1114 and 1116, Tosetus de Tolosa granted these institutions to the Hospitalers. With the addition of their brother Peter William Pilistortus, they were among those applauding the count's grant founding the New or Daurade Bridge circa 1135. Three years later Peter William witnessed the count's foundation of the town of Montauban. It is therefore probable that these persons were of much distinction and were members of the count's service cadre. Although Peter William is seen until 1152 and Pilistortus until 1163, we know little more about them, but the succession of a Bernard Raymond Pilistortus can be traced (see Table 8).[1]

Dead by 1170, Bernard Raymond had three sons named Bernard Raymond, Peter William, and Raymond Garsias. In that year the brothers divided their inheritance. Bernard Raymond received rents in the City and Bourg, the profits of the bakery of the New Bridge, a mill at "Sposterla" on the Garonne, lands at Blagnac, and vineyards at Buguet and Montaudran. His brothers got the family house in Toulouse, the "bovaria" at Braqueville on the left bank of the Garonne, a Villanova "pignus" of 1000 shillings, and other undisclosed properties.[2] Bernard Raymond Pilistortus thereafter disappears from the charters, but it is worth noting that there was a Pons or Pons William Pilistortus de Suburbio who had died by 1192, but whose sons Pilistortus de Portaria and Arnold William Pilistortus are seen from 1187 until 1201 and 1225 respectively, persons called on for service in the wartime consulates.[3]

---

[1] Malta 1 43 (undated but possibly 1114 or 1115), anent Saint-Rémézy; Daurade 145 (for the date see note 3 in the Caraborda family history) witnessed by all three brothers; PAN, JJ 19, fol. 169v (October 1144) Montauban; Grandselve 3 ii (February 1152, copied in 1194/5) Peter William Pilistortus along with other notables; Lespinasse 24 (July 1163) written by the scribe Vital "in porticu" of Pilistortus' house in Toulouse; and Saint-Étienne 227 (26 DA 1 9) (November 1163, copied in 1205 and 1238) Bernard Raymond Pilistortus' property in the tithing of Braqueville.

[2] Saint-Étienne 227 (26 DA 2 102) (October 1179, copied in 1198) among other witnesses were the brothers William and Peter William de Castellonovo.

[3] Grandselve 2 i (November 1187) Pilistortus and Arnold William Pilistortus his brother; E 575 (June 1191) Pilistortus and wife Orbria with consent of her father Bertrand

TABLE 8: CASTRONOVO DE STRICTIS FONTIBUS

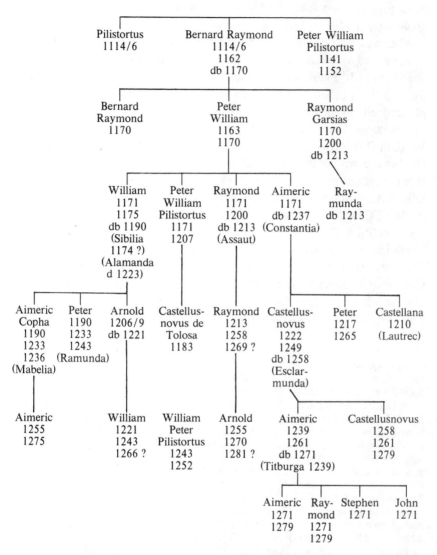

We are better served for Peter William Pilistortus and Raymond
Garsias. The latter is seen from 1170 onward largely dealing with his

de Palatio; E 506 (March 1192) Pilistortus son of Pons William Pilistortus de Burgo;
E 510 (January 1199) de Portaria; Grandselve 4 (April 1201) Pilistortus son of quondam
Pons William de Suburbio; E 509 (September 1219) Arnold William Pilistortus; TAM, AA
1 75 (March 1222) Arnold William as councilor of the consuls; E 504 (April 1223) Arnold
William; and Saint-Sernin 502 (1 1 42) (March 1225) Arnold William's property outside
the Arnaud Bernard gate.

"bovaria" of Braqueville where he was in conflict with the canons of Saint-Étienne, and also with his tithes at Balma to the east of Toulouse. He apparently lived at Montaygon (modern Place Saint-Georges), was a knight, was never called anything other than Raymond Garsias, appears to have had no sons but instead a daughter named Ramunda, and was dead by 1213.[4] Peter William was the one who appears to have made the fortune. In 1163 a Gausbert de Castellonovo (Castelnau-d'Estretefons) pledged all his property at Saint-Jory to him. Either he or his sons so expanded or consolidated their holdings in that region that most of Peter William Pilistortus' heirs adopted the name Castronovo (Castellonovo). During the war year of 1213, Count Raymond VI placed the capstone on this construction when he gave Peter William's son, the distinguished knight Aimeric de Castronovo "probushomo," lifetime possession of the castle of Castelnau-d'Estretefons "pro beneficio, honore, et servicio," on the condition that "habeamus de predicto castro in causa et guerra auxilium et valenciam."[5]

Before narrating this complicated family history, it is useful to list the Castronovo properties as identified in the appended footnotes (see Map 5). On the left bank of the Garonne, the family had interests in Braqueville, Larramet, Cornebarrieu, and Blagnac; on the right bank north of town at

[4] For October 1170 see note 2 above; Saint-Etienne 117 (26 DA 2 50) (January 1181) his "condamina" in Braqueville/Saulonar; Malta 116 12 (January 1188) a tithing at Balma; Saint-Étienne 227 (26 DA 1 17) (November 1189) a suit before the vicar between Saint-Étienne and Raymond Garsias, who was enlarging his "curia," enclosing pasture, etc.; E 505 (April 1190, copied in 1218) Raymond Garsias and Peter William Pilistortus; Saint-Étienne 227 (26 DA 1 18) (June 1190) acquisition at Braqueville by Raymond Garsias attested by Raymond de Castellonovo and his brother Peter William Pilistortus; ibid. (26 DA 1 19) (March 1193) witnessed by the brothers Peter William Pilistortus, Raymond, and Aimeric de Castronovo, and by Raymond Garsias; ibid. (26 DA 1 22) (November 1197) settlement between Saint-Étienne and Raymond Garsias about Braqueville; ibid. (26 DA 1 17) (November 1198) more litigation before the vicar of the same about the same; Malta 15 100 ii (September 1198) Raymond Garcias called knight; Saint-Sernin 599 (10 35 16) 5th of 8 membranes tied together iii (January 1200, copied in 1219 and 1220) Raymond Garsias; and Malta 135 41 (January 1213, copied in 1229) sale of property at Larramet to Peter de Castronovo, Master of the Temple, by Aimeric de Castronovo "probushomo," his nephew Raymond, the brothers Aimeric and Peter, and by Ramunda, daughter of the quondam Raymond Garsias, the Castronovo for half and Ramunda for the other half. In TBM, MS 609, fol. 58v a witness said in 1245 that she saw Raymond Garsias, his wife, and family (none named) in his house on Montaygon circa 1220. The witness' memory was faulty as to time.

[5] PAN, J 330 13 (May 1238) where the count bought his property back from Aimeric and his son Castellusnovus. The act contains a vidimus of the transfer of this property at "Castrumnovum de Instrictis Fontibus" dated February 1213. This included the castle and all rights of the count there including 14 families and half of two other families, to be returned on payment of 5000 shillings.

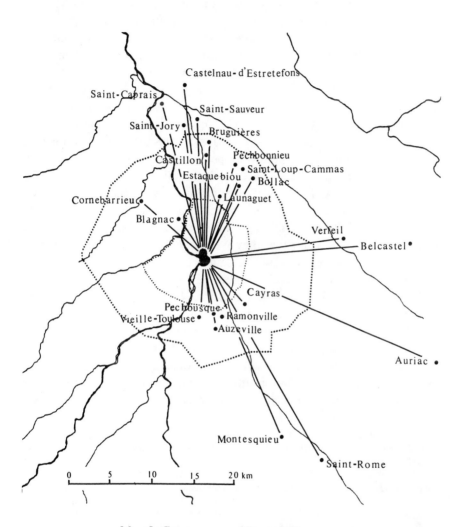

MAP 5. CASTRONOVO DE STRICTIS FONTIBUS

Lalande, Saint-Caprais, Launac (Launaguet), Estaquebiou, Saint-Loup-Cammas, Castillon, Pechbonnieu, Saint-Sauveur, Saint-Jory, and Castelnau-d'Estretefons itself. East of town, they were at Verfeil and Belcastel toward Lavaur, and, nearer town, at Buguet and Montaudran. To the south, they gave their name to Pechaimeric (near Pechdavid) and held property there and along the Garonne river (Flamolriu), further out at Ramonville, Auzeville, Vieille Toulouse, and Pechbusque, and as far south as Saint-Rome near the later Villefranche-en-Lauragais, Cayras, Auriac, and Montesquieu. In town, the family was primarily in the City with a residence in the "partita" of Saint-Rome, but also once had had holdings in the Close of Saint-Sernin.[6] Just as was the case of the Pilistorti seen above, furthermore, there were people called Castronovo who were decidedly not of the social level of the family investigated here. The placename Castelnau is common, after all, and there is therefore no reason to assume that the sailor or sheepskin dealer or artisan who bore the name were of this family. On the other hand, given the social range of a large family, one cannot assert that they were not. Moreover, not all of those who were almost certainly of the clan are sufficiently identified in the documents to fit them into the present genealogy.[7]

Peter William Pilistortus had four sons, William de Castronovo, Peter William Pilistortus, Raymond de Castronovo, and Aimeric de Castronovo, who, because of the appearance of a nephew bearing the same Christian name, was later to be called "maior" or "probushomo." These sons appear together in charters of 1171 through 1175, during which time we see them giving the church tithes and busy in land credit operations, activities typical of the landed and entrepreneurial families of the time.[8]

---

[6] Puylaurens, *Chronica*, p. 64 and TAM, II 10 (March 1271-July 1272) for which see note 32 below. This document concerned City folk only, and specifically mentioned Castellusnovus and his heir and Aimeric de Castronovo in the "partida" of Saint-Rome. PAN, JJ 21, fol. 69r published in *HGL*, vol. 8, No. 127 has Aimeric, Raymond Garsia, Oldric, Peter William Pilistortus, Aim "iuvenis" and his brother Peter admit that the "domus et capelle" and the "planum Montaygone" were public property, Saint-Quentin in Saint-Sernin 679 (20 70 12) (May 1249) together with the mention of a house owned by the knight Arnold de Castronovo on Romenguières just off the Place Montardy in *HGL*, vol. 10, Proof No. 55 xxxviii col. 226 (dated 1287 and 1289). Douais, *Saint-Sernin*, Appendix No. 55 (May 1171) states that half of a third part of a tower and lot were owned by William de Castellonovo and his brothers Peter William Pilistortus, Raymond, and Aimeric.

[7] A William Durand de Castronovo in Grandselve 2 (September 1185); a "pelegantarius" Peter in Grandselve 7 (October 1232); and the "nauta" Peter in MADTG, A 297, fol. 862r (September 1244). For members of the family, see also the Oldric in March 1207 in the note above, and the Bertrand who married Stephana David in Malta 118 179 (June 1184).

[8] For May 1171 see note 6 above; Malta 135 121 (June 1174, copied in 1234) grant of a

It will be convenient to run down Peter William Pilistortus' succession
son by son. William, presumably the oldest, was perhaps initially married
to a woman named Sibilia,[9] but, if so, was later married to an Alamanda
by whom he had two sons, Aimeric, called "iuvenis" or "Copha" (the
knight's cap) to distinguish him from his uncle, the "probushomo," and
Peter. A knight who served as vicar of Toulouse in 1184, William had
died by 1190, and his widow Alamanda's obit is dated 1223.[10] His two
sons, especially Aimeric, were active in the public life of their community,
and together appear in documents referring to them as nephews of their
uncles or as brothers from 1190 to 1233.[11] There is a mystery concerning
William's children, a missing son named Arnold who is never mentioned
in the charters cited above. As the brother of Aimeric "iuvenis" and Peter,
and as the father of a William, Arnold appears only when dead in
documents of 1221 and 1223.[12] But this sparse evidence is confirmed by
the historian Puylaurens when he informs us that the knights and brothers
Aimeric "Copha" and Arnold de Castronovo were among the leaders of
the White Confraternity created by Bishop Fulk to attack heresy and

---

tithe at Larramet to Saint-Étienne by William, Peter William Pilistortus, Raymond, and
Aimeric, sons of Peter William de Castellonovo; and Saint-Sernin 600 (10 36 10) (June
1175) where Raymond del Castelnau, son of Peter William Pilistortus, sold a "pignus" to
Saint-Sernin for 400 shillings.

[9] Douais, *Saint-Sernin*, No. 599 (December 1174) gift of properties at Saint-Sauveur
and Castillon by a William del Castelnou and wife Sibilia.

[10] TAM, AA 1 71 (January 1184) as vicar; Malta 2 167 i (April 1190, copied in 1218 and
1233) where Raymond de Castronovo and Alamanda, together with her sons Aimeric and
Peter, children by the deceased William de Castronovo; and Lahondès, *Saint-Étienne*,
p. 44 No. 2 recording the obit dated 1223 of the canoness of Saint-Étienne Alamanda,
widow of the knight William de Castronovo, Lahondès misconstrued the date as 1123.

[11] For April 1190, see the note above; Saint-Étienne 230 (27 2 unnumbered) ii (October
1198, copied in 1244) Peter William Pilistortus and his brother Raymond de Castronovo
and their nephew Aimeric; PBN, Doat 48, 1374 (November 1198) cession of the tithe of
Saint-Caprais to Grandselve by Raymond de Castronovo, son of Peter William Pilistortus,
and his nephew Aimeric; TAM, AA 1 19 (June 1202) Peter at signing of peace with
Rabastens; an Aimeric (either "Copha" or his uncle) took oath to the faith in PAN, JJ 21,
fol. 78r (December 1203); for March 1207 see note 6 above; sale of property at Larramet
in January 1213 by Aimeric "probushomo" and his nephews, namely Raymond and the
brothers Aimeric and Peter in note 4 above; *HGL*, vol. 8, No. 197 (January 1218) Aimeric
"maior," Raymond de Castronovo, Aimeric "minor," and Arnold Pilistortus; Malta 17 27
and 28 (January 1222) sale by Aimeric de Castronovo, son of the quondam William; TAM,
AA 1 75 and 80 (dated respectively March and September 1222) among the councilors of
the consuls were Arnold William Pilistortus, Arnold Pons de Castronovo, Peter,
Raymond, Aimeric "probushomo," his son Castellusnovus, and his nephew Aim
"iuvenis"; and Malta 3 167 ii and iii (dated respectively March 1218 and October 1233)
mention the same cast and Aimeric's wife Mabelia and Peter's wife Ramunda.

[12] For the document of April 1221, see note 14 below, and Douais, *Paléographie*,
No. 18 (March 1223) William son of the deceased Arnold.

usury sometime in or just after 1206.[13] In 1221, furthermore, when the count enfeoffed the fortress of Belcastel to the east of Toulouse, he entrusted a third of it to a knight from Lavaur and the rest to Aimeric "iuvenis," his brother Peter, and their nephew William, son of the quondam Arnold.[14] We also hear of Aimeric's wife Mabelia and Peter's wife Ramunda, and William surely lived until 1243 and may have been the knight of that name who took personal oath to Alphonse of Poitiers in 1249.[15] Aimeric and Mabelia sold their share of Saint-Rome near Ville-franche-en-Lauragais to the count in 1236.[16] Although documents are becoming too few to count on, this Aimeric may have had a son who bore his name. This later Aimeric lived far to the south of Toulouse at Issel, was in economic difficulties in 1255, and was lightly flicked by the whip of the Inquisition in 1275.[17] If this is so, this branch of the family was rusticating rapidly, having less and less to do with the town.

To turn back to the children of the original Peter William Pilistortus, his second son bore his own name Peter William Pilistortus. Never called Castronovo, Peter William is seen from 1171 to 1207.[18] One of his sons was named Castellusnovus de Tolosa, and he, together with his father, is seen handling family property in 1183.[19] Thereafter nothing is known of Castellusnovus, but it may well be that a William Peter Pilistortus seen in the twelve-forties and fifties derives from this line. Because we have no documents concerning property, however, one cannot do more than mention this worthy.[20]

---

[13] Puylaurens, *Chronica*, p. 64.

[14] PAN, J 325 23 (April 1221). Belcastel lay toward Lavaur.

[15] *HGL*, vol. 8, No. 218 (March 1222) William and Aimeric "probushomo"; PBN, Doat 21, fol. 152v (February 1237) attested by the knights Raymond and Peter; PAN, J 305 29 (February 1243) oath to uphold the Peace of Paris includes Castellusnovus (given correctly as Castrumnovum, a rare grammaticism!) Gerald, Peter, Raymond, and William; PAN, J 308 71 (December 1249) William with his nephew W; and E 546 (February 1266) sale of property at Montesquieu to William. For the wives, see the acts of March 1218 and October 1233 in note 11 above.

[16] PAN, JJ 19, fol. 8v (December 1236).

[17] PBN, Doat 84, fol. 312r (November 1255) where Aimeric, son of quondam Aimeric, and his wife Ramunda de Rupeforte lost property for reason of poverty to a "jurisperitus" of Mas-Saintes-Puelles, property between Recaure and the tithing of Sainte-Marie-d'Ayros. In PBN, Doat 25, fol. 202r (March 1275) this knight of Issel informed the inquisitors that he had had no commerce with the Cathars.

[18] For the following dates, see the following notes: May 1171 note 6 above; June 1174 note 8; April and June 1190 and March 1193 note 4; October 1198 note 11; the consulate of 1201-1202; and March 1207 note 6. For September 1200 see note 27 below.

[19] PBN, MS lat. 9994, fol. 161v (January 1183) where he enfeoffed property at Baniols near Grisolles north of Toulouse on the Garonne to the monks of Grandselve.

[20] William Peter at the oath to the Peace of Paris in February 1243 above note 15 and MADTG, A 297, fol. 880r (August 1252) as an executor of Bertrand Descalquencis.

Peter William Pilistortus' third son was Raymond de Castronovo. He was first seen in 1171 and was presumably dead by 1213.[21] We know nothing about his religious adhesion, but his wife Assaut was engaged in Catharism at the time of her first marriage to Raymond Unaldus, a baron of Lanta, and was sentenced as relapsed in 1246.[22] Either by her or by an earlier wife, Raymond had a son named Raymond. This younger Raymond appears from 1213 to 1258. He twice served as a consul during the war years, and was finally sent to Paris as an hostage in 1229. He may have been the consul and knight of that name in 1268-1269.[23] His son was Arnold. A knight, Arnold is seen in family documents in 1255 and 1268, and may have been the consul of this name in 1258-1261, 1273-1275, and 1280-1281.[24]

To turn back again, Peter William Pilistortus' fourth son was Aimeric, the knight who was called "probushomo" to distinguish him from his nephew Aimeric "Copha" or "iuvenis." He was a distinguished man, serving frequently as a consul and being one of the two notables, who, together with the bishop, arranged the terms of the peace between the count and the town in 1189, the start of what is describable as the republican period of the history of Toulouse.[25] In spite of this, or perhaps because of it, he was close to the count and his court, and, as we have seen, received the castle of Castelnau-d'Estretefons in 1213 for the duration of the war. Testimony of the social level with which we are dealing, the "probushomo's" daughter, appropriately but somewhat forbiddingly named Castellana, married the second son of the viscount of Lautrec with the substantial dowry of 2600 shillings in 1210. Incidentally,

[21] For May 1171 see note 6 above; June 1174 note 8; PAN, JJ 21, fol. 43r (March 1181 or 1182) in the court of the count; June 1190 and March 1193 note 3; and Saint-Étienne 226 (DA 1 18) (June 1190) Raymond de Castronovo and his brother Peter William Pilistortus. For September 1200 see note 27 below.

[22] TBM, MS 609, fol. 66r refers to her as the widow of Raymond Unaldus in the late 1220s and as being active in Catharism, and Douais, *Inquisition*, 2: 17 (May 1246) recording her as the wife of Raymond de Castronovo. She was No. **243** in the amnesty of 1279.

[23] For January 1213 see note 4 above; *HGL*, vol. 8, No. 250 (May 1226) Aimeric "major" and Raymond; PAN, J 310 45 (April 1229) for his role as hostage; for October 1233 note 11; and MADTG, A 297, fol. 85v (April 1258). Consuls of this name 1199-1200, 1211-1212, and 1225-1226.

[24] PBN, Doat 78, fols. 394r and 397r, two instruments of April and May 1255 recording the alienation of the tithe of Saint-Pierre-del-Payro to Grandselve by Aimeric, son of Castellusnovus, and witnessed by Peter de Castronovo and Arnold de Castronovo, son of Raymond; also PBN, Doat 73, fol. 47v (December 1268) where he is titled knight.

[25] He was a chapterman and consul in 1186-1187, 1189, 1200-1201, and perhaps 1214-1215. Either he or his nephew Aimeric "Copha" took oath to the faith in December 1203 for which see note 11 above.

to illustrate the social milieu in which the Castelnau-d'Estretefons family moved, Lautrec's older son, who was dead by 1207, had married the count's own natural sister India in 1203.[26]

Rich, active, and acquisitive, the "probushomo" is seen from 1171 to 1230, and was dead by March 1237.[27] Married to Constantia, Aimeric had two sons, Castellusnovus and Peter. Although it may have been his own cousin with the same name, a Peter was consul in 1217-1218 and 1257-1259,[28] and was also a knight with properties in Castelnau-d'Estretefons, Flamolriu, and Verfeil seen from 1258 to 1265.[29] His successor may have

[26] HGL, vol. 8, No. 119 i (October 1203) Peter Ermengavus de Lautrico married his son Gilbert to India giving a "dotalicium" of 100 marks (2600 shillings) on Fiac (modern department of the Tarn); ii (February 1207) Bernard Jordan de Insula married India, widow of Gilbert, she bringing "dos" of 5000 shillings and was promised a "dotalicium" of 5000 shillings more, thus 10,000 shillings; iii (March 1210) Castellana married Hugh, son of the Peter Ermengavus above (see iv [January 1211]), and the count gave her all the "dos" India could claim in Fiac.

[27] For the following dates, see the following notes: May 1171 and March 1207 note 6 above, January 1213 note 4 (where he was first called "probushomo"), February 1213 note 5, March 1222 note 15, September 1222 note 11, and May 1238 note 5. Saint-Sernin 599 (10 35 16) 5th of 8 membranes tied together iii (January 1200, copied in 1219 and 1220) alienation of enormous properties by Sarracena de Noerio to Aimeric who is expressly called "miles"; Malta 15 69 (September 1200) acquisition of large properties from William de Turribus, witnessed by Raymond de Castronovo and Peter William Pilistortus; Malta 3 190 (May 1203) Aimeric and Constanca sell Hospital half of rights on Garonne at Flamolriu acquited from Pons David, called "maior" in Malta 1 112 (October 1214, copied in 1232); and he and his son Castellusnovus attested a comital act in HGL, vol. 8, No. 290 (October 1230). Perhaps dead by June 1232 because E 436 mentions an arrangement about property once mortgaged by him. Malta 123 11 (March 1237) where two Turribus released what Aimeric "probushomo" gave the Hospital at Estaquebiou and Bolencs "pro salute sue anime," witnessed by Gerald de Castronovo de Auriaco; Grandselve 7 (September 1240) records that Aimeric had paid 1300 shillings of a debt of 3000 shillings to Grandselve and his son Castellusnovus the rest. For the "probushomo's" Catharism and that of his wife Constantia and his son Castellusnovus, see TBM, MS 609, fols. 60r, 197v and 203r, with references dating from the mid 1220s to the early 1230s, touching both the "probushomo" and his nephew "Copha," and their wives Constanca and Mabelia. The citation on fol. 60r is confused because it mistakenly describes Constantia as Castellusnovus' wife when it meant his mother. For other evidence of the father's and son's involvement in Catharism, see PBN, Doat 24, fol. 94r approximately 1237 together with Alaman de Roaxio. In the amnesty of 1279 (for which see the list in Chapter 5 above) Aimeric is listed as No. 2, his son as No. 4, and their wives respectively as 134 and 136.

[28] Other than as a consul, Peter also appeared in TAM, AA 1 75 (March 1222) (although this is possibly the Peter, son of William, mentioned above), and PAN, J 308 76 (also in HGL, vol. 8, No.516) (May 1266) where he, as a knight, and Raymond de Castronovo (Curtasolea) "burgensis" represented the consulate before the count. For the Curtasolea, see the family history below. See also the material in note 30 below.

[29] Lespinasse 24 (February 1258) where, with the consent of their mother Esclarmunda, Aimeric de Castronovo and his brother Castellusnovus arranged the payment of their father Castellusnovus' bequest to the nunnery of 500 shillings of Tours

been a knight with the same name who was consul in 1275-1276 and is seen in the 1290s.[30] Peter's brother was also a knight, and, like his father and mother, he and his wife Esclarmunda were condemned for heresy sometime before 1237. This married couple was released from imprisonment by 1238, and Castellusnovus evidently preserved much of the family property at the time of his death by 1258.[31] An inquiry of 1271/2 cited Castellusnovus and his heirs and his cousin Aimeric "Copha" as examples of how rich rural seigniors paid taxes as citizens of Toulouse.[32]

Castellusnovus and Esclarmunda, furthermore, had two sons, Aimeric and Castellusnovus who flourished in the 1250s.[33] First seen with his wife Titburga and his parents in 1239, the knight Aimeric is last seen in 1267,

---

over a three years period, in a charter attested by Peter, son of the dead Aimeric de Castronovo "probushomo," and Gerald de Castronovo de Auriaco; Malta 184 120 (June 1258) where a vineyard at Castelnau-d'Estretefons was sold to Ferrando de Alfario, and a person who was among those who "omnes sunt ejusdem castri" was Peter de Castronovo, son of the deceased Aimeric de Castronovo; Molinier, *Correspondance ... d'Alphonse de Poitiers*, No. 2058 (around 1265) Peter spoke for the consuls to the count and was there called "dominus," hence a knight; Malta 4 197 and 198 (July and October 1260) with property near that of the deceased Aimeric on the Garonne; for May 1255, see note 24 above; and E 493 (April 1265, copied in 1272) property at Verfeil owned by "dominus" Peter.

[30] Possibly the earlier Peter, a knight of this name is in TAM, II 61 (April 1270 and November 1277); also in MADTG, A 297, fol. 883r (December 1292) as an executor for a Sancto Barcio; and the latter Peter is mentioned in the commentary of 1296 on the custom of Toulouse for which see Gilles, *Coutumes*, p. 167.

[31] For the following dates, see the above notes: mid 1220s as a Cathar note 27; March and September 1222 note 11; October 1230 note 27; May 1238 note 5; E 65 (May 1239) his property at Cayras; September 1240 note 27; February 1243 note 15; April and May 1255 note 24; and February 1258 note 29. As to his marriage, see Fournier and Guébin, *Enquêtes d'Alphonse de Poitiers*, pp. 323-324 (April-May 1270) where Bertrand de Garrigiis said he had acquired property at Auzeville 33 years previously from Aimeric "probushomo" and his daughter-in-law Esclarmunda, about 1237. Malta 27 52 (January 1243) one of several membranes tied together, Castellusnovus, son of the dead Aimeric "maior," sold property (acquired in March 1185 or 1186) to Guy de Turribus. Called knight, he, his wife Esclarmunda, his son Aimeric, and the latter's wife Titburga settled with Grandselve about a "bovaria" near the bridge of Bruguières in Saint-Sernin 679 (20 70 12) (May 1239). That he was dead by February 1258 is shown in note 29 above.

[32] TAM, II 10 (March 1271-July 1272) where Peter Niger de Portaria said that, when he was consul in 1255-1257, "comunalerii dicebant eisdem consulibus tunc, et ante audiverat dici, quod dominus Aimericus de Castronovo dederat" taxes on properties in and out of Toulouse. John de Galhaco, once "comunalerius" in the "partida" of Saint-Rome, said the same about Castellusnovus and his heirs.

[33] PBN, Doat 78, fol. 354r (April and May 1255) Aimeric alienated a tithe to Grandselve; Dossat, *Saisimentum*, p. 92 note 11 says Aimeric was one of the lords of Puybusque (anciently Pechbusque); for February 1258 see note 29 above; and E 502 (July 1261) where the two brothers appear together.

and probably left issue.[34] Castellusnovus was still alive in 1279 when he petitioned for the release of heretical inheritances. He was joined in this enterprise by the brothers Aimeric and Raymond de Castronovo "domicelli" who served as proctors.[35] It seems probable that these were the sons of Castellusnovus' deceased brother Aimeric, and we know that these noble worthies, together with their brothers Stephen and John, were the premier lords of Castelnau-d'Estretefons in 1271.[36]

To summarize the history of this great Toulousan clan, the most illustrious figure was Aimeric "maior" or "probushomo." An adult in 1171, he was last seen in 1230 and was dead by 1237, therefore well into his seventies when he died.[37] When still in his thirties, he, together with Bishop Folcrand and Toset de Tolosa, had helped arrange the terms of peace when the town defeated Raymond v in 1189. Thereafter he was inactive in the political life of the town, possibly because he leaned toward the count and away from the town. At the time of the Albigensian war, he was clearly in the Cathar opposition to the crusade. Both he and his son Castellusnovus were listed, together with their wives, among the sentenced heretics in the last of 1279 and are seen as Cathars in other sources as well. As we know, also, his brother Raymond's wife was listed there too.[38] As shall be seen below, the "probushomo," although already late in his fifties, may even have emerged to be one of the leaders of Toulouse in the war against the crusade.

In the meantime, Aimeric "maior's" nephew, Aimeric "iuvenis" or "Copha," demonstrated the versatility of a large family in the face of conflicting interests and difficult circumstances. "Copha" served in the consulates after 1189, and he, together with his brother Arnold, was one of the four leaders of Bishop Fulk's confraternity against heresy and usury. This confraternity initially supported the crusade, sending provisions, and even, against the express veto of Count Raymond vi,

[34] For May 1239, see note 31 above; Clares (January 1266-April 1267, copied in 1298) where the knight Aimeric acts with Raymond de Castronovo de Burgo and his son Stephen and a Jordan de Castronovo is a witness. These last Castronovos were Curtasolea.

[35] See the names in Chapter 6 (March 1279) above.

[36] Dossat, *Saisimentum*, pp. 111 and 139 (October-November 1271) reports that Aimeric was a noble of the vicarage of Toulouse and that he and his brothers were the lords of Castelnau-d'Estretefons. For Aimeric in 1301, see J. Contrasty, *Histoire de Saint-Jory* (Toulouse, 1922), pp. 38-41.

[37] May 1171 in note 6 above was the first charter in which we see him acting as a major.

[38] The amnesty of 1279 (Chapter 5 above) lists them all and shows that the men were picked up fast: Aimeric is No. **3**, his son **4**, their wives **134** and **135**, and Assaut, wife of Raymond, **243**. See also notes 22 and 27 above.

volunteers to help the crusaders at the siege of Lavaur in 1211. Shortly
after the fall of that place, the crusader army tried to take Toulouse by a
coup de main in June 1212, and, faced by that assault, Fulk's confraternity
broke up, the majority going over to the count in order to defend the
town.[39]

What "Copha's" role in these events was we do not surely know, and it
is not certain whether it was he or his uncle the "probushomo" who led
the resistance to the crusade after the occupation of the town by Simon of
Montfort. Probably written by a Toulousan, the famous *Canso* of the war
states that a knight and citizen named Aimeric left the town under
safeguard during the re-occupation of the town by the crusaders after its
unsuccessful rising against Simon in August 1216. The poet has him say
that his prominence in the resistance caused him to fear crusader
vengeance. He was soon back, however, being sent ahead by Raymond vi
to incite what was to be the successful revolt of the town in mid-
September 1217, and he may also have been the Aimeric who helped
defeat a crusader force at Baziège in 1219.[40] What makes it probable that
we are here seeing a "Copha" who had radically changed sides is not only
the fact that the "probushomo" was relatively old, but also that "Copha"
and his wife had played with Catharism during wartime. This opinion is
reinforced by learning that Aimeric and his brother Peter were among
those given the fortress of Belcastel by Count Raymond in 1221. Still, to
change sides does not necessarily make a man the leader.[41]

Whatever happened to "Copha's" line, nothing is clearer than the depth
of the involvement in heresy of his uncle's, the "probushomo's," line.
Even collaterals seem to have been in it. We hear, for example, of a close
relative named Gerald de Castronovo de Auriaco (Auriac, near Caraman
in the Lauragais) who attested family documents of the "probushomo's"
line in 1237 and 1258 and who was surely a Toulousan citizen.[42] In 1245
Gerald's wife Honors testified that she had attended a meeting with Cathar
dignitaries at the house of a "domina" Bermart in Toulouse.[43] But Gerald,

[39] Puylaurens, *Chronica*, pp. 64-70, and Vaux-de-Cernay, *Historia Albigensis*, 1: 216-
217, 219-220, and 239-240.
[40] *Canso*, 2: 222, 241, 269, and 3: 259. Martin-Chabot, the learned editor, conjectures
that the Aimeric at Baziège was an Aimeric de Clermont.
[41] For "Copha" and Mabelia dabbling in heresy, see TBM, MS 609, fol. 203r
(approximately 1225). For Belcastel, see note 14 above. Note, however, that the charter
was attested by the "probushomo," evidence then of a reconciliation between nephew and
uncle.
[42] For March 1237 see note 27 above; for the oath to keep the Peace of Paris in
February 1243 see note 15; and for February 1258 note 29.
[43] TBM, MS 609, fol. 90v (November 1245) about events circa 1235. The name Bermart
seems garbled.

like other Castronovo, appears to have survived. Well into his seventies, he was a witness for the crown around 1274. Rather accurately, he told about the political history of the town from the days of Simon de Montfort, several times asserting that he had served in harness for Toulouse at that time.[44]

One final Castronovo must be mentioned. A petitioner for the amnesty of 1279 was a Johanna de Castronovo, whose spokesman was her husband William de Garrigiis "iuvenis." [45] Since one of the Garrigiis had property relations with the Castronovo family, one guesses that she was a true blue Castronovo, those of Castelnau-d'Estretefons, and not a person of a lesser line, the Curtasolea Castronovo, of which the history is written below.

---

[44] PAN, J 305 32, fol. 9r-v where he says he "interfuit in predicta guerra" with Simon, and then against both Amaury de Montfort and Louis VIII. The text describes him as "dominus" (which usually meant knight) and as "de Auriaco," a country cousin, in short.

[45] See the list in Chapter 6 (March 1279) above. For the relationship, see note 31 above April-May 1270 where a Bertrand de Garrigiis said he had acquired property from Aimeric "probushomo" at Auzeville some 33 years previously.

Corregerius

Named from and presumably exercising the craft of belt or strapmaking, a Peter Corregerius first appeared in 1179 (see Table 9). He acquired a bit of land and a vineyard in the immediate region of the Bourg, and a house in that area paying 12 pence annual rent.[1] The strap-maker died sometime between 1193 and 1200, and a charter gives us to understand that his widow Willelma managed the estate for a time.[2] In 1216, acting with the approval of her three daughters, Ermesendis, Mabriana and Blancha, "domina" Willelma arranged to give her three sons, Arnold Corregerius, Peter de Tolosa, and Raymond Corregerius all her property. She reserved usufruct of her goods until death, stating that, if she wished to leave the house and enter an order, she should have 300 shillings and her "panni," but, if she died at home, she was to have 100 shillings to give to charity. Her sons pledged themselves to transmit this property to each other were anyone of them to die without legitimate heirs.[3]

The sons could not have been well off during the war years. Peter de Tolosa and Raymond Corregerius sold a rent in 1215, and, in 1218, we hear that an "arpent" of their land was pledged to Arnold Rogerius.[4] The last mention of this little family is in 1242 when Orbria, the widow of Raymond Corregerius, and Peter Corregerius, the son of Peter de Tolosa, sold the house the latter's grandfather had bought.[5]

---

[1] E 575 (October 1179) vineyard of Peter at Siculnea near Montvincent; E 475 (May 1181) where Peter rents arable "ad Gravarias" near Castelmaurou; Saint-Bernard 138, fol. 61r (January 1186) reference to the property of 1179 above; ibid., 36 (March 1187) the house; and ibid. (March 1193).

[2] E 510 (June 1200) where the widow acted about arable.

[3] Grandselve 5 (August 1216). The special clauses are: "Set si exire volebat de domo quod ipsa voluisset mittere in ordinem quod haberet de predictis rebus .ccc. sol. tol. et suos pannos et non amplius, et, si de domo non exiebat usque ad finem, retinuit quod de predictis rebus darent sui filii predicti .c. sol. tol. pro amore dei et anime eius ...." "Et ibidem predicti fratres ... fecerunt convenientiam inter eos unusquisque alteri quod, si de aliquo eorum descedebat, scilicet quod descederet absque infante uxoris, quod tota sua pars de predictis rebus remaneret aliis pro omni eorum voluntate inde facienda, et, si de duobus descedebant, scilicet quod descenderent sine infante uxoris, quod tota eorum pars de predictis rebus remanerent tercio pro omni sua voluntate inde facienda."

[4] Saint-Bernard 138, fol. 148r sale of the rent "ad Gravarias," and ibid., fol. 61r and also in E 538 (October 1218) Arnold Rogerius' "pignus."

[5] Grandselve 8 (October 1242).

TABLE 9: CORREGERIUS

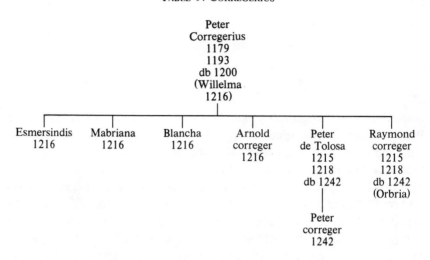

One mystery here is why the son named Peter styled himself (de) Tolosa. The other is whether our Raymond Corregerius above was the Cathar sentenced in the 1240s.[6]

---

[6] Listed as No. **259** in the amnesty of 1279 published in Chapter 5 above.

Cossano

An Arnold de Cozas is seen in 1143 or 1144 and again in 1156 with property at the Pouzonville Gate in the Bourg.[1] The heir of this property and presumably Arnold's son was a Bernard Peter de Cossano who appears in 1167 (see Table 10).[2] Perhaps because of his expertise in law, Bernard Peter enjoyed an immense political success. Starting in 1180, he was thrice a member of the count's chapter, was a consul and "judex" at the time of the count's defeat in 1189-1190, and, until his final term in 1212-1213, was a consul for at least six terms.[3] During this period, he was one of the most active examples of the pre- or proto-jurist age of Toulousan law, the age when arbitrative justice had not been weakened by the evolution of the consul's court and by emerging professionalism. He also served the count as a judge, was often an arbitrative judge in the courts of the count's vicar, the bishop, the seigniorial court of the archdeacon of Saint-Sernin, and was especially busy as a judge both among the consuls and as judge in their arbitrative courts.[4] Although a true expression of twelfth-century Toulousan republicanism, he seems to have wavered during the great war. As seen above, he was a consul before the defeat of Toulouse and its count at Muret, but is reported to have served the Montfort regime.[5] He may eventually have fallen foul of

[1] Douais, *Saint-Sernin*, No. 310 (March 1143 or 1144) as "de Cosanis"; Malta 120 390 (October 1148) as "de Coza"; Grandselve 1 (May 1155) as "de Cozas"; and Douais, *Saint-Sernin*, No. 37 (January 1156).

[2] Grandselve 4 (January 1167) as "de Coza" with property at Gratalauze.

[3] 1180-1181, 1183-1184, 1186-1187, 1189-1190 (the old chapter was composed of two "judices," two "advocati," and the rest were "capitularii"), 1190-1191, 1192-1193, 1194-1195, 1198-1199, and 1212-1213.

[4] *HGL*, vol. 8, No. 3 (dated to 1200 or 1201) the count's court; Saint-Étienne 227 (26 DA 1 17) (November 1189) the vicar's court; Douais, *Saint-Sernin*, Appendix No. 30 (January 1191) the bishop's court; and Saint-Sernin 680 (20 72 unnumbered) (November 1196) private parties before the seigniorial court of Saint-Sernin. A selection of his work in arbitrative courts supervised or regulated by the consuls is to be seen in my *Toulouse*, Chapter 11, especially p. 350 note 28 in 1177, p. 351 note 31 in 1173/4, and p. 354 note 47 in 1188, 1191, and 1192/3. For Bernard Peter's acquisition of property at the Portaria, see Saint-Bernard 36 i and iv (February 1191 and July 1210, copied in 1229). He took oath to the faith to the legates in PAN, JJ 21, fol. 78r (December 1203).

[5] See PAN, J 304 32, fol. 8v around 1274 where a contemporary named Bernard Hugh de Sesquieras reported on his role.

the occupation government, however, because his property seems to have been threatened by confiscation. In 1222 he gave his son Peter his claim on a rent of 20 shillings alienated to Saint-Antoine "in dominatione Symonis Montisfortis,"[6] a matter that was eventually settled between Peter and this priory of Lézat in 1225.[7] In the charter of that settlement, we also learn that Bernard Peter was dead. In passing, it may be noted that Bernard Peter had been appointed one of the guardians of William Arnold "medicus'" hospital later called Sainte-Catherine's in 1199.[8]

TABLE 10: COSSANO

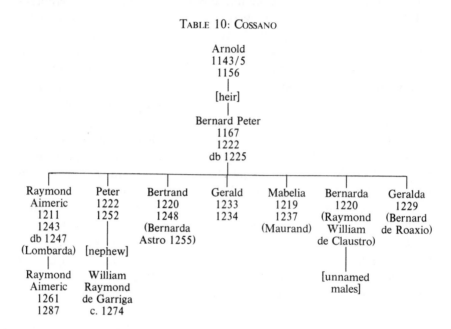

Arnold
1143/5
1156

[heir]

Bernard Peter
1167
1222
db 1225

Raymond Aimeric 1211 1243 db 1247 (Lombarda)	Peter 1222 1252	Bertrand 1220 1248 (Bernarda Astro 1255)	Gerald 1233 1234	Mabelia 1219 1237 (Maurand)	Bernarda 1220 (Raymond William de Claustro)	Geralda 1229 (Bernard de Roaxio)
Raymond Aimeric 1261 1287	[nephew] William Raymond de Garriga c. 1274				[unnamed males]	

Bernard Peter had at least four sons and several daughters. To treat the latter first, we learn in 1219 that Mabelia, the wife of Maurandus "vetus," was his daughter because Bernard Peter intervened "nomine doni vel matrimonii" to confirm an action by her husband.[9] Mabelia's history was tragic. Married with the very substantial marriage portion of 3000 shillings, she, like her husband, was found to be a Cathar, and was

---

[6] PBN, MS lat. 9189, fol. 231v (February 1217) and fol. 229v (October 1222).
[7] Ibid., fol. 230 (July 1225).
[8] E 973 iv (probably March 1199, copied in 1202) as one of three notables.
[9] Saint-Bernard 138, fol. 173v (April 1219).

condemned as relapsed in 1237.[10] Another daughter was Bernarda, the wife of Raymond William de Claustro or de Burgo, whose sons lost the substantial farm of Fontanas mainly as a result of resisting the crusader occupation of the town.[11] A third daughter (although this person may have been the child of one of his sons) was Geralda, the wife of Bernard de Roaxio. Evidence of this family's sense of its quality is the fact that, although married to an undoubted patrician, Geralda is seen in 1229 proudly carrying her own family name.[12]

Bernard Peter's sons were Raymond Aimeric, sometimes called simply Raymond, Peter, Bertrand, and Gerald. Raymond Aimeric appears from 1211 to 1243.[13] Bravely following in his father's footsteps, he served as consul in 1211-1212 and 1217-1218, but his later years were clouded. He is described as dead in 1247 in the record of the condemnation to life imprisonment of his widow Lombarda by the Inquisition.[14] That the unhappy pair had a child, however, is almost certain. Raymond Aimeric, son of the deceased Raymond Aimeric, petitioned in 1279 for the amnesty.[15] The same person, once called Raymond and then Raymond Aimeric, is seen from 1261 to 1287, and appeared as one of a group of creditors of the lords of l'Isle-Jourdain who paid off debts owed by that notable to the Barravi. Together with a Peter Iudex, he had been assigned the revenues of Saint-Sulpice (sur Lèze?).[16]

Seen first in 1222, Bernard Peter's second son Peter appears to have picked up where his brother left off. He served as a hostage for Toulouse

---

[10] PBN, Doat 21, fol. 150v (February 1237), and in the list of 1279 (Chapter 5 above) as No. **179**. Her marriage portion is mentioned in Saint-Sernin 599 (10 35 11) (November 1233). For Mabelia, see the Maurandus family history below.

[11] See the Claustro family history in my "The Farm of Fontanas at Toulouse: Two Families, a Monastery, and a Pope," *BMCL*, n.s. 11 (1981) 29-40. Her relation to her spouse and her father is shown in Saint-Bernard 138, fol. 10v (May 1220) when, as a widow, Bernarda acted with her father's consent "nomine doni vel matrimonii."

[12] MADTG, A 297, fol. 609v (March 1229) wherein she consented to an action by her husband.

[13] Other than this terms as a consul, he is seen in Saint-Bernard 138, fol. 52v (March 1217) with his father; *HGL*, vol. 8, No. 210 (October 1220) again with the same; the document of 1222 cited in note 6 above where he was a witness; E 538 (December 1226) as an executor; Saint-Sernin 599 (10 33 15) (April 1234) where he and his three brothers fulfilled the terms of their father's testament; and PAN, J 305 29 (February 1243) in which Raymond, Bertrand, and Peter take oath to preserve the Peace of Paris.

[14] Douais, *Inquisition*, 2: 44 (August 1247), and, appropriately enough, she was listed as No. **197** in the amnesty of 1279, for which see the list in Chapter 5 above.

[15] See the list of March 1279 in Chapter 6 above.

[16] Grandselve 41 (December 1261) where we see Raymond Aimeric de Cossano, son of the dead Raymond Aimeric, and MADTG, A 297, fols. 464r and 550r (respectively May 1274 and December 1287) in partnership with Peter Iudex.

and was sent to Paris in 1229.[17] He lived busily until 1251 when we hear of him alienating his rights at Les Leus near Lalande just north of town and see him as a consul in the term 1251-1252.[18] Peter had a nephew named William Raymond de Garriga who related around 1274 what his uncle had had to say about the government of the town in and just after the Albigensian war.[19]

Next in line was Bertrand. Bertrand was an executor of the wealthy Stephen Astro's will in 1220, and was again an executor of another Astro will in 1248, which is the last we know of him.[20] In 1225, moreover, we learn that he had married Stephen Astro's daughter Bernarda, who had brought with her a dowry of 1000 shillings.[21]

Gerald, the last and youngest brother, is seen only in 1233 and 1234.[22]

After the death of the celebrated Bernard Peter, there are few documents concerning this family. Perhaps the heir of an up country immigrant from Coussa near Pamiers, Bernard Peter had made the family fortune. His daughters were married off very elegantly, and so was at least one son. Curiously, no male Cossano is known to have been involved in Catharism in spite of the fact that a daughter who married into the Maurandi family was sentenced for this belief. The unhappy Mabelia had probably adopted the belief of her husband. But that does not say it all. The Maurandi, we shall see, were notoriously Cathar. To permit a daughter to marry into that family meant that the young woman was more than merely likely to enter that faith. As we have seen, moreover, the wife of Raymond Aimeric was also condemned for this divergence. The Cossano prove what the contemporary historian Puylaurens said, namely that, before the start of serious repression at the end of the war, the "orthodox" tolerated the "deviant."

[17] For October 1222, see the reference cited in note 6 above.

[18] For July 1225, see note 7 above; PAN, J 310 45 (April 1229) as Peter de Cociano; April 1234 as in note 13 above; Malta 27 65 (January 1240); February 1243 as in note 13 above; E 896 (September 1248) as "de Cosseanis"; and Saint-Sernin Canonesses 34 ii (May 1251, copied in 1260) involving his rights in the "curia Leuzinorum" (Les Leus near the modern Lalande and Frenchman's Road).

[19] PAN, J 305 32, fol. 6r (about 1274) where the uncle Peter was reported to be deceased.

[20] Grandselve 5 (March 1220) for Stephen's testament; for April 1234 and February 1243 see note 13 above; and E 896 (September 1248).

[21] Grandselve 6 (May 1225), thus, together with the husband's gift, making a rich marriage portion for the bride of about 1300 shillings.

[22] Saint-Sernin 599 (10 35 17) 8th of 9 membranes tied together (November 1233), and, for April 1234, note 13 above.

Curtasolea

Whatever their origins, and they may have been from Caraman in the Lauragais,[1] a family initially named Curtasolea early appeared in the documents.[2] The family name subsequently vanishes from the charters, and does not appear again until 1191. At that date, an arbitral court decided in favor of Saint-Sernin and refused John Curtasolea the right to collect the tithes on his "honores" at Gravarias just north of the Bourg.[3] Subsequently, in 1204, we hear of a sale by John, Stephen, Peter Raymond, and their minor brother Bernard Curtasolea.[4] The John of 1191 was therefore either the father of the brothers of 1204 or the oldest sibling (see Table 11). Thereafter references become more plentiful. From 1202 to 1211, John and Stephen served as guardians for the children of Raymond Maurandus,[5] and Peter Raymond was a business partner, as a creditor or usurer, of course, of the latter's brother Peter Maurandus.[6] This evidence tells us that, although perhaps the junior partners, the Curtasolea were already people of worth. Stephen possessed an eighth part of the "bovaria" or great farm of Valségur, and "honor" that, as we shall see, had been largely acquired by the Maurand family.[7]

---

[1] One gambles without putting much stock in it because of several things: (1) the forename Jordan and the surnames Castronovo and Caramanno were used by the Curtasolea in the thirteenth century, and (2) the fact that the main family Castronovo described above initially had property in the Close of Saint-Sernin makes it not impossible that the Curtasolea were a cadet line of the greater family. Whatever the case, the pertinent documents are: Douais, *Saint-Sernin*, No. 447 (August 1165) where Donat and Jordan de Caraman and their brother William del Castelnou surrendered the tithe at Blagnac, and Malta 1 24 xxv published in C. Molinier, "La question de l'ensevelissement du comte de Toulouse Raimond VI en terre sainte (1222-1247)," *Annales de la faculté des lettres de Bordeaux*, n.s. 2 (1885), 78-79 (August 1184) where the count tells Saint-Sernin that William de Castronovo and William Peter de Caramanno had no claim on Blagnac's tithe.

[2] Douais, *Saint-Sernin*, No. 546 (1075 to 1078) where Peter Bernard Curtasola witnessed the foundation of the Hospital Saint-Raymond.

[3] Douais, *Saint-Sernin*, Appendix No. 30 (January 1191).

[4] Grandselve 4 i (June 1204).

[5] See the history of the Maurandus family below.

[6] As an example, see Malta 58 unnumbered (January 1211).

[7] Douais, *Documents sur Languedoc*, pp. 13-14 in the inventory of September 1234.

TABLE 11: CURTASOLEA

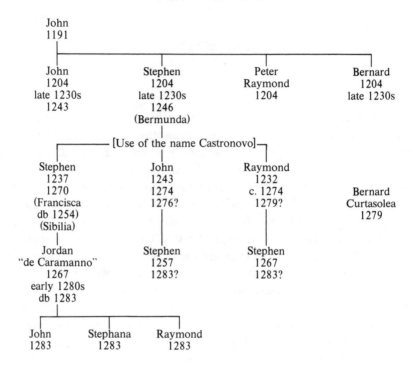

The economic connection between the two families translated easily into ideological and religious ones. The Curtasolea were clearly members of the war party at Toulouse and served as consuls during four wartime terms.[8] Again, like the Maurandi, at one of whose houses they are known to have worshipped, the Curtasolea were remarkably heretical. Of the four siblings of 1204, John, Stephen, and Bernard were all condemned Cathars, and shared this fate with their unnamed sisters and the wives of the first two brothers here listed. All these persons were sentenced before February 1237, sometimes well before.[9] A curious result of this catastrophe was that the family gradually changed its name and increased in wealth.

[8] John was consul in 1214-1215 and 1224-1225, Bernard in 1223-1224, and Stephen in 1225-1226.

[9] TBM, MS 609, fol. 111r where, in the early 1230s, Stephen and his wife Bermunda were in Maurandus "vetus"' house in the Bourg. In the amnesty of 1279 (Chapter 5 above), these deceased persons are listed in the following order: John 12, Stephen 13, Bernard 132, their sisters (at least two) 141 and 142, John's wife 143, and Stephen's wife Bermunda 144. The latter woman was not named in the amnesty, but see the beginning of this note.

How this came about is complicated. Along with his brother John, Stephen took oath to defend the Peace of Paris in 1243.[10] It is therefore likely, that the brothers, by delation, oiling palms, or other means, had escaped the full burden of the effects of their earlier condemnation, or, alternately, that they had "repented" and were then picked up later either for omissions in their testimony or for falling back, and were again condemned. Still, the family persisted. Not only did the later Castronovo of this line not forget their father Stephen Curtasolea's name, but also a Bernard Curtasolea appeared as a petitioner in 1279, an unabashed spirit who was surely the son or grandson of John, one whose name perhaps commemorated the Bernard Curtasolea who had vanished forever.[11] We know much more about Stephen than we do about his brother John Curtasolea. Stephen is seen dealing with his properties at Estaquebiou in 1245 and with his share of Valségur in 1246,[12] but it was his three sons who were to regild the family arms.

The son named Stephen de Castronovo struck it rich. In 1237 Bernard de Miramonte, one of the wealthiest men in Toulouse, set aside for the dowry of his daughter and only heir Francisca (Francisqua, etc.) the lordly sum of 3000 shillings. The father's will stated that the husband was to be Stephen, and, in fact, the marriage was consummated.[13] Francisca had died by 1254, however, and Stephen had married a woman named Sibilia, but, what is more, had inherited a quarter of Miramonte's estate.[14] Unsuccessfully charged with usury in 1244, Stephen was involved in a lawsuit from 1266 to 1270 trying to recuperate his fourth part of the "bastide" of Castillon "wrongfully" seized by Count Raymond VII.[15] 1270 also produced an instrument wherein the count ordered his vicar to settle a suit decided sometime before in favor of Stephen de Castronovo and his brother John against the rural lord Jordan de Saissaco.[16] This Stephen had

[10] The Curtasolea-Castronovo in PAN, J 313 95 (February 1243) were John, Raymond and Stephen all called "de Castronovo," and John and Stephen Curtasolea.

[11] See March 1279 in Chapter 6 above.

[12] Malta 123 15 (April 1248, copied in 1252) and, for Valségur, the inventory of September 1246 in note 7 above.

[13] PAN, J 328 24 (August 1237).

[14] TAM, II 39 (March 1254, copied in 1286) records the division of the inheritance with the brothers Niger and Galhaco, one involving all property save the "bastida" of Castillon.

[15] Blanc, *Jacme Olivier*, June 1255, witness No. 20 said Stephen got 260 shillings for a loan of 60 shillings, but the end of the roll states "non probatum contra Stephanum de Castronovo ...." Had Stephen received what was said, his profit would have been three and a third times his original investment. For the suit against the count see Fournier and Guébin, eds., *Enquêtes d'Alphonse de Poitiers*, pp. 211, 231-232, 297b, and 328b (November 1266 to 1270), and also PAN, J 317 (November 1266).

[16] Molinier, *Correspondance d'Alphonse de Poitiers*, No. 1397 (January 1270), the other creditor being William Laurencii, also a "civis."

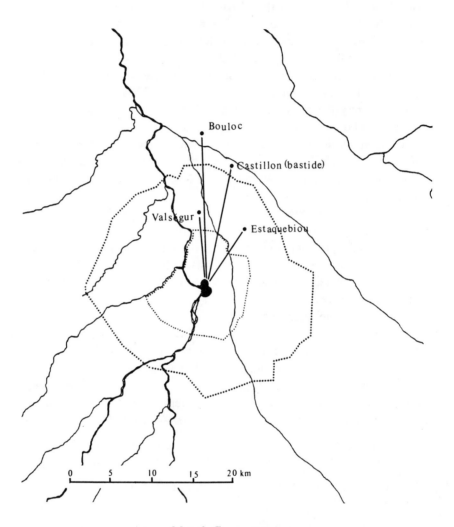

MAP 6. CURTASOLEA

a son named Jordan de Castronovo, sometimes also called "de Cara-manno." [17] He is seen busy protecting his rights at Lespinasse (?) and Bouloc near Fronton in 1268 and 1270, and selling his share of the tolls in the Bourg to the crown in 1273.[18] Testimony in the early 1280s mentions him as a prominent wine merchant, and he was dead by 1283 when he left his issue, John, Stephana and Raymond, under the care of a Stephen de Castronovo, one of his cousins, the son of one of his uncles, of either John or Raymond to be seen below.[19]

Stephen's brother John is seen as early as 1243 swearing to uphold the Peace of Paris just as all the rest of the family was doing. We know little about him except that we see him in charters of 1270 and 1274, and presume that he was the consul of that name in 1275-1276. He also had a son named Stephen, who is seen once in 1257, but who may have been alive in 1283.[20] Likewise at the oath of 1243, John's brother Raymond was a man of greater weight. Called a merchant in 1232, Raymond initially strongly supported Raymond VII's seizure of the town govern-ment, serving as consul in the long period from 1242 to the reaction of 1246. He then changed his tune and served in the free consulate of 1247-1248. Although we lack private documents, Raymond de Castronovo de Burgo was alive in 1267 and again about 1274,[21] and was probably the one of that name who petitioned for himself and for the heirs of his deceased brother John in 1279.[22] In 1267 we know that Raymond had a

---

[17] PAN, J 324 6 x (November 1273) where "Jordanus de Castronovo qui alio nomine appellatur de Caramanno, filius quondam Stephani Curtasolee burgensis Tholose" and Bruna his wife, sell the tolls mentioned below for 20 pounds of Toulouse.

[18] Molinier, *Correspondance d'Alphonse de Poitiers*, No. 801 (June 1268) involving the "nemus" "de Castro Spinacii" (Lespinasse?) and "Fonteregali" wherever that may have been; Fournir and Guébin, eds., *Enquêtes d'Alphonse de Poitiers*, p. 328b in 1270; and the act of November 1273 in note 17 above.

[19] MADTG, A 297, fol. 791r (Novembr 1283).

[20] Grandselve 9 (June 1257) referring to the son Stephen, but not describing his father as dead; MADTG, A 297, fol. 464r (March 1274) where John was one of the three guarantors of the debts of the baron of l'Isle-Jourdain to the Barravi; Grandselve 11 (May 1271) where he sold his house on the rue des Couteliers to the knight Arnold de Falgario. For the possibility that his son Stephen was alive in 1283, see note 19 above. The John de Castronovo "sutor" in PBN, Doat 73, fol. 47r-v (January 1269) attending a general assembly was surely not our man.

[21] Clares 24 (January 1266-April 1267, copied in 1298) where we see Raymond de Castronovo de Burgo, his son Stephen and Jordan de Castronovo; and PAN, J 305 32, fol. 2r where William de Seres (Septinis) testified correctly that they were in the same consulate, and that, at the time he gave testimony, both Raymond and Berengar de Portalli of that consulate were still alive, that is, approximately 1274.

[22] See March 1279 in Chapter 6 where Raymond de Castronovo de Burgo spoke "pro se" and for the heirs of John.

son named Stephen, and, as seen above, he may have served as guardian for the children of his uncle Stephen.[23]

In fine, the Curtasolea-Castronovo survived their threatened extinction at the time of the assault on Catharism, and went on to flourish in the latter half of the thirteenth century.

[23] See the testament in note 19 above.

David

A family bearing the name David as a surname was among the largest shareholders of the mint of Toulouse in the years around 1200.[1] Toulouse's minters were a curious and select group. Initially, because of their function, they were in the count's service. As the authority of that prince diminished in the late twelfth century and that of the consuls rose, the minters gained a more independent role, and, being, as it were, suspended between count and consulate, came to enjoy hereditary rights in the mint. Along with the brothers Puer (Macip or Mancipius is the other form of the name), Pons David, who is described below, quite adequately represents this stage in the history of the mint and its minters.[2] In my earlier study of the history of Toulouse, I suggested that, to judge by such names as Ispaniolus, Amoravis, and Floranus, some of the minter families seem to have derived from Spanish and perhaps Jewish antecedents.[3] Given the use of "their" Jews by secular princes in this period, this conjecture still seems reasonable. All the same, the relations of people like the David to the Jewish community may reflect nothing more than the fact that the Jews themselves were closely connected to the count's administration.

The name David was not uncommon as a Christian name, and, since forenames often became surnames, it is not surprising that we have one or more families called David in town. Pechdavid, the name of a locality south of the town, poses the problem as to whether the name of the family came from that of the place or vice-versa. Because the rural properties of the David family of the City lay in the arc Lespinet, Saint-Agne, Pouvour-

---

[1] E 501 (March 1199) (published in Boyer, *Mélanges*, 1: 152 and my *Toulouse* No. 9) where the sons of Ispaniolus, Arnold Raymond de Frenariis, the Amoravis family, that of Puer or Mancipius, that of Floranus, and Bernard Belotus confirm the fact that Bertrand and Pons David have a quarter part of the mint, and also record the acquisition that the Davids' father Bernard had made from Pons de Claromonte and his family.

[2] See Boyer's article (originally published in 1950) cited above, and my *Toulouse*, pp. 28, 30, and 108-109.

[3] My *Toulouse*, pp. 30 and 53, but there is nothing to the conjecture about Pons David in pp. 242-243, note 5. I had merely misread my notes on the charter.

ville, Pechdavid, and the waterfront of the Garonne river south of town, it seems more likely that the family gave its name to the place.[4]

The earliest known David are a Bonetus, a David de Labrausa, and a Pons David de La Brauza of the 1130s, the latter having a house on the rue de Bouquières in the City.[5] From one of these, perhaps Bonetus, derived a family named David located in the Bourg, a group whose history shall not be treated here for want of material.[6] There is no reason to assume that this little family is not related in its origins to that whose history we shall trace here, but there is also no way of showing it. Along with his wife Sibilia, a Bernard David appears in the period 1156-1158, and the charters refer to properties in the Close of Saint-Sernin and Flaugas east of Toulouse on the way to Balma(?). This property links this Bernard to the two David de La Brauza mentioned above and perhaps even to Bonetus David, as well as to the line deriving from Bernard, thus assuring us that the family derived from La Brauza, wherever that may be.[7]

Presumably the same as the Bernard seen above or his direct descendant, Bernard appears again in 1160 with property next the church of Saint-Pierre and Saint-Géraud in the City on the Place de la Pierre, and vineyards in the Close of Saint-Pierre, outlying property of this church located somewhere in the Pouvourville and Pechdavid neighborhood.[8] In 1180 we learn that Bernard and his two sons, Bertrand and Pons, owned

---

[4] See the document cited below, and especially Malta 1 100 (April 1180) where what was later called Pechdavid is simply named "Podium." Note also ibid., 58 14 an undated record of testimony taken sometime after Pons David's death describing properties once in his hands in and around Pechdavid. A nearly contemporary dorsal note reads "De Ponz David."

[5] Douais, *Saint-Sernin*, No. 11 (May 1125) Bonetus with property at Busquet near Balma; ibid., No. 72 (undated) and No. 101 (March 1126 or 1127) David de la Brauza, land in Flaugas in the outlying Close of Saint-Sernin; E 501 undated but dateable from 1121 to 1139 with Pons David de Labrauza as a witness; and Grandselve 3 i (June 1154, copied in 1195) the latter's house on the "carraria de Boqueriis."

[6] A Peter in Saint-Bernard 138, fol. 1r (April 1161); ibid., fol. 73v (September 1171); a Stephen married to a Petrona in Grandselve 2 (April 1170) at Lascrosses gate; ibid., 1 (January 1172) the same at the "ser" or close of Saint-Quentin; Malta 118 179 (June 1184) mentioning also his married daughter Stephana and land near the Pont-des-Clèdes; the brothers William and Bernard who had married two sisters from whom one received various properties and a quarter and a half of another quarter of a mill at the Bazacle in Grandselve 2 (March 1188 or 1189).

[7] Douais, *Saint-Sernin*, Nos. 69, 70, 78, and 79 (variously dated October 1156, October 1157, and September 1158) mentioning the wife Sibilia and the place of Flaugas, for which see March 1126 or 1127 in note 5 above.

[8] Saint-Pierre and Saint-Géraud (April 1160) two and a half arpents of vineyard in the Close of Saint-Pierre and the town properties.

an undetermined portion of the mint, that Bernard was married to a Rica, and that Pons surrendered all claims on family property in the region of Saint-Agne, Flaugas, and the adjacent Las Combas, the Close of Saint-Pierre, adjacent to the church of Saint-Pierre and Saint-Géraud, and in the Salvetat (presumably the southern part of the City). Pons retained the region around Pechdavid and the waterfront on the Garonne, and a third part of the family right in the mint. The document also states that Bertrand was married to Brus Martina, that his brother Pons was married to Bruna, a daughter of the distinguished Toset de Tolosa, and that their sister Bonafos was married to Raymond Ispaniolus, a minter and a son of the onetime vicar of Toulouse, Ispaniolus.[9] In 1182 we learn that Bernard had probably died, and that he had had another son named Galhard who had become an Hospitaler.[10]

Although the charter of 1180 clearly states that the shares of Bertrand and his brother Pons had been separated, we know that the two siblings remained close probably because Pons, although perhaps the younger of the two, was decidedly the richer. They acted together in the 1180s, confirmed their acquisitions of a fourth part of the mint in 1199, together sold to the town government houses on the Place de la Pierre in 1203, houses that were both their own and those about which they had a say as executors of the estate of Raymond Monachus, a onetime vicar of Toulouse.[11] The brothers knew this region well because we know that they lived on this square.[12] Further testimony to the closeness of the

[9] Malta 1 100 (April 1180) when Bernard and his son Bertrand, together with their wives Rica and Brus Martina, and Bonafos with her husband Raymond Ispaniolus, gave Pons all family holdings from the "tegularium Curvi [de Turribus]" down the waterfront to Flamolriu and Pechdavid inclusive, and retain for themselves all the rest, including all "pignora" held beyond the Hers river. Thereupon Pons, with the consent of Bruna and Toset de Tolosa, surrendered all claim to these, "excepta moneta quia Poncius David retinuit terciam partem in illis iuribus monete que Bernardus David habebat in moneta, scilicet in magistratione et in dominatione, excepta domo que est monete ante domum Arnaldi Bitobo, quia in predicta domo habet terciam partem quamdiu moneta operabitur, et quamdiu non operabitur moneta, Poncius David non habet ibi quicquam, et si predicta moneta mutabitur ad operandum alibi, Poncius David habet ibi suam terciam partem sicuti in aliam habet."

[10] Malta 1 76 (September 1183) where Bertrand, with Pons' consent, gave the Hospital 12 pence rent and a tithe acquired from his father, thus fulfilling a gift their father had promised the Hospital "pro Galiardo filio suo."

[11] Malta 3 88bis (September 1183) where Bertrand and his wife with Pons's consent sell a lot in the outlying Close of Saint-Pierre to the Hospital, the property seen in the act of March 1199 seen in note 1 above; Bernard also had two thirds of the family right to the mint, and the two are seen alienating property on the "planum Sancti Petri" to the consuls in TAM, AA 1 43, 48, and 50 (dated March to May 1203).

[12] Mentioned in Malta 145 22 (May 1187) and E 501 (June 1187) their house was bounded by properties of a Roaxio, of the minter Yspaniolus, the church of Saint-Pierre

brothers is seen when Pons provided very liberally for Bertrand in his testament, buying him entry into the Hospital as one of the senior brethren, or, if he preferred, a substantial annual pension from the order.[13] Bertrand outlived Pons and is seen in the documents until 1235.[14] Oddly enough, in spite of the facts that Pons made the Hospital his general heir, that he endowed a priest to sing masses there, that his brother Galhard was an Hospitaler, and that, in 1208, he himself had the option of becoming one by the terms of his brother's will, Bertrand David was a Cathar, being listed among those sentenced for that belief in the amnesty of 1279.[15] Still another oddity is that, although Pons was a far more successful man than his brother, a street named after Bertrand was to be found near Saint-Pierre and Saint-Géraud. Somehow, Bertrand had captured the fancy of his concitizens.[16]

Much more is known about Pons than about Bertrand. Pons was twice married, first to Bruna de Tolosa, as we know, and then to Pagesia, daughter of Hugh Surdus. The latter outlived him, and the documents about her widow's settlement and the special gift Pons left her in addition tell us much about this minter's social status and the practices of the businessmen of the time. Replacing all others, he drew his final will in 1208, but was still alive and busy in 1210.[17] He had died by July 1213, when the Hospital, which was his heir, gave his widow her settlement of 1400 shillings, a substantial sum, but not that of a millionaire.[18] A partial payment of the additional 500 shillings gift he had left his widow Pagesia

and Saint-Géraud, and a public street, probably the one later named after his brother, for which see note 16 below.

[13] The testament in Malta 1 17 (January 1208, copied in 1214, 1221, 1227, and 1239), and the pension given Bertrand is described in note 21 below.

[14] Although obviously not as rich as Pons, Bertrand had two thirds of the family right in the mint and usually precedes Pons in the acts where they appear together, thus implying that he was the older sibling. Other than the acts seen above, Bertrand is in Malta 3 168 iv and v (dated respectively March 1221 and March 1235); ibid., 7 87 (published in G. Saige, *Les Juifs de Languedoc* ... [Paris, 1881], No. 26) and E 406 (November 1230), the actor being a Jew named David; Saint-Étienne 227 (26 DA 2 47) (November 1230); and the act of March 1235 in Malta 3 168 immediately above.

[15] As No. **79** in the list in Chapter 5 above, therefore an early condemnation. No petitioner of this family is seen in 1279.

[16] According to Chalande, this is the present rue de la Colombe. The medieval name is seen in E 467 (April 1309).

[17] The testament of January 1208 is in note 13 above. Pons was collecting on loans amounting to 1500 shillings in E 508 (April 1210).

[18] E 505 (July 1213), the money and the usual "lectum bene munitum de pannis." The "rachat" on one of his properties was not paid until Malta 3 140 v (July 1215, copied in 1218).

was not made until 1226.[19] This delay was not abnormal, but it must be confessed that the heir's other obligations were paid off very slowly indeed. A godchild's legacy was honored in 1230, and that to the church of Saint-Barthelémy only in 1240.[20] Perhaps the Hospitalers thought that God could wait, and for upwards of thirty years! Still, the good knights were obliged to invest to get this "hereditas." Pons gave just under 3000 shillings to ecclesiastical and charitable institutions and just over that sum to layfolk, to which may be added a fair amount of real property and four possible pensions for layfolk at the expense of the order, one of them expensive.[21]

Among the legacies to layfolk was one that, although not called so, looks much like a specific restitution for usury.[22] Pons was undoubtedly a moneylender, and his will assigned 2000 shillings to be distributed by his executors to those who sued the estate for restitution. Pons was a creditor of the Toulousan Jew Provincialis and of various other lay parties, gentle and humble, one of whom was being taken at the rate of over 33 percent annually.[23] That contemporaries thought him to be a manifest usurer is shown not only by a tenant's rent strike against his heir in 1213,[24] but also

[19] The "laixa" or payment is in E 504 (November 1226), and was given to two of her family, the Surdi clan, and to two others, only 300 shillings of the promised 500 shillings.

[20] E 504 (July 1230) 20 shillings to Bona daughter of William Badallus and Bona, and E 501 (May 1240) 50 shillings to the proctors of the fabric of Saint-Barthelémy, then called Sainte-Marie "de Palacio."

[21] January 1208 in note 13 above where pensions at the Hospital were assigned to two men and to Pons' "pedisecca" Audiarda who could, however, take 100 shillings instead. Pons willed his brother food and clothing in the Hospital "sicut uni dominis" of the house, if he needed it, but, if he did not want to receive "sua necessaria" there, the Hospitalers were to grant him "pro stipendie" 2 "cartones" of grain, 1 "modium" of wine, and 20 shillings "pro indumenta" annually.

[22] The bequest of 200 shillings to the wife and daughter of a Raymond Pelliparius and the return of a vineyard at Restaque near Lespinet which Pons had "in pignore" is a "certa" restitution, the "pignus" being admittedly usurious. The general bequest for restitution mentioned in the next sentence is to the conventional "conquerentibus suis de usura."

[23] In PAN, J 318 13 (December 1207) the sons of the quondam vicar Bernard Seillanus received 400 shillings for a "pignus" on vineyards at Lespinet, "scilicet pro omnibus illis baratis et debitis que Bernardus Sillanus pater eorum qui fuit firmaverat pro predicto Provinciale iudeo vel pro fratribus vel pro nepotibus suis aut pro aliquo eorum erga Poncium David." In short, Provincialis had mortgaged them to Pons. E 508 (May 1194) a loan of 28 shillings to an Arnold Crosatus with monthly interest ("de lucro") of nine pence and a half penny (2.8 percent monthly; 33.9 percent annually), payment of capital and lucre on the creditor's demand. Malta 3 190 (May 1203) where Aimeric de Castronovo sold the Hospital the shore, water, and fishing rights near Flamolriu he had bought from Pons. See also the act of April 1210 in note 17 above.

[24] Malta 1 21 (June 1214) an action on consular order by the "nuncius" Falquetus, published in my *Toulouse*, No. 14 where it was mistakenly dated 1213 and the word "premium" or rent misprinted as "primum."

by a decision of 1215 by the bishop's court on usury against the Hospitalers requiring restitution to the "fideiussores" or guarantors of a debt owed Pons by a knight named Boson. The rate of interest recorded in this sole example of the activities of Bishop Fulk's tribunal was 20 percent.[25]

Given his business, a curious quality of Pons David, to judge by his will with its legacies to his nieces, godchild, and his "pedisseca" Audiarda and her son, etc., is that this usurer, unlike the far richer and equally generous Pons de Capitedenario, seems to have been a thoughtful and rather warm man.

A final note: it is not inconceivable that Bertrand or even Pons had a son. We hear of a Raymond David with property near that of the line of Bertrand and Pons in 1231, and, in 1254, of a Raymond David of Pechdavid called Rossellus.[26]

---

[25] E 508 (November 1214) also published in my *Toulouse*, pp. 208-209 with a misprint and an omission: "Villamurensi" for "Villamurensis" and "apponentes quod" for "apponentes et mandantes quod."

[26] Malta 58 19 (April 1231), and Saint-Étienne 24 (30 4 unnumbered) (March 1254) "de Podiodavid qui vocatur Rossellus."

Descalquencs

The name of this family derives from the Village of Escalquens not far from Castanet to the southeast of Toulouse (see Map 7), and appears in a variety of spellings, de Escalquencs, Scalquencs, Escalquencis, Descalquenxs, Descalquenchis, etc. The first persons bearing this name are a Montarsinus and his brother Bastard. Active in town government from 1141, Bastard is seen until 1158,[1] and is probably the one who gave his name to the block in the City called the Four Bastard. Montarsinus' property was around Castanet, but in 1163/4, he donated much to the cathedral chapter and entered as a canon, his wife joining as a canoness.[2] At about the same time, a William who held lands at Escalquens entered the monastery of Saint-Sernin as a canon bringing with him property at the community for which he was named. As seen above, the family seems similar to other rural notables who owed service in town to the count or ecclesiastical institutions.[3] Mysteriously the curious name Montarsinus persisted. Not called Descalquencs, a Montarsinus was a consul for the City in 1215-1216. In 1239 a person with the same name was called "de plano Sancti Stephani," took oath to the Peace of Paris in 1243 together with a Bernard Montarsinus, and served as a consul in 1247-1248.[4]

Having for long some property at Escalquens, a family bearing the surname (but not necessarily related to that seen above) appeared in the 1180s, Peter Raymond first seen in 1180, his brother Arnold Raymond in 1186, and the last of the three brethren William Raymond in 1187 (see

---

[1] Douais, *Saint-Sernin*, No. 538 (undated) where Montarsinus and Bastard donated a serf at Saint-Sauveur toward Montaudran; E 573 (May 1141) Bastard; Douais, *Saint-Sernin*, No. 143 (November 1141) the same; Malta 5 292 i (May 1152, copied in 1230) Bastard consenting to an action of the Tolosa family; and Douais, *Saint-Sernin*, No. 104 (1158) again Bastard.

[2] G. Catel, *Mémoires de l'histoire du Languedoc* ... (Toulouse, 1633), p. 884 (March 1163 or 1164). See also *Gallia Christiana*, vol. 13, No. 29 where in March 1163 or 1164 the bishop gave the canons the tithe on Montarsinus' "honor" of Castanet defined as between the Hers river, the "strata Francisca," Auzeville and Pechabou.

[3] Douais, *Saint-Sernin*, Nos. 539 and 545 (respectively January 1162 and March 1165 or 1166) and ibid., No. 692 (March 1164 or 1165).

[4] E 65 (May 1239) as a witness. PAN, J 305 29 (February 1243).

Table 12).[5] Whatever its social origins, the most obvious claim to attention of this family was expertise in legal and political matters, in a manner not unlike that of the Bernard Peter de Cossano described above. Both William Raymond and Arnold Raymond attested copies of acts by public scribes, and were therefore known to be literate and legally expert persons in the age before the judges and lawyers were rigorously separated from the notaries.[6] All three brothers served also as arbitral judges in private courts, in that of the archdeacon of Saint-Sernin, and as agents of the consuls in these private and seigniorial courts or as members of consular public "curie jurate."[7] One or another of the brothers were consuls almost every year in the 1190s and the early 1200s.[8] The brothers exemplify with peculiar clarity the oligarchical political and legal structure of Toulouse between the defeat of the count in 1189 and the acquisition of

---

[5] See Saint-Bernard 138, fol. 61r (January 1186) Arnold Raymond; Grandselve 6 (November 1187, copied in 1227) William Raymond; ibid., 7 i (March 1186 or 1187, copied in 1237) William Raymond; PBN, MS lat. 9994, fol. 238r (April 1188) William Raymond; Malta 123 5 vi (February 1192) William Raymond and his brother Arnold Raymond; Douais, *Saint-Sernin*, No. 33 (April 1198) Arnold Raymond; A. Jouglar, "Monographie de l'abbaye de Grandselve," *Mémoires de la société archéologique du Midi de la France*, 7 (1853-1863), Proof No. 5 (November 1201) Arnold Raymond; PAN, J 318 16 (October 1208) Arnold Raymond a creditor for 390 shillings and "lucrum"; E 506 (July 1213) Arnold Raymond; Saint-Bernard 138, fol. 172r (March 1216) Peter Raymond's property; Grandselve 6 vi (June 1218, copied in 1227) sale of lots at Mossa Pisca to Arnold Descalquencs witnessed by William Raymond Descalquencs; Saint-Bernard 138, fol. 181v (May 1218) Arnold Raymond; E 472 (December 1219) Arnold Raymond; Malta 116 24 (July 1222) Arnold Raymond and Arnold; E 504 (April 1223) Arnold Raymond; Saint-Bernard 138, fols. 86v and 95r (respectively dated December 1225 and January 1226) property of William Raymond. Drowning in material, I have omitted many references, and also advise the reader that others will be found in the notes immediately below.

[6] E 508 (July 1189, copied in July 1190), the copy being attested by William Raymond; Grandselve 2 (March 1190, copied in March 1193) attested by Arnold Raymond; and E 501 i (February 1214, copied in August 1215 and 1230), that of 1215 being attested by Arnold Raymond.

[7] For November 1196 see note 8 below; for that of October 1205 note 9 ; E 510 iv (January 1207, copied in 1212 and 1214) William Raymond; E 573 (March 1225, copied in 1233) Arnold Raymond as judge in a consular court assigning property for payment of debt; and Grandselve 6 (May 1225) the same together with Raymond and Bertrand Descalquencs as witnesses.

[8] The capitulars and consuls of this line are Peter Raymond 1180-1181, 1189-1190, 1190-1191, 1192-1193, William Raymond and his brother Arnold Raymond 1193-1194, Peter Raymond 1194-1195, Peter Raymond and Arnold Raymond 1196-1197, William Raymond 1197-1198, Peter Raymond 1198-1199, Arnold Raymond 1199-1200, Peter Raymond 1201-1202, Arnold Raymond 1211-1212, Arnold Raymond 1214-1215 and 1224-1225. Peter Raymond and his brother took oath before the legates for the faith in PAN JJ 21, fol. 78r (December 1203).

consular office by a popular group or party in 1202. In 1196, one brother was a judge arbiter in the seignorial court of Saint-Sernin, another the consul assigned by the consuls to oversee the workings of that court for the benefit of the community, and the third was a consul in the same consulate that assigned his brother to Saint-Sernin's court! [9]

TABLE 12: DESCALQUENCIS

The brothers were also the first Descalquencs to show an interest in the regions to the north and northwest of the town on both sides of the Garonne river. In 1183 Peter Raymond began an association with the Caraborda in lands near Saint-Jory along the Garonne. In 1205 he served as an arbiter, and William Raymond as a witness, for a suit of the inhabitants of Seilh against the abbot of Mas Garnier (Masgrenier).[10] These busy persons disappeared during the war. Peter Raymond is not

[9] Saint-Sernin 680 (20 72 unnumbered) (November 1196) the seigniorial court of the archdeacon.

[10] Peter Raymond with the Caraborda at Saint-Jory and south in Malta 1 24 (May 1183) and PBN, MS lat. 9994, fol. 238r (April 1188). For Seilh see MADTG, A 297, fol. 821v (October 1205), the arbiter being Peter Raymond and a witness William Raymond.

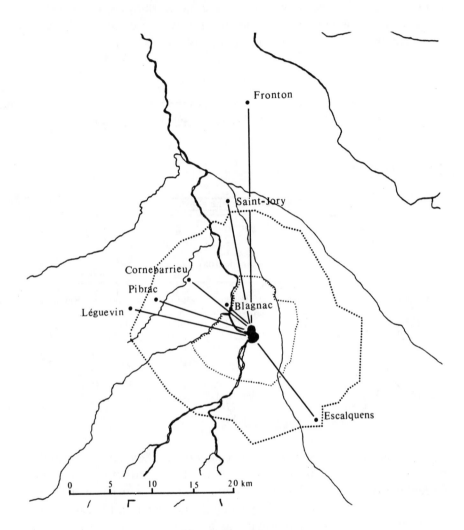

MAP 7. DESCALQUENCS

seen after 1216, Arnold Raymond after 1225, and William Raymond after 1226. Although their properties were clearly transmitted to the individuals described below, little is known about the issue of the brothers, save that Peter Raymond had a son named Raymond who twice served in the consulate in 1212-1213 and 1217-1218, and who is seen from 1190 to 1225.[11]

The successors of the three brothers (and probably of Raymond as well) were an Arnold and a Bertrand. First seen in 1218, Arnold was several times a consul during the war years, and was of sufficient presidency to be chosen to be one of the hostages sent from Toulouse to Paris in 1229.[12] He was surely a university trained jurist, being titled "jurisperitus" in 1248 and 1251.[13] He served as an executor of the will of Bertrand Descalquencs, mentioned above and described below, in which document he was called "probushomo" to distinguish him either from his own son Arnold or Bertrand's son of the same name.[14] Arnold "probushomo" was last seen in 1258 when he was described as one of the lords of Pibrac, a community northwest of Toulouse, a castle and village he shared with Bertrand's sons and with the lord of l'Isle-Jourdain.[15]

The "probushomo" had two sons, Arnold and William. William was probably the one of that name seen as early as 1243, was at least once

---

[11] E 508 (July 1180, copied in July 1190) which copy was attested by Raymond; PAN, J 1024 i (May 1200) as a "fideiussor"; the members of this family who were councilors for the consuls in TAM, AA 1 75 (March 1222) were Arnold, Arnold Raymond, Bertrand, and Raymond; PAN, J 330 9 (July 1222) Arnold and Raymond witnessed the count's agreement with the butchers of the City; for Raymond in May 1225 see note 7 above.

[12] For May 1218 and July 1222 see note 5 above; Arnold also attested a decision of a consular court on debts, one of whose judges was Bertrand Descalquencs in E 573 (March 1225, copied in 1233); TAM, II 92 (May 1227) Arnold; PAN, J 310 45 (April 1229), the name being garbled to "Ernaud de Calqueins"; Grandselve 7 (April 1231) a division between Arnold and Bernard Guilabertus of property ranging from Escalquencs through Belsoleil to the east of the town to Fronton far to the north; Saint-Sernin 599 (10 35 8) (July 1233); (10 35 17) first of a group of membranes tied together (July 1234); and the Descalquencs who swore to keep the Peace of Paris in PAN, J 305 29 (February 1243) were Arnold, Bertrand, and Peter Raymond Descalquencs.

[13] G. Sicard, *Aux origines des sociétés anonymes: Les moulins de Toulouse au moyen-âge* (Paris, 1953), p. 367 (September 1248), and PAN, J 311 69 (June 1251) where Arnold and his son William are listed among the "jurisperiti" being called to revoke the will of Raymond VII by his successor Alphonse of Poitiers.

[14] See the will of Bertrand Descalquencs of August 1252 in note 26 below.

[15] Grandselve 8 (January 1247); MADTG, A 297, fol. 1382r (June 1254) where Arnold and his son William are seen; Saint-Sernin 675 (19 65 7) (March 1256) Arnold and his son William; and the settlement concerning Pibrac between the lord of l'Isle-Jourdain and his co-seigniors Arnold Descalquencs, Vital Durandus, Durand de Sancto Barcio, and Peter Raymond Descalquencs the latter's brother in MADTG, A 297, fols. 890r and 892r (respectively May 1256 and May 1258).

a consul, but, far more important, was a professional jurist ("jurisperitus" or "legista") who served the consulate of his native town but especially the renascent power of the counts.[16] His possessions are infrequently mentioned but we know that he had property in the region of Saint-Michel-du-Touch.[17] He had inherited, moreover, a rent from an Aymengarda Centulla who, together with her husband, Raymond Centullus, had been condemned for Catharism in and before 1237.[18] One therefore conjectures that Aymengarda was his own, or, more likely, his father's sister. Arnold was dead by 1279 when we also hear of his deceased wife Comdors. He and his wife appeared in the list of the petitioners for the amnesty of 1279 partly because of an unknown ancestor of Comdors, partly because of Aymengarda, and perhaps because of someone unknown.[19] William's family is last seen in 1296, when we hear of his son Raymond William and his house near the tower of Ugolenus (the modern Bourse in the City).[20]

William's brother Arnold was also a jurist. Twice consul, we hear of his property at Beauzelle, not far from Pibrac, and in the town.[21] He was last seen when appointed councilor in the will of Peter Raymond, a son of Bertrand, in 1277.[22] He was dead when listed along with his brother as a petitioner for the amnesty of 1279. The man who spoke for him and for

[16] For February 1243 see note 11 above; consul 1261-1262; E 296 (May 1251) as judge for the count's court on debts; seen in the note above for June 1254 and March 1256; PAN, J 328 1 xxvii (May 1261) as "legista"; HGL, vol. 8, no. 509 v (April 1264) as "locumtenens vicarii Tholose"; E 531 ii (April 1268) where his brother Arnold purchased property and William witnessed; in the business of tax "reform" and the troubles of 1268-1269 in PBN, Doat 73, fols. 47v and 63v and, along with Arnold, in PAN, J 129 b; TAM, AA 3 128 (June 1270); TAM, II 9 (November 1270 – January 1271) as syndic for the town; and 9 (January 1274), where the brothers William and Arnold are called "cives et jurisperiti."

[17] Clares 24 (January 1266 – April 1267, copied in 1298) at Leyrac, and Daurade 157 (March 1274) with the Caraborda.

[18] Grandselve 10 (December 1262) where William gave Grandselve a rent he had been given by the deceased Aymengarda. This woman, the wife of Raymond Centullus, was condemned as relapsed in PBN, Doat 21, fol. 129v (March 1238), and her husband is described as cited in 1235 and thereafter sentenced in Pelisson, *Chronicon*, pp. 101 and 111, Raymond was No. **1** in the list of 1279 (Chapter 5, above) and his wife No. **166** (between February-September 1237).

[19] In Chapter 6, above (March 1279) the family was represented by Stephen Descalquenchis who served as executor for the heirs of the brothers William and Arnold, both dead, and Comdors deceased wife of William, and Bertrand and Raymond.

[20] E 502 (March 1297), a large house and some stores near a stone tower.

[21] Consul in 1258-1261 and 1264-1266. For September 1248 see note 13 above and for 1268-1269 and January 1274 note 16 above.

[22] For January 1274, see note 16 above, and also see note 28 below for his appearance in August 1257.

his brother at that time was a Stephen Descalquencs who was obviously a
child of one or the other brother.[23]

We now turn back to Bertrand, the contemporary of the Arnold
"probushomo" who was last seen as one of the lords of Pibrac in 1256.
Bertrand first appeared in 1222 and 1225, but thereafter we know little
about him until 1243 and his consulate of 1246-1247.[24] He had not been
idle in the meantime. He had been early sentenced for Catharism, and had
probably spent the time until 1243 in punishment and clearing his name.[25]
His testament was drawn up in 1252. We there learn that his wife was
named Aymengarda, his sister Alfavia was assigned five years of income
from goods at Pibrac, his son Arnold a property at Cornebarrieu, and his
son Peter Raymond his stone hall and great house or "albergum" in town.
The rest of the inheritance was divided among four of his sons in equal
portions, Peter Raymond, Durand de Sancto Barcio, Arnold Raymond,
and Raymond.[26] The surname Sancto Barcio for one of his sons is of
interest because the old family of that name appears to have been
extinguished in its male line around this time, and both the name and the
fief of Pibrac associated with it went over to the Descalquencs by
marriage.[27]

Arnold Raymond and Arnold vanish after 1257,[28] but Peter Raymond
and Durand lived longer. They arrranged the lordship of the castle and
town of Pibrac with l'Isle-Jourdain in 1256 and 1258,[29] and served three
consular terms in the sixties and seventies. One of these evoked a protest
that tells us that Peter Raymond had once been condemned to pilgrimage
or other penalty for heresy.[30] Peter Raymond composed his testament in

[23] See Chapter 6, above.

[24] For March 1222 see note 11 above; E 501 (March 1225, copied in 1233) as judge
for a consular court; for May 1225 note 7; Malta Garidech 1 i and ii (respectively dated
May 1233 and June 1235, copied in 1238) for Bertrand as an executor of Vital Rotbertus;
and February 1243 in note 12 above.

[25] In the list of 1279 (Chapter 5) as No. **25**, and therefore quite early.

[26] MADTG, A 297, fol. 820r (August 1252) including among his executors Arnold
Descalquencs "probushomo."

[27] Malta 1 33 (June 1253) Durand "nepos" of the dead Durand de Sancto Barcio.

[28] Malta 27 99 (August 1257, copied in 1261) attested by Arnold Descalquencs de
Cornebarillo (Cornebarrieu).

[29] For this settlement of 1256 and 1258 see note 15 above; A. Du Faur, *Pibrac*
(Toulouse, 1882), p. 33 (May 1256) an action of their brother Raymond; Malta Garidech
8 6 i (January 1260, copied in 1270) Durand witness at Cornebarrieu; Saint-Sernin 599
(10 35 22) ii (February 1269) Peter Raymond son of Bertrand; and Malta Garidech 8 19
(May 1270) Durand.

[30] Durand consul in 1264-1256 and 1275-1276, Peter Raymond in 1270-1271. PAN,
J 318 107 (undated) claimed that the consuls Peter Raymond and Aimeric de Roaxio had
been "crucesignati," and it is true that both were consuls in 1270-1271.

1277, at which were present numerous relatives, especially his son and heir Bertrand and his brothers Durand de Sancto Barcio and Raymond Descalquencs as well as the "legista" Arnold.[31] In 1279 his son Bertrand and brother Raymond were petitioners for the amnesty of heretical inheritances, and Bertrand and his two uncles, Durand de Sancto Barcio and Raymond, confessed in 1281 that they held the village of Léguevin in fee of l'Isle-Jourdain.[32]

A careful reader of the notes of this family's history will have noticed that there are members of this family whose history has not been traced. Among these was the "frater" Raymond de Eschalquenchis, "gardianus" of the Franciscans of Toulouse in 1273.[33] There is also evidence of a modest artisan family bearing this surname.[34]

Derived from the community south of Toulouse that gave them their name and possibly also from the service family of Montarsinus and Bastard, the main line of the Descalquencs entered vigorously into the political life of the town in the 1190s and began to acquire lands and interests to the west and north of the town at about that time. Although dyed by Catharism, the thirteenth-century family flourished, producing jurists, lords of Pibrac and Léguevin, and landlords of no mean wealth. The family was able to change from being exemplars of the oligarchical republicanism of the 1190s with its amateur jurisprudence to becoming professional jurists often seen in the service of the prince. No member of this family, at once burgher and seigniorial, is known to have been titled knight in the period discussed.

---

[31] MADTG, A 297, fol. 877v (May 1277). Restoring usury, the testator made his son and heir the only executor, with his two uncles and Arnold "legista" as "consiliarii." Two Peters were among the witnesses, one being Peter Descalquenquis de Pibraco.

[32] MADTG, A 297, fol. 886r (April 1281).

[33] PAN, J 324 6 xi (November 1273), surely a member of this big family because he was a "consiliarius" of the will of a rich Brugariis.

[34] Malta 15 114 a series of acts on the same parchment recording the acquisition of a small lot by an Arnold in November 1222, and the sale of the same by Arnold's daughter Sibilia with the consent of her widowed mother Aycelina in March 1230. In Malta 15 133 iii (January 1243, copied in 1253) Sibilia's brother William concurred in the sale. In TAM, II 49 (dated to the 1250s) a William Descalquencs "carpentarius" was involved in the mills and lived in the Bazacle area.

Embrinus

The family begins with an Embrinus (Aibrinus, Ibrinus, Embry) and a
Peter Embrinus. The former is seen from 1183 to 1196, served as a
chapterman for the count in 1183-1184, and acquired property just to the
north of the Bourg.[1] More important for us is the Peter Embrinus, son of a
quondam Peter (see Table 13). First seen in 1183, he was thrice a consul
during the 1190s and, in 1203, we learn that he was married to Oliva.[2] He
surely lived until 1207 and perhaps longer.[3] Peter and Oliva had four
sons, Embrinus, Peter, Arnold and William. Nothing is known about
William save that he existed.[4] Arnold is also a very shadowy figure. He
was, together with his two brothers Embrinus and Peter, a councilor of
the consuls in 1222.[5] He is seen in 1224 again, and is said to have
"adored" a Cathar "perfectus" around 1228. It is conceivably a scribal slip
that recorded the name of the sentenced heretic as Raymond in 1237,[6]
because Arnold's "hereditas" is listed among those of the deceased Cathars
amnestied in 1279.[7]

---

[1] Grandselve 58 Roll II verso iii (November 1183) Abrinus lord consent to a sale by
Peter Aibrannus, son of Peter Aibrannus; Saint-Sernin 674 (19 63 12) (February 1195,
copied in 1258 and 1260) at Colombier Beroart as "pignus" holder; and Saint-Bernard
138, fol. 54v (February 1196) Ser Saint-Quentin.

[2] Consul in 1194-1195, 1197-1198, and 1199-1200; in November 1183 as in above
note; Grandselve 1 iii (July 1197) a partner of Bernard de Capitedenario; E 538
(November 1198) the same; Saint-Sernin 599 (10 35 16) 3rd of a group of membranes tied
together (January 1200); E 538 and Saint-Bernard 138, fol. 25r (April 1203) a sale by Peter
and wife Oliva of arable and a vineyard in the close of Saint-Sernin outside of town.

[3] E 575 (April 1205) pledge with Bernard Peter de Cossano of arable "in feodo de
macellis"; Grandselve 4 (May 1206); and Malta 15 110 (April 1207) as landlord of a house
with a stone hall, tower, a bakery, etc. in the Daurade area (for which see the act of March
1224 in note 6 below). Which of the two Peters, the father or the son, was consul in 1212-
1213 and again in 1217-1218 is impossible to say, but one leans to this Peter.

[4] Saint-Sernin 600 (10 35 12) (January and March 1244) which deals with the "curia"
of Castillon which William once held. See the discussion about this farm below.

[5] TAM, AA 1 75 (March 1222) where Embrinus, Peter and Arnold all served as
advisors and were described as brothers.

[6] Malta 15 115 (March 1224) as heir to the property owned by his father in April 1207
in note 3 above; PBN, Doat 23, fol. 293v recording the "adoration" in testimony of 1243;
and ibid., 21, fol. 145r, and especially fol. 146v (July 1237) where a Raymond is recorded
as excommunicated, hence as having fled.

[7] The Embrini in the amnesty of 1279 (Chapter 5) are Peter No. **59**, Bernard No. **60**,
Arnold No. **108**, and Embrinus No. **112**.

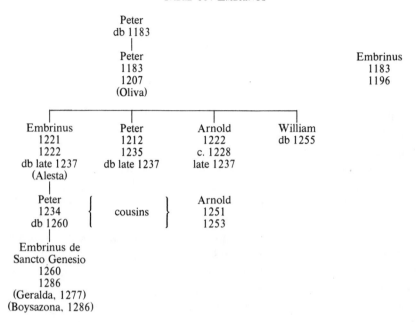

TABLE 13: EMBRINUS

More is known about the two other brothers. Possibly consul in 1212-1213, certainly councilor in 1222, we hear of Peter in 1225 and again as a consul in 1235.[8] His term in office was certainly brief because he had died before 1237 when, with his deceased brother Embrinus and his mother Oliva, he was condemned for Catharism. We know nothing about his children, if he had any. Peter's brother Embrinus was also sentenced for this divergent belief, and so was his wife Alesta.[9] Embrinus had a son, however, named Peter, who is first seen in 1243 and was dead by 1260.[10] His property in the "curia" of Estaquebiou in Saint-Geniès is seen in 1245,[11] and we know that he alienated his "villa" of Launac (Launaguet) to the count in 1249 probably in order to buy off that prince into whose

---

[8] Douais, *Paléographie*, No. 19 (March 1225) where we hear that he or his father had been the "fideiussor" for the weighty debts of the notable Jordan de Villanova.

[9] Pelisson, *Chronicon*, p. 110 mentions Embrinus "maior," his wife Alesta, his brother Peter, and Oliva their mother as all dead and disinterred. For Oliva in April 1203 see note 2 above. Embrinus is also seen in Saint-Bernard 138, fol. 81v (June 1221).

[10] PAN, J 305 29 (February 1243) the oath for the Peace of Paris, and Grandselve 11 (June 1260) with goods at Negaport near Aurival and Le Buguet owned by Embrinus, son of the deceased Peter Embrinus.

[11] Malta 123 15 (April 1245, copied in 1252) a farm shared with Stephen Curtasolea.

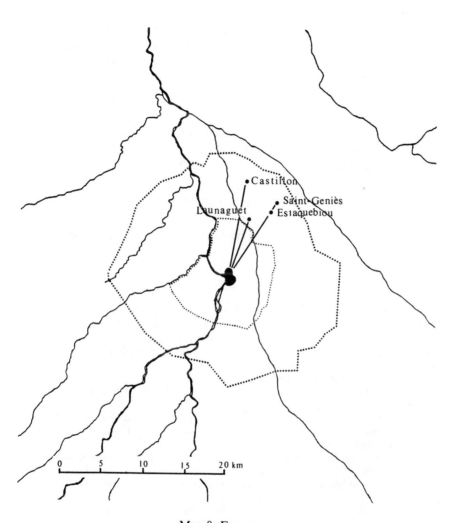

MAP 8. EMBRINUS

"incursus" his father's "hereditas" had fallen.[12] In 1255 he acquired the "curia" or farm of Castillon.[13] This transaction is of some interest. The price of this farm was 5000 shillings. He had raised this money by selling the large family house with its stone halls, tower, etc. located adjacent to similar Maurandi property on the edge of the Close of Saint-Sernin for 6600 shillings. The farm had once been willed to William, a son of his grandfather Peter. The purchaser of this town house was his cousin Arnold who is seen in the 1250s but whose father cannot be identified.[14]

Peter was dead by 1260 when we hear of his son Embrinus who was sometimes appropriately called "de Sancto Genesio" (Saint-Geniès). He was seen with his first wife Geralda in 1277,[15] and, in 1279, was one of the petitioners for the amnesty of that year.[16] We see him again in 1285 and 1286 with his second wife Boysazona.[17]

Two other persons bearing this surname were involved in the petition of 1279, a proctor named Peter and a William.[18] William was the son of a Bernard Embrinus who was dead by 1266 and who had been condemned for heresy at some time in the past.[19]

---

[12] PAN, JJ 19, fol. 148r (March 1249) described as Peter, son of Embrinus and grandson of Peter Embrinus. See also PAN, JJ 24A 2, No. 46, fol. 6 (March 1260 or 1261 – the date is unclear) where the count allowed the Franciscans his claim for the "incursus" on the house Peter Embrinus sold them, a house in the Bourg, once owned by his father Embrinus, the Cathar "credens."

[13] The act of January and March 1255 in note 4 above.

[14] E 286 (May 1251) as witness, and Grandselve 9 (October 1253) as witness with Peter Embrinus his cousin.

[15] For June 1260 see note 10 above, and Malta 123 19 second of 5 membranes tied together (November 1277) Embrinus, son of Peter, and his wife Geralda.

[16] See the Embrini in March 1279 listed in note 18 below.

[17] Malta 123 19 first and fifth of 5 membranes tied together (respectively dated November 1285 and June 1286) where Embrinus de Sancto Genesio is called son of the deceased Peter and his wife's name is given as naBoysazo and "domina" Boysazona.

[18] See the list in Chapter 6 (March 1279) for Embrinus, son of the dead Peter, Peter Embrinus the proctor, and William, son of the deceased Bernard Embrinus.

[19] Grandselve 15 i (October 1266, copied in 1298) where William is described as the son of the dead Bernard. For Bernard see his name in note 7 above.

Gamevilla

The first person listed to bear this surname and certainly deriving from the area of Saint-Orens-de-Gameville just to the south of Toulouse was a Bernard who is seen in the charters from 1158 or 1159 to 1165. At that latter date, he shows himself to be a man of worth because he served as an arbitral judge in a case involving notables of the town and especially a Peter de Tolosa.[1] Next to bear this surname are Pons and William. The former was a member of the town chapter from circa 1180 to 1184, and the latter was a consul in 1194-1195.[2] That the two were closely related to each other and to the Bernard who preceded them is shown when, in 1187/8, they together witnessed the division of the property of the daughters of Peter de Tolosa.[3] Little else is known about these persons. William is seen again in 1207, but it is not likely that he was the one of this name who was among the councilors of the consuls in 1222.[4] Pons is probably the Gameville whose wife Aurimunda had commerce with the Cathars around 1220, and who was himself described as alive and a "credens" by Pelisson in 1236.[5] If we presume that he remarried, it may have been our Pons who, in his sixties, was sentenced as a relapsed heretic

[1] Saint-Bernard 36 ii (March 1158 or 1159, copied in 1205) as a witness with Adalbert de Villanova; PAN, J 321 6 (January 1159) witness near Castanet; PAN, J 304 ii (February 1166) marriage of Raymond de Valberald (Belberaud near Gameville); PAN, J 320 4 (March 1175); and Malta 1 9 (August 1165) case of the son of Peter de Tolosa with two of the four arbiters being Bernard de Gameville and Adalbert de Villanova.

[2] Pons' years in the chapter are 1177-1180, 1181-1182, and 1183-1184.

[3] Malta 3 191 (March 1187 or 1188) simply as witnesses and not identified as brothers or cousins.

[4] E 502 (December 1207, copied in 1224) sale to the Villanova (for this clan, see the family history below) witnessed by William and Raymond Aton, son of Peter de Tolosa; E 538 i (December 1207) William and Oldric de Gameville and the latter's wife Austorga; and TAM, AA 1 75 (March 1222) listing Oldric and William. This William is almost surely the William "iuvenis" who, it might be noted was last called "iuvenis" in the act of August 1212 in note 10 below. It is therefore probablye that our William had died between 1212 and 1222.

[5] TBM, MS 609, fol. 60r where a witness from Baziège reports a meeting in the house of Sicard de Gamevilla in Toulouse where Aurimunda was with the wives of Bertrand de Sancto Luppo and Castellusnovus some 30 years previously. See also Pelisson, *Chronicon*, p. 111.

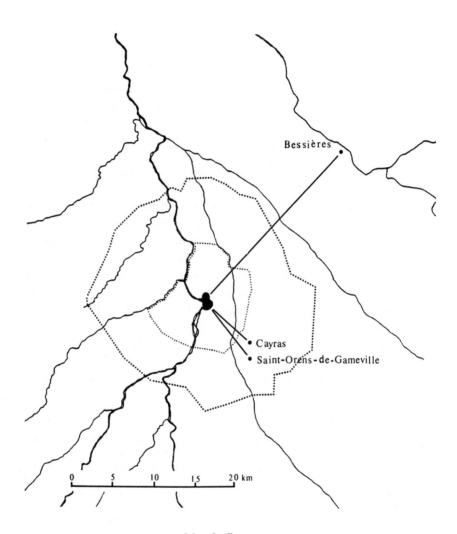

MAP 9. GAMEVILLA

in 1246 and whose wife Titborxs (Titburga in Latin) was given fifteen years imprisonment.[6]

Others bearing this surname (who were possibly children of the above and certainly close relatives) were Oldric, William "iuvenis," and Sicard. Oldric appeared first in 1206, and, in the next year, served as a coexecutor of a will together with the William de Gamevilla mentioned above. Active in the consulate during the war years,[7] Oldric several times attested acts of William "iuvenis" at the latter's seigniory at Bessières as well as a document in which William gave up property at Cayras near Gameville to a Castronovo in exchange for other property.[8] Oldric does not appear after 1241, probably for good reason: he was listed among the deceased and condemned Cathars in the amnesty of 1279.[9]

William "iuvenis" was the one who best weathered the storm. That he was related to the earlier Pons and William and to Oldric seems undoubted. Not only was he called "iuvenis" to distinguish him from the other William, but also one of his earliest appearances shows him witnessing a document concerning the heirs of Peter de Tolosa, and he was also closely associated with Oldric and a nephew named Bernard Raynald (Reginald) de Tolosa.[10] Evidence of his prestige and wealth is shown by his marriage in 1223 to the daughter of Peter Bernard de Paolaco, a rural magnate. Clara de Paolaco brought with her a principal share of the lordship of the community of Bessières to the northeast of

---

[6] Douais, *Inquisition*, 2: 2 and 6 (March 1246) where Pons was described as a "civis." The reader is cautioned that there is no way of knowing if this is our Pons, because it is equally likely that this is a Gameville of the next generation. It is also to be noted that there was a family resident at Gameville, father, son and grandson, Pons, William and Bernard, closely related to a William de Tolosa de Gomervila, of which the father and grandson were burned by the Inquisition circa 1243. This testimony was rendered by William de Gomervila, the son, and by others in TBN, MS 609, fols. 46v, 59v, and 206r. That this was a local farming family and not that with which we are dealing is shown by the fact that William shaved the "perfectus" William de Solerio for money. Doubtless our William de Gamevilla could shave someone, but he would not have taken money for it. Likewise the Pons de Gomervila seen in the testimony of William Carreira in June 1254 in TADHG, MS 124, fol. 201v is surely the farmer William.

[7] Consul in 1217-1218 and a councilor in March 1222 in note 4 above. See also Grandselve 4 (December 1206) a charter of the Carbonellus-Prinhaco family, one of whom had property at Bessières, and for December 1207 see note 4 above.

[8] For the references to Bessières and Cayras, see note 13 below, and PAN, JJ 19 39 (January 1241) as a witness.

[9] The persons bearing this surname in the amnesty (Chapter 5) are Oldric No. **111**, Fais No. **169**, her mother Blancha No. **186**, Sicard No. **190**, and Pons No. **215**.

[10] E 538 (December 1222) as "iuvenis"; ibid. (August 1212) as "iuvenis" together with an heir of Peter de Tolosa named Bernard Aton de Portaria; probably in March 1222 as in note 4 above; and, for his nephew, see November 1239 and October 1244 in note 13 below.

Toulouse on the Tarn river, including 73 "homines proprii" or dependent citizens.[11] Once the wars were over, William resided at Bessières from 1231 to 1245, a removal from town that did not prevent him acting as a citizen and serving as a consul in 1251-1252.[12] Although the powers were shared with a co-seignior named William Capel, a squire and a veteran of service with the crusaders, and with the community itself, William lived like a lord in this modest town with its castle, barbicaned gate, defensive wall, public streets, church, and hospital. His house was itself located in this town or village, and we see him there busy together with the parish priest, and having his documents drawn by the public notary of Bessières.[13] Perhaps because his family was gravely compromised by heresy, Clara and William sold the third part of their lordship to the count in 1245.[14]

This pair had three children, Bertrand, Pons and Mabriana. The two males are first seen in 1252 and last in 1262, by which time we know that their father was dead. Along with the brothers Turribus, Pons was among the defenders of Isarn Jordain in the famous litigation against his cousin german Jordan IV, lord of l'Isle-Jourdain, in 1259 and 1260, and the knightly and very rich Guy de Turribus was the husband of his sister Mabriana.[15]

---

[11] PAN, J 325 1 (April 1223), although at first the couple handed over the keys to the seigniory to the bride's uncle Gerald Bernard de Paolaco, probably because of the war.

[12] PAN, J 304 29 (February 1243) where William and Pons de Gamevilla swore to uphold the Peace of Paris.

[13] When aged, William Capelli de Vesseriis gave testimony about his service on the side of Simon de Montfort in about 1274 in PAN, J 305 32, fol. 8v. All acts listed below mention William and the vast majority are vernacular charters written by William Repolier "escrivas comunals de Vessieras" and are mostly found in PAN, J 325 (hereafter in this note referred to by the sigla #) # 6 (February 1231) attested by Sicard de Tolosa; # 9 (December 1235) citing "la porta de Veseiras e la barbacana"; # 11 (June 1237) act rendered in Latin at Toulouse witnessed by Bernard Raynald nephew of William; # 3 and # 4 (April 1237) charter of testimony written on order of the "prohoms" of Bessières; # 19 (March 1239) attested by Noaldric de Gamevilla; # 23 and # 24 of same date, mentioning the "portal," "paret," and the "careira comunal" of the town; E 65 (May 1239) Latin charter from Toulouse about Cayras witnessed by Oldric; # 29 (November 1239) attested by Bernard Raynald de Tolosa; PAN, J 330 26 (January 1241) written by the notary public of Montastruc-la-Conseillière; # 30 (January 1241) the hospital of Bessières; # 40 (October 1243) with the parish priest before "la gleia de S. Prim e de S. Clar"; # 20 (October 1244) "la paret del castel de Veseiras"; # 46 (October 1244) Raymond Raynald de Tolosa; and # 46 (November 1244) "devant la maio del sobredig seinor W. de Gamevila."

[14] PAN, JJ 19, fol. 61r (January 1255).

[15] Malta 27 69 (January 1251) the two brothers; PBN, MS new acq. lat. 2046 (December-April 1259 and 1260); and Malta 2 157 (January 1262, copied in 1265) the two brothers and Mabriana wife of Guy de Turribus.

To turn the clock back to Sicard, the Gameville of this name was described by Pelisson as a knight. He was also sometime named Sicard de Tolosa perhaps because he also had relationships with that family as did other Gamevilla. Heard of from about 1215, this person attended the wedding of Clara and William in 1223, and was in the retinue of the count in the early 1230s.[16] His career was blasted by the fact that he was a Cathar, and first fingered in 1235, he was sentenced in the next year or just thereafter.[17]

The list of Gamevilla Cathars includes some women whose husbands and parents cannot be identified. Active in Cathar circles around 1225, Blancha de Gamevilla and her daughter Fais were condemned when already dead in 1237.[18]

The petitioner for the amnesty in 1279 was named Sicard de Gamevilla, clearly a scion of the family. Our last glimpse of the clan shows them in the City. Still related to the Turribus, we hear of their house on the square called Montardy, owned in 1290 by a squire named Oldric, heir of the squire Bastard de Gamevilla.[19] It is worth remarking that the last name and the place are a curious reminiscence of the twelfth-century Descalquencs family described above.

To conclude, the Gamevilla family was clearly half rural and half urban. The relative infrequency of documents drawn at Toulouse argues that, although citizens and bearing the burdens of citizenship, the family largely lived on its rural properties. Although one knows nothing about this until the days of Sicard, it seems likely that the family was a knightly one.

[16] For him and his house in Toulouse around 1220 see the reference in TBM, MS 609 in note 5 above and, for him in February 1231 note 13. He is also seen as a tutor to a descendant of Peter de Tolosa in Malta 5 291 (May 1215, copied in 1218 and 1222); Malta 3 145 ii (September 1221); Malta 3 170 ii (June 1230, copied in 1235); ibid., v (November 1232); ibid., vi (June 1235); PAN, J 325 2 (February 1231) and ibid., 3 (October 1231); and Malta 5 293 (December 1233).

[17] Pelisson, *Chronicon*, pp. 101 and 111 describes him as a "credens," a knight, and as both "de Tolosa" or "de Gamevilla." PBN, Doat 21, fols. 145v and 148v (August 1237) has him excommunicated. The amnesty of August 1279 (Chapter 5) lists both Sicard de Tholosa as No. **32** and Sicard de Gamevilla as No. **190**, so he may have been burned as relapsed.

[18] TBM, MS 609, fol. 203r and PBN, Doat 21, fol. 150r (February 1237) for Fais; and Pelisson, *Chronicon*, p. 111 describes both mother and daughter as dead.

[19] Chapter 6 (March 1279) the petitioner Sicard; Malta 8 66 (June 1278) where the squire Audric de Gamevilla rented a house next that of Guy de Turribus for 10 pounds of Tours; E 502 (January 1286) the squire William de Turre rented property to Bastard de Gamevilla "domicellus"; and E 510 (April 1290, copied in 1303) rental of the same house on the square called Montarsin by William de Turre to Oldric de Gamevilla, as "domicellus," a house acquired by the latter from Bastard de Gamevilla. The "Planum de Montarsin" or "Planum Montarzinum" is the place near the northeast wall of the City later called the Pré Montardy.

Guido

In 1169 we hear of the brothers William and Raymond Guido (Table 14). Of the former, we know nothing save that he was dead by 1237, may have married Rica, and that he had a son named Arnold. Distinguished from his cousin Arnold by his title of "maior," this Arnold was an active person, being a consul in 1204-1205 and again in 1218-1220.[1] He was early spotted as a Cathar, however, and composed his testament before going to the Holy Land as his penitence in 1237. His heir was his cousin Arnold "iuvenis," but he gave a share in the mills to his cousin's sister and his house (next door to that of his cousin) to this relative's son.[2] If, as seems likely, Rica was his mother, she was also sentenced for Catharism in 1237.[3] It is also possible that Arnold survived his voyage to the east, because an Arnold de na Rica is seen in 1247.[4]

As observed above, William's brother was Raymond. Raymond was heard of in 1193 and became consul in the popular party's victory of 1202-1203. Although dead by 1228, he may have been consul in 1226-1227.[5] His heirs were an Arnold called "iuvenis" to distinguish him from his older cousin, and Bruna, the wife of Bernard Raymond de Ponte. Arnold "iuvenis" was thrice a consul, had a store in the Bourg, and was in

[1] Malta 3 114 (February 1169) mentioning both Raymond and William Guido. Arnold is called "maior" in the consular lists.

[2] Pelisson, *Chronicon*, p. 101 describes him as "vetus" and as a "credens" in 1235. Daurade 117 (March 1237, copied in 1238) where the testator, son of the quondam William, "volens ire in partibus transmarinis ratione penitentie sibi iniuncte a domino Romano apostolice sedis legato," gave the Daurade 4s 6d, his "ancilla" Brayda 25 shillings and an "archa," his grandnephew Bernard, the minor son of his cousin Arnold, son of the quondam Raymond, a house next to his cousin's, and his share in the mills constructed near the "carraria Sancti Cipriani" and the "fons Augerii" to his cousin Bruna. Arnold "maior" was listed in the amnesty as No. **16**.

[3] PBN, Doat 21, fol. 182v (September 1237) Rica mother of Arnold Guido. Which Arnold she mothered is, of course, the question. Listed in 1279 (Chapter 5) as No. **182** so between February and September 1237.

[4] Malta 17 60 ii (June 1250) where he witnessed the sale of property resulting from the will of Bernarda Guisona, for which see note 8 below. Just as people sometimes used the names of their fathers as a second name, so could they use those of their mothers, and, by that time, the name Arnold Guido had been in some sort preempted.

[5] For February 1169 see note 1 above; Malta 3 1143 (November 1193) as a creditor of a "pignus"; MADTG, A 297, fol. 472r (August 1228) Arnold, son of Raymond Guido deceased, among the creditors of 80 shillings at l'Isle-Jourdain.

the Garonne wine trade. Alive in 1255, he may have been the Arnold "probushomo" seen in 1259.[6] His son Bernard was alive in 1237 and 1243, but may have died by 1247. In that year, a close relative named Bernarda Guisona rendered her testament. Other than her daughter Stephana who was married to a glover, she gratified her nephews Raymond, son of the deceased Bernard Guido, and William Guido. Nothing more is known of William, but Raymond was a consul in 1239-1240 and again in 1249, being thrown out of office when the town rose on the news of the count's death. Raymond was dead by 1257.[7]

TABLE 14: GUIDO

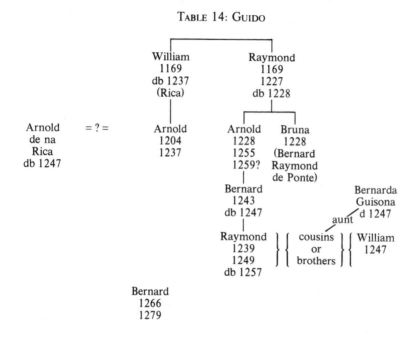

[6] Called "iuvenis," consul in 1217-1218 and 1225-1226; as only Arnold at the oath to the Peace of Paris in 1243 and consul in 1248-1249; TAM, AA 6 129 (January 1225) Arnold "iuvenis"; August 1228 in note 5 above; PBN, MS lat. 9189, fol. 241va (August 1229) as "iuvenis"; Clares 24 unnumbered (May 1235) as "iuvenis"; March 1237 in note 2 above with his sister Bruna; Daurade 117 (March 1239) as among the Barravi (had he married one?) with rights on the New Bridge; Malta 9 139 (February 1245); *Calendar of the Patent Rolls*: Henry III, p. 456 (July 1245) as a burgess of Toulouse owing money to two burghers of Castelsarrasin; Malta 9 139 (January 1254) the same property mentioned under February 1245 above; Blanc, *Jacme Olivier* (May 1255) witnesses Nos. 11 and 12 report on his "operatorium" in the Bourg; Clares 24 unnumbered (January 1257, copied in 1259) "junior" as a witness; and TAM, II 61 (March 1259) Arnold Guido "probushomo," implying another "iuvenis."

[7] Bernard was a minor (below 25 years) in 1237, but in PAN, J 305 29 (February 1243) took oath to the Peace of Paris together with his father and his own son Raymond. Bernarda's will is in Malta 17 60 i (November 1247, copied in 1250). Note also property once owned by Raymond in Grandselve 9 (September 1257).

Although several later Guido were possibly members of this family,[8] the only certain member of the clan is a Bernard who is seen in 1266, 1270 and 1271, and who, coming from the Borguet-Nau, was a petitioner for the amnesty in 1279.[9] In 1285, also, we hear of the brothers Bernard and William Guido, members almost surely of the same line.[10]

[8] A consul Arnold in 1269-1270, and along with Bernard Guido, Raymond Guido a "confrater" of the confraternity of Saint-Sernin in Saint-Sernin 626 (14 13 14 and 15) (dates respectively March 1270 and May 1271).

[9] Clares 24 unnumbered (June 1266-April 1267, copied in 1298) where he served as a proctor; ibid., 25 unnumbered i (May 1268, copied in 1292); for 1270 and 1271 see the note above; and chapter 6 (March 1279).

[10] Clares 24 unnumbered (November 1285). Since the documents about the later history of this family all derive from the same archival collection, it is probable that we are dealing with descendants of the earlier Guido.

Maurandus

Although the earliest Maurandi appear early in the twelfth century and are connected to Saint-Sernin,[1] the first of this name to appear regularly in the charters was Bonmacip (Bonus Mancipius or Bonus Puer, i.e., Good Servant or Good Slave) Maurandus. In 1141 and again in 1147, Bonmacip served as a member of the count's chapter, the institutional predecessor of the later consulate. Seen until 1162,[2] Bonmacip was the father of the Peter Maurandus (see Table 15), who abjured Catharism in 1178 and also of another son named Maurandus, founder of a collateral line of the family whose history will be traced after that of the main line deriving from Peter.

A leader, witness, and participant of the mission of 1178, the Abbot Henry of Clairvaux remarked that Peter was "aetate grandaevus" at the time of his trial before the missionaries. This is surely so because Peter, having already attained his majority, served as a witness to a document in 1143 or 1144 together with his father. It may also be that, as Henry implied, Peter was a Cathar "perfectus," one of the higher and priestly order of this religion whose members were forbidden to shed blood, take oaths, and other things required in ordinary civil life. If that is the case, he probably never served in the court's court and later consulate, the Peter seen there being his son named Peter.[3] For this history, see Chapter One above.

Following the condemnation and confession of faith in 1178, it is uncertain if Peter went to the Holy Land according to the terms of his penance. If he did, he probably returned to Toulouse, and there acquired

[1] Douais, *Saint-Sernin*, No. 286 (approximately 1106) Maurannus and William Maurannus witnessed the return of the archdeaconry of Villelongue to the house. An initial sketch of the Maurand family is to be seen in my "Une famille Cathare: Les Maurand," *Annales: ESC* (1974) 1211-1223, which is here corrected and enlarged.

[2] Saint-Sernin 600 (10 36 5) (November 1135); Malta 123 4 (July 1141); PBN, MS lat. 9189, fol. 243ra (March 1143 or 1144) Bonmacip and his son Peter; Grandselve 1 (January 1151) Bonmacip and his son Peter; Saint-Sernin 599 (10 35 1) (August 1165, copied in 1181 and 1234) where Maurandus, son of Bonmacip, had property adjacent to that of Bonmacip and Peter Maurandus.

[3] For Henry, see his *Gesta* (Rolls Series 49) 1: 215. Peter could have been a chapterman in 1183-1184, however, and converted thereafter.

TABLE 15: MORANDUS – LINE OF PETER MORANDUS

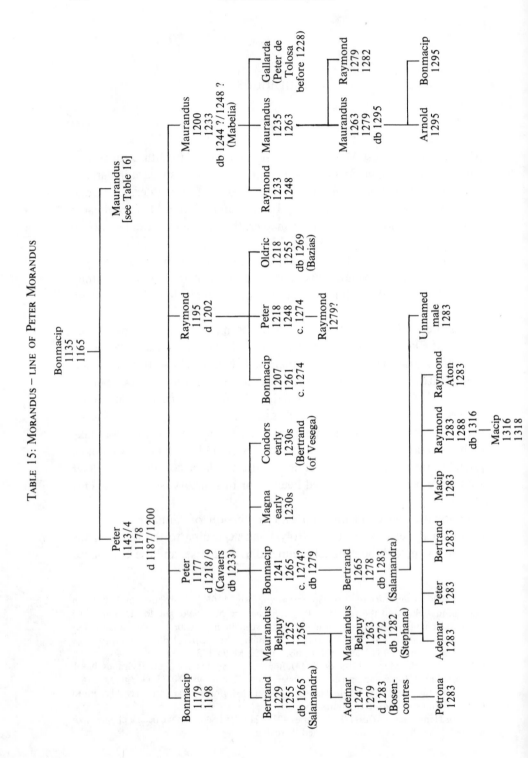

properties in the fief or "bovaria" of Valségur, especially from other Maurandi, in 1187.[4] The first sure evidence of his death is from 1210 when his son Maurandus confirmed Saint-Sernin's possession of the tithes and property mentioned in an earlier settlement of 1179 where Peter Maurandus and his sons Bonmacip and Peter, acting for themselves and their brothers, surrendered the tithes of Valségur, Launac, and Castillon to the canons.[5] It is likely, however, that the old Peter had died before 1204. In 1228 a consular court declared that his son Maurandus had held the fief of Valségur for at least 25 years.[6] It seems sure that Maurandus' capacity to act concerning Valségur without his brothers had resulted from a division of the parental inheritance among the siblings. Peter had probably died even earlier. His son Maurandus acted alone in acquiring rights at Valségur in 1202, and, even before that, his three sons Peter, Raymond and Maurandus were jointly held responsible for some rents there in 1200.[7] It is therefore probable that Peter died sometime between 1187 and 1200, and that his inheritance was divided among his sons, giving Valségur to Maurandus sometime beween 1200 and 1202 or, at the latest, by 1204.

Peter's eldest son Bonmacip appears in the charter containing the settlement about tithes with Saint-Sernin in 1179, and only once again in 1198. He had probably died by 1200, although there is a chance that 1219 is a better date. As stated above, his brothers Peter, Raymond and Maurandus had been held jointly responsible for rents in 1200, and Bonmacip was not mentioned in the charter. Guessing that the brothers had not yet divided their parental inheritance, this implies that Bonmacip had died. Certainly, he was gone by 1219. Properties once owned by him were mentioned as adjacent to other lots owned by his siblings in 1219.[8]

---

[4] Saint-Sernin 599 (10 35 16) 5th of 6 membranes tied together ii (February 1187) where property was sold to "Petro Maurando et suis filiis." This could have, of course, referred to his son Peter.

[5] Dated 3 January 1179 two originals are in Saint-Sernin 594 (10 32 4) and 599 (10 35 2), one published in Douais, *Saint-Sernin*, No. 688. The act was dated by the "conscriptio" and not by the "actio." In Saint-Sernin 599 (10 35 2) 3rd of 3 membranes tied together (March 1210), Maurandus repeated the cessions earlier made by his father and two older brothers, Peter having held them "ad diem sui obitus."

[6] Saint-Sernin 599 (10 35 4) (February 1228).

[7] Saint-Sernin 599 (10 35 16) 5th of 6 membranes tied together iv (January 1200) and v (April 1202).

[8] Saint-Sernin 599 (10 35 16) 5th of 6 membranes tied together ii (February 1187) records a sale by Stephen Maurandus, son of Maurandus, to Peter Maurandus and his sons; Malta 123 5 iv (March 1198, copied in 1225 and 1234); and Saint-Bernard 138, fol. 174v (April 1219). Note also that, in the acts of the 1230s contained in "liasse" 599 of Saint-Sernin, Maurandus "vetus" was often called "Maurandus filius Petri Maurandi," but

The second son of the Peter of 1178 was also named Peter. He appears to have been the workhorse of the family. He served as a member of the count's court and as a consul five times from 1183 to 1215.[9] He was the principal guardian of his deceased brother Raymond's sons from 1202 through 1207. He shared this chore with his younger brother Maurandus and with two brothers of the Curtasolea family, John and Stephen seen above. Peter also lent money in partnership with yet another Curtasolea brother, Peter Raymond.[10] He died sometime in 1218 or early 1219, and his wife Cavaers was gone by 1233.[11]

Raymond, the third son of the Peter Maurandus of 1178, was active in business in 1195, and probably a consul in two annual terms from 1197 to 1200. He died between September and December of 1202, leaving his sons, who were minors, in the charge of his brothers Peter and Maurandus and the two brothers of the Curtasolea family, as has been noted above.[12]

The remaining son is the Maurandus who lost the "bovaria" or "forcia" of Valségur. He served as a guardian for his brother Raymond's children after that sibling's death in 1202 and also as an executor of his will. Maurandus also acquired rents at Valségur from the Tolosa family in

---

nearly as often "Maurandus frater Petri Maurandi." One referred to his father and the other to his brother.

[9] Putting aside the term 1183-1184, he was surely consul in 1192-1193, 1198-1199, 1201-1202, and 1214-1215, although the latter term may have been that of his brother Raymond's son named Peter.

[10] Grandselve 2 iii (February 1203, copied in 1205) Peter and John Curtasolea act "post mortem Raimundi Maurandi"; Saint-Sernin 599 (10 35 16) 5th of 6 membranes tied together vi (March 1204) again Peter and John Curtasolea with Maurandus and Stephen Curtasolea "qui sunt domini predicti honoris pro bailia filiorum Ramundi Maurandi qui fuit"; PAN, J 327 1 i (October 1205 with "conscriptio" dated April 1206) Peter and John Curtasolea about Cépet; Saint-Bernard 138, fol. 7r (December 1207); and Malta 58 unnumbered (January 1211) where the Hospitalers paid a debt of 850 shillings owed to Peter and Peter Raymond Curtasolea.

[11] Saint-Bernard 138, fol. 186v (May 1218) Peter's property; and ibid., fol. 173v (April 1219) property once of Peter. Several charters of the 1230s listing his brother Maurandus' debts mention Peter as a "fideiussor," and this may lead some to think that Peter was still alive. I discount this because the notaries were describing instruments and not persons. One such charter in Saint-Sernin 599 (10 35 10) (November 1233) records the claims of two sons of a dead father to debts worth 200 shillings in these words: "quod Maurandus frater Petri Maurandi Vitali Geraldo eorum patri debet et de quibus Petrus Maurandus est ei debitor et donator sicut in cartis illorum debitorum quas Poncius Arnaldus [notarius publicus] scripsit continetur." Ibid., 599 (10 36 6) ii (November 1233) where Cavaers is recorded as dead.

[12] Grandselve 2 ii (December 1195, copied in 1205). He was alive in Saint-Sernin 599 (10 35 16) 5th of 6 membranes tied together and TAM, AA 1 42 (respectively April and September 1202), but dead in Grandselve 2 iii (December 1202, coped in 1205).

1202.[13] He was called "vetus" and "senex" in Pelisson's chronicle, which also names his sons Maurandus and Raymond "luscus" (one-eyed), and asserts that their father was a "perfectus." [14] Unless, as is likely, it was his nephew Maurandus de Bellopodio, he may have been the Moranz listed among the nineteen notables who were sent as hostages to Paris in 1229.[15] Pelisson also lists him as burned after the fall of Montségur in 1244, but, if so, his sons were not yet sure of it when almost all the sons of all three brothers, himself included, surrendered their rights in Cépet in 1248.[16]

The members of the next generation may start with Bertrand, Peter's oldest son (grandson of the Peter of 1178). Bertrand is seen from 1229, was a lord of Castelmaurou, and was dead by 1265, leaving a wife named Salamandra.[17] His brother Maurandus de Bellopodio (lord of Beaupuy or Belpech) [18] – called so to distinguish him from his uncle Maurandus de Vallesecura or "vetus" and also from Maurandus "iuvenis," the "vetus'" son – was a consul in 1235-1238 and 1251-1252, and also a merchant who boasted among his debtors the king of England.[19] Peter's third son,

---

[13] See the document of April 1202 in note 7 above.

[14] *Chronica*, pp. 101, 104-105, and 111. The first reference describes him as a "credens," the second narrates the attempted arrest at his house and his sons' attack on the Inquisitors, and the last reports that he had become a "perfectus," and mentions that many of the persons among whom he was listed were burned at Montségur.

[15] PAN, J 310 45 (April 1229).

[16] PAN, J 330 26 ii (January 1248) wherein Bertrand and Maurandus de Pulchropodio for their dead father Peter and themselves, and Bonmacip and his brothers Oldric and Peter Maurandus for their deceased father Raymond and for themselves, and Maurandus and his sibling Raymond Maurandus for themselves and their father Maurandus, not described as dead, surrender their rights in Cépet.

[17] Malta 123 1 14 i and ii (November 1229) Bertrand a witness; Saint-Sernin 699 (10 36 6) ii (November 1233) Bertrand and Maurandus, sons of Peter and Cavaers, and their uncle Maurandus "vetus"; Malta Garidech 1 (1 1) (November 1237) Bertrand at Castelmaurou; Archdiocese 793 (Register), fols. 45r-51v (November 1247) mentioning properties of Bertrand, his presumed daughter "domina" Magna, and the bishop at Castelmaurou, Granhague, Belsoleil, those of Maurandus de Bellopodio (Pulchropodio) at Belsoleil, and witnessed by Bonmacip Maurandus "maior," Maurandus de Bellopodio, Maurandus son of the quondam Maurandus, Oldric Maurandus, Ademar Maurandus, and Bonmacip Maurandus "junior"; January 1248 in note 16 above; Blanc, *Jacme Olivier* (May 1255) where witness No. 2 speaks of Bertrand's "operatorium"; Malta Garidech 1 (1 4) (September 1265, copied in 1272) Bonuspuer, son of the dead Peter, and Bertrand his son surrender claim to goods of his deceased brother Bertrand with the consent of Bertrand's widow Salamandra, attested by Ademar Maurandus. Salamandra is spelled variously, see, for example, Scalamandria in note 34 below.

[18] Variously called Pulchropodio, Pulchrovidere, and Belpech.

[19] E 531 (March 1225, copied in 1233) judge on a consular "curia jurata"; Saint-Sernin 599 (10 35 17) 8th and 9th membranes tied together (respectively November 1233 and December 1234) listing Maurandus "vetus," Bertrand, and Maurandus de Bellopodio at Valségur; November 1247 in note 17 above; *Calendar of the Patent Rolls*: Henry III, pp. 296, 405, and 412, (respectively November 1253 and March and June 1244) involving a debt of 1080 marks for wine to Maurandus and his partner.

Bonmacip, was condemned to pilgrimage for heresy in 1241,[20] but was back in circulation by 1243. Thereafter he was seen especially at Garidech until 1265 where, in spite of his past, he and his son Bertrand entered into violent litigation with the Hospitalers. The testimony for the arbitration that eventually settled the matter tells that an Hospitaler party of fourteen horse was charged by Bonmacip and his son Bertrand with their retinue, the latter shouting against the "capellanus" "ad carnem, moriatur, moriatur!" Lances, crossbows, and helmets were employed in this small war.[21] Peter also had two daughters. Inquisitorial notes about the early 1230s mention him, his sons Maurandus (de Bellopodio) and Bonmacip, and his daughters Magna and Condors, the latter the wife of Bertrand, a lord of Baziège.[22]

Raymond's children were minors at his death. His eldest son Bonmacip remained under guardianship until at least 1207, but had surely reached majority by 1218 when he spoke for his brothers.[23] In 1222, he and his brother Peter acted "for all their brothers." [24] Their only known brother was an Oldric, who was a consul in 1235-1238, had a farm at Valségur in 1246, and was dead by 1266, when we see his widow Bazias.[25]

The two Bonmacips mentioned above are hard to distinguish. Both were listed among those who swore to uphold the Peace of Paris in 1243, and both, one called "maior" and the other "junior," appeared in November 1247.[26] Since the Bonmacip who was the son of Raymond was

[20] PBN, Doat 21, fol. 178v (September 1241) pilgrimage to Rocamadour, Vienne, Saint-Gilles, twice to Saint-Dénis, Le Puy, and Vezelay, and visits to all parish churches of Toulouse the first Sunday of each month, etc.

[21] Malta Garidech 1 (1 6) (dated 1244) his property there; as Bonmacip "maior" in November 1247 in note 17 above; PAN, J 328 1 xii (October 1252); Archdiocese 793 (Register), fol. 51v (May 1258) called Bonmacip "maior"; Malta Garidech 1 (1 5) (July 1264) his property; ibid., 8 (August 1265) where mention is made of the dead Peter, his son Bonmacip, and the latter's son Bertrand.

[22] Testimony about the early 1230s in TBM, MS 609, fols. 58v, 111r and 197v mentioning all the above people together with Maurandus "maior." Note Magna in November 1247 in note 17 above.

[23] For the minority of these children, see note 10 above, and also Saint-Bernard 138, fol. 7r (May 1218).

[24] Saint-Bernard 138, fol. 8r (April 1222) and E 573 (March 1225, copied in 1233).

[25] PAN, JJ 19 45 (April 1243) where the cousins Maurandus de Bellopodio and Raymond's son Oldric served as executors for Bernard William de Brugariis; Oldric was a witness in November 1247 in the act in note 17 above; Clares 24 (January 1266-April 1267, copied in 1298) where the instrument states that Bazias was the sister of a quondam Gerald Arnaldus, and was witnessed by Raymond Maurandus, son of Peter Maurandus.

[26] PAN, J 305 24 (February 1243) includes seven Maurandi: Bertrand, the two Bonmacips, Maurandus "iuvenis" (the son of "vetus"), Maurandus de Bellopodio, Oldric, and Peter. Raymond "luscus" was the only member of this generation not included. For November 1247, see note 17 above.

older, he was probably the one who served in a consular "curia jurata" in 1224, and was termed "maior" and "probushomo" in 1258 and 1261.[27] Raymond's son also had property at Castillon, Le Fossat, and Verfeil, and probably also a farm at Valségur.[28] Owing to the other Bonmacip's history of heresy, it is likely that Raymond's son was the consul in 1238-1239, possibly again in 1246-1247, and was one of the commissioners for Count Raymond vii's testament.[29] But it cannot be determined which Bonmacip was the person who, at about seventy years of age, testified about the history of his town around 1274. Equally aged, another witness was Peter, presumably the son of the Raymond mentioned in the paragraph above.[30]

Maurandus "vetus'" sons Raymond and Maurandus "iuvenis" were adults in 1235 when Pelisson describes them beating up the inquisitors who had come to arrest their father at home. Raymond "luscus," indeed, had witnessed an act of 1233 dealing with the property of Peter de Tolosa, the husband of his sister Gallarda. Gallarda had married Peter sometime before 1228. Other than in 1248, Raymond is not seen again, but Maurandus appears in 1247 (?) and 1263.[31]

Although the document of 1248 about Cépet is the last wherein we can see the whole clan assembled, the five petitioners of the amnesty of 1279 enable us to pursue the family somewhat.[32] The first is Ademar, sometimes called "de Bellopodio." A son of Maurandus de Bellopodio,

---

[27] Douais, *Paléographie*, No. 19 (May 1224) for the consular court; in note 21 above dated May 1258 he was called Bonmacip "maior"; and the Bonuspuer Maurandus "probushomo" is in Grandselve 41 (December 1261).

[28] Malta 123 113 (October 1237, copied in 1240) Le Fossat; MADTG, A 297, fol. 108v (October 1253) exchange with the bishop at Verfeil; Saint-Sernin 600 (10 36 12) (January and March 1255) Castillon property shared with his brother Oldric and cousin Bertrand; and Douais, *Documents sur Languedoc*, 2: 19-20 (September 1246) inventory of Saint-Sernin: "Et boaria de Vallesecura ... est proprietas dicti monasterii, ... excepta octava parte terrarum, que est cujusdam burgensis, scilicet Stephani C[urt]asola, et excepta boaria quam habet ibi Bonus[mancipius Mauran]di, et except boaria quam habet ibi A[ldric]us Maurandus." He was once called "Vallissecure" in Saint-Sernin 599 (10 35 13 and 14) (February 1235).

[29] For his career in the count's service, see Fournier and Guébin, eds., *Enquêtes d'Alphonse de Poitiers*, pp. xxi-xxii.

[30] PAN, J 305 32 1v and 6r.

[31] Malta 5 294 ii (June 1233) Raymond Maurandus de Suburbio; Saint-Sernin 599 (10 35 7) (November 1233) Peter de Tolosa records having received 1000 shillings for his eighth part of Valségur; PAN, J 320 48 (April 1235) Raymond; Maurandus son of the dead Maurandus in November 1247 in note 17 above; and the same person described in Grandselve 41 (February 1263). The last reference could also refer to the son of this Maurandus who was also named Maurandus, for whom see note 36 below.

[32] See the names in Chapter 6 above.

Ademar is seen from 1247, and, in 1268 is joined in the charters by his brother Maurandus de Bellopodio. This Maurandus was consul in 1271-1272 at which time he was also described as a noble of the vicarage of Toulouse, Maurandus de Bellopodio was dead by 1282, and his brother Ademar wrote his own testament in 1283.[33] Childless except for a natural daughter, Ademar's heir were his nephews. The children of his deceased cousin Bertrand, the son, that is, of the onetime Cathar Bonmacip, were gratified but left unnamed. Bertrand had been seen in 1265 and thereafter battling the Hospitalers at Garidech, and again in 1273 when we learn that his wife Salamandra was a rich and very young Villanova, and that his father Bonmacip was still alive. Bertrand last appears as a petitioner in 1279.[34] Ademar's principal heirs were his brother Maurandus de Bellopodio's six sons, Ademar, Peter, Bertrand, Macip, Raymond, and Raymond Aton.[35] Two other petitioners in 1279 were Maurandus and Raymond Maurandus, sons of the deceased Maurandus. These were the sons of Maurandus "iuvenis," son of Maurandus "vetus," the Cathar described above.[36] Dead by 1295, this final Maurandus left two sons, Arnold and Bonmacip, who are seen in that year at Verfeil.[37] The remaining petitioner was Raymond, son of Peter, presumably the son of the Peter who, as an aged man, gave testimony about 1274.[38]

As noted above, the Maurandi were unusually Cathar. Pelisson's chronicle of the Inquisition and also inquisitorial records document this

[33] November 1247 and September 1265 in note 17 above for Ademar; E 531 ii (April 1268, copied in 1268) Ademar and Maurandus de Pulchropodio as witnesses; Malta 4 233 (March 1282) property of Maurandus and wife Stephana, the latter a Tolosa woman; and Saint-Sernin 696 (22 74 2) (January 1283, copied in 1285) Ademar's will mentioning his wife Bosencontres and the others listed in the text below.

[34] For Bonmacip and his son Bertrand in August 1265 see note 21 above; MADTG, A 297, fol. 255v (July 1271) Scalamandria and her husband Bertrand dispose of her property; and PAN, J 324 6 vii (November 1273) where we see Salamandra, Bertrand, and his father Bonmacip. The wife was a cousin of the knight Pons de Villanova and younger than 25 years of age.

[35] For January 1283 see note 33 above. The nephew named Raymond Maurandus was probably the one alive in Saint-Sernin 696 (22 74 1) (dated 1288) but dead by E 599, two acts respectively of August 1316 and November 1318, where property at Flourens of Macip, son of the quondam Raymond Maurandus de Bellopodio, is mentioned.

[36] Grandselve 10 (March 1270) town property of Maurandus, son of the quondam Maurandus, and his brother Raymond; the same in Saint-Bernard 21 (April 1282, copied in 1295).

[37] E 493 (December 1295) property at Verfeil of Arnold and Bonmacip, sons of the dead Maurandus.

[38] PAN, J 305 32, fol. 6r (about 1274) where Peter was 70 or more years old when testifying. His son Raymond attested an act of January 1266-April 1267 seen in note 25 above.

fact, as does the royal amnesty of 1279.[39] These sources tell us that Maurandus "vetus," the youngest son of the Peter of 1178 was a "perfectus," and that his wife Mabelia was a relapsed heretic in 1237. A year later their two sons Maurandus "iuvenis" and Raymond "luscus" were sentenced to pilgrimage.[40] In 1241 Bonmacip, the son of Mauran-dus "vetus'" elder brother Peter, was also dispatched on pilgrimage.[41] Additionally, three deceased Maurandi were mentioned in the amnesty of 1279. The first is Bertrand, probably the eldest son of the Peter who died in 1219. The second is Oldric "pedas" (the tongue), possibly Raymond's third son. The name of the third, Mauranda, smacks of the family; she was probably the widow of Arnold de Brantalone.[42] Two wives were also listed: Bernarda, wife of Bonmacip, and another named Johanna Mauranda, a sister of the Curtasolea brothers.[43] Besides, fate added insult to injury. Whichever of the two possible Bonmacips was the consul in 1246-1247 (and it was probably Raymond's son) had the grisly duty of witnessing the condemnation of Bernarda, the wife of his cousin Bonmacip, to a life sentence for Catharism.[44]

The family also suffered economically. In 1228 the consuls ordered the "bovaria" of Valségur sold to pay Maurandus "vetus'" debts. The court estimated the value of this farm at 15,500 shillings. Maurandus' many creditors appear in the charters of "liasse" 599 of the collection of Saint-Sernin. They included his wife Mabelia for more than her "dos" and "dotalicium" of 3000 shillings, his deceased brother Peter, other Maurandi, other patricians of Toulouse, and people of the humbler

---

[39] In order of their appearance in the list (Chapter 5), they are: Maurandus "senior" No. **89**, Johanna Mauranda "soror Curtasolee" **92** (a member of that family closely related to our Maurandi and clearly married to one), Oldric **128**, Bertrand **147**, Bonmacip **153**, Mabelia wife of Maurandus de Vallesecura or "senior" **179**, Bernarda de Massos wife first of William de Massos, then of the Bonmacip Maurandus mentioned above **220**, and Mauranda wife of the quondam Arnold de Brantalo[ne] **253**.

[40] PBN, Doat 21, fols. 177v-178r (March 1237) Maurandus to go to Compostella, Le Puy, and Saint-Gilles, etc., and (April 1238) Raymond to go to Rome (40 days), Le Puy, and Saint-Gilles, but the trip to Rome was commuted because of sickness to Compostella and Rocamadour.

[41] September 1241 in note 20 above.

[42] See note 40 above. Arnold de Brantalone was a public notary who was the son of another Arnold de Brantalone, Saint-Étienne 227 (26 DA 2 50) (January 1181) Arnold a witness; PBN, MS lat. 9189, fol. 221v (December 1190) Arnold "qui manet apud crucem Baranhonis"; Malta 17 79 i (October 1203, copied in 1254) Arnold de Brantalone "iuvenis" a witness; Douais, *Paléographie*, No. 7 (July 1181, copied in November 1203 and October 1206) both copied in by the notary Arnold; E 501 i (dated 1157/8, copied in August 1207 by Arnold).

[43] See note 40 above. Which Maurandi was her husband is not known.

[44] Douais, *Inquisition*, 2: 16 and 36 (July 1246).

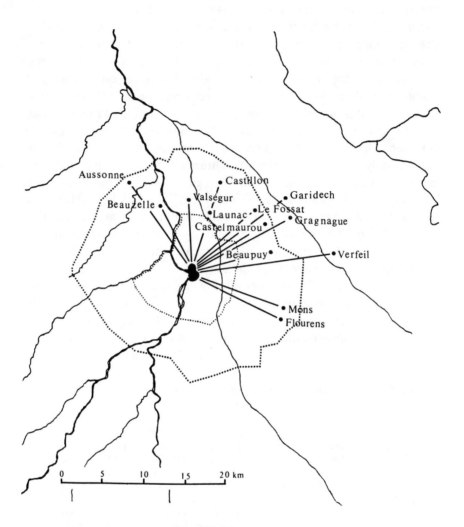

MAP 10. MAURANDUS

classes.[45] Saint-Sernin was Maurandus' beneficiary. The canons took over his debts, and our unhappy Cathar confirmed this arrangement with a formal sale of his rights at Valségur to them in 1235.[46] Interestingly, this sale occured before Maurandus was condemned for Catharism. Moreover, he had already begun to diminish his rights there sometime before 1228 by giving his daughter Gallarda one-eighth of the "forcia" as her dowry.[47]

Although there were undoubtedly difficulties, this family was anything but ruined. It ended the thirteenth century possessing very considerable properties on the left bank of the Garonne at Beauzelle and Aussonne; on the right bank to the north of the town at Launac, Castillon, and Valségur; to the north and east of town, at Le Fossat, Garidech, Verfeil, Gragnague, Beaupuy, Mons, and Flourens. In spite of Catharism, therefore, and resulting persecution, this patrician and eventually noble family had successfully weathered the storm.[48]

The original home of the Maurandus family was in, or in the region of, the Close of Saint-Sernin, although a branch later lived in the region of Cuisines.[49]

---

[45] Saint-Sernin 599 (10 35 4) (February 1228) the consuls decision; ibid., (10 35 17) 3rd of 9 membranes tied together (April 1235) concerning Mabelia; and the rest of the acts in the "liasse" 599. Note ibid., (10 35 6) ii (November 1233) where Peter has served as "fideiussor" for debts to others.

[46] Saint-Sernin 599 (10 35 6) ii and ibid., (10 35 7) first of 9 membranes tied together (November 1235).

[47] See the act of November 1233 in note 31 above. The actual marriage charter of sometime before is no longer extant.

[48] Wolff, *Estimes*, pp. 74-75 and items Nos. 4 and 700 on pp. 130 and 258 not only shows that the Maurandi were a rich family at the end of the 1200s but also that they held property at Valségur valued at 1600 pounds of Tours (16,000 shillings of Toulouse). A few references to other and later Maurand properties are: the will of January 1283 in note 33 above mentions Castillon, Flourens, Gragnague, and Mons as well as Beaupuy; MADTG, A 297, fols. 790v and 792r (both dated August 1283) acquisitions at Beauzelle and Aussonne by Arnold Maurandus de Coquinis; Saint-Sernin 599 (10 35 20) (June 1287) lots at Valségur of Stephen and Maurandus, sons of the quondam Bonmacip, and of Arnold Maurandus; E 493 (December 1295) property at Le Fossat of Arnold and Bonmacip, sons of the quondam Maurandus, with the consent of their mother and tutrix Emengardis; E 559 (May 1299) Ademar Maurandus at Flourens; and Saint-Sernin 599 (10 35 16) 2nd of membranes tied together (September 1311) Oldric, son of quondam Stephen, at Valségur.

[49] Catel, *Mémoires*, pp. 135-136 mentions a tower supposedly of the Peter Maurandus of 1178 on the emplacement of the later College of Périgord, a matter studied by Meusnier, "Collège de Périgord," *AduM* 63 (1951) 211-220. There is a good eighteenth-century map of the college and tower in the PAN, S 3253 Haute-Garonne. Grandselve 10 (June 1265) records a suit between the consuls and Grandselve over the destruction of some stores inherited by the monastery from Pons de Capitedenario describing the property as being "in loco qui dicitur claustrum Sancti Saturnini iuxta domum que fuit

TABLE 16: MAURANDUS – LINE OF MAURANDUS, BROTHER OF PETER

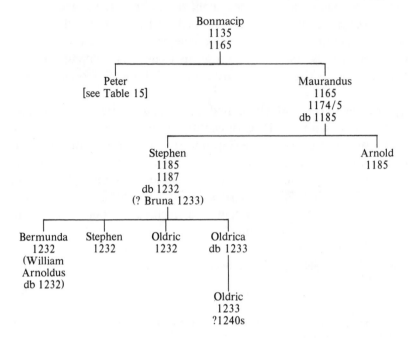

The attentive reader will perhaps remember that the Peter Maurandus of 1178 had a brother named Maurandus. Maurandus was dead by 1185 (see Table 16) when his sons Stephen and Arnold Maurandus divided his substantial holdings at Valségur, including houses with halls and towers.[50] In 1187 Stephen sold his rights there to Peter Maurandus and his sons,[51] and we know that he was dead by 1232. In that year a Bermunda, widow of William Arnaldus sold four arpents "pro recuperare suum sponsalicium et pro suis necessariis" with the consent of her brother Oldric Maurandus, the son of a deceased Stephen Maurandus, and, later in the same year, another Stephen, also a son of a Stephen, sold much at

---

quondam Aldrici Maurandi." For the Maurandi near or in Cuisines, see the acts of August 1283 in note 48 above.

[50] Saint-Sernin 599 (10 35 1) (August 1165, copied in 1181 and 1233) as the son of his father Bonmacip; Saint-Bernard 36 ii (March 1174 or 1175, copied in 1220) property on way from Pont-d'Alned to Valségur; and Saint-Sernin 599 (10 35 16) 5th of 6 membranes tied together i (November 1189) but recording the division of the inheritance four years previously.

[51] Saint-Sernin 599 (20 35 16) 5th of 5 membranes tied together ii (February 1187).

Valségur to the main line of the Maurandi.[52] One of these Stephens had a brother named Arnold who gave a substantial gift to Saint-Sernin in 1233.[53] After the death of one of these Stephens, also, the widow Bruna entered Saint-Sernin as a pensioner or canoness in 1233, together with her grandson Oldric, the child of her deceased daughter Oldrica.[54] Owing to the closeness of the dating, one cannot tell which Stephen was Bruna's husband. It is more probable than not, however, that Bruna was the wife of the Stephen first seen in 1185, and that he and she had had four children, Bermunda, Stephen, Oldric, and Oldrica. But this is guess work. At any rate, the young Oldric presumably entered Saint-Sernin as an oblate, but may have taken his vows to the Cistercians of Grandselve. An Oldric Maurandus became "cellerarius maior" of that house in the early 1240s, and is often seen in its documents.[55]

The Maurandi who drank deeply of Catharism seem to have done better than those who were orthodox.

[52] E 510 i and ii (February 1231), and Saint-Sernin 599 (10 35 17) 8th of 9 membranes tied together. The latter document was wrongly dated by the notary, but the "feria" and the day of the month work for November 1232.

[53] Saint-Sernin 599 (10 35 17) 6th of 9 membranes tied together (November 1233) where Arnold turned over a debt owed him by Maurandus "vetus" to the canons.

[54] Saint-Sernin 599 (10 34 8) (July 1233).

[55] Grandselve 8 ii (March 1243, copied in 1248) is the earliest reference.

Montibus

Surely deriving their name from the community of Mons to the east of Toulouse toward Verfeil was the family Montibus. The first of this line traceable at Toulouse are the brothers Raymond Aton de Montibus and Peter Aton, sons, it appears, of a William Aton who was perhaps the one of that name seen at Lanta and Belberaud to the south of the town (see Table 17).[1] Raymond Aton is the only brother who has left substantial traces in the instruments. He is seen from 1159 until 1183, was an arbitral judge for Saint-Sernin, and surely had interests at Verfeil.[2] His succession is not known.

The next generation of this line is constituted by two persons, nowhere stated to be related, a Bertrand de Montibus and an Aton de Montibus. Bertrand appeared in 1183 to attest an act concerning the mills of the Château Narbonnais together with the Raymond Aton mentioned above. He was several times a chapterman and consul and last appears around 1200 when he was termed "maior" to distinguish him from a junior of the same name and family.[3] His younger contemporary Aton was rather

---

[1] PAN, J 321 7 (February 1161) at Lanta, and ibid., 13 (March 1165 or 1166) at Belberaud.

[2] Douais, *Saint-Sernin*, No. 104 (February 1159) where Raymond, also called Raymond Aton de Montibus, and his brother Peter Aton had property at Saint-Sauveur on the Girou river; Malta 178 1 (April 1168) at Verfeil Raymond Aton son of William Aton; Malta 1 63 (April 1172) the brothers Raymond Aton and Peter Aton; Douais, *Saint-Sernin*, Appendix No. 68 (March 1173 or 1174) Raymond Aton as arbiter in a case between Saint-Sernin and a notable from Verfeil; Malta 135 121 (June 1174) a canon Peter Raymond de Montibus and Raymond Aton were witnesses; PAN, J 328 1 viii (February 1175) Raymond Aton; Douais, *Saint-Sernin*, No. 690 (May 1177) Raymond Aton as arbiter between the Surdi and Saint-Sernin; Malta 13 58 (July 1183) Raymond Aton; and TAM, DD 1 1 1 (Mot, *Le moulin du château narbonnais*, No. 1) (January 1183, copied in 1280) Bertrand and Raymond Aton de Montibus.

[3] Chapterman in 1180-1181; for January 1183 see the note above; Malta 1 24 xx (April 1184); E. Léonard, *Catalogue des actes de Raimond v* (Nîmes, 1932), No. 122 (September 1186); Malta 4 191 i (March 1186 or 1187, copied in 1203 and 1283) property at Escalquens and Belberaud pledged; Malta 3 98 (August 1187, copied in 1221) at Rosers; chapterman in 1189-1190; E 503 (June 1192, copied in 1199 and 1204); MADTG, A 297, fol. 802v (November 1195) l'Isle-Jourdain; consul 1199-1200; Saint-Sernin 599 (10 35 16) 5th of group of membranes iii (January 1200, copied in 1219 and 1220) as "maior" with Peter de Montibus; and ibid., 501 (1 1 52) 1st of 5 membranes tied together (September 1201) where a Bertrand de Montibus freed a servile family.

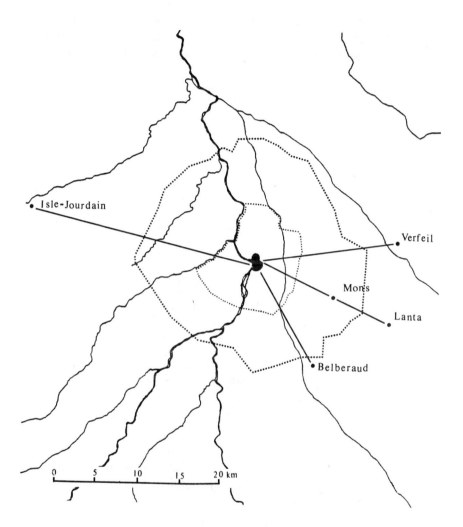

MAP 11. MONTIBUS

more famous. Twice a consul, he was interested in Verfeil, and we know that he had rights at Montaygon in Toulouse. He even appears in a papal letter, it being charged that Bishop Raymond de Rabastencs had been illegally elected as a result of a plot among the canons that transpired in his house, presumably near Montaygon. Aton was last seen in 1211.[4]

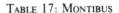

TABLE 17: MONTIBUS

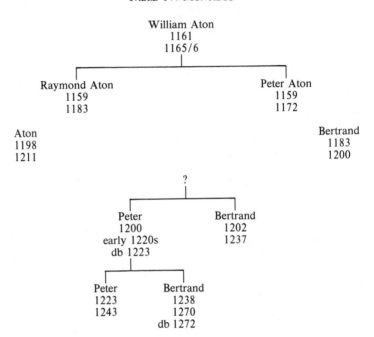

The subsequent generation is composed of two brothers, Peter and Bertrand de Montibus. That these individuals were related to the generation mentioned above cannot be proved but is strongly indicated. The older Bertrand was once, it will be recalled, called "maior," and the younger Bertrand "junior." Both the younger Bertrand and his brother

[4] He was consul in 1198-1199 and again in 1201-1202; TAM, AA 1 64 (June 1203) when he and Peter de Montibus witnessed a treaty between Toulouse and Verfeil; PL. 215: 683 (Potthast 2561) (July 1205) papal charge that Mascaron had swung the election "in domo Attonis de Montibus"; PAN, JJ 21, fol. 69r (March 1205) where Aton and Bertrand de Montibus with other notables admitted that the "capella" and "domus" in the "planum Montaygonis" were public property; PAN, J 320 28 (November 1208) Aton as witness; and MADTG, A 297, fol. 841v (April 1211) where he witnessed the marriage of William de Turre and the daughter of a lord of Verfeil.

Peter were also either interested in, or had rights at, Verfeil, Lanta, etc. just like the Aton we have seen above. Whatever the exact relationship, Bertrand is first seen in 1202 and last in 1237, when he was described as "probushomo," showing that there was yet another younger Bertrand of the family. He was clearly a successful businessman and creditor and is seen active from l'Isle-Jourdain to the west of Toulouse to Verfeil and Lanta to the east and south. He was consul in 1214-1215, again in 1225-1226, and served as a hostage for the town to Paris in 1229. Thereafter Bertrand disappears and it seems that this coincides with his condemnation for Catharism sometime before February 1237.[5]

Although possibly mentioned in the sources concerning Catharism, his brother Peter was spared this fate, perhaps because he was dead by 1223. We know that he too was interested in l'Isle-Jourdain, Lanta, and Verfeil.[6] He left two sons, Peter and Bertrand, Peter was first seen in 1223 and is last heard of taking oath to maintain the Peace of Paris together with his brother Bertrand.[7] Bertrand does not unequivocally appear until 1238

---

[5] Possibly September 1201 as in note 3 above; TAM, AA 1 69 (June 1202) Bertrand de Montibus "iunior"; PAN, J 318 7 (October 1202) where the brothers Bertrand and Peter are "fideiussores"; TAM, AA 1 70 (April 1204) where both attest a consular act; PAN, J 317 11 (August 1205) attested by Bertrand and Peregrin de Montibus; March 1205 as in act cited in the note above, having rights at Montaygon; MADTG, A 297, fol. 407r (August 1206) where the two siblings are guarantors of the debts of the Unaldi of Lanta and another; ibid., fol. 793r (October 1208) Bertrand and Peregrin; PAN, J 318 16 (October 1208) Bertrand and Peter guarantors for pledged properties at Lanta, Belberaud, etc.; PAN, J 320 30 (November 1208) ditto; Saint-Sernin 501 (1 1 57) (April 1212) where Bertrand freed a servile family; and PAN, J 330 9 (July 1222) Bertrand as a witness to an act of the count. Bertrand may have been the hostage sent to Paris in PAN, J 310 45 (April 1229), but it is obvious that we do not know when this Bertrand ends and his nephew Bertrand begins. The last reference to the older Bertrand in PAN, JJ 19, fol. 121r (February 1237) Bertrand "probushomo." Anent his Catharism, TBM, MS 609, fol. 58v mentioned conventicles in a house adjacent to those of Bertrand and of Alaman de Roaxio, hence in the regions Montaygon and Saint-Étienne. He is listed in the amnesty of 1279 (above, Chapter 5) as No. **133**, hence condemned before February 1237.

[6] For January 1200 see note 3 above; August 1205 note 5 above; June 1203 note 4 above; TAM, AA 1 54 (June 1203) Peter de Montibus a witness; April 1204 note 5 above; MADTG, A 297, fol. 406v (May 1205) as "fideiussor" for the lord of l'Isle-Jourdain; August 1205 note 5 above; MADTG, A 297, fol. 414r (October 1206) where Peter pays off the debts of the lord of l'Isle; the second act of October 1208 in note 5 above; TBM, MS 609, fols. 130r and 197v references to a Cathar meeting in his house in Toulouse and in a house near his sometime in the early 1220s; PAN, J 318 26 (March 1223) payments of debts once owed to Peter and his brother Bertrand by our Peter described as son of the quondam Peter; and PAN, J 310 25 (March 1223) about the same matter.

[7] See the first act of March 1223 in the note above; PAN, J 329 39 (December 1225) restitution of usury to Peter de Montibus for Lanta debts owed the brothers Bertrand and Peter de Montibus; PAN, J 310 45 (April 1229) hostage to Paris; PAN, J 330 25 (May 1235) the testament of Hugh Johannes whose three executors were Bertrand, Francis

when he was called "iuvenis" to distinguish him from his uncle, the "probushomo" of the same name. It is probably "iuvenis" who served as a consul in 1257-1258, but he was certainly dead by 1272 when witnesses from the City remarked that his heirs had paid taxes on all holdings both in town and out.[8] A possible heir is the knight Bertrand de Montibus seen in 1270.[9] Curiously, although the family had boasted at least one Cathar, no person of this name appears in connection with the amnesty of 1279.[10]

The name Montibus, Montz, or Mons was carried by other families in and around Toulouse. We hear of an oil dealer and a miller with this name.[11] There were also persons and probably families at both Lanta to the south and Verfeil to the east called such, families notable for their devotion to Catharism.[12] A religiously orthodox and somewhat monoto-

(Franchischus), and Peter de Montibus; PAN, J 327 2 ii (November 1241) Peter at the settlement of the Noerio family inheritance; PAN, J 320 50 (April 1242) the brothers Peter and Bertrand; and PAN, J 305 29 (February 1243) where the brothers swore to uphold the Peace of Paris.

[8] It is possible that the Bertrand who was a consul in 1225-1226 and hostage in1229 was this one and not his uncle, and, given the latter's problems with the Inquisition, it is likely that Hugh Johannes' executor in May 1235 (see the note above) was our Bertrand. Other references to him are Malta 178 5 (March 1236) where the Hospital commended all it had at Verfeil to him for life; PAN, J 330 14 (June 1238) where Bertrand acted as executor of Hugh Johannes; PAN, JJ 19, fol. 14v (May 1238) Bertrand de Montibus "juvenis"; for April 1242 and February 1243 see the note above; PAN, J 320 55 (June 1245) Bertrand, son of the quondam Peter de Montibus; PAN, J 330 27 (October 1247) concerning the inheritance of Hugh Johannes; and a reference to his heirs in TAM, II 10 (March 1271 to July 1272).

[9] TAM, AA 3 128 (June 1270).

[10] An Arnold de Montibus was listed in the amnesty. Whether he was a member of our family is unsure, but is possible because an Arnold, along with Bertrand, was listed among the councilors of the consul in TAM, AA 1 75 (March 1222), a somewhat elegant body. According to Dossat, Inquisition, p. 305 (based on PAN, JJ 24B, fol. 6r No. 49 [dated 1257]) his "hereditas" was given to one of Alphonse of Poitiers' officers. Arnold's number in the list of 1279 was **265** which means he was condemned after 1248.

[11] Peter de Montibus "olearius" in Saint-Bernard 138, fol. 178r (December 1209), and E 538 (May 1216) where his widow sold some of his holdings to her second husband John Garnerius. Since the Montaygon was the oil market of Toulouse, this person may have been related to our family, but he seems just a bit too modest. The same is true of another Peter de Montibus "molnerius" in TAM, II 60 (December 1261) who sued another miller and his wife for pulling him off his mule and beating him up. Bernard Guy, De fundatione, p. 37 (dated about 1263) records that this person lived on the street of the millers or of Arnold Barravus on the site of the present Jacobins.

[12] A Pons de Montibus of Lanta was active in Catharism there about 1230 in TBM, MS 609, fol. 200v, and he or a predecessor with the same name is seen in Douais, Saint-Sernin, Appendix No. 68 (March 1173 or 1174) at Verfeil together with Raymond Aton de Montibus, and PAN, J 317 5 and 6 (dated respectively March and April 1198) where he pledged his house at Lanta. Note also the Assalit de Montibus in PAN, J 327 1 i (October 1206) whose widow Berengaria was given a life sentence for Catharism in Douais, Inquisition, 2: 44 (August 1247).

nous troubadour named At de Mons flourished in and after the mid-thirteenth century.[13] Although our family is probably related to the persons or families at Verfeil and Lanta, it seems almost sure that it had little or nothing to do with the rather humble oil dealer or the miller of this name. The testimony of around 1272 records our family among those with substantial rural holdings, and it is therefore sure that, weaknesses of documentation aside, it was a partly rural and probably knightly clan that, for a time, had residence and citizenship in Toulouse.[14]

---

[13] For this person, see my "Urban Society and Culture," p. 246.

[14] It is possible that the male line died out. Molinier, *Correspondance ... d'Alphonse de Poitiers*, Nos. 237, 1267 and 1268 (dated respectively May 1267 and June and July 1269) records a suit about Mons by the Toulousan citizen Arnold de Ponte against Lombarda, widow of Berengar Alemanni.

Ponte

A difficulty of the name "of the Bridge" or "de Ponte" is that anyone who lived near the Old or New Bridges on the Garonne waterfront was liable to be so called. Many therefore carried this soubriquet, and it is likely that not a few families bore it as a surname. Here, however, only one rather thin line will be traced for four or five generations. It is thin because the family is curiously weak in private documents. Perhaps it did not invest as much in land and rents as in trade and moneylending.

TABLE 18: PONTE

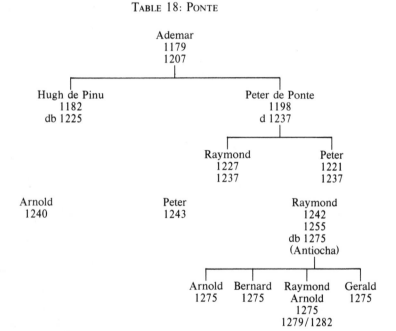

The first to appear is Ademar de Ponte in 1179 (Table 18). He served not infrequently as a chapterman and consul, and is last seen in 1207.[1]

[1] PAN, J 321 28 (April 1179) as a witness; chapterman in 1180-1181 and 1186; E 502 i (June 1192, copied in 1199 and 1204); consul in 1196-1197; and PAN, J 318 13 and 14 (December 1207) together with Bernard Peter de Ponte.

Later information tells us that he was the father of the brothers Peter de Ponte and Hugh de Pinu.[2] Seen from 1182, Hugh is referred to in a document of 1225 wherein we learn that he had died at Montpellier, and that one of his heirs was Peter de Ponte "iuvenis."[3] Hugh's brother Peter, who was eventually called "maior" to distinguish him from the "iuvenis" mentioned in the last sentence, appeared in 1198, was thrice a consul, and died between March and November of 1237, leaving sons, the Peter "iuvenis" seen above and Raymond de Ponte.[4]

Both Peter and Raymond were important personages in town during the 1220s, Peter being twice a consul and Raymond serving as a hostage to Paris in 1229.[5] The brothers were, however, condemned for Catharism sometime in the late 1230s.[6] Although it is possible that they performed a penance and were forgiven, and therefore that the Peter we see taking oath to maintain the Peace of Paris in 1243 and the Raymond who served as consul in the 1240s and 1250s were the same persons,[7] it is more likely that one of these persons had a son named Raymond. Whatever the case, Raymond, who was active until 1255, was clearly of their line.[8] In 1275 we learn that Antiocha, widow of Raymond de Ponte, had modest rights on the tolls of the town which she, along with her sons Arnold, Bernard,

[2] Malta 4 205 (March 1247, copied in 1240, 1241, and 1242) Peter de Ponte son of the deceased Ademar de Ponte and Raymond Stephen de Ponte, concerning a sale of property adjacent to that of an Arnold de Pinu; and PAN, J 317 24 (November 1237) in which Raymond de Ponte and others arrange about debts owed to Peter de Ponte, father of the above Raymond, or to Hugh de Pinu his brother, and to others.

[3] E 573 (March 1225, copied in 1233) wherein Peter de Ponte "maior" appears as the executor of a creditor of Arnold de Villanova and Peter de Ponte "iuvenis" gives testimony that the same owed Hugh de Pinu 260 shillings which the latter gave in his testament rendered at Montpellier to the said Peter de Ponte and his brothers. Other references to Hugh are Malta 116 20 i and ii (respectively June 1182 and May 1196), involving property at La Devèze, and the second act of November 1237 in note 2 above.

[4] Douais, Saint-Sernin, Appendix No. 52 (February 1198) Peter as a witness; consul in 1202-1203, 1213-1214, and 1220-1222; for March 1225 as "maior," see note 3 above; and for March and November 1237 note 2 above.

[5] Peter was consul in 1221-1222; described as "iuvenis" in March 1225 for which see note 3 above; consul in 1225-1226; Malta 116 25 (January 1227) Peter and his brother Raymond with property at the Pont-des-Clèdes on the Hers river; and Raymond in the act of November 1237 cited in note 2 above.

[6] Described as brothers and listed as Nos. **57** and **58** in the amnesty (Chapter 5), and hence condemned very early.

[7] PAN, J 305 29 (February 1243) Peter taking oath; a Raymond as consul in 1242-1244 and 1251-1252. Forgiveness was certainly possible, but it is unlikely that a man would be twice a consul so soon after rehabilitation.

[8] Grandselve 8 (March 1255) Raymond a witness. The material in notes 9 and 11 below show that Raymond was of this line.

Raymond Arnold, and Gerald, then sold to the crown.[9] Arnold was perhaps the "cambiator" who is seen from 1240 to this date.[10] Bernard was certainly the petitioner for the family in 1279, and Raymond Arnold was described as having been a merchant in the wine trade in 1279/83.[11]

[9] PAN, J 306 88 (January 1275) involving a small rent Antiocha had brought or acquired from the Baranoni, thus implying she was of that family.

[10] Malta 4 205 iii (November 1240, copied in 1241 and 1242) as "cambiator," and among those taking oath to the Peace of Paris in 1243. But this Arnold is possibly one of the unnamed brothers of March 1225 mentioned in note 3 above. Also Molinier, *Correspondance ... d'Alphonse de Poitiers*, Nos. 236, 1267, and 1268 (dated respectively May 1267 and June and July 1269) where Arnold acted as testamentary executor of Peter Barravus and also for himself as a creditor of imprisoned debtors and as a defendant in a lawsuit.

[11] Bertrand, son of Raymond de Ponte, as a petitioner in Chapter 6 (March 1279), and TAM, II 63 (dated from 1279 to 1283 inclusive) where Raymond Arnold was mentioned as having been a wine merchant by Hugh de Roaxio and Bertrand Bequini.

Roaxio

Although many charters list members of this family as actors and witnesses, the unfortunate fact is that the Rouaix had the center of their power in the City "apud Roaxium" (the modern Place de Rouaix), on the streets centering on the principal market called the Place de la Pierre, and adjacent to the church of Saint-Victor whose tithes were held for a time by the family. What is unfortunate about this circumstance is that this area depended largely on the cathedral of Saint-Étienne and somewhat on the monastery of the Daurade whose archives have been almost wholly lost. Luckily, Saint-Étienne held property at Braqueville on the left bank of the Garonne (some of whose documents still exist) and the Hospitalers around Castanet, and in both of these areas the Rouaix were also prominent.

TABLE 19: ROAXIO

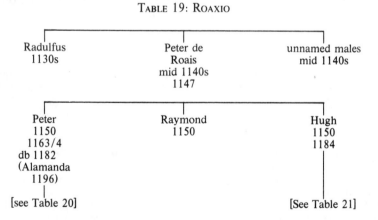

What is known is nevertheless enough to illustrate the extraordinary extent or reach of this clan. In 1205 we have a reference to a gift to the church of Saint-Victor of a part of the tithe of Saulonar (region Saint-Cyprien and Braqueville) by Radulfus "volens pergere Iherusalem" (see Table 19), his cousin Bernard Rogerius, his brother Peter de Roais, and their other brothers in an abbreviated copy of a charter originally written by the notary Pons Vitalis who instrumented from approximately 1141 to 1162. Because the second crusade took place in 1147, the original may be dated as somewhere in the mid-1140s.[1] Radulfus may also have been the one who was described as vicar (presumably) of Toulouse in the celebrated act of Count Alphonse Jordan concerning the foundation of the New or Daurade Bridge approximately 1135.[2] At about the same time, Peter de Roais was among those supporting the Templars at Toulouse, witnessed the count's foundation of Montauban in 1144, and was probably the chapterman of that name in 1147.[3] It therefore seems that the family was initially part of the count's service personnel in Toulouse, a role that does not necessarily imply that it was among the richest inhabitants in this early period. It may, in fact, have been quite modest.[4]

In 1150 a Peter, Raymond, and Hugh de Roaxio, together with their uncle Gerald, divided property and dependent tenants at Péchabou to the south of Toulouse a long way from Saint-Caprais to the north of the town where Peter's wife Alamanda seems to have shared property with her husband in the 1140s and in 1152.[5] It is probable that this Peter is the same as the brother of Radulphus seen earlier (it will be recalled that they had other siblings), but it is only sure that it was he who was a chapterman and a councilor for the town in 1152, 1158, and 1163/4, and that he sold a tower and a locality in the Close of Saint-Sernin in 1163. Of the two brothers, Raymond is seen only in 1150 and Hugh again only in 1184, but it seems probable that, like their brother, they had issue.[6]

---

[1] Saint-Étienne 227 (26 DA 2 53) an act confirming the inserted material from the original of Pons Vitalis, dated October 1205, witnessed at that later date by Raymond, son of the dead Arnold de Roaxio.

[2] Daurade 145 (dated circa 1135) – see the Caraborda history note 3 above.

[3] Malta 1 45 published by Albon, *Cartulaire de l'Ordre du Temple*, No. 20 and there dated as from 1128 to 1132, perhaps a trifle too early; PAN, JJ 19, fol. 169v (October 1133) foundation of Montauban; and Douais, *Saint-Sernin*, No. 27 (tentatively dated early 1140s) about property of Peter de Roais and Alamanda in the tithing of Saint-Hilaire, an unidentified church in the region of Montmazalguer in or near modern Saint-Caprais north of the Bourg.

[4] Anent wealth, the average annual grant promised to the Templars in the act published by D'Albon cited in the note above was about 11 pence (26 males pledging), but Peter promised only 6 pence. He was listed among the mixed "milites" and "pedites." The nine members of the confraternity of the Dalbade church, all "pedites" we may be sure, offered a bit over two pence average. Our family may have derived from the hamlet called Rouais near Saint-Léon in the Lauragais.

[5] See the act of approximately 1140s in note 3 above; Douais, *Paléographie*, No. 4 (May 1150) property at Rover (Rosers?) and Péchabou; and Douais, *Saint-Sernin*, No. 117 (May 1252) Peter, his wife Alamanda, and their unnamed children, give a tithe at Montmazalguer.

[6] Douais, *Saint-Sernin*, No. 64 (November 1163) where part of this property had been sold earlier, and was adjacent to the "planum" or square of Saint-Sernin. For Hugh in May 1187 see note 25 below.

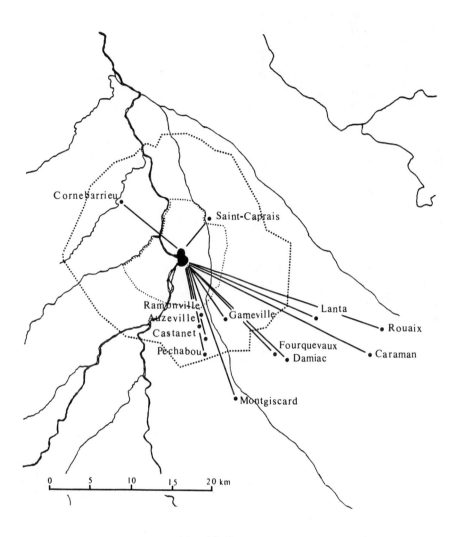

MAP 12. ROAXIO

TABLE 20: ROAXIO – LINE OF PETER AND ALAMANDA

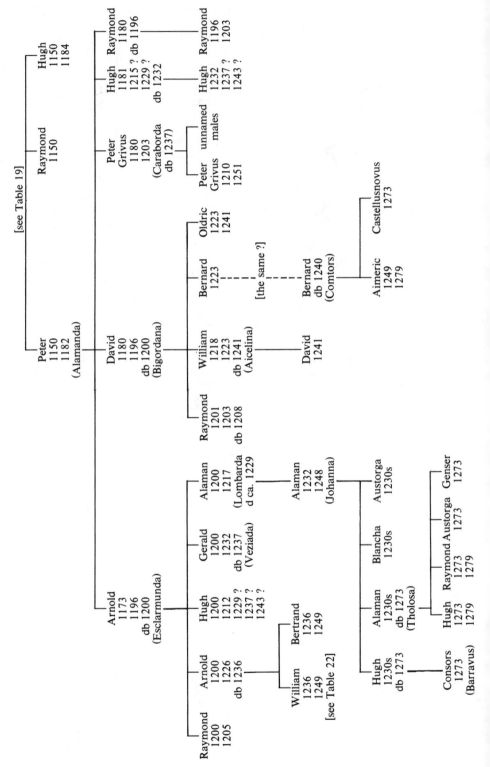

It is perhaps best to start by tracing the line of the brother named Peter (Table 20). Married to Alamanda, as we have seen, Peter was dead by 1182, but his widow lingered until 1196.[7] Later but sure information enables us to see that Peter and Alamanda had five sons, Arnold, David, and Peter called Grivus (from "greu," meaning hard or heavy?), Hugh, and Raymond. Not only were these brothers frequent chaptermen/consuls, but they acted in concert not infrequently about their properties. The last general round up of the family available is a charter of 1200.[8]

Peter and Alamanda's oldest son was apparently Arnold. First seen in 1173, Arnold last appears as an executor for his brother Raymond in 1196, and was dead by 1200 or 1202 when his widow Esclarmunda and her five sons Raymond, Arnold, Hugh, Gerald, and Alaman, the latter

---

[7] Douais, *Saint-Sernin*, No. 7 (September 1158) a property at Bel Olmel just north of the Bourg; Grandselve 5 iii (February 1182, copied in 1212 and 1213) property of Alamanda widow of Peter de Roaxio; and the same in Saint-Bernard 138, fol. 54v (March 1196).

[8] PAN, J 328 1 i (August 1173) Arnold a witness of an enfeoffment by the count; Saint-Étienne 227 (26 DA 2 unnumbered) (December 1177) Arnold de Roaxio and members of the Guilaberti family with property at Las Bosqueras in the region of Braqueville and Saint-Cyprien; Malta 3 70 (February 1180) Raymond as a witness; Saint-Étienne 227 (26 DA 2 39) i (November 1180, copied in 1183) Braqueville with Arnold and the Guilaberti, attested by Raymond and David de Roaxio; Saint-Étienne 227 (26 DA 1 12) (March 1180 or 1181) acquisition at same by Arnold; ibid., (26 DA 2 50) (January 1181) David a witness; Douais, *Paléographie*, No. 7 (July 1181) property and tithes at Merville, Péchabou, Auzeville, and Crozils (?) in the general region of Castanet given to Arnold de Roaxio in a charter witnessed by Raymond, David, and Hugh. Some of these properties had been mentioned in the act of May 1150 noted in note 5 above; Malta 9 4 three acts (with the date of March 1181/2) with Arnold as an executor of a minter; Malta 1 76 (September 1183) Bernard and David as witnesses; PBN, MS lat. 9189, fol. 49v (December 1184) the "domus" and "curia" of Péchabou with the Guilaberti and Arnold de Roaxio, attested by Peter Grivus, David, and Peter Rogerius, son of Bernard Rogerius; Saint-Étienne 227 (26 DA 2 39) ii (March 1185 or 1186, copied in 1193) Guilaberti act about Braqueville witnessed by the brothers Arnold and David, and mention of property there of Peter de Roaxio; Malta 20 25 (July 1186) Hugh executor of person with rights at Campferrand near Montaudran; Saint-Étienne 227 (26 DA 1 16) (January 1186) land at Braqueville of the brothers Peter and Hugh; ibid., (26 DA 2 21) i (November 1187, copied in 1197) Arnold lord of property at Braqueville; Saint-Bernard 138, fol. 110r (April 1196) David's small property in the Bourg; Malta 3 120 (October 1196) sale of some rural goods to the Hospital by Raymond, son of the deceased Raymond, with the consent of his father's executors, Arnold, Peter Grivus, Hugh, and Bertrand de Roaxio; Saint-Étienne 227 (26 DA 2 57) (January 1200, copied in 1258) sale of rights at Braqueville by Raymond and Arnold for themselves and for their brothers Hugh, Gerald, Alaman, and with the consent of Esclarmunda, their mother and the widow of Arnold de Roaxio; and PAN, J 326 36 (May 1200) reception of "rachat" by Peter Grivus and his brother Hugh, their nephew Raymond, son of their brother Raymond, for themselves and for Bertrand and all their nephews, the sons of Arnold, and for the sons of David de Roaxio, for what appear to be properties in town.

two being minors, dealt with their rights at Braqueville.[9] To trace these children is more difficult. Arnold was certainly seen as a consul in 1212-1213, again in 1226, and it may very well have been he who was dead by 1236, when an Arnold left two heirs, the brothers William and Bertrand, who are both seen again in 1249.[10] The last reference to the brother named Raymond is from 1205. With Hugh we do somewhat better, but the matter is confused by the fact that his uncle Hugh likewise had a son named Hugh. Arnold's son Hugh was certainly seen as a consul in 1211-1212, may have been the Hugh called "maior" in 1237, and may also have been one of the two Hughs of this family seen in the oath to keep the Peace of Paris in 1243.[11] The brother named Gerald is not known to have had issue. He was a councilor of the consuls in 1222, a witness in 1232, but may have been dead by 1237.[12]

Alaman, the last of Arnold's sons, started a family that was to have a very lively history. He seems to have been minded to become a country gentleman. Perhaps through his wife Lombarda, he acquired property at Villèle in the Lauragais in 1217, and, in 1222, we learn that his son named Alaman was in training to become a knight in the household of the lord of Lanta, and that he himself had obtained property in that community.[13] Alaman probably died in the late 1220s and his wife

[9] For the references up to 1200, see the previous note and PBN, MS lat. 9189, fols. 247va and 252rb (respectively May 1195 and December 1184) for Arnold's properties. Saint-Étienne 227 (26 DA 2 118) (March 1202) lists the five sons. Arnold was also consul in 1181-1182 and 1198-1199.

[10] Saint-Étienne 227 (26 DA 2 86) (April 1226) where Arnold sold to his brother Alaman property at Braqueville acquired by their dead father Arnold; PAN, JJ 19 174 (December 1236) William and Bertrand, sons of the deceased Arnold; and HGL, vol. 8: No. 410 (March 1249) the brothers William and Bertrand in an act of the count. Anent their father, his consulate of 1212-1213 is certain because his parentage is there mentioned, but the Arnold who served as a councilor in 1222 and as consul in 1225-1226 may be a later Arnold to be seen below.

[11] Concerning Raymond, see him in October 1205 in note 1 above. Persons with the name of Hugh served as consuls in 1224-1225 and 1246-1247. Hugh "maior" appeared as a witness in PAN, Doat 21, 153 (February 1237). He may have been alive in PAN, J 330 20 (July 1241) where the witnesses were Alaman "iuvenis" and Hugh, son of the quondam Arnold.

[12] PAN, JJ 19, fol. 174r (May 1232) witness to a comital act, and PBN, MS lat. 9189, fol. 240ra (July 1237) Veziada widow of Gerald.

[13] For the acts of May 1200 and March 1202, see notes 8 and 9 above; PAN, J 328 6 (July 1217) the testament of William de Busqueto of Lanta with gifts to Alaman and his wife Lombarda of goods at Lanta and Villèle; and PAN, J 323 70 (November 1222) where William Unaldus noted that Alaman, son of Alaman, was his godson and requested his executor, Sicard de Montealto, another baron, this one of Montaut, to make him and a young gentleman from Villèle into knights ("faceret eos milites"), and also granted the father Alaman property presumably in his lordship of Lanta.

Lombarda right after the Peace of Paris of 1229. This did not prevent her being condemned for Catharism in 1237.[14] Her son Alaman the younger, the squire and would-be knight of 1222, appears as a creditor of the count for 4000 shillings in 1235, but was already in trouble with the church. He was sentenced to a penitential voyage to the Holy Land in 1229, which he apparently refused to undertake, was condemned again in 1237, and finally sentenced to life imprisonment in 1248, his wife Johanna having received the same sentence two years before.[15] Before this final seclusion, we see him and his wife and their homes and possessions at Lanta, Villèle, and Damiac in the Lauragais during the 1230s and 1240s, and also hear of their children, their sons Hugh (nicknamed Bego) and Alaman "junior," and daughters Blancha and Austorga.[16] Save for a reference to Alaman "junior" in 1241, we do not see these children until two trials took place before a royal court of judge delegates of 1272-May 1273 about a farm or "bovaria" named Ribalta (Ribaudin or Ribaut) in the tithing of Gameville.

---

[14] Alaman was surely alive and flourishing in April 1226 as we see in note 10 above. Although there is a possibility of confusion with his son who bore the same Christian name, and although the dating of testimony given twenty years later is not sure, I shall list inquisitorial evidence about these two persons. TBM, MS 609, fol. 200v (around 1228) mentions Alaman and wife Lombarda in their home in Toulouse; ibid., fols. 202v-203r (about 1226) a reference to Lombarda as the "quondam uxor Alamanni," that is, as widow of the same; and ibid., fol. 213v the pair again at Toulouse (approximately 1228). PBN, Doat 23, fol. 294v mentions Alaman at Toulouse with the deeply Cathar Rocovilla family, rural knights from the Lauragais in residence there, and, on fol. 16r, refers to Lombarda in 1226. PBN, Doat 21, fol. 184r (September 1237) tells us that Lombarda, "uxor quondam Alamanni," had died "statim post pacem" and that she was condemned as a Cathar.

[15] PAN, J 320 436 (February 1235) where Alaman aquits the count of all the latter owes him including a pledge on the count's "condamina" held for a debt from January 1232 to date, a debt of 4150 shillings. Pelisson, Chronicon, p. 111 notes his condemnation. PBN, Doat 21, fol. 143v (May 1237) tells us that he reneged on the penitence imposed by Cardinal Roman and was condemned to life imprisonment. Douais, Inquisition, 2: 72 (January 1248) repeated the same sentence and added the requirement that he annually give 50 shillings to a Pons "qui stetit cum" Raymond Scriptor, the quondam "officialis" of Toulouse who had been assassinated at Avignonet. Ibid., p. 27 (June 1246) condemned Johanna his wife to life. Alaman was No. **130** and his wife No. **131** in the amnesty (Chapter 5).

[16] PBN, Doat 23, fol. 21r-v (circa 1233) Alaman and Johanna and Blancha, Austorga, Bego (Hugh) and Alaman junior. Some of the references in TBM, MS 609 are: fol. 45v (approximately 1237) Alaman "de novo" condemned; fol. 130r (around 1227) Alaman and his children Blancha, Bec, and Austorga; fol. 201r (about 1237) Alaman had participated with others and with two "perfecti" in the heretication of William de Garnes of Lanta when the latter was being executed at Toulouse; fol. 202r (approximately 1231) in a wood at Lanta with wife Johanna and circa 1244 at Lanta itself; fol. 202v (around 1234) Alaman, Johanna, and all the children in their "boaria" at Lanta; fol. 207v Alaman had a bailiff at Fourquevaux in 1244; fol. 208v Alaman's property at Damiac; and fol. 210v (early 1240s) Alaman's house in Lanta and Bego.

We there learn that the family had had property confiscated because of Alaman's Catharism, that Alaman junior and his wife Tholosa were dead by this time, and that they had had two sons named Hugh and Raymond and two daughters, Austorga and Genser. The trials also tell us that Alaman junior's brother Hugh was likewise deceased, but that he had had a daughter named Consors who had married a Barravus.[17] Hugh and Raymond are subsequently seen as petitioners for the amnesty of heretical inheritances in 1279.

To turn back to the children of Peter de Roaxio and Alamanda, the second son was David. First seen in 1180, David last appears alive in a charter of 1196 and was dead by 1200. A sign of the station of this family, David's house was sufficiently large to serve as a temporary residence for Count Raymond VI, his son, and their wives, when the bishop of Toulouse took over the Château Narbonnais for the crusaders in 1213 after the defeat of the southern side at Muret.[18] David and his wife Bigordana, who was still alive in the 1230s, had four sons and at least one daughter who may well have married Hugh de Palatio.[19]

David's sons were named Raymond, William, Bernard, and Oldric. Raymond, who acted for his brothers in 1201 and again in 1203, early separated from the family, possibly because he was a merchant. He was

[17] For July 1241, see the act cited in note 11 above. Fournier and Guébin, eds., *Enquêtes d'Alphonse de Poitiers*, No. 92 (p. 294) a reference in 1270 to property of the condemned Alaman at Villèle. The trials of Hugh and Raymond started in 1271 and ended in May 1273, and are in PAN, KK 1228, fols. 52r-54v and 54v-57r (the foliation of this much destroyed register is a hopeless mess, the medieval numbering being 99r-101r and 101v-104r). The same register contains a trial of the bishop of Toulouse for properties wrongfully acquired from heretics, including (on fol. 58v or 105v) a house in or near the Close of Saint-Étienne acquired from the said Alaman. The building was used for the bishop's court according to the record in October 1273: "domus que dicitur curia officialis."

[18] David was chapterman and consul in 1180-1181 and 1190-1191; Saint-Étienne 227 (26 DA 2 50) (January 1181) David a witness; for July 1181 see note 8 above: Malta 1 76 (September 1183) whose witnesses were Bernard and David; for December 1184 and March 1185 or 1186 see note 8 above; Saint-Bernard 138, fol. 110r (April 1196) David a witness; for May 1200 where David is deceased leaving heirs, see note 8 above: Malta 3 126 i (July 1201) Peter Grivus, Hugh, and Bertrand de Roaxio, executors for David, act with the consent of David's son Raymond who speaks for himself and his brothers; and Malta 3 45 (April 1203) exactly the same cast of characters along with Raymond, son of the quondam Raymond de Roaxio. Puylaurens, *Chronica*, p. 90 remarks that in late 1213 the count and his party "in domum David de Roaxio descenderunt."

[19] Bernard Guy, *De fundatione*, p. 40 reports on acquisitions by the Dominicans from Roger de Palatio and from a "quidam Vasco qui manet cum domina Bigordana de Roaxio, avia dicti Rotgerii de Palacio." Since Roger's father was Hugh, one guesses that one of Bigordana's daughters married that worthy. Vasco is too common a name to do anything with.

dead by 1228, and died in Montpellier, where he had made his brothers his heirs, an action that resulted in his siblings being forced to pay one of his creditors, Bertrand de Pozano, by virtue of a consular decision. Before his death, in 1223, his three brothers divided their properties in a document mentioning stone halls, houses, stores, and other properties in the City especially on the "carreria bancorum maiorum" (modern rues des Changes and Saint-Rome), localities in the Bourg, and lands near Ramonville, Castanet, and Montgiscard down in the Lauragais. William probably was the person of that name who was vicar of Toulouse in 1218. Oldric is seen for the last time in 1241 when he attested a charter by David, the son of his brother William, who was dead by that time.[20] As to the remaining brother named Bernard, I forbear from speaking of him because there is another Rouaix with the same Christian name, both of whom shall be treated later on. Interestingly, Aicelina or Aiglina, the wife of William, who appeared in charters of 1223 and 1231, was sentenced for Catharism as relapsed in 1237.[21]

The third son of Peter and Alamanda was another Peter, sometimes called Grivus presumably to distinguish him from the son of his first cousin Bertrand who was also called Peter. Grivus is seen from 1180 onwards and was very active in family affairs, as well as being a moneylender of some (ill) repute.[22] It seems likely that the first Peter

---

[20] For July 1201 and April 1203 see note 18 above; Malta 1 24 ii (December 1218) where William is described as vicar of Toulouse; TAM, AA 1 75 (March 1222) the Rouaix who were councilors of the consuls in this year were Bernard, Bertrand, Gerald, Hugh, Oldric, and Peter Grivus; Douais, *Paléographie*, No. 18 (March 1223) a division between William, Bernard, and Oldric, sons of David and grandsons of Alamanda, of property in town and at Mervilla near Castanet, Pompertuzat, "Claromonte" (possibly Clermont on the Ariège river in the same general region), and the Pont-des-Clèdes over the Hers river – Aiglina, wife of William, gave her consent to this division; TAM, II 45 (March 1228) – also in TAM, AA 6 132 – an award of over 130 shillings to Bertrand de Posano for debts owed by the deceased Raymond to be paid by William, Bernard, and the absent brother Oldric; Malta 3 160 i (October 1231) sale of stores on the "carraria de Esporterla" (the Sack or Basket?) near the Garonne river to the Hospital by William, son of David, with the consent of his wife Aiglina and his mother Bigordana; and Malta 2 135 i (May 1241, copied in 1251) where David, son of William de Roaxio deceased, sold a house in an act attested by Oldric de Roaxio.

[21] For March 1223 and October 1231, see the note above. PBN, Doat 21, fol. 151r (February 1237) sentencing of Aicelina de Roaxio as relapsed.

[22] Peter was chapterman in 1180-1181; called Grivus for the first time in December 1184, for which see note 8 above; called simply Peter in March 1185 or 1186 and January 1186 for which see the same note; Peter Grivus as consul 1192-1193; executor of his brother Arnold in October 1196 in note 8 above; Peter Grivus as consul 1197-1198; May 1200 as Peter Grivus in the family document in note 8 above; Peter Grivus as consul 1201-1202; for his work as an executor of his brother David in July 1201 and April 1203 see note 18 above; and Saint-Étienne 221 (22 3 7bis) (September 1214, copied in 1259) the

Grivus died sometime after 1203 because the next person bearing the same name and nickname was described in 1210 as a nephew of Hugh, the older Peter Grivus' brother. Sometimes simply called Grivus, Peter junior had brothers whose names escape us and also had a rather distinguished career in the service of the last count of the Raymondine line, Raymond VII. He was a commissioner in 1249 for Raymond's testament, and is last seen serving in a court of judges delegated by the count in 1251.[23] Catharism touched this branch of the family also. A Caraborda "mater Grivi" was condemned when dead in 1237, thus giving us to understand that the wife of the first Peter Grivus was a Caraborda woman and that she was heretical.[24]

The fourth son of our original Peter and Alamanda was Hugh. Seen as early as 1181, he was probably alive in 1210 and possibly in 1215, but was certainly dead by 1232. Several times a consul, Hugh may have been the hostage sent to Paris in 1229. The charter of 1232 adverted to above also tells us that Hugh had a son named Hugh.[25] Hereafter we are faced by

---

testament of the rural notable Raymond de Montelauro willing to an heir the restitution for usury owed him by Peter Grivus on a debt of 200 shillings on which he had paid 30 shillings in usury annually for 12 years, thus 15 percent annually or, in 12 years, a total of 180 percent on the investment. As is obvious, the debt had been contracted for in 1201.

[23] Cresty, *Repertoire Saint-Étienne*, 1: fol. 32r (lost charter catalogued CC 1 14) (dated 1210) recording a donation of the tithe of church of Saint-Victor by Hugh and his nephew Peter G[rivus]; PAN, J 326 23 (April 1221) Peter, son of Bertrand de Roaxio, Hugh, and Grivus witnessed an important comital act during the war; Peter Grivus a councilor for the consuls in March 1222 in note 20 above; as Grivus a consul in 1224-1225; Saint-Étienne 230 (27 2 unnumbered) v (September 1230, copied in 1235 and 1244) the brothers Bertrand and Toset de Roaxio and Peter Grivus were executors of the deceased Peter de Roaxio for properties at Bonagazanha at Montaudran; Saint-Étienne 227 (26 DA 1 32) ii (February 1232) Peter Grivus acting for himself and his brothers with Hugh, son of the dead Hugh, on property at Braqueville; as Grivus consul 1235-1238; Grivus at oath for Peace of Paris in 1243; PAN, J 326 37 (April 1249) where Grivus witnesses an act of Aimeric, son of the deceased Bernard de Roaxio; Fournier and Guébin, eds., *Enquêtes d'Alphonse de Poitiers*, p. xxii as one of the commissioners of Raymond VII's will, that is, from 1249 to 1251; and Malta 118 8 and E 286 (May 1251) Peter Grivus as a judge delegated by the count of Toulouse involving the plaintiff William de Roaxio.

[24] PBN, Doat 21, fol. 179v (September 1237) sentence of the dead woman. Somewhat garbled, she is mentioned in the amnesty of 1279 (Chapter 5) as No. **184**.

[25] Hugh is seen in July 1181 in note 8 above; consul in 1181-1182; Malta 20 25 (July 1186) Hugh de Roacxio executor of a man named Savatus; ibid., 145 22 (May 1187) acquisition of a house near Saint-Pierre and Saint-Géraud; consul 1196-1197; as executor of his deceased brother Raymond in October 1196 in note 8 above; consul 1199-1200; in family dealings in May 1200 in note 8 above; as executor for his brother David in July 1201 and April 1203 see note 18 above; for 1210 see the reference to Cresty in note 23 above; Malta 5 291 (May 1215, copied in 1218 and 1221) a reference to Hugh, son of Hugh, the latter not described as dead; therefore possibly the Hugh, hostage at Paris in PAN, J 310 45 (April 1229); and the same son Hugh described as fathered by the deceased Hugh in February 1232 in note 23 above.

a confusing gaggle of Hughs in this family. The reader will remember that the older Hugh's brother Arnold had a son named Hugh, and that Arnold's son named Alaman had both a grandson and great grandson named Hugh. Which of these was the Hugh that appears several times in documents of the thirteenth century is not known. Nor can it be said which Hugh was the one who, at the age of about 70 years, gave testimony in 1279/83 that he had been busy in the wine traffic for about 35 years, and that he lived "apud Roaxium," the Place de Rouaix.[26]

The fifth and last son of Peter and Alamanda was Raymond. Active in 1180, nothing more is known about him save that he was dead by 1196 leaving a son named Raymond who was seen again in 1200 and 1203.[27]

The reader may remember that Peter, the husband of Alamanda, had two brothers, Raymond and Hugh. To put Raymond and a mysterious Bernard who may be related to him aside for a moment, Hugh, who may have last been seen in 1184 (Table 21), appears to have had an heir, perhaps a son, named Bertrand. Closely related to the five brothers mentioned above, Bertrand is seen from the late 1170s until 1203 when we learn that he sold property on the later Place de la Pierre to the town government. He was probably still alive in 1221, when we also hear of his son Peter, and he may have served as a consul in 1222-1223. Indeed, Bertrand may still have been alive in 1227, but the matter is unclear, and one suspects that he was dead. By this time we hear of a Bertrand and his brother Peter, who sound suspiciously like the children of the Bertrand whose history I have been describing. At the same time, as we shall see below, nothing can be less sure than this identification, because there are quite several Bertrands at this time.[28]

[26] Two Hughs appear at the oath in 1243 and it cannot be ascertained which Hugh appeared in the consulate or its council in 1222, 1224-1225, and 1246-1247. In Fournier and Guébin, eds., *Enquêtes d'Alphonse de Poitiers*, No. 128 (p. 324) (April-May 1270) a Hugh de Roays sought 4 pounds of Toulouse from the count who had confiscated the property of his debtor, the deceased Raymond Rogerius. The wine merchant Hugh gave witness in TAM, II 63 (dateable to between 1279 and 1283).

[27] Note 8 above contains references to him in November 1180, October 1196 when Raymond, son of the deceased Raymond, was active, and May 1200 with Raymond the younger and his uncles; the son Raymond appears with his uncles, etc. in April 1203 in note 18 above. Which of the available Raymonds was consul in 1212-1213 cannot be known.

[28] TAM, AA 1 43 and 58 (March and October 1203) sale by Bertrand of a place in order to enlarge the Place de la Pierre or the grain market in the center of town. Owing to the proximity of this property to that of the David family seen above, it seems probable that Bertrand had inherited this land and house from Hugh, who had acquired it in Malta 145 22 (May 1187) cited in note 15 above, when he obtained the possession ("dominium utile") to a place adjacent to property of the Davids and to that of the church of Saint-Pierre and Saint-Géraud; a Bertrand was chapterman in 1177/1180; an executor of

TABLE 21: ROAXIO – LINE OF HUGH DE ROAXIO

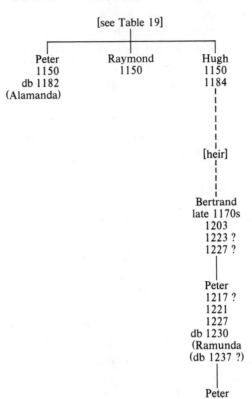

Little is known about Bertrand's son Peter. First surely seen in 1221, he had perhaps been a consul a few years earlier and was again seen in 1227. He was surely dead by 1230 when we have an action by the executors of his will.[29] Although there is a chance that it was his father's wife, his wife

Raymond in October 1196, and with the family in May 1200 both in note 8 above; an executor of David in July 1201 and April 1203 in note 18 above; for the act of April 1221 when Peter was described as the son of Bertrand who was not described as deceased see note 23 above; Malta 17 26 (October 1221) action taken by Peter de Roaxio and his brother Bertrand; and TAM, II 92 (May 1227) where a Bertrand acquired property near the Palatio, that is, either near the town hall or the Château Narbonnais. The charter was attested by Peter de Roaxio and Hugh, son of the deceased Arnold de Roaxio.

[29] A Peter not described as Grivus was a consul in 1217-1218; for the act of April 1221 see note 23 above; for the charters of October 1221 and May 1227 see the note immediately above; Saint-Étienne 230 (27 2 unnumbered) v (September 1230, copied in 1235 and 1244) where the executors of the deceased Peter are the brothers Bertrand and Toset, and Peter Grivus de Roaxio.

Ramunda was sentenced when dead for Catharism in 1237.[30] Peter's own son Peter was active in Catharism and seems to have been condemned as relapsed in 1237, but was back in circulation in 1243 when he took oath to uphold the Peace of Paris. He subsequently fell definitively into the hands of the Inquisition. He was sentenced as relapsed in 1246, and two years later the count assigned his confiscated "hereditas" to one of his supporters.[31]

The executors of the first of the two Peters described above are themselves interesting. One was our familiar Peter Grivus, but the other two are the brothers Bertrand and Toset de Roaxio (see Table 22). Although we never see the latter person again, his name tells us something. Toset was a Christian name customarily used by the Tolosa family (whose history is to be seen below) which fact leads us to believe that Peter had married a woman from that distinguished clan.[32] Owing to the way in which executors were chosen, furthermore, it is certain that these brothers were close relatives of the deceased Peter, if not his brothers. Since Toset appears only to disappear, so to speak, we are left with Bertrand.

Bertrand poses a problem because he had a contemporary Rouaix with the same Christian name who was, as we have seen above, the son of Arnold, grandson of the Peter and Alamanda of the original line. One of these Bertrands lost a lawsuit to the parishioners of Saint-Pierre-des-Cuisines over a private passage next to his house in 1247.[33] And the one who was serving a prison sentence in August 1247 was viewed as a martyr by the Cathars. Happily for this Bertrand, he was released from imprisonment by Innocent IV sometime before the end of his pontificate in

---

[30] Our sources are in conflict. PBN, Doat 21, fol. 179r (September 1237) reports Ramunda condemned as deceased and describes her as the wife of Peter. Pelisson, *Chronicon*, p. 110, on the other hand, says she was an inhabitant of the Bourg who was married to Bertrand de Roaxio.

[31] Although it seems likely that the whole family were Cathars, it is not easy to discover which Peter is meant in the Inquisitorial records. PBN, Doat 23, fol. 296r records a Peter adoring some "perfecti" in Saint-Julia near Revel in the Lauragais about 1240. In Douais, *Inquisition*, 2: 2 (March 1246) Peter, described as a "civis," was condemned as relapsed and probably in flight, a reference that fits an earlier one in Pelisson, *Chronicon*, p. 111 to a Peter condemned in 1237. The Peter listed in 1279 (Chapter 5) is No. **214** referring to the later condemnation. Malta 2 142 (February 1248, copied in 1250 and 1255) states that the count gave Odo Escotus of Linars "omnem hereditatem qui fuit Petri de Roaxio quondam filii Petri de Roaxio ratione seu nomine incursus."

[32] September 1230 for which see note 29 above.

[33] TAM, AA 6 94 (March 1247). The parishioners won. Incidently, the Bertrand, son of Arnold, clearly had a son named Bertrand. See PBN, MS lat. 9186, fol. 238ra (December 1245) concerning the property seen above in note 9 in charters of December 1184 and May 1195.

1254. The same document also tells us that, in 1270, the count restored Bertrand's inheritance to his widow Alamanda, his son Raymond, and his daughter Sibilia.[34] It also seems likely that it was Bertrand's son Raymond, who, according to a hostile witness, was a Cathar in refuge in Cremona and Piacenza approximately 1253-1254, and who had there stolen some money.[35]

TABLE 22: ROAXIO

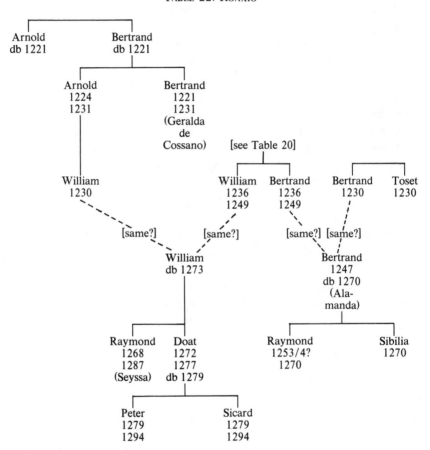

[34] Douais, *Inquisition*, 2: 112 (August-November 1247) containing the extraordinary testimony of Peter Garsias de Borguet-Nau who claimed that Bertrand was a saint and mentioned that he was in prison at that moment. PAN, JJ 24 A 2, fol. 34v, No. 189 – also in PBN, Doat 32, fol. 69r (May 1270) – records the government's return of property to the 'liberi et heredes" of the said Bertrand, who is described as having been long in prison and released by the pope. Bertrand is No. **158** in the amnesty of 1279 (Chapter 5) so he must have gone to prison sometime in February-September 1237, so anywhere from 10 to 27 years.
[35] TADHG, MS 124, fol. 201v (August 1257) testimony of William Furnerius.

To return again to the generation of Peter and Alamanda and Peter's brothers Raymond and Hugh, it may be that one of these siblings had a child named Bernard. Serving as a witness along with David de Roaxio, Bernard is seen in 1183.[36] Further mention of this person is lacking, but, in 1221, we hear of a Bernard, son of a deceased Bernard de Roaxio, who, together with his equally deceased brother Arnold, had been creditors of the Rossellus family for the sum of 352 shillings.[37] The new Bernard of 1221 (see Table 22) also seems to have had a brother named Arnold who is seen with him in 1224, 1230, and 1231. We also learn that the new Bernard was married to Geralda de Cossanis, had property at Corne-barrieu west of Toulouse, and that his brother Arnold may have had a son named William.[38].

There are two problems here. The first is that there were two Rouaix of this generation bearing the name Bernard. The first was the son of David and grandson of Peter and Alamanda; the second the Bernard described above. An English document tells us that one of these Bernards was a wine merchant in 1260.[39] The other Bernard was dead by 1240. Married to a Comtors, who, to judge by the names of her children, was a Castronovo, Bernard had two sons, Aimeric and Castellusnovus (Table 20). Aimeric is first seen in 1249 when he surrendered to the count his claim on the inheritance of his mother's uncle that was confiscated for reason of heresy. He witnessed a riot in town in 1268, and was a consul in 1270-1271. When consul, he was titled "dominus," an honorific that, at that time, implied that he was a noble. As a citizen, he paid taxes on his rural possessions, notably at Caraman according to the notary Paul in 1272.[40] Residence at Toulouse did not prevent him from directing the

---

[36] For September 1183 see note 18 above.

[37] Grandselve 6 (June 1221) Bernard takes the action in the name of his dead father Bernard and the latter's brother Arnold.

[38] E 273 (February 1224) the brothers Bernard and Arnold as witnesses; MADTG, A 297, fol. 609r (March 1230) where Bernard sold rents at Cornebarrieu with the consent of his wife and of his brother Arnold. A witness there was William, son of Arnold; and E 501 ii (October 1231, copied in 1233) where the brothers Arnold and Bernard admit they owe money to Raymond Centullus.

[39] *Calendar of the Patent Rolls* (June 1260) lists a Bernard de Roys, "civis," associated with Bertrand de Palacio and Arnold del Unde in the wine trade. Both are well known Toulousans in this traffic.

[40] PAN, J 326 37 – also PAN, JJ 19, fol. 33r – (April 1249) where Aimeric, son of the deceased Bernard, vacates his claim to the inheritance of Arnold Gauffredi, the uncle of his deceased mother. Grivus de Roaxio was among the witnesses; PAN, J 192 b (events of 1268, inquiry of February 1269); TAM II 10 (datable to 1272) with prominent mention of his property at Caraman; and he and his brother Castellusnovus, sons of Comtors, were sued by the crown in PAN, KK 1228 1v, in 1271 and March 1273.

fortunes of the community of Caraman in the Lauragais. He was a consul there in 1249 and again (or still consul) in 1271.[41] So important was the family there, in fact, that a hamlet just to the north of Caraman eventually bore the name of Rouaix. Aimeric is last seen as a proctor for heretical inheritances in 1279.[42]

The second problem is that there were also two Rouaix named William, and both were sons of Arnold. One was then the son of Arnold, the brother of the Bernard seen above, and the other the son of Arnold, the son of Arnold and grandson of Peter and Alamanda. The name William de Roaxio is frequently mentioned in the instruments from the 1230s forward, and one or both of the Williams was rich and important.[43] One William may have died by 1268, and it may be his wife Ramunda who sued for her dower property just outside of Montauban.[44] One of the Williams had two sons, Raymond and Doat. Raymond was seen in 1268, was married to Sayssa, owned a part of the tolls collected in the City and Bourg, served as the petitioner for himself and his dead brother Doat's children in 1279 in the matter of the heretical inheritances, and is probably last seen as a consul in 1286-1287.[45] Doat or Donat is seen in 1277, and had died by 1279. He left two sons, a Peter and a Sicard, who are briefly seen in 1294.[46]

Besides the Rouaix mentioned above, there are two others in the documents. A Roger was briefly seen in the 1240s.[47] A Stephen is seen in

[41] *HGL*, vol. 8, col. 1263 (December 1249) Aimeric as consul of Caraman, and Dossat, *Saisimentum*, No. 81 par. 15 (p. 220), (December 1271) as the same.

[42] See Chapter 6 above.

[43] PAN, JJ 19, fol. 174r (December 1236) a William and Bertrand, son of the deceased Arnold de Roaxio; there were consuls named William in 1238-1239, 1251-1252, and 1261-1263; and a William also at the oath to uphold the Peace of Paris in 1243.

[44] *Layettes du Trésor*, vol. 4, No. 5455 (December 1268). The link is not sure partly because the name is garbled to Roanxio and partly because Montauban is just a bit far away from Toulouse, but it will be remembered that the family were often merchants.

[45] In PAN, J 192 b (events of 1268, testimony of January 1269) Raymond also gave evidence; Molinier, *Correspondance ... d'Alphonse de Poitiers*, No. 1314 (July 1269) where Raymond was listed as a detainer of tolls; a Raymond consul 1271-1272; TAM, II 12 (November 1273) with the consent of his wife Sayssa, Raymond, son of the deceased William "burgensis Tholose qui moratur in Tholosa prope Roycium" (Rouaix, that is) sold his share for 200 pounds of Toulouse; and Chapter 6 above (March 1279) as proctor.

[46] TAM, II 77 (dated 1272) Donat sent to Paris for the consuls; PAN, J 302 5 (June 1277) Doat "burgensis" sold rents on a "quondam aula," house, and stores owned by some Jews near the Carmelites to the crown; dead as in the act of March 1279 cited in the note above; and Malta 20 19 (February 1294) where we see the landlords Hugh de Palatio, knight, and Peter and Sicard, sons of the deceased Doat.

[47] At the oath to maintain the Peace of Paris and again as consul in 1247-1248. The oath of 1243 (PAN, J 305 29 [February 1243]) makes it clear that both he and the Stephen

the 1230s and 1240s, and was deeply involved in Catharism, for which he gained life imprisonment in 1246.[48] One final Rouaix Cathar is a Petrona de Roaxio who was sentenced when dead in 1237.[49]

What is perhaps most striking about this large family is that, in spite of the interruptions in our lines of filiation, everybody bearing this surname can be shown to have really been members of the Rouaix family. The Rouaix was also a clan that had been penetrated by Catharism more deeply than the lists of those mentioned above or contained in the amnesty of 1279 indicate. When Aimeric de Roaxio de Caramanno was consul of Toulouse in 1270-1271, he was described as serving illegally (according to the Peace of Paris and the statutes of the count) because, in the past, he had been sentenced to wear the cross for reason of heresy.[50] It will also be remembered that, in that consular list, Aimeric was titled "dominus," a term that, as we have seen, implied nobility. The reader will also recall that an earlier Rouaix, Alaman, had either become or been about to become a knight before his condemnation for Catharism. In fine, the family did well enough in spite of the persecution it had suffered at the hands of the Inquisition, but its early attempts to enter the nobility had been retarded by its devotion to divergent thought.

---

mentioned below were of this family. On lines 30-31, the list of the names of persons bearing this surname standing together to take oath reads: Hugh, William, Grivus, Hugh, Roger, Bertrand, Stephen, and Peter. Only one of the family, the second Peter, was not in this group.

[48] PBN, Doat 23, fol. 298r records that Stephen "adored" (approximately 1231); among family in February 1243 in note above; Douais, *Inquisition*, 2: 16-17 (May 1246) where he was sentenced to life; and he is listed as No. **241** in the amnesty.

[49] PBN, Doat 21, fol. 179r (September 1237).

[50] PAN, J 318 107, an undated note referring to Aimeric as a onetime "crucesignatus" serving with a similarly tainted person, Peter Raymond Descalquencs, mentioned above. Both were in the consulate of 1270-1271.

Tolosa

Just as in the case of the name Castronovo, the name Tolosa was never wholly the monopoly of what may be called the main line bearing that name. For example, the appellation Tolosa was originally, and continued to be, applied to the family of the viscounts of Toulouse or of Saint-Sernin. As I argued in my earlier book on Toulouse, the ambitions of the viscomital line of Toulouse had been defeated by the counts during the late eleventh and early twelfth centuries, and the family had largely retired to the region of Montauban at Bruniquel and Monclar.[1] Members nevertheless occasionally appeared at Toulouse where they retained vestigial holdings. Son of William de Monteclaro, a Pons de Tolosa "vicecomes" is seen at Saint-Sernin in 1173 dealing with the properties of the original viscomital line.[2] It is also likely that the Pons "le Ros" de Tolosa, viscount of Monclar, who formed part of the garrison of Montferrand during the siege by the crusaders in 1211, was a successor of this family.[3]

Even at Toulouse, furthermore, the name Tolosa was applied to families or individuals other than the principal one to be described below. This was partly because, whatever his craft designation or real family name, a Toulousan who traveled outside of town was naturally called "of Toulouse," an appellation that might easily stick to him when at home. The name was obviously also one of those that no clan, however great, could monopolize. I have elsewhere narrated the history of a burgher family called Tolosa. These Tolosa lived in the Bourg and may have been the group from which Peter Raymond de Tolosa, sometimes simply called Raymond, a well-known troubadour, derived.[4]

---

[1] See my *Toulouse*, pp. 23-24 and 193. References to Ademar, viscount of Bruniquel and Toulouse abound, as, for example, in Douais, *Saint-Sernin*, Nos. 133, 251, and 291, the first two undated and the last one July 1098.

[2] Douais, *Saint-Sernin*, No. 689 (August 1173) referring to rights at Grisolles, the old fief of the viscounts of Toulouse.

[3] *Canso* 1, "liasse" 73, 176-177.

[4] For the history of this family, see my "Urban Society and Culture: Toulouse and Its Region," p. 244. For yet another example of the general use of this surname, see the Peter de Tolosa in this history of the Corregerii family mentioned early in these family histories.

TABLE 23: TOLOSA – LINE OF BERNARD RAYMOND TOLOSE

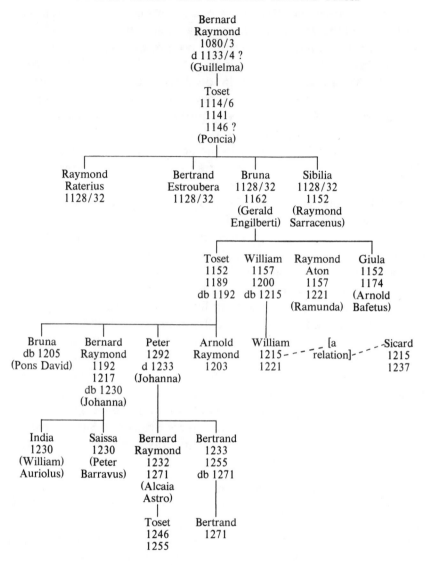

To turn now to the principal Tolosa clan, that of the City, it was already of great weight at the end of the eleventh century. A curious list of land credit operations or "pignora" partly written in the first person by one Regimundus (Raymond) seems to concern this family largely because it deals with property in Saint-Cyprien near the Old Bridge and with the tithing of Lespinet near Pouvourville where the later Tolosa are known to have had extensive holdings. One of the transactions recorded in this list concerned the celebrated Bishop Isarn, and thus occurred between 1071 and 1105, and the document mentions Raymond's brother Peter going to Spain, a Peter Regimundus "vicarius" presumably of Toulouse, and a Bernard Raymond Tolose and his unnamed wife (Table 23).[5] Bernard Raymond Tolose is also seen in documents of the 1080s, acts of significance in the settlement of differences between state and church in that period.[6] As shall be seen, furthermore, a document whose "conscriptio" is dated 1133 or 1134 refers to extensive holdings along the waterfront of the City enfeoffed to the heirs of one Toset de Tolosa (or Tolose) by the lords of Calmont (a place near Cintegabelle to the south of Toulouse), and describes them as goods that had earlier been given to Bernard Raymond and Toset.[7] To add to this, an act dated 1114-1116 records the gift by a widow named Guillelma, her son Toset and his wife Poncia, together with their unnamed children (soon to be seen below) of the hospital and church of Saint-Rémézy of Toulouse to the recently founded order of the Hospitalers.[8] It is therefore highly probable that we may trace the main clan of the Tolosa back through Toset to his presumed father Bernard Raymond Tolose and his mother Guillelma.

Toset had helped introduce the Hospitalers to Toulouse, and his children played the same role in regard to the Templars. By the time they did so in 1128-1132, Toset himself may have gone eastward, being recorded as in Jerusalem in 1141. The gift of 1128-1132 appears to have been of the original emplacement of the Temple in the City, and was made by Toset's sons Raymond Raterius and Bertrand Estroubera (a nickname meaning "the spur" ?) and by his daughters Bruna and Sibilia, together with their husbands Gerald Engilbertus and Raymond Sarracenus.[9] After

---

[5] Saint-Étienne 227 (15 DA 2 79) (undated) titled "Breve de pignoris [lege pignoribus]."

[6] Magnou, *Réforme Grégorienne à Toulouse*, Appendix Nos. 14 and 15 (dated around 1080) and Douais, *Saint-Sernin*, No. 290 (July 1083).

[7] See the document of March 1133 or 1134 described in note 10 below.

[8] Malta 1 43 i and ii, in May during the latter part of the reign of William, count of Poitou and Toulouse (1097-1108 and 1113-1119, there being two occupations by this prince). The church was sold for 396 shillings and half of the pre-existing hospital next to the Daurade was pledged for 60 shillings. Subsequent gifts and pledges are recorded in Malta 1 43 iii, and 1 44, the former being dated in the latter part of the episcopate of Amelius (1105-1139). Others than our Tolosa were involved, the seigniors of Auterive and an Unald of Lanta, thus showing the social level of Toset and his line.

[9] Malta 1 45 published and dated in Albon, ed., *Cartulaire ... de l'Ordre du Temple*, No. 20. In his notes, Albon conjectured that Toset was in Jerusalem from 1132 to 1152, but a glance at Röhricht, *Regesta regni Hierosolymitani 1097-1291*, No. 205 gives only one reference to a Toset de Tolosa there in February 1141. The others are to a simple Toset, a name that could have been carried by another.

this, Raymond and Bertrand are never seen again, and, as we shall see, it was through Bruna, their sister, that the name Tolosa was transmitted or given new life.

Adverted to above, the charter of 1133 or 1134 informs us that the lords of Calmont granted Gerald Engilbertus and Raymond Sarracenus and their wives who, be it noted, were named and expressly described as the daughters of Toset, pasturage, docking, fishing, and milling rights along the waterfront of the City from the count's meadow to the Old Bridge, in short, an ample area including the later Ile-de-Tounis. Calmont also granted Gerald and Raymond the tithing of Saint-Rémézy together with the "vicaria Tolose et Burgi," that is, of the City and Bourg, a grant that tells us something not perceived in my earlier book on Toulouse, namely that the vicarage of Toulouse was in the possession of the lords of Calmont.[10] Furthermore, since the grant of 1133 or 1134 was designed to protract a long standing relationship between the Calmonts and the Tolosa, it comes as no surprise to learn that Gerald Engilbertus, the husband of Toset's daughter Bruna, is called vicar in other sources from 1125 to 1127.[11]

To pause for a moment, it is obvious that the Tolosa were members of the count's service cadre, and it seems that the family held the vicarial office for at least three generations. The role of the Tolosa as vicars and then as chaptermen was supplemented by their power over the local church. As may be seen in these pages, they held the tithing of Saint-Rémézy or a substantial part of it, and also had a major portion of the Dalbade church. And, when they sold or surrendered this direct owner-ship of ecclesiastical facilities in the twelfth century, they replaced it by occupying offices in the local church, the Templars, for example, and the cathedral chapter of Saint-Étienne.[12] In short, the Tolosa, like the counts

---

[10] Malta 3 177 (March 1133 or 1134, copied in 1186 and 1221) where Dozo de Calmonte and his brother Augerius agree to give Gerald Engilbertus and Raymond Sarracenus and their wives Bruna and Sibilia, daughters of Toset de Tolosa, both expressly described as such in the act, what their family had earlier granted Bernard Raymond Tolose and Toset. This consisted of the "aqua," "capitium," fishing, milling, etc. "de prato comitis usque ... ad caput pontis" (the Old Bridge) and extending from the river to the public road. In addition, they gave them the "decima Sancti Remegii et vicariam Tolose et Burgi." In payment for this "fevum Ramundus Sarracenus fuit homo Dozonis ... et Geraldus Engilbertus fuit homo Augerii," and, on their deaths or that of their wives, the lords are to have a "rachat" of 50 shillings.

[11] See my *Toulouse*, pp. 33-34, 39, and 171.

[12] Among others, note the master of the Temple Peter in 1167-1179 and Arnold in 1221-1224 listed in Du Bourg, *Ordre de Malte*, p. 24, and the cathedral canons Bertrand and Pons in PAN, J 322 56 (July 1235).

themselves, received the remuneration or salary for their offices as much from ecclesiastical as from secular goods. During the century we are now examining, the Tolosa, just like their prince, were, so to speak, secularizing.

To return to the daughters of Toset and Poncia, we see Sibilia and her husband Raymond Sarracenus in 1137, but hear nothing of them after 1152 when Sibilia, acting for herself and her husband, gave the Hospital her rights in the Dalbade church.[13] It may be here suggested parenthetically that it is probable that Sarracena de Noerio, the wife of the seignior of Noé and founder of a Toulousan family bearing the name Noerio, was a daughter or descendant of this pair.[14] Bruna's descendants, however, bore the name Tolosa and carried it into the future. In 1152, she, her husband Gerald Engilbertus, their son Toset, and Arnold Bafetus, the spouse of their daughter Giula, stood together in an instrument dealing with the holdings at Rosers.[15] Bruna is seen until 1162, her daughter Giula until 1174 (her history being then linked with that of the Bafetus and Maillaco families), and her three sons William, Raymond Aton, and Toset de Tolosa acting together about holdings at Pouvourville and Pechdavid south of Toulouse, and at Braqueville on the west bank of the Garonne.[16] Thereafter, the histories of the brothers begin to diverge.

[13] Malta 1 3 (December 1137) enfeoffed by Gerald Engilbertus and Raymond Sairacenus and their wives Bruna and Sibilia; TAM, AA 1 2 (July 1147) Toset witnessed a comital privilege to the town; Malta 2 50 (August 1147) where property near the Dalbade is enfeoffed to the Hospital by Raymond Sarracenus and Sibilia and by Arnold Bafetus and his wife Giula; Grandselve 3 ii (February 1152, copied in 1195) Raymond Sarracenus and wife Sibilia and Gerald Engilbertus and wife were landlords of property on the street called Bouquières in the City; see May 1152 in note 15 below; and Malta 25 2 (December 1152) where Sibilia, daughter of Toset, and her husband Raymond Sarracenus gave the Hospital her rights in the Dalbade church.

[14] E 510 (December 1152, copied in 1190 and 1206) concerning goods at Ysola Rando (the modern Redon near Belsoleil) in the lordship of Raymond Sarracenus and Sibilia, and E 510 iii (June 1184, copied in 1207) adjacent property among whose lords were Walter de Noerio and his wife Sarracena.

[15] Malta 5 292 i (May 1152, copied in 1230) enfeoffed property "ad Rosarios," a place with meadows near the Hers river, probably near the modern Le Palais and Lespinet (l'Espinet).

[16] To review the evidence chronologically, note that Toset was seen in an act of July 1147 cited in note 13 above, and one of May 1152 in note 15; Raymond Aton and his wife Ramunda in Malta 1 53 (August 1157) pledged their portion of the tithing of Saint-Rémézy across the Garonne; Malta 1 5 (December 1157) Bruna and her sons Toset, Raymond Aton, and William Tolose enfeoffed property "ad Punctam" near Launac (Launaguet) to the north of the town; Malta 12 3 (April 1161) enfeoffment of land in the region of Pouvourville and Flamolriu (near Pechdavid) by Arnold Bafetus, Giula his wife, and Bernard Hugh their son, with the consent of Giula's brothers Toset (and Bernarda his wife), Raymond Aton, and William Tolose, some of the property being located at the

The oldest brother, Toset, was the most distinguished, being a chapterman, an arbitral judge, and a person of decisive and recognized weight in 1189. At that date, he, Aimeric de Castronovo, and the bishop of Toulouse were the principal notables entrusted with drawing up the terms of the settlement between the town and the count.[17] 1189, in fact, is the last time we see Toset alive. Starting in 1192, all subsequent references speak of him as dead, but they also give much information about his holdings along the town waterfront and in the mills of the Château Narbonnais and the Daurade.[18] Toset's younger brothers were longer lived. William was seen until 1200 and was stated to be dead by 1215, but Raymond Aton was still alive in 1221.[19]

"podium" called Font Balmar (Pechdavid and Pechaimeric) which had come to Giula "in divisione quam fecerunt cum Toseto et cum predictis suis fratribus"; Malta 3 55 (February 1162) where Toset Tolose, Raymond Aton, and Wiliam Tolose sold rents at Férétra to the Hospital; Malta 12 4 (August 1162) enfeoffment of goods at Rocastrictorum (Roche-des-Étroits on the Garonne) and the "podium" of Fontana Balmar by the above three brothers, called sons of Bruna, and with the consent of their sister and her husband; Malta 1 60 (February 1163) the same actors with property at Férétra; Malta 1 75 (January 1169) Toset de Tolosa a witness; PAN, J 328 1 i (August 1173) the same; Malta 3 145 i (November 1173, copied in 1182 and 1221) where the three brothers were lords of a "casal" adjacent to holdings of the Temple and the town wall; and Saint-Étienne 227 (26 DA 2 36) (August 1174) where the three brothers, their sister and her husband sell land at Braqueville.

[17] Chapterman in 1180-1181 and 1183-1184; councilor in 1181-1182; arbitral judge assisting the abbot of Lézat in PBN, MS lat. 9189, fols. 249r and 251r (December 1179); and TAM, AA 1 8 (January 1189).

[18] Malta 1 100 (April 1180) Toset and his daughter Bruna or Brus Martina, wife of Pons David, arrange about her dowry; PBN, MS lat. 9189, fol. 250v (January 1181) Toset a witness; TAM, DD 1 61 1 (January 1183, copied in 1212, 1241, and 1280) refers to property of Toset at the mills, and was attested by his brother Raymond Aton, Bertrand, son of Arnold Bafetus, and Bertrand and Raymond Aton de Montibus; PBN, MS lat. 9189, fol. 252rb (November 1189) a witness is William de Tolosa "frater Toseti"; PAN, J 330 5 (December 1192) holdings of the sons of Toset de Tolosa near the mills of the Château Narbonnais; TAM, AA 1 22 (April 1199) in which a consular judgment adverts to a suit between the Daurade and Toset in the past; and finally Saint-Sernin 599 (10 35 16) 5th instrument in group of membranes tied together iv (January 1200) where Aimeric de Castronovo sold Bernard Raymond and Peter de Tolosa, sons of the deceased Toset, property at Launac (Launaguet), Pont-d'Alned, and Puncta.

[19] Grandselve 2 (November 1177) where William de Tolosa sold a meadow at Rosers; ibid., (June 1178) William for himself and his brother Raymond Aton enfeoffed a meadow there; see the act of January 1182 in the note above for Raymont Aton "frater Toseti"; Malta 3 98 (August 1187) sale at Rosers and Campvital by the brothers Raymond Aton and William Tolose, the heirs of their sister Giula, and other landlords; for William, see November 1189 in the note above; E 505 (April 1190, copied in 1218) property and persons mentioned above under August 1187; Raymond Aton de Tolosa a consul in 1196-1197; PBN, MS lat. 9189, fol. 250r (March 1200) where William de Tolosa and Bernard Raymond his nephew were witnesses; Malta 5 291 (May 1215, copied in 1218 and 1221) where land at Rosers was sold to the Temple with the consent of the Bafetus and Maillaco family, that of Noé, and of Raymond Aton de Tolosa for himself and Sicard de Tolosa as

Pitifully little is known about the children of the brothers Raymond Aton and William. William had a son who bore his name. Seen in 1215 and 1221, the younger William was on both occasions in the "bailia" of a Sicard de Tolosa, a tutorship that tells us that William was either a minor or incapacitated.[20] Sicard, however, is an interesting person. Owing to his tutelage of the above mentioned William, he may well have been the son of Raymond Aton. On the other hand, there were surely other Tolosa lines about which we know little, and one of these appears in 1155 alienating in the form of a "pignus" the church of (Ramonville-)Saint-Agne to a William de Tolosa. The persons involved were a Raymond Massuirri (a nickname?) and his sons Bonmacip, Toset, and Sicard.[21] Sicard, in short, may have derived from this group. At any rate, he was a knight who was close to the count throughout the 1230s, but his promising career was ruined by the fact that he was a Cathar and was sentenced as such in 1237.[22]

Before turning back to the line derived from Toset de Tolosa, it may be remarked parenthetically that the name Raymond Aton disappeared from the Tolosa family after the generation of Toset, and was not to reappear there until later in the thirteenth century. In the meantime, the reader may observe that several families habitually carried the name Aton, and one of them was an Aton who carried the name Peter de Tolosa de Portaria.

---

tutor of William, son of the deceased William de Tolosa; and Malta 3 145 ii (September 1221) where Raymond Aton de Tolosa, acting for William de Tolosa, confirm the acquisition by the Temple of 6 arpents at Rosers once made by the three siblings Toset, Raymond Aton, and William.

[20] See the acts of May 1215 and September 1221 in the note above.

[21] Malta 4 191 one of a bundle of membranes tied together (November 1155). The William de Tolosa will be seen below in May 1157 in note 31.

[22] Malta 3 170 i and ii (May and June 1230) Sicard a witness; ibid., iii (July 1230) Sicard bought the rent of a property "ad Celatam" at Lespinet (l'Espinet); ibid., iv (March 1232) reference to an adjacent holding once sold by the dead Bernard Peter de Tolosa to a Bernard Molinerius, which new vineyard Peter de Tolosa, son of Toset, then held; ibid., v (November 1232) where Sicard bought the rent on that property; and ibid., iv (June 1235) where the latter sold it to the Temple. pan, J 325 2 and 5 (respectively dated February and October 1231) Sicard as a witness to acts of the count. See the act of December 1233 in note 28 below where Sicard witnessed an action by the grandchildren of Toset de Tolosa, showing once again the link to the main line of the family. Pelisson, *Chronicon*, pp. 101 and 111 calls him a knight, and once says he was cited for heresy and once as sentenced for it. Pelisson's first reference is confusing because it calls him "de Gamevilla seu de Tolosa." This may have been a slip because the amnesty of 1279 (Chapter 5) records two condemnations, one of Sicard de Tolosa as No. **32** and the other of Sicard de Gamevilla as No. **190**. The earlier number fits perfectly with the record of the condemnation and excommunication of Sicard de Tolosa in pbn, Doat 21, fols. 145v-148v in July 1237. See also the Gamevilla family history above.

Furthermore, in order to exemplify the complexity of the matter, the reader should examine the history of the Montibus family given above. Here, too, the name Aton was common.

As has been seen, the distinguished Toset de Tolosa had died by 1192, but the happy news is that he had at least one daughter and three sons. The daughter named Bruna or Brus Martina was married to the minter and usurer Pons David, by arrangement between the fathers. She is heard of in 1180 and never again thereafter, and her husband Pons remarried.[23] The sons were a Bernard Raymond, Peter, and Arnold Raymond, the latter of whom appeared in 1203 and is never seen again.[24] Both Bernard Raymond and Peter were very active individuals. Starting in 1196, both were several times consuls, and Bertrand Raymond has the dubious distinction of being a member of Simon de Montfort's government of the town. Peter, however, regilded the family escutcheon by being one of the hostages sent to Paris in 1229.[25] From 1196, the brothers are frequently seen dealing with their holdings in Launaguet, Saint-Agne, and their houses on or near the rue de Comminges in the City. Bernard Raymond is last seen in 1217, and was dead by 1230. His brother Peter lasted longer, and seems to have died between June and October 1233, leaving a widow named Johanna.[26]

---

[23] See the first document of April 1180 in note 18 above, and note also Pons David's history in that of his family above.

[24] Malta 4 191 2nd of a group of membranes tied together (November 1203) where all three attested a sale by Titburga and her husband Peter de Montebruno.

[25] Peter a consul in 1196-1197, Bernard Raymond in 1197-1198, Peter in 1198-1199, Bernard Raymond in 1199-1200, and Peter in 1201-1202. Bernard Raymond was a "curialis vir" for Simon in 1217, and Peter an hostage in PAN, J 310 45 (April 1229). Both brothers took oath to defend the faith in PAN, JJ 21, fol. 78r (December 1203).

[26] See the references to December 1192 and January 1200 in note 18 above; for their service in government, see the note above; TAM, AA 1 27 (August 1201) where Bernard Raymond headed the "probihomines" "qui in carraria Convenarum permanebant," protesting the residence of prostitutes there (rue de Comminges, now rue des Moulins); Saint-Sernin 599 (10 35 16) 5th of a group of membranes tied together v (April 1202, copied in 1219 and 1220) where Bernard Raymond and his brother Peter gave Maurandus "vetus" rights at Launaguet; for November 1203 see note 24 above; MADTG, A 297, fol. 724r (December 1203) the two brothers serving as arbitral judges about properties at Cornebarrieu and Colomiers; Malta 1 17 (January 1208, copied in 1239) the two again being executors of the will of Pons David and recipients of testamentary bequests; Malta 5 292 ii (February 1209, copied in 1230) where the Bafetus and Maillaco family sold the brothers all between the Hers river and the Meiana (possibly a reference to the main channel of the Garonne?) except the Portaria (a port on the river near the mills of the Château Narbonnais, and not the Portaria now located at the present Place du Capitole), and all rents between Portet, Larramet, and Blagnac on the left bank of the Garonne; Malta 1 108 (May 1209) Bernard Raymond took over a debt owed by a Barravus to Peter Maurandus of 720 shillings and "lucrum"; Malta 5 292 iii (October 1230) where India,

Possibly also married to a Johanna, Bernard Raymond appears to have had no other issue than his daughters India and Saissa, respectively married to William Auriolus and Peter Barravus, who appear in the charters from 1230 to 1233.[27] Peter and Johanna, however, had two sons, named Bernard Raymond and Bertrand. Seen from the early 1230s, when they appeared with their widowed mother and their cousins, the brothers continued to share property and activities. Last seen in 1255, Bertrand was dead by 1271, at which time he left a son named Bertrand still in tutelage.[28] Bernard Raymond was more successful. He was a consul in 1246-1247 and was titled both knight and "dominus." By 1246, he was widowed by Alcaia Astro from whom he had a child named Toset, then a minor. Toset appears once again in 1255 as a major.[29] His knightly father was still alive in 1272, and was one of the guardians of his deceased brother's son Bertrand in 1271 when he and many other members of the Tolosa clan, the Bafetus and Maillaco line, and others arrranged about their rights in the waterfront region of the Ile-de-Tounis.[30]

Although not a few persons called Tolosa appear in the documents and cannot be linked to our genealogy, there were some who must have been

wife of William Auriolus, and Saissa, wife of Peter Barravus, daughters of the dead Bernard Raymond de Tolosa sold rights acquired above in February 1209 with the consent of their uncle Peter; Malta 1 128 (June 1232) action by Peter and his nieces about a house on the waterfront; Malta 148 13 1st of two membranes tied together (August 1232) Peter de Tolosa and his son Bernard Raymond witnessed an act about mills on the Save river; Malta 5 294 (June 1233) where Peter acquired a "curia" and much else at Lantourville near Gameville from a Noé; and for October 1233 see the note immediately below.

[27] On Johanna as a heretic, see note 51 below. For October 1230 and June 1232 see the note above. Malta 3 167 ii (October 1233) Bernard Raymond de Tolosa and his cousins India and Saissa and their husbands approve a transfer of meadows on the Hers river.

[28] Malta 5 293 i (December 1233) a sale by the two siblings Bertrand and Bernard Raymond with the consent of their mother Johanna of part of their goods at Rosers, an act attested by Sicard de Tolosa; Malta 4 215 (February 1253) the two brothers as witnesses; Malta 4 200 (November 1255) concerning lands near Lespinet (l'Espinet), Bernard Raymond de Tolosa "miles" and his brother Bertrand, and Bernard Raymond's son Toset are witnesses; Malta 7 117 (March 1271) among the Tolosa was "dominus" Bernard Raymond acting for himself and for Bertrand, son of the quondam Bertrand, acting about the region of the Ile-de-Tounis and Portaria on the Garonne.

[29] For the earlier references, see the two previous notes. PAN, JJ 21, fol. 79v − published in HGL, vol. 8, No. 395 − (November 1246) where one of the litigants is Bernard Raymond de Tolosa, widower of Alcaia, for his son Toset; see the note above for November 1255 with Bernard Raymond and his son Toset; E 506 iii (January 1260, copied in 1260) the knight Bernard Raymond de Tolosa as a witness; and E 508 (May 1268) the same.

[30] For March 1271 see note 28 above, and TAM, II 10 (March 1271-July 1272) where "dominus" Bernard Raymond testified that he paid taxes on all his rural property and also spoke about the Falgario brothers who had refused to do so.

closely related to it. Among these was a family springing from a William
de Tolosa (Table 24) who owned property at Ramonville and Saint-Agne,
Rosers, and other places where the main line described above had theirs.
Married to a Titburga, William was an active landed entrepreneur who is
seen as early as 1150, and was dead by November 1177.[31] His son Peter,
whose wife was Austorga, was dead by March 1187-1188, the date of
the division of their inheritance made by his daughters, Titburga and
Willelma. These were very rich young women, but because, although
they also acquired a farm and other real property, much of their fortune
consisted of rents derived from mortgage ("pignora") service charges, one
imagines that William or Peter probably had sons of whom no record has
been found. The principal real properties of the sisters stretched from the
walls of the town southward to Mervilla and southeast to Gameville, but
more impressive than that is the far wider range of the investments in
"pignora" that covered the whole region of Toulouse.[32]

TABLE 24: TOLOSA – LINE OF WILLIAM DE TOLOSA

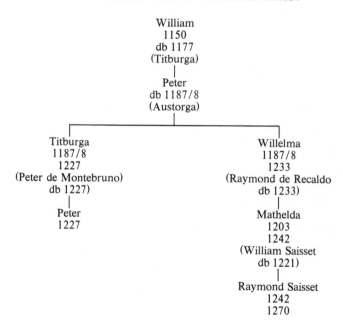

William
1150
db 1177
(Titburga)

Peter
db 1187/8
(Austorga)

Titburga
1187/8
1227
(Peter de Montebruno)
db 1227)

Peter
1227

Willelma
1187/8
1233
(Raymond de Recaldo
db 1233)

Mathelda
1203
1242
(William Saisset
db 1221)

Raymond Saisset
1242
1270

---

[31] Malta 4 191 one of a group of membranes tied together (May 1150) recording the
pledge of part of the tithing of Saint-Agne to William; another of the same group
(November 1155) where Raymond Massuiri's sons pledged the same to the same; another
of the same (May 1157) where Arnold de Sancto Genesio and Raymond de Capitedenario
pledged the church of Saint-Agne to the same William.

[32] Malta 4 191 another of the group of membranes tied together i (March 1187 or
1188, copied in 1203). For goods of the deceased William de Tolosa at Rosers adjacent to

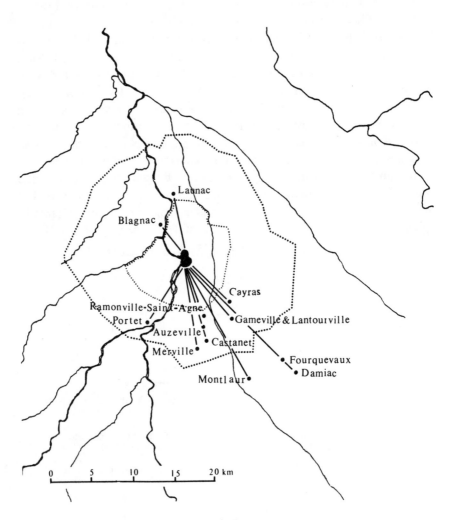

MAP 13. TOLOSA

By 1187-1188 Titburga had married a rural lord named Peter de Montebruno (Montbrun near Montgiscard southeast of Toulouse), and the couple are seen together until 1214 when Montebruno was constituted an heir of another rural notable, Raymond de Montelauro (Montlaur in the same region).[33] Peter was dead by 1227 when we see his widow and her son, also named Peter, selling possessions near the Palace (Château Narbonnais) to Bertrand de Roaxio.[34]

Titburtga's sister Willelma was married to Raymond de Recalto (Recaut, etc., from Ricaud near Castelnaudary), a gentleman in the service of Count Raymond VI, who rose to become the first vicar general of the Toulousain, an office renamed that of the seneschal in 1210.[35] As befitted one bound up with the fortunes of the count, Raymond was not only a participant in the defeats of the Albigensian war (his flight from the battlefield of Castelnaudary being immortalized in William of Tudela's *Canso*), but was also refused admission to the hospital called the Mainaderie by Bishop Fulk of Toulouse in 1214. Weary, Raymond had wished to retire from the world and head that institution.[36] He was still alive in 1221, but his wife was a widow when we last see her in 1233.[37] In the meantime, the child of this pair, Mathelda, had married one of the lords of Laurac in 1203. So important was this match that her dower

that of the William de Tolosa and his brother Raymond Aton, see the two acts of Grandselve 1 (November 1177 and June 1178) quoted in note 19 above. And for William's heir's property there, see the act of October 1233 in note 37 below.

[33] Malta 4 191 – as in the note above – ii and iii (both dated November 1203) alienation by Titburga and Peter de Montebruno of two parts of a tithe acquired from Bernard and Pons David at Flamolriu near Pechdavid and of the church of Saint-Agne. The same act transferred the instruments concerning the property to the Hospital. The witnesses included Bernard Raymond, Peter, and Arnold Raymond de Tolosa, the sons of the deceased Toset. Saint-Étienne 221 (22 3 7bis) (September 1214, copied in 1258) where the testator left Peter some houses and properties in town, his "forcia" at Vieillevigne, all possessions between the tithing of Bruguières up to that of Gardouch, all he had at Combel, and a serf at Baziège.

[34] TAM, II 92 (May 1227) where the two sold Bertrand all "locales domorum" fronting among other places on the "honores" "quos ipsi dederant in palacio," together with 4s 7d of "oblie" on nearby properties.

[35] See my *Toulouse*, pp. 111-112 and 125. As seneschal, he represented the count at the oath to maintain the faith administered by the legates at Toulouse in PAN, JJ 21, fol. 78r (December 1203).

[36] For his early activities and Castelnaudary, see "liasses" 38 and 104 of the *Canso*, and for his attempt to defend Lavaur, Vaux-de-Cernay, *Historia Albigensis*, 1: 219 and 3: 76, and *HGL*, vol. 8, No. 373, col. 1148. For the Mainaderie, see Puylaurens, *Chronica*, Chapter 23. His retirement took place after the defeat of the southern side at Muret. The story is discussed in my "Charity and Social Work in Toulouse 1100-1250," p. 250.

[37] Malta 3 167 ii (October 1233) speaking of property of "domina Willelma de Recaldo" at Rosers adjacent to that of the heirs of Toset de Tolosa.

charter was attested by great notables including the count of Toulouse.[38] William Saisset, her husband, was dead by 1221, but we hear of her and her son Raymond in 1242 negotiating with the count about Belcastel near Lavaur, and it is probably her son who is seen again in 1263 and 1270.[39]

TABLE 25: TOLOSA – LINE OF MACIP AND PETER DE TOLOSA

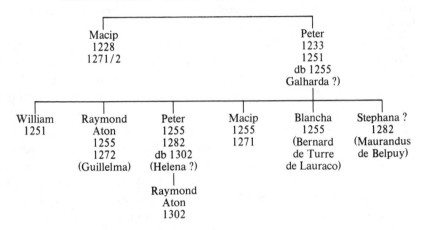

A pair clearly related to these lines of the Tolosa family are the distinguished brothers Macip and Peter de Tolosa (Table 25). Macip and Peter not only shared in the general family possessions, especially along the waterfront of the Garonne in the City, but also had rights in the same localities that Titburga, the daughter of Peter and granddaughter of William mentioned above, had, notably at Montlaur, Fourquevaux and other places. They were therefore closely related not only to the line of Toset charted above but also to that of the two heiresses. They might also have been related to Sicard, the condemned heretic, because it is from these siblings that one of the two known petitioners for the amnesty of 1279 bearing the name Tolosa were to appear.

Whatever their parentage, Macip (Massip and Mancipius) is seen from 1228 and Peter from 1233, if we assume that it was he who was married to Galharda, the daughter of Maurandus "vetus." The brothers thereafter appear frequently.[40] Both were active in Count Raymond VII's administra-

---

[38] PAN, J 320 21 (October 1203).

[39] Fournier and Guébin, eds., *Enquêtes d'Alphonse de Poitiers*, Nos. 42 and 146 (pp. 140b and subjoined notes, and 304ab).

[40] Malta 3 156 (February 1228) Macip a witness; note that the Peter de Tolosa serving as a hostage to Paris in PAN, J 310 45 (April 1229) was probably not this man but instead the Peter of the line of Toset mentioned above, but one cannot be sure; Saint-Sernin 599 (10 35 7) (November 1233) Peter (hopefully this Peter) returned to the creditors of Maurandus "vetus" the eighth part of the "bovaria" of Valségur given him as dowry of his

tion and were frequent witnesses to his acts. Macip was presumably the bailiff of Avignonet who arrested three of the participants in the massacre of the inquisitors there in 1242, and he may have served as Raymond's seneschal of the Venaissin in 1239.[41] Macip outlived his sibling Peter, and was called "maior," "senior," or "probushomo" to distinguish him from a son of his brother also named Macip. Macip appears in the documents until 1271 and 1272 when he was also titled "dominus," surely indicating that he was a knight.[42]

Macip's brother Peter's most spectacular service was as vicar of Toulouse from sometime between July and September 1235 until March or April 1243. His term of office coincided both with the attempt of the count to limit the power of the Inquisition and with the expulsion of the

---

wife Gallarda; Macip was consul 1238-1239; PAN, J 328 21 (April 1245) both brothers witnessed an act of the count; MADTG, A 297, fol. 603v (May 1245) a bailiff of "dominus" Macip for his holdings at Quint, southeast of Toulouse; PAN, JJ 19, fol. 36v (April 1246) the brothers sell to Raymond VII acquisitions at Damiac, etc.; Peter "miles Tolose" took an individual oath of loyalty to Alphonse of Poitiers in PAN, J 308 71 (December 1249), and Malta 2 147 ii and iii (October 1251) where William, son of Peter, acquired a house and gave it to the Templars as a "donatio inter vivos," his father consenting and his uncle Macip attesting.

[41] TBM, MS 609, fol. 140r for the arrests in 1242, and *HGL*, vol. 8, No. 324 (May 1239) for the Venaissin.

[42] Malta 4 200 (November 1255) a sale of holdings at Lespinet (l'Espinet) by a Bernard de Turre de Lauragesio "miles" and his wife Blancha, and by Macip and his nephews Raymond Aton, Peter, and Macip. The instrument was attested by Bernard Raymond de Tolosa "miles," his brother Bertrand and son Toset, thus showing the link with the main line described above; E 65 (July 1257) a suit in the vicar's court against dependents in Castanet and Marvilla brought and won by Raymond Aton and his brother Macip, sons of the dead "dominus" Peter, and witnessed by their uncle Macip; MADTG, A 297, fol. 319v (February 1259) where Guillelma, daughter of Raymond de Alfaro, widow of Raymond Jordan de Tillio (Thil near Grenade), present wife of Raymond Aton de Tolosa, reports that Jordan de Insula, seignior of l'Isle-Jourdain paid 3000 shillings owed to Alfaro. Witnesses were Macip de Tolosa "probushomo" and Bernard de Tolosa "miles." Note parenthetically that it is possible that latter knight was Macip's son. In PAN, J 328 1 vi (March 1251) a witness to a charter about Gémil is a Bernard Mancipius de Tholosa. Had the charter recorded Bernard Mancipii [the genitive] de Tholosa, this would surely have been Macip's son; PAN, J 328 1 xxviii (May-June 1261) Macip "maior"; Malta 7 117 (March 1271) where possessions on the present Ile-de-Tounis and Portaria were rented to a Bernard Raymond "fusterius" in order to build a bridge. The landlord's shares were divisible into 16 parts, 8 of which were the count's, 5 parts those of Macip "senior" and Peter his nephew, 1 part shared equally between Bernard Raymond "miles" and the tutors (Pons de Malhaco de Villamuro, the above Bernard Raymond, and Macip de Tolosa "junior") of Bertrand, son of the deceased "dominus" Bertrand, another to Bernard de Turre "miles" de Lauraco (or Lauraguesio), and a final part to the Barravus family; and TAM, II 10 (March 1271-July 1272) where "dominus" Macip de Tholosa gave testimony about City taxation.

Dominicans from Toulouse by the consuls in 1235, an event that led to the excommunication of both the consuls and our vicar Peter.[43] This knight was still alive in 1251, but was dead by 1255.[44]

Other than his son William, who is not seen after 1251, we learn that Peter had five other children, Raymond Aton, Peter, Macip (also called Macip de Montelauro and Macip de Tolosa "minor" to distinguish him from his uncle of the same name), and their sisters Blancha, the wife of a knight named Bernard de Turre de Lauragesio or Lauraco (Laurac in the Lauragais), and possibly Stephana, wife of Maurandus de Bellopodio. Seen from 1255, these persons, save the sisters, were all together for the last time in 1271 dealing with the waterfront properties. Thereafter Macip disappears and Raymond Aton is not seen after 1272.[45] Their brother, the squire Peter, lasted longer, and acted together with his presumed sister Stephana alienating family holdings at Lespinet (l'Espinet), Rosers, and Campvidal in 1282.[46] After that, track is lost of this family save that, in 1302, an Helena, widow of a squire named Peter de Tholosa, and tutrix of her son Raymond Aton de Tholosa, enfeoffed some lands at Cayras.[47]

A view of the social level of this branch of the family is shown by charters of 1259 about the 3000 shillings Morlas dowry brought by Guillelma, the wife of Raymond Aton de Tholosa. Willelma was the daughter of Raymond de Alfaro, the lord of Saint-Jory and a onetime seneschal of Agen, and, in her first marriage, had been joined to Raymond

---

[43] Guilhalmonus Dalart was vicar in PAN, J 322 56 (July 1235) and Peter was in office in PAN, J 320 47 (September 1235); PAN, J 330 13 (May 1238); PAN J 314 21 (September 1241); PAN, J 302 73 (February 1242); PAN, J 314 24 (February 1243); and PAN, J 314 23 (March 1243). Berengar de Promilhaco was called vicar first in PAN, J 314 72 (September 1243).

[44] He was still in the count's service even after his vicarage for which, see the index of the *Layettes du Trésor*, vol. 2. For his individual oath of 1239 to Alphonse of Poitiers and his appearance in 1251 see note 40 above. It was probably his son Peter who was consul in 1251-1252, but perhaps himself.

[45] For the appearances of these brothers in November 1255, July 1257, February 1259, and March 1271 see note 42 above; PBN, Doat 73, fol. 336r (July 1270) where Raymond Aton served as an arbiter between the bishop and the Carmelites of Toulouse; described as a squire, Raymond Aton was a consul in 1271-1272; and he acquired property near Castanet in E 65 (March 1272). His brother Macip was last seen in 1271. For Stephana, see the note below, but observe also that she may have been a sister of the next generation of the family.

[46] PAN, J 302 4 (May 1276) the sale of rent to the crown on a house on the "carraria Pilisarditis joculatoris" (modern rue des Filatiers) by the squire Peter, son of the knight Peter; for March 1279 see note 50 below; Peter as a consul in 1280-1281; and Malta 4 233 (March 1282) Peter and Stephana, widow of Maurandus de Bellopodio, Peter still being a "domicellus."

[47] E 65 (April 1302).

Jordan, lord of Thil, and son of Odon Bernard de Terrida, third son of Jordan III, lord of l'Isle-Jourdain.[48] Blancha's husband, the knight Bernard de Turre, was also a distinguished man. He was a companion on crusade of Alphonse of Poitiers and one of the lords of Saint-Sauveur near Laurac.[49]

The religious sentiments of this large clan cannot be discerned, but, like most knightly and patrician houses of Toulouse, they appeared to have tasted Catharism somewhat. Two petitioners bore this surname. One was the squire Peter, son of the knight Peter, whose career has been rehearsed above. The other was Oldric de Prinhaco acting as tutor for the infants of a deceased "dominus" William de Tholosa, a person whose history we do not know.[50] Sicard was the only Tolosa known to have been sentenced for this divergence. The inquisitors of the mid-forties also uncovered evidence that Johanna, wife of one they called Bernard Raymond Tozez de Tholosa, had witnessed an heretication in the mid-twenties.[51] This is clearly the wife of our familiar Bernard Raymond, the son of Toset de Tolosa, but one does not know if anything came of that. There are no unattached Johannas and no unnamed Tolosa wives in the list of 1279.

---

[48] For the details see February 1259 in note 42 above, and the actual payment of the 3000 shillings to Raymond Aton is in the same MADTG, A 297, fol. 323r (November 1259). As lord of Thil near Grenade, Raymond Jordan had granted that community its customs in May 1246 in MADTG, A 297, fol. 315r. On Raymond and the other members of this clan see Fournier and Guébin, eds., *Enquêtes d'Alphonse de Poitiers*, p. lxxii, and Contrasty, *Histoire de Saint-Jory*, especially pp. 32-33.

[49] PAN, J 319 1 (April 1258) Bernard de Turre shared the criminal justice at Saint-Sauveur near Laurac and Fanjeaux with the crown. In Molinier, *Correspondance ... d'Alphonse de Poitiers*, No. 729 (June 1268) he owed the count 400 pounds of Tours for debts contracted while on crusade.

[50] Chapter 6 (March 1279). In TBM, MS 609, fols. 45r, 59r, 206v, there was a William de Tolosa at Gameville in the 1230s and 1240s who was associated with the Cathars, but there is no evidence that this person was a citizen of Toulouse, and the list of 1279 contains only citizens.

[51] TBM, MS 609, fol. 80r testimony by a knight from Saint-Michel-de-Lanès in the Lauragais that his sister had hereticated in the mid-1220s at Toulouse and that Johanna had been there.

Trageto

In 1222 an Arnold de Trageto was a councilor for the consuls, and he attained the grade of consul himself in 1227-1228. His advancement was cut short when he was sentenced for heresy sometime before February 1237.[1] In the meantime, a Bernard de Trageto "iuvenis" appeared in 1230, a person whose identification tells us that there was then a Bernard de Trageto "maior."[2] Such a person soon appears. In 1243 an Arnold Bernard, and Bernard "iuvenis" take oath to the Peace of Paris, and, in 1251, we see a Bernard "probushomo" and "maior" twice so identified in the charters. One of the documents of 1251 records the testament of Bonafos, wife of Bernard John de Trageto. Living in the Dalbade parish, Bonafos distributed 100 shillings in charity and gifts, and left her paraphernal properties (an arpent of vineyard and an "honor" adjacent to the Temple and the City wall) to her three minor children, her sons Arnold and Bernard and her daughter Geralda. The "probushomo" Bernard attested this testament as did a "cultellarius."[3] The presence of this cutler is indicative because, the year before the will was written, the Arnold de Trageto seen in 1243 was also called "cultellarius."[4] This was, in short, a family of craftsfolk.

After this, mentions of this surname are rare. A Bernard de Trageto, son of the deceased Bernard, was a consul in 1269-1270, and, in 1271 or 1272, Bernard and Bernard John de Trageto of the Dalbade quarter gave testimony in an inquiry about taxes in the City.[5] A Bernard of this name was consul in 1278-1279, and a final and sure member of this family appeared in 1279. This was Bernard Arnold de Trageto, a minor under the tutelage of Bernard Hugh de Dealbata, who petitioned for the amnesty of heretical inheritances.[6]

---

[1] TAM, AA 1 75 (March 1222). He was No. **33** of the list of 1279, for which see Chapter 5 above.

[2] Malta 3 1700 ii (June 1230, copied in 1235) a witness.

[3] PAN, J 305 29 (February 1243). Malta 2 147 i and ii (respectively June and October 1251, copied in 1252). In the first act the name is Trajeto, and our Bernard was there called "probushomo." In the second act, he was "maior." The cutler was William de Borrello.

[4] E 509 iv (November 1250, copied in 1255).

[5] TAM, II 10 (between April 1271 and July 1272).

[6] Chapter 6 (March 1279).

Turre

Because there were many towers and at least one street named Turre (the modern rue Larrey), the name Turre (Latour) was common in Toulouse. It was also widely used in the countryside, and one rural knight of this name was married into the family named Tolosa in town.[1] There were, moreover, individuals in such varied occupations as a barber, weaver, and tailor of this name who cannot be related to the lines of the City and Bourg described below.[2]

TABLE 26: TURRE, OF THE CITY

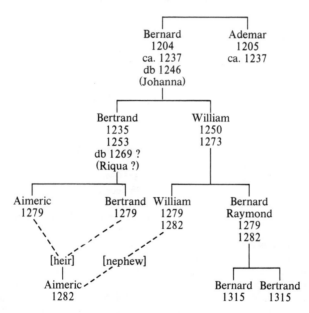

---

[1] See the history of the Tolosa above. Note also in PAN, J 324 6 xi (November 1273) where we see a John de Turre, brother of the squire William de Brugariis, who had predeceased him.

[2] A Peter de Turre consul in 1231-1232, and, called "sartor," was listed in the amnesty of 1279 as No. **47**, condemned therefore before February 1237; PBN, MS lat. 9189, fol. 237ra (May 1238) has a Bernard de Turre "raditor barbarum"; and a Bernard de Turre "textor" in PAN, J 327 4 xviii (February 1275) was a member of the Carmelite confraternity.

Although there are earlier Turrenses or persons bearing the family name, the first members of the City family to offer a coherent line are the brothers Bernard and Ademar (Table 26). First appearing as consuls in 1204 and 1205, they were thereafter seen intermittently, but were then both sentenced as heretics by February 1237.[3] Perhaps Bernard's wife Johanna was a broadminded woman. When a widow and in retirement as a nun at Lespinasse in 1246, she was condemned for having listened to both the Cathars and the Waldensians.[4]

Bernard and Johanna seem to have had two sons. One was Bertrand who first appears in 1235 as an executor for one of the Roberti de Burgo. He then served as an executor for a Descalquencs in 1252 in a charter where he was called "de Civitate," and was dealing with the Roberti again in 1253.[5] These connections show that Bertrand had means, but they also pose a problem because of a Bertrand de Turre who was given life imprisonment by the Inquisition in 1247.[6] Even though condemned heretics sometimes obtained releases from Rome or perhaps even from other ecclesiastic authorities, it is difficult to imagine such a person serving as the executor of an important man five years after his own imprisonment.[7] There may, therefore, have been two persons bearing this name. Whatever the case, a widow of Bertrand de Turre was gradually collecting her marriage jointure as late as 1269, and her dowry and marriage gift totalled a very substantial 2300 shillings.[8] The last news of

[3] Bernard in the term of 1204-1205, and Ademar in 1205-1206; E 43 (January 1214) the two described as brothers; Malta 1 114 (February 1216) where they have properties in the region Lespinet (l'Espinet) and Montaudron; Bernard in TAM, AA 1 75 (March 1222) as a consular councilor; E 510 ii (December 1225, copied in 1228) where the siblings Bernard and Ademar de Turre appear together; E 506 (November 1230) Ademar as a witness to a charter involving Jews and Bertrand David; both listed in the amnesty of 1279 (Chapter 5) as Nos. **95** and **96**; and Ademar expressly mentioned as sentenced in PBN, Doat 21, fol. 181r (September 1237).

[4] Douais, *Inquisition*, 2: 31 (June 1246).

[5] Malta Garidech 1 (1 2) ii (June 1236, copied in 1238) where the executor Bertrand was absent and owed the dying Vital Robertus 100 shillings; PAN, J 305 29 (February 1243) oath to the Peace of Paris; MADTG, A 297, fol. 880r (August 1252) "de Civitate"; Grandselve 9 (June 1253) where a witness is Bertrand, son of the dead Bernard de Turre.

[6] Listed in the amnesty of 1279 as No. **199** and specifically in Douais, *Inquisition*, 2: 44 (August 1247) with life imprisonment.

[7] See, however, the case of Bertrand de Roaxio freed from prison by Innocent IV sometime between 1247 and 1254 in the Roaxio family history above.

[8] Saint-Sernin 599 (10 35 22) i and ii (February 1269) in which Rigua admits to having received 1000 shillings of her jointure from her husband's executors. The property was half a farm at Valségur, including a tower and a dovecote, and the executors were a Franciscan and the rector of Saint-Sernin, spoken for by a "domicellus" and another layman.

the line of this Bertrand, or of that of one of these Bertrands, derives from 1279 and 1282. At the former date, the brothers Aimeric and Bertrand, sons of the dead Bertrand, petitioned for the amnesty of heretical inheritances, and, in 1282, Aimeric is seen in an act working together with his uncles.[9]

The uncles appear to have derived from a brother of the older Bertrand mentioned above, another child of the original Bernard and Johanna. His name was William. William is seen from 1250 when we learn that he, sometimes called "de Urbe," had a house on the "carraria piscatorum" (the southern or City section of the modern rue des Blanchers).[10] In 1269 and 1273, we learn that he sold the crown his share of the town's tolls for 80 Toulousan pounds, and that he was the son of a deceased Bernard who lived on the street "de Turre." [11] In 1282 we hear that William, then called an "olierius" or oil merchant, and his brother Bernard Raymond de Turre were handling a property together with their nephew Aimeric, mentioned in the paragraph above.[12] Before that, in 1279, William and Bernard Raymond had been active in seeking the amnesty, one being a proctor and the other a petitioner.[13] Lastly, we catch a glimpse of Bernard Raymond's succession when we hear of Bernard and Bertrand de Turre, sons of the quondam Bernard Raymond de Turre "burgensis Tholose," with a holding on the "carraria piscatorum" in 1315.[14]

The bourghal family named Turre begins with a John and a William (Table 27). William is seen from 1192 onward and John from 1196, but the first time we get a grip on this clan is in 1215 and 1216.[15] Because of

[9] Chapter 6 (March 1279) lists Aimeric and Bertrand, brothers and sons of Bertrand de Turre deceased. For February 1282 see note 12 below.

[10] Bernard Guy, *De fundatione*, pp. 36 and 39 (circa 1250) with the house on the "carraria piscatorum"; TAM, DD 1 1 3 iii (December 1262, copied in 1267 and 1270) William de Turre, son of the dead Bernard, bought a house near the mills of the Château Narbonnais; and TAM, DD 1 1 4 ii and iv (dated respectively September 1263 and June 1264) acquisition of more property there by William de Turre de Urbe.

[11] Molinier, *Correspondance ... d'Alphonse de Poitiers*, No. 1314 (July 1269) and PAN, J 324 6 iv (November 1273) sale by William de Turre "civis," son of the quondam Bernard de Turre, who lived on the "carraria de Turre," and whose wife's name was Bernarda.

[12] E 480 (February 1282) where the knight Hugh de Palacio refers to the lords of a piece of property on the "carraria piscatorum" who are William and Bernard Raymond de Turre who act for themselves and their nephew Aimeric de Turre.

[13] Chapter 6 (March 1279) William de Turre "olierius" and Bernard Raymond de Turre. William was called "olierius" there because another proctor was named William de Turre "legista."

[14] Daurade 169 (February 1315).

[15] William de Turre was consul 1192-1193, 1194-1195, and 1198-1199, and John in 1205-1206. John is seen as a witness in MADTG, A 297, fol. 798r (December and February 1196 and 1197); William sold a house in E 506 (January 1205); he was a witness in PAN, JJ 21, fol. 69v (March 1207); and had property in E 538 i (December 1207).

their links with the substantial Astro family, we then see three brothers, John, William, and Vasco. Important worthies, described as "de Suburbio," these persons are last seen toward the end of the great war, one in 1226 and the others in 1229.[16] Vasco, the husband of Dias Astro, was surely the most active of the siblings. He was a consul in 1221-1222, 1224-1226, and again in 1230-1231, but his success was cut short by being condemned for Catharism before February 1237. His presumably older brother William was sentenced for the same deviance shortly after his sibling.[17]

TABLE 27: TURRE, OF THE BOURG

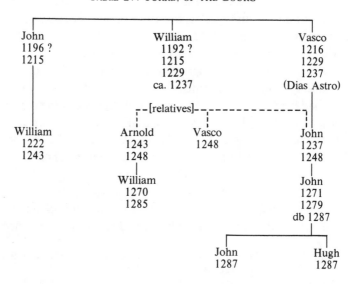

These unhappy brothers had issue. John had a son named William, who is seen only in 1222 and 1243, and is not seen thereafter.[18] Either

---

[16] E 501 i (March 1215, copied in 1233) the brothers John and William; PBN, MS lat. 9189, fol. 241v (May 1216) where three executors of William Pons Astro were John, William, and Vasco de Turre. William was to be "in loco parentis" together with Astro's widow to raise his minor son, and Vasco (either the above or his son) was the second husband of Astro's daughter Dias; ibid., fol. 240v (March 1217) has Astro's widow and John and William acting together; in E 573 (March 1225, copied in 1233) the brothers William and John act together; William was a consul in 1225-1226; and in PBN, MS lat. 9189, fol. 241v the brothers William and Vasco agreed about an Astro matter in August 1229.

[17] In the amnesty of 1279 (Chapter 5) Vasco was No. **56** and William No. **100**.

[18] As councilor for the consuls in TAM, AA 1 75 (March 1222), and taking oath to the Peace of Paris in PAN, J 305 29 (February 1243).

William or Vasco had children named Arnold and Vasco, and the older Vasco certainly had a child named John. Whoever their fathers may have been Arnold, John and Vasco, brothers or cousins, are seen active from the late 1230s until 1248.[19]

After 1248, there is a gap in the family history. It is possible that the Arnold mentioned in the paragraph above was a "jurisperitus," and the father of a William de Turre de Burgo, himself a lawyer, who appears from 1270 to 1285. This William served in 1279 as a proctor for the amnesty and was therefore a relative of the line described above.[20] A second successor was John, son of the deceased John de Turre, who appears in 1271. John was a petitioner in 1279, and was dead by 1287 when his sons John and Hugh sold their substantial house in the Portaria to the lord of l'Isle-Jourdain.[21]

Perhaps the most intriguing fact in the history of these two families is that they were both hard hit by the attack on Catharism, and nevertheless both survived and even flourished. Four of the five members of the two sets of brothers seen in these pages had been sentenced for heresy, as had one of their sons, but the families continued.

---

[19] PAN, J 317 24 (November 1237) mentioned John de Turre, son of Vasco (himself still alive) as a member of a group of creditors; both Arnold and John took oath to the Peace of Paris in 1243; and Arnold, John and Vasco are mentioned in E 896 (September 1248) where John is an executor of an Astro.

[20] E 579 (January 1270) William, son of the quondam Arnold de Turre; TAM, II 61 (April 1277) where William, son of the dead Arnold de Turre "jurisperitus," served as proctor; Chapter 6 (March 1279) records a William de Turre, "legista de Burgo," as proctor for the amnesty; and TAM, II 61 (February 1285) where the consuls and a noble "compromise" their case in the hands of two laymen, one being "Magister" William de Turre.

[21] Grandselve 10 (March 1271) John de Turre, son of the deceased John de Turre; Chapter 6 (March 1279) John as a petitioner; MADTG, A 297, fol. 89r (June 1287) where John and Hugh sons of the quondam John de Turre sold rents paid on a stone house and stores "prope Portariam" adjacent to the church of Saint-Quentin.

Unde

The name Unde (Unda, Onda, and Aonda) derived from Ondes, a place north of Toulouse. During the war years, two persons with this name were consuls, Arnold in 1218-1220, and Peter in 1226-1227. These persons were both condemned well before February 1237 for Catharism.[1] The last blow fell in 1246 when we learn that Ramunda, wife of an Arnold Unde, was given life imprisonment for heresy.[2]

Three years before this last disaster, another Arnold took oath to uphold the Peace of Paris, and, in 1248-1249, a person of the same name was a consul.[3] In 1262 we again hear of this Arnold (presumably) and of his brother Peter who are described as the sons of Arnold Unde de Cruce Baranhoni (modern Croix Baragnon in the City).[4] Arnold was again a consul in 1268-1269, in 1270 a witness to a consular act, and was mentioned as living in the quarter of Saint-Pierre and Saint-Géraud and paying taxes on all holdings both rural and urban by a witness in 1271 or 1272. In 1276 Arnold objected to his tallage of 40 shillings, and threatened the consuls with an appeal to the royal tribunal.[5] This tallage probably means that his estate was estimated to be worth 80,000 shillings of Toulouse.[6] Lastly, what ties this wealthy person had to the condemned Arnold and Peter of the 1230s are shown by the fact that Arnold served as

---

[1] In addition to the consular terms, Arnold Aonda was seen as a witness in Malta 3 147 v (February 1224), and Peter Onda was a judge of a consular court on debts in TAM, II 45 (February 1228). In the amnesty of 1279 (Chapter 5) Arnold and Peter were Nos. **8** and **9**.

[2] Douais, *Inquisition*, 2: 17 (May 1246) for Ramunda. The text describes her as the wife and not the widow of Arnold. It is therefore obvious either that the Arnold mentioned in this paragraph was still alive and presumably in prison, or that Ramunda was the wife of the first (?) Arnold described in the paragraph below.

[3] PAN, J 305 29 (February 1243).

[4] E 504 (February 1262) a sale of rents by Arnold Peter Petricola, son of the butcher Petricola.

[5] TAM, AA 3 128 (June 1270); TAM, II 10 (March 1271-July 1272) testimony of the notary Pons de Albeges (Albigesio); and ibid., 63 (August 1276) stating that Arnold lived on the street called "de Forguas" (a street not identified in Chalande and Cau, *Rues de Toulouse*).

[6] In the act of March 1271-July 1272 cited in the note above, the notary Bernard Aimericus stated that the Falgario family had been assessed at the rate of sixpence per 1000 shillings sometime before.

a proctor requesting the amnesty of 1279.[7] What this child or descendant of condemned Cathars did to rebuild the family wealth is not known, but he is thrice mentioned in English sources as a merchant busy in the wine trade with England, having initially been an assistant or agent of the greater merchant Bertrand de Palatio.[8]

---

[7] See his name in Chapter 6 (March 1279) above.

[8] *Calendar of the Close Rolls*, Henry III, dated 1253, p. 477: "Ernaldus de Unde vadlettus Bertrandi de Palatio," and the *Calendar of the Patent Rolls*, Henry III, October 1255 and June 1260, respectively p. 445 and p. 79, in which we see Arnold del Unde associated with Bertrand de Palatio and also with Bernard de Roys (Roaxio), being owed over 758 English pounds, etc.

Villanova

Because the name Villanova was common around Toulouse and also designated a quarter of the Bourg of Toulouse, there were persons of every social level named Villanova in that town.[1] The family I intend to concentrate on here probably derived its name from Villeneuve-Tolosane near Cugnaux and its subordinate family name of Bovilla from a place near the modern Lardenne, both of which sites lie to the west of the Garonne river.[2]

In 1141 Pons Capiscol, Raymond Arnold, and the brothers Pons and Adalbert de Villanova enfeoffed land.[3] The family deriving from the last two persons shall be treated first (Table 28). Pons had been seen as early as approximately 1120, and he and his brother were nephews of Augerius de Calvomonte, one of the two lords of Calmont (near Citegabelle south of town) seen earlier in the history of the Tolosa family to which they had enfeoffed the vicarage of Toulouse. After 1141 the brothers Pons and Adalbert were not seen together again until 1162, when an arbitral court held at Adalbert's farm found in favor of the Hospitalers against a Tolosa claim that was argued by his brother Pons as the tutor of a minor.[4] In the

---

[1] See, for example, E 501 ii (May 1164, copied in 1207) where Peter de Villanova sold property to give 100 shillings to his brother John's widow in order to remarry, and, as we see in ibid., v and vii (respectively dated July 1201 and August 1206), an heir of this family was Ademar de Villanova. Note also in MADTG, A 297, fol. 619r (April 1225) a Pons de Villanova "textor" in Toulouse. From time to time, the notes below will mention the Villanova from Montréal (far to the south of Toulouse) and those from Caraman (southeast of town), the latter of which families was related to Vital Galterius of the Carbonellus and Prinhaco families.

[2] The matter is discussed in C. Higounet, "Le style du 1er avril," *AduM* 49 (1937) 164-172, where he also published the acts of June 1192 and March 1200 respectively referred to in notes 7 and 9 below.

[3] E 573 (May 1141) where the rent was 18 pence annually and the location at La Celata (La Salada just north of the Bourg?).

[4] Pons a town councilor approximately 1120; *HGL*, vol. 5, No. 537 (dated 1138 without month) recording the renunciation by the count of his right of spoil to the bishop, attested by Pons de Villanova and Raymond Arnold de Bovilla; TAM, AA 1 2 (July 1147) a comital grant to the town witnessed by Pons; TAM, AA 1 28 (December 1148) Adalbert at another comital grant; Grandselve 58 Roll I verso iii (June 1149) Augier, his "nepos" Pons and the latter's wife Mabriana, free a serf; Pons a chapterman in 1152; Malta 1 59bis, undated act wherein Pons and Mabriana enfeoffed an "alberga" of 6 knights and 1

meantime and until 1167, we see a lot of Pons, his wife Mabriana, and his alienation of a share in the tithe of Saint-Rémézy which, as we know from the history of the Tolosa family, was gradually being given or sold to the Hospitalers.[5] The brothers are seen together again in 1174 or 1175, which was Adalbert's last appearance, but Pons persisted longer, dying not long before 1183 when we see his widow, his oldest son Jordan, and hear of his other minor children.[6] Unlike his brother also, Pons had been active in government. He several times witnessed acts of the counts, served as a chapterman in 1152, as both vicar and chapterman in 1164, and as chapterman again in 1181-1182. At death, Pons was surely in his seventies and had been married to Mabriana for over thirty years.

In 1192 Pons' sons Jordan, Pons, and Stephen divided the family holdings in a document that mentions their cousin Pons, the son of Adalbert, and two other close relatives, Arnold and Bertrand, possibly also Adalbert's sons.[7] The charter only records Jordan's share of the division with his siblings. We learn that he had property in town around the square called Montaygon (modern Place Saint-Georges) and the Croix Baragnon. To the south of the town, he had rents and lands extending from the Garonne and the count's meadow (Pré Comtale) to Pouvourville and Lespinet (l'Espinet). On the left bank of the Garonne his rights were even more extensive, including much around Villeneuve-Tolosane, half the "condamina" of Frouzins, the church of Saint-Simon, and half the "forcia" of Colomiers.

---

sergeant in their part of the tithe of Saint-Rémézy to the Hospitalers, with the agreement of unnamed children; Malta 1 55 (dated 1157 without month) where Pons and Raymond Arnold de Bovilla give a "casal" on the street of Saint-Rémézy, Pons promises 100 shillings at death, Adalbert one third of his gifts "pro anima" at death, and both swear to enter the Hospital and only that house if they leave the world; Malta 3 52 ii (August 1159) pledge of more of the tithe by Pons and Mabriana; Malta 12 3 (April 1161) Pons a witness; Malta 3 182 i (May 1163) Pons and Mabriana and the tithe again; in 1164 Pons was both vicar of Toulouse and chapterman, and Raymond Arnold de Bovilla was chapterman; and Malta 1 9 (August 1165), published in my *Toulouse*, pp. 194-196, where Pons, as "curator," pleaded in the "curia" of Adalbert who also sat as one of the judges.

[5] Malta 1 59bis (January 1167) further surrender of tithe by Pons and Mabriana in a charter attested by Adalbert. For other such actions, see the note above.

[6] Saint-Etienne 227 (26 DA 2 111) (October 1170, copied in 1198) Adalbert de Villanova; Malta 135 121 (June 1174) Adalbert a witness about Larramet; PAN J 320 4 (March 1174 or 1175) the two brothers as witnesses; Malta 25 19, an undated charter of a suit dateable to between October 1179 and sometime in 1181 in which Pons was a judge; Pons a chapterman for the City in 1181-1182; and E 510 (December 1183) where Jordan and his mother Mabriana act as tutors or guardians of the other children.

[7] E 503 i (June 1192, copied in 1199 and 1204).

TABLE 28: VILLANOVA – LINES OF THE BROTHERS, PONS AND ADALBERT

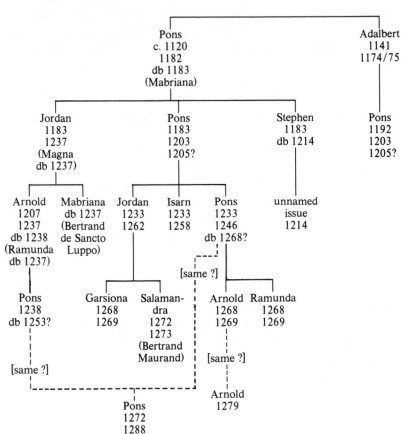

Little is known about Jordan's brothers Stephen and Pons or about his cousin Pons, Adalbert's son. Adalbert's Pons was a consul in 1198-1199, and it is sure that the two Pons were alive in 1202 and 1203, but, although we see one of them in 1205, the only sure thing is that the brothers Pons and Stephen were dead by 1214, both leaving issue.[8]

---

[8] Pons a consul in 1198-1199; E 505 (December 1202, copied in 1224) purchase by Jordan of land at Essart Gayrard on way to Fons Sancti Martini (near Montaudran) witnessed by Bertrand and Pons de Villanova "iuvenis," the latter term being an obvious attempt to distinguish between the two cousins named Pons, but which of the two was the junior is not known; TAM, AA 1 50 (March 1203) Pons "iuvenis" a witness; MADTG, A 297, fol. 407r (May 1205) a witness of a debt owed by the lord of l'Isle-Jourdain is a Pons; and E 43 (January 1214) where the children of Pons and Stephen de Villanova are among the lords of holdings at Motte Saint-Hilaire north of the Bourg.

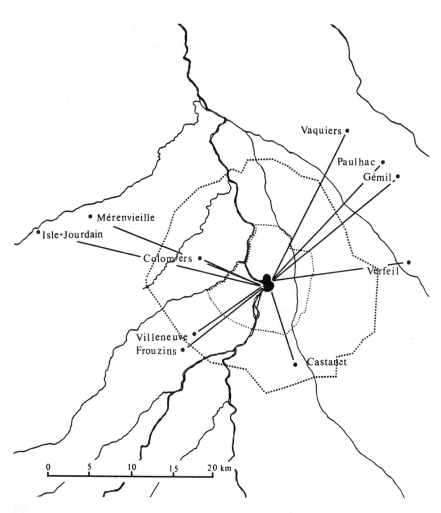

MAP 14. VILLANOVA

Stephen and Pons' brother Jordan was the success of the family. A knight, he was thrice a consul, a creditor of Saint-Sernin, and we see him dealing with his holdings at Montaygon, and on the Garonne and at Braqueville until 1230.[9] Jordan had two children, Arnold and his sister Mabriana who married the knight Bertrand de Sancto Luppo (Saint-Loup-Cammas, north of town). A curiosity of this history is that our sources, the Dominican Pelisson and the later amnesty of 1279, intimate that Jordan's wife Magna had been, in an earlier marriage, the mother of Jordan's son Arnold's wife Ramunda.[10] In more ways than one, indeed, Arnold followed his father's footsteps. Active from 1207, he was also a knight, served as a consul, and, like his father, step-mother, and wife, was a Cathar. Oddly enough, also, the women were dead when sentenced for this divergence in 1237, but both their men were still alive. As a relapsed heretic, Jordan was given life imprisonment in 1237, and Pelisson reports that Arnold was among those "perfecti" who were slain at Montségur in

[9] Jordan was consul in 1196-1197; E 503 ii (March 1200, copied in 1200 and 1204) a sale by him of property at Belsoleil near Montaudran; Jordan consul 1201-1202; for December 1202 see the note above; Saint-Sernin 594 (19 33 8) (May 1203) where Jordan and two other partners lent the monastery 900 shillings in return for the tithe of Saint-Jory and an "alberga" there for ten years; TAM, AA 1 54 (March 1205) where various owners of property at Montaygon confess that the square is public, as are its church, etc. Among those so declaring were Jordan, Bertrand, and Raymond Arnold de Villanova; Grandselve 4 (June 1205) where Jordan and Arnold de Villanova deal with their holdings north of the Bourg; Saint-Étienne 227 (26 DA 2 68) (October 1205) in which Jordan and Arnold, son of the deceased Arnold, deal with property at Braqueville; E 504 (January 1207) with the consent of his wife Magna and son Arnold, Jordan pledged 8 arpents of vineyard and 15 of land at Essart Gayrard to Capitedenario and the Aiscii; Jordan a consul in 1214-1215; PAN, J 326 23 (April 1221) Jordan witness to a comital act; the Villanova councilors of the consuls in TAM, AA 1 75 (March 1222) were Arnold, son of Jordan, Jordan, and Raymond Arnold; Saint-Bernard 138, fol. 83r (June 1222) a sale by Jordan and his son Arnold with the consent of their wives Magna and Ramunda of goods at Essart Gayrard; Saint-Étienne 227 (26 DA 2 68) (November 1222, copied in 1236 and 1246) where Jordan and Arnold, son of the dead Arnold de Villanova, enfeoffed property at Braqueville, TAM, II 46 (February 1227) a court appointed by the consuls judged that Jordan must pay a debt of 114 shillings as "fideiussor" of the deceased lord Isarn de Viridifolio (Verfeil); Saint-Étienne 227 (26 DA 2 47) (November 1230, copied in 1249 and 1256) a judgment against the sons of the deceased Arnold de Villanova, Arnold, Arnold Raymond, and Rabastencs, part of which is to be charged to a willow grove on the Garonne ("albareda") owned half by the debtors and half by Jordan.

[10] Pelisson, *Chronicon*, p. 111, describing the condemned deceased heretics from the City in 1237 wrote: "Magna, uxor Jordani de Villanova, et Ramunda, ejus filia, uxor Arnaldi de Villanova, et filia Jordani praedicti, uxor Bertrandi de Sancto Lupo militis." The pertinent passage from the amnesty of 1279 (Chapter 5) reads: "Jordanus de Villanova, Arnaldus ejus filius, et eorum uxores Ramunda et Magna."

1244. This may not have been the case because we hear of a Pons, son of a deceased Arnold de Villanova, in 1238 and 1243.[11]

This Pons, the son of Arnold, is seen from 1238 until 1257.[12] He was one of the many creditors of the seigniors of l'Isle-Jourdain in 1243, may have had property at Montaygon, and assuredly sold much at Gémil, Paulhac, and Vaquiers to the count's bailiff at Buzet including debts owed to his grandfather Jordan by local people. It was probably this Pons whose erstwhile possessions at Verfeil are mentioned in 1253, but it is hard to know because he had a great-uncle also named Pons, the son of Pons de Villanova, the brother of Jordan and Stephen.[13]

[11] Pelisson, *Chronicon*, p. 111 is not really sure that Arnold was a perfect nor that he died at Montségur, but intimates it. TBM, MS 609, fol. 60r reports that about 1216 Mabriana, wife of Bertrand de Sancto Lop (Luppo), was among the heretics at the house of Sicard de Gameville in Toulouse. On fols. 64v, and 66r, the knight Estult de Rocovilla, reported in February 1246 that the now dead knight Arnold de Villanova had been in his house near the Croix Baragnon around 1225 to 1227 "adoring" heretics. The Rocovillas perhaps rented this house from the Villanova. PBN, Doat 21, fol. 149v records the condemnation of the knight and citizen Jordan in February 1237, assigning him life imprisonment because he had relapsed; ibid., fol. 179v (September 1237) condemnation of the deceased Mabriana, wife of Raymond de Sancto Luppo. The confusion here is the name of her husband because both Pelisson and the amnesty of 1279 give the name Bertrand; and ibid., fol. 179v (September 1237) sentencing of the deceased Ramunda, wife of Arnold de Villanova. In the list of 1279 (Chapter 5) these persons are numbered as follows: Jordan **22**, Arnold **23**, Ramunda **24**, Magna **25**, and Mabriana **185**. For the last references to Arnold, now dead, but referred to in relation to his son Pons, see Clares 24 (May 1238) where Pons de Villanova, son of the dead Arnold de Villanova, served as a witness, and PAN, JJ 19, fol. 27r (March 1243) where the count received the homage of Comminges attested by Pons de Villanova son of the quondam Arnold, and by Jordan de Villanova. The quondam Arnold had been seen in January 1207 (see note 9 above), was a consul in 1217-1218, and appeared in March and June 1229 (again in note 9 above).

[12] For Pons in May 1238 and March 1243 see the base on the note immediately above. In PAN, J 305 29 (February 1243) the oath to the Peace of Paris lists the Villanova singly or in groups as follows: Pons, Bertrand de Bovilla, Arnold and Raymond Arnold, Raymond, Bertrand and Jordan, and Bernard. Two observations may be made. One cannot tell which of the two possible Pons was the one at the oath taking. Also, the Raymond de Villanova mentioned above in the list is surely not a member of our family. He is probably the person who rented a house from the Daurade church in Daurade 189 rent roll dated 1227, is in PBN, MS lat. 9189, fol. 31rb described as a "bursellarius," received an undetermined sentence in Douais, *Inquisition*, 2: 5 (March 1246), and is No. **225** in the amnesty of 1279, for which see the list in Chapter 5 above.

[13] MADTG, A 297, fol. 383v (October 1243) the Villanova creditors to whom money was owed by the lord of l'Isle-Jourdain are Bernard, Arnold for money, of which some was owed to him himself and some to Raymond Arnold de Villanova, Pons, the son of Arnold de Villanova deceased, and for money owed Arnold Berengar de Villanova (one of the Caraman Villanova), and Isarn for money owed Pons de Villanova, his dead father; Saint-Étienne 239 (30 3 unnumbered) (January 1247) – published in Saige, *Juifs*, No. 37 – Bernard and his brother Raymond Arnold de Villanova, acting with the consent of their wives Geralda and Grisa, the two brothers being sons of the dead Raymond Arnold de

We last saw Jordan's brothers Stephen and Pons when they were described as dead in 1214 leaving heirs. Nothing is known about Stephen's issue, but Pons' children are well known. They were the brothers Jordan, Isarn, and Pons. All three are seen together from 1233 until 1246, and Jordan and Isarn until 1258.[14] A consul in 1261-1262, Jordan was a knight and served as a guarantor for the premier lord of l'Isle-Jourdain in 1259 and 1260. We later learn that he had two daughters, a Garsiona who is seen in the late 1260s and a Salamandra who appears in 1272 as the wife of Bertrand Maurandus selling her portion of the lordship of Mérenvielle on the Save river near l'Isle-

Villanova, sold a property in the Close of Saint-Étienne to a Jew in a charter attested by Pons, son of the quondam Arnold de Villanova; TAM, AA 1 103 (January 1248) a document where a Pons de Villanova de Monteaygono is contrasted to a Pons de Villanova de Monteregali (Montréal), but which of our two Pons the former is cannot be said; PAN, JJ 19, fol. 148r (August 1248) a charter of the count witnessed by the brothers Isarn and Jordan, and by Pons, son of the quondam Arnold; Clares 24 (January and September 1257, both acts copied in 1259) with Pons son of the deceased Arnold de Villanova; PAN, J 330 29 (July 1260) the same Pons sold large holdings at Gémil, etc.; MADTG, A 297, fol. 108v (October 1253) property at Verfeil once owned by the dead Pons de Villanova. Incidently, Verfeil is in the direction of Gémil, and it will be noted in the document dated February 1227 in note 9 above that his grandfather Jordan had been a "fideiussor" for a debt of the lord of Verfeil.

[14] For January 1214 see note 8 above; Saint-Étienne 239 (30 2 unnumbered) (December 1233) where Isarn and his siblings Jordan and Pons sell rents on the street of the Four Bastard in the City to the provost of Saint-Étienne; PAN, J 328 10 i (March 1236) where Isarn and Pons attested an act of the count; PAN, JJ 19, fol. 121r (February 1237) where the same witnessed an act of the same prince; for Jordan and possibly Pons in February 1243 see note 12 above; PAN, JJ 19, fol. 45r (April 1243) Isarn and Jordan as executors of a Brugariis; for Jordan in March 1243 see note 11 above; for Isarn and possibly Pons as creditors of the lords of l'Isle-Jourdain in October 1243 see note 13 above; TAM, II 60 (January 1246) an important act involving l'Isle-Jourdain attested by Isarn and his brother Pons; MADTG, A 297, fol. 393r (April 1246) where Isarn, Jordan, and their sibling Pons acquit the lord of l'Isle-Jourdain for payment of his debts; Douais, *Inquisition*, 2: 16 (May 1246) Jordan a councilor of the consuls of Toulouse; Isarn consul 1247-1248; for Pons de Villanova de Monteaygone in January 1248 see note 13 above; for Isarn and Jordan in August 1248 see the same note; MADTG, A 297, fol. 423r (May 1249) a marriage of Peter de Bordello of l'Isle-Jourdain witnessed by Bertrand, Isarn, and Arnold Raymond de Villanova; Saint-Étienne 227 (26 DA 2 78) (May 1253, copied in 1256) in which Arnold, Arnold Raymond, and Raymond de Rabastenquis, sons of the deceased Arnold, settled their debts by surrendering properties along the waterfront and on the Four Bastard in the City in an act attested by Jordan de Villanova; Saint-Sernin 600 (10 36 12) i (March 1255) Isarn a witness; MADTG, A 297, fol. 219v (April 1255) a sale at l'Isle-Jourdain attested by the brothers Isarn and Jordan; Malta 138 1 (November 1255) Isarn and Bertrand de Villanova give witness at Cugnaux; MADTG, A 297, fol. 890v (May 1256) Isarn called knight serving as an arbiter in a case between the lords of Pibrac and those of l'Isle-Jourdain; ibid., fol. 892r (May 1258) a second stage in the same suit with Jordan now giving an attestation; and Archdiocese 793 (register), fol. 51v (May 1258) mentions Bertrand de Villanova and Jordan de Villanova and his brother Isarn.

Jourdain. A year later, together with her cousin Pons, she alienated part of her family's tolls in the town.[15]

Jordan's brother Isarn was also active in government and at l'Isle-Jourdain. A knight, he was last mentioned in 1258, and it is not known whether or not he had children. The last brother Pons was surely alive in 1246, but afterward is easily confused with Pons, son of the heretical Arnold a-d grandson of the heretical Jordan. Because the latter Pons had his principal properties stretching from Buzet on the Tarn river to Verfeil to the northeast of the town, it is my guess that the Pons who was dead by 1268, leaving two children Arnold and Ramunda in litigation with Garsiona, the daughter of the Jordan whose other daughter Salamandra has been seen above as a lord of Mérenvielle near l'Isle-Jourdain to the west of Toulouse, was the brother of Jordan and Isarn.[16] If such is the case, it tells us who the squire named Pons, son of the knight named Pons, was. A cousin of Jordan's daughter Salamandra, he owned some of the tolls of the town and many waterfront rights on the Garonne at Toulouse in 1272 and 1273. This same person was the premier lord of Mérenvielle for which he gave homage to l'Isle-Jourdain in 1288.[17]

A final person from one of these lines was an Arnold de Villanova who was the only petitioner for the amnesty of 1279 for this clan.[18] Whoever he was, whether the Arnold mentioned two paragraphs above or a child derived from Pons, the son and grandson of the heretics Arnold and Jordan, cannot yet be determined.

It may be remembered that far back in 1141 one of our original participants was a Pons Capiscol or Capiscolis. We do not know Pons'

---

[15] PBN, MS nouv. acq. lat. 2046 (December 1259-April 1260) the knight Jordan offered to guarantee the lord; Molinier, *Correspondance ... d'Alphonse de Poitiers*, No. 844 (July 1268) and No. 1226 (May 1269) concerning the suit before the vicar's court between Garsiona, daughter of the dead knight Jordan, and Arnold de Villanova and his sister Ramunda, children of the deceased knight Pons, over the disputed inheritance of the dead Jordan; MADTG, A 297, fol. 255v (July 1272) where Salamandra (Scalamandria), daughter of Jordan, with the consent of her husband Bernard Maurandus, sold Jordan de Insula a third of a half of the lordship of Mérenvielle; and PAN, J 324 6 vii (November 1273) 360 pounds of Toulouse worth of tolls sold by Pons "domicellus," son of the dead Pons "miles," and by his cousin Salamanda, daughter of the dead Jordan "miles" and wife of Bertrand Maurandus, with the consent of her mother Aimengardis and of her father-in-law Bonmacip Maurandus. The young woman was less than 25 years of age.

[16] For the careers of Isarn and Pons, see the two preceding notes.

[17] For the acts of July 1272 and November 1273 see note 15 above. Pons was a person of stature for which see PAN, J 324 6 xi (November 1273) where he, described as a "civis" and a "domicellus," was one of the executors of a Brugariis. For the earlier relationship of the two families, see above April 1243 in note 14. In MADTG, A 297, fol. 1538r (March 1288) the squire rendered homage for Mérenvielle.

[18] Chapter 6 (March 1279).

succession, but we do know that a Raymond Capiscolis was alive in 1181-1182, and had a daughter named Mantelina. Named Raymond Stephen, this woman's son made Arnold and Bertrand de Villanova his heirs for his property at Bovilla in 1194.[19] Who these persons were and what their degree of relation to each other and to the other Villanova already treated is not known. There is no doubt, however, that they were close relatives. They and their heirs shared possessions with the other lines, and, furthermore, both Arnold and Bertrand attested the division of property between Jordan, Pons, and Stephen in 1192.[20]

TABLE 29: VILLANOVA – LINES OF BERTRAND AND OF ARNOLD

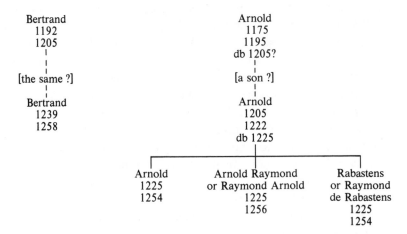

Bertrand (see Table 29) was several times a consul and had holdings in 1205 in the square called Montaygon.[21] He thereupon vanishes from the

---

[19] Whatever its origins, the name Capiscolis was a family surname, and not the title of an ecclesiastic officer. A layman named Raymond Capiscol is in Saint-Sernin 586 (8 27 1) (July 1098) at the founding of the hospital of Saint-Raymond. The William Capiscolis who was a canon of Saint-Étienne is seen in Saint-Étienne 227 (30 DA 1 5) (March 1144 or 1145) to ibid., 227 (26 DA 1 11) iii (January 1168, copied in 1180) with several intervening references in the same collection. The Raymond Capiscolis we are here considering is one seen among the town councilors and chaptermen in 1165/6, 1178, and in 1181-1182, and in Malta 1 100 (April 1180) when his possessions in the City are mentioned. The charter described in the text above is in Archdiocese 704 (register), fol. 49r containing a list of the property of the hospital of the Arnaud-Bernard gate wherein was given in January 1309 the tenor of a document written in February 1194 by the notary Magnes.

[20] See the document of June 1192 cited in note 7 above.

[21] He was consul in 1192-1193 and 1197-1198; for December 1202 see note 8 above and for March 1205 note 9.

record, but another Bertrand – perhaps, in fact, the same one – appears as a consul in 1239-1240, is seen at l'Isle-Jourdain in 1243 with other members of the family, and last is seen in an instrument concerning Bovilla in 1258.[22] An associate in the Capiscol inheritance of the earlier Bertrand who was named Arnold had a more interesting history. An individual with this name appears in charters and in town government from 1175 to 1195.[23] In 1205, however, we hear of an Arnold, the son of a dead Arnold.[24] It is obvious that this Arnold may be the same one seen earlier because it is about 1205 that Arnold, the son of Jordan, makes his appearance in the charters, thus requiring a distinction to be made between the various Arnolds of the same family.[25] Whatever the facts, Arnold, son of Arnold, was himself deceased by 1225 when we hear of his son Arnold acting for himself and his minor siblings. The young Arnold was then cited for refusing to attend a consular court that assigned for sale the family "curia" at Castanet valued at 20,000 shillings in order to pay his father's debts.[26] We subsequently learn that Arnold's brothers were Arnold Raymond de Villanova, sometimes called Raymond Arnold, and Rabastencs, sometimes called Rabastenquis. These brothers were again adjudged in default on a debt in 1230, were among the creditors of the lords of l'Isle-Jourdain in 1243, and were still paying off their father's debts at Toulouse in 1254. Raymond Arnold, the last of the brothers, appears in 1256.[27]

[22] Bertrand was consul in 1239-1240; for March 1243 see note 12 above; consul again in 1246-1247; for May 1249 and November 1255 see note 14 above; in an act of May 1258 together with Jordan de Villanova and his brother Isarn for which see note 14 above; and Puybusque, *Généalogie Puybusque*, pp. 48-53 (November 1258) a testament mentioning Bertrand's property at Bovilla. Bovilla is there described as being at l'Ardène, today's Lardenne.

[23] PAN, J 328 1 viii (February 1175) a witness about a matter at Gémil; chapterman in 1180-1181 and in 1189-1190; for June 1192 see the document in note 7 above; for February 1194 the last reference in note 19 above; and PBN, MS lat. 9189, fol. 248ra (May 1195) a sale by Arnold.

[24] For the act of October 1205 in which this Arnold appears see note 9 above.

[25] If so, this Arnold was probably the son of the Arnold first seen in February 1175 in note 23 above.

[26] For November 1222 about property at Braqueville held together with Jordan see note 9 above; E 501 i (March 1225, copied in 1233) and E 573 (the same date) settling debts totalling 6230 shillings (the total was surely much more but these instruments record only the assignments to individual creditors) by selling the "curia" or farm. The court received a quarter of the sale price.

[27] Saint-Étienne 227 (26 DA 2 47) (November 1230, copied in 1249 and 1256) recording a debt of 300 shillings and requesting an assignement on the property of the brothers Arnold, Arnold Raymond, and Rabastencs; for February 1243 and for the act of October 1243 for the debts of l'Isle-Jourdain, see notes 12 and 13 above, noting that, in

TABLE 30: VILLANOVA-BOVILLA

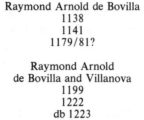

Raymond Arnold de Bovilla
1138
1141
1179/81?

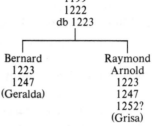

Raymond Arnold
de Bovilla and Villanova
1199
1222
db 1223

Bernard	Raymond
1223	Arnold
1247	1223
(Geralda)	1247
	1252?
	(Grisa)

To turn back to the original cast of 1141, the reader may recall Raymond Arnold de Bovilla (Table 30). First seen in 1138, this person probably served as an arbiter in a consequential case between the Dalbade church and the Hospitalers in 1179 or 1181.[28] After that, a Raymond Arnold de Bovilla, who was also called Villanova, is seen in the consulate of 1199-1201.[29] Raymond Arnold de Villanova had possessions on Montaygon, was alive in 1222, and deceased in 1233, when we see his children Bernard and Raymond Arnold enfeoffing his house in the close of Saint-Etienne.[30] Both these men were knights, and Bernard was of such prestige at Toulouse that he was the hostage from this family sent to Paris in 1229. We know that both brothers were sentenced for heresy. In 1241,

---

the latter, Arnold's brother was there called Raymond Arnold; Puybusque, *Généalogie Puybusque*, pp. 20-33 (dated 1244) a charter with Arnold as a witness; for Arnold Raymond de Villanova in May 1249 see note 14 above; Saint-Étienne 227 (26 DA 2 78) (May 1254, copied in 1256) final payment of debt of 300 shillings on waterfront holdings and rents from the street of the Four Bastard in which Rabastencs is called Raymond de Rabastenquis; and MADTG, A 297, fol. 38v (June 1256) in which Raymond Arnold de Villanova, son of the dead Arnold, witnessed an act of the chapter of Saint-Étienne.

[28] For 1138 and 1157 (both charters without month) having details on Raymond Arnold, see note 4 above; and Malta 25 19 (undated but dateable between October 1179 and sometime in 1181) by the personalities therein listed.

[29] The consulate had an unusual two year term.

[30] For Montaygon in March 1205 and for Raymond Arnold as a councilor of the consuls in March 1222 see note 9 above; Saint-Étienne 242 (32 4 5) (December 1223, copied in 1247) where he enfeoffed a house once of Mosse de La Caustra by Saint-Étienne to the issue of the deceased Raymond Arnold, that is Bernard and Raymond Arnold de Villanova. Their father had acquired the right to this house from the Jew Aster.

Bernard had completed lengthy penitential pilgrimages and Raymond Arnold was condemned to perform the same and to provide much material for building a prison for the Inquisition.[31] Both were soon back in business, Bernard being a consul for the count in 1242(?)-1245, and both swore to maintain the Peace of Paris in 1243. The two brothers are seen with their wives in 1247 selling a house in the Close of Saint-Etienne. Lastly, a Raymond Arnold may have been the consul of that name in 1251-1252.[32]

Although obviously originating in the service aristocracy of the counts of Toulouse, the Villanova were among the leaders of the town in the consulate once it had won its freedom in 1189. The family was not as politically active after the popular victory of 1202, but reentered the consulate during the war years. Thereafter, it appears to have been more or less on the count's side in the struggle with the town, and to have held office in the consulate only in the usual intermittent manner of the old families in the thirteenth century. It also began to parade its knightly title during the same time. As was seen above, also, the family was shot through with Catharism, and that fact, together with the great war and attendant economic difficulty, hurt it badly. One may presume that much property owned by Jordan and his son Arnold was confiscated, and we also know that the non-heretical branch of Arnold, Raymond Arnold, and Rabastencs lost much, including the farm of Castanet. On the whole, however, the Villanova weathered the storm, and, in the testimony about the Falgario and taxation in Toulouse, witnesses chose the thirteenth century Jordan and his heirs to exemplify a citizen rich in property outside of the town.[33]

---

[31] PAN, J 310 45 (April 1229) Bernard as a hostage; PAN, JJ 19, fol. 39r (January 1241) both siblings as witnesses to an act of the count's government; PBN, Doat 21, fol. 172v (May 1241) Raymond Arnold de Villanova "miles et civis" assigned wide pilgrimages and taxed to build the prison to the tune of 2,000 "lateres plani," 10 "modia calcis," and 100 "saumate harene cernite"; and ibid., fol. 178v (August 1241) pilgrimages for Bernard de Villanova "miles et civis."

[32] Bernard was consul 1242-1245, and both brothers took the oath in February 1243, for which see above note 12; Saint-Étienne 239 (30 3 unnumbered) (January 1247) – published by Saige, *Juifs*, No. 37 – the house, perhaps the one mentioned in note 30 above, going to the Jew Bonuspuer.

[33] TAM, II 10 (March 1271-July 1272) the onetime treasurer of the quarter of Saint-Rome, John de Galhaco, testified that the following deceased "domini" had paid taxes to the town on their rural holdings: Bertrand de Montibus, Castellusnovus, and Jordan de Villanova and their heirs.

Bibliography

A. Archival Documents and Manuscript Texts

The documents used in this monograph are found in cartularies or registers, rolls, or individual parchments. Individual acts in cartularies or registers are referred to by foliation (recto and verso). If the act or document is of modest size only the first folio is cited. If a document being cited is large or if a part well after its start must be signalled, additional folio numbers will be specified. Rolls are handled in the conventional manner, an attempt being made to number the documents. Two large rolls in the collection called TADHG Grandselve have, however, never been numbered, and I have proposed a system described below under that archive's rubric. Individual documents are referred to by Archive Abbreviation (not used in the case of TADHG, the Archives départementales de la Haute-Garonne, the most extensively used of all the repositories in this list). Series Letter (in the case of archives other than TADHG), and Collection Name (for which, see below), followed by specific identifying materials. Materials common to all documents save those contained in cartularies or registers are shown by the following example: Collection [Saint-Bernard, for example] 36 2nd of four membranes tied together iii (August 1232, copied in 1245 and 1256). After the Collection Name, this reference means container or folder no. 36, the second of four membranes tied together, the third document copied on the same membrane, written in August 1232, and copied in 1245 and 1256. All dates are modernized in this book. The style of the beginning of the year at Toulouse was initially the Annunciation and then, starting roughly about 1190, the 1st of April (presumably because of the date of the annual installation of the new town consulate), both employing the Florentine computation. During the thirteenth century, the inquisitors sometimes used Nativity (common in maritime Languedoc), and the royal administration favored the northern French new year's day of Easter, but, if and when needed, these variants will be signalled.

In this listing of documentary resources, the national archives at Paris are followed by the local ones housed at Angers, Montauban, and Toulouse, and the same rule holds true of the libraries, themselves appended at the end of the list.

PAN: Paris, Archives nationales

J – Followed by a box number, a document number, and the date, this simple reference refers to the documents housed in the Archives Nationales and calendared and occasionally published in the *Layettes du Trésor des Chartes*, 5 vols. (Paris, 1863-1909). When this collection is used without consulting the original parchment, the document will be cited by its number in the published series, the editors of the five volumes having had the prescience to number and date all the charters seriatim (with the exception of some "acta omissa"). The dates of the documents and their numbers in each of the five volumes are the following: vol. 1: 755-1223, Nos. 1-1590; vol. 2: July 1223-1246, Nos. 1591-3573; vol. 3: 1247-1260, Nos. 3574-4663; vol. 4: 1260-1271, Nos. 4664-3744, and "acta omissa" Nos. 239bis-5763bis; vol. 5 – "series olim saccorum": 632-1270, Nos. 1-903.

JJ – Registers of the Trésor not described in the publication mentioned above.

KK – A register of lawsuits of the early 1270s, referred to by folio number. Described in the body of this study, this register is badly damaged and reference is made more difficult by the fact that it contains two sets of foliations.

AADML.: Angers, Archives départementales de Maine-et-Loire

H – Lespinasse, a register of this affiliate of the order of Fontevrault. Some Lespinasse documents are housed at Toulouse and are mentioned below.

MADTG: Montauban, Archives départementales de Tarn-et-Garonne

A – A 297 is the enormous and celebrated cartulary of the Armagnac Collection. Dealing with the barony (later county) of l'Isle-en-Jourdain, it is often called the Saume de l'Isle, and contains documents from the year 899 to 1555. Cited by folio. A complete photographic exemplar is housed in my office.

G – The collection of the famous Benedictine house of Moissac, used here because of its dependencies, the monasteries of the Daurade in Toulouse and of Lézat with its appendage of Saint-Antoine located outside the town's walls. Individual parchments are cited in the manner described above. One of the documents is a register, and will be referred to by folio.

TADHG: Toulouse, Archives départementales de la Haute-Garonne

The documents from this archive are so frequently used that the specific reference to the archive itself (TADHG) shall be omitted in this monograph. Furthermore, the series letters and the numerical identifications designating the major segments of this great collection by modern archivists are also omitted because they are not necessary in order to consult the appropriate collections. They are 4 D (educational establishments, hence Saint-Bernard), 1 E (family history, which letter will, however, be retained because there is no other series identification), 1 and 4 G (respectively the archdiocese and the cathedral chapter of Saint-Étienne), and H (all regular clergy – Saint Sernin is 101 H, for example, the Daurade is 102 H, the Dominicans 112 H, etc.). One collection recently integrated into the archives, that of the Bazacle, has no identifying letter. It shall simply be called "Bazacle."

The collections are:

Archdiocese – The archdiocese of Toulouse. Save for the "liasses" concerning Braqueville and one or two other places, most of the individual charters of this series have been lost, but there are some important registers, notably 347 (Cartulaire blanc).

Bazacle – The mills of the Bazacle, whose archives had been in the possession of a private corporation until after the Second World War. They have recently been integrated into the Archives départementales.

Clares – The order of the Clares associated with the memory of Clara, the celebrated follower of Francis of Assisi.

Dalbade – A parish in Toulouse depending on the Benedictines of the Daurade. Only one document of this small collection is cited, a register numbered 91.

Daurade – A parish church and a monastery depending on the Benedictines of Moissac. The monks of the Daurade provided the priest for the parish, and the abbot of Moissac provided the prior of the Daurade, at least, when the two institutions were not locked in combat.

E – A few documents from this collection utilized in my earlier book on Toulouse and in this manuscript as well are now housed in the Malta collection. This was because, in 1946, I noted that some of the instruments used by G. Saige in his *Juifs de Languedoc* had derived from the Malta collection, but had been put into that of series E (whence others of his documents had derived) when they were returned to the archives after the death of Mme Saige, or so I was told. There was, of course, no intention of theft here. To take documents out of the archives was normal practice in past times, and I was myself offered a register to take home in order to continue work during the Easter break. Unfortunately, the excellent M. Alibert who reintegrated the documents in the file forgot to send me the list, and I have never had quite enough time at Toulouse to collate them all myself. All documents that suffered this fate cited in this book and in my earlier one are found in photographic copies housed in my office.

Grandselve – A Cistercian house northwest of Toulouse. The collection is cited in the normal manner, save for two rolls. These, at the time I published my first book on Toulouse, were in "liasse" 2 of the collection, and have now been put in "liasse" 58. Since the documents in these two rolls have not yet been numbered and catalogued, I have assigned them the following designations: Roll I recto i (September 1147)-xvii (January 1177); verso i (probably January 1177), ii (January 1169)-xix (August 1169), and xx (possibly 1171); Roll II recto i (June 1148)-ix (May 1179) and x (undated); verso i (December 1173)-vi (October 1131).

Lespinasse – A house depending on the order of Fontevrault just north of Toulouse.

Malta – An abbreviated reference for Series H, Order of Malta, Grand Priory of Toulouse, Commandery of Toulouse, Houses of Toulouse, Estacabuou, and elsewhere in the Commandery. Since all the houses in the Commandery are numbered sequentially in the archives, there is no need to mention the specific houses in the references. A typical reference will read Malta 1 12 followed by the date. The two appended digits ("1", meaning the House of Toulouse, and "12", the twelfth document in its collection) derive from an anonymous eighteenth century catalogue in two volumes (of which a photographic copy is in the Library of Congress in Washington D.C.). A manuscript concordance converts the old identifications to the modern ones. Several rolls from the Malta collection have been published in Molinier "Ensevelissement de Raimond vi" (Malta 1 24, the cartulary of Raymond vii), and Ourliac, "Les sauvetés du Comminges" (the cartulary of Saint-Clar in Malta 360 1) for which titles, see the bibliography below.

Malta-Garidech – Grand Priory of Toulouse, and Commandery of Garidech.

ms 124 – This cartulary consists of two fragments of inquisitorial testimony, the first collected by the inquisitors Raymond Resplandi and Arnold of Gouzens in 1254 and the second by John of Saint-Pierre and Reginald of Chartres in 1256. Modern foliation has been imposed, and is used here.

Saint-Bernard – The College of Saint-Bernard derived from the Hospital or Hospice of Grandselve in Toulouse. The reference system is the same as that described at the head of this section, except for D Saint Bernard 138 (the Capdenier cartulary) where foliation is used.

Saint-Étienne – The Cathedral Chapter of Saint-Étienne. The method of reference is more complicated than usual because there is a manuscript catalogue by Claude Cresty, *Répertoire des titres et documents concernants les biens et droits du chapitre de Saint-Étienne*, 2 vols., and another of tables (1734-1737). A typical reference will read: Saint-Étienne 227 (26 DA 2 47) (November 1230). The number "229" refers to the modern "liasse," and the material in the first set of parentheses refers to Cresty's archival identification. Since Cresty's "sacks" and other eighteenth century containers have long since been replaced by modern paper "liasses," I forbear from defining their parts. A photographic copy of Cresty's inventory is found in the Library of Congress, Washington, D.C.

Saint-Pierre and Saint-Géraud – A priory of the cathedral located on the Place de la Pierre in the center of the City.

Saint-Sernin – The regular canons of the famous basilica. Cresty catalogued this collection also in his *Répertoire des titres et documents concernants les donations ... et divers autres droits appartenants à l'auguste chapitre de Saint-Sernin*, 2 vols. and another of tables (1728-1730). A typical reference will read: Saint-Sernin 132 (20 70 12) July 1222. The rules formulated for Saint-Étienne apply here also, and a photographic copy of Cresty's inventory is likewise in the Library of Congress. The large cartulary contained in this collection was published by C. Douais, Saint-Sernin, in 1887, for which see the bibliography below.

Saint-Sernin Canonesses – A few thirteenth century documents are found in the "liasses" of this little order.

TAM: Toulouse, Archives municipales

AA – Acts of public authority referred to by the numbers assigned to them by Ernest Roschach, *Inventaire-sommaire des archives communales de la ville de Toulouse antérieures à 1790*, vol. 1 (Toulouse, 1891). Cited, for example, as AA 1 34 followed by date. AA 1 and 2 have been published in Limouzin-Lamothe, *La commune de Toulouse*, for which see the Bibliography below.

BB 204 – The matricule of the notaries of Toulouse. Referred to by folio.

DD – The archives of the mills of the Château Narbonnais.

II – The onetime "Layettes," catalogued by Odon de Saint-Blanquat in his *Inventaire des archives de la ville de Toulouse antérieures à 1790*, vol. 2 in 2 parts (Toulouse, 1976-1977).

PBN: Paris, Bibliothèque nationale

Doat – Conventionally called "Collection Doat" after the principal scribe who prepared authenticated copies of original documents to grace the library of Jean Baptiste Colbert, the part of this massive seventeenth-century collection used in this book largely consists of materials taken from the archives of the Inquisition at Carcassonne and Toulouse. These are referred to by volume number and folio. Photographic exemplars of most of the Doat volumes containing material about heresy are available in the Columbia University Library.

MS lat. 6009 – A cartulary of Grandselve, the Cistercian house to the north of Toulouse, by which the College of Saint-Bernard in town was founded.

MS lat. 9189 – The cartulary of Lézat, a Benedictine monastery to the south of Toulouse that had a priory with an attached hospital called Saint-Antoine in the southern suburb (Saint-Michel) of that town. Like the Daurade monastery in town, Lézat was a dependency of Moissac, but had its own abbot.

MS lat. 9994 – A cartulary of Grandselve.

MS lat. 11008 – A cartulary of Grandselve.

MS lat. 11010 – A cartulary of Grandselve.

MS nouv. acq. lat. 2046 – A partly truncated document bound in the form of a book containing the pleas in a suit in the court of the vicar of Toulouse dated December 1259 and January-April 1260. The litigants were the paramount lord of the barony of l'Isle-Jourdain, Jordan de Insula, and his cousin Isarn Jordan. The bound parts of the dismembered roll have been numbered as pages, but since, in these pages, only the first two pages have been utilized, I here refer to the manuscript alone.

TBM: Toulouse, Bibliothèque municipale

MS 609 – Once housed in the Bibliothèque municipale of Toulouse where Miriam Sherwood and I photographed it, the register has now been taken to the Institut de Recherche des Textes at Paris. A copy together with a transcription done by Austin P. Evans' students presently rests in my office. The depositions were copied into MS 609 on the orders of William Bernard and Reginald de Chartres, inquisitors at Toulouse, sometime between 1258 and 1263. Although the vast bulk of the depositions derive from 1245-1246, the last is dated October 1258. This collection of testimony about Catharism is cited by folio.

B. Published Documents and Texts

Albon, Guigues Alexis Marie Joseph André, Marquis d', ed. *Cartulaire général de l'Ordre du Temple 1119-1150*. Paris, 1913.

Benedict of Peterborough. *Gesta Henrici secundi Benedicti abbatis*. Rolls Series 49. 2 vols. London, 1867.

[Benedictus XII, pope.] *Le registre d'inquisition de Jacques Fournier, évêque de Pamiers (1318-1325)*. Ed. Jean Duvernoy. 3 vols. Toulouse, 1965.

Boutaric, Edgard, ed. *Les Olim*. In *Actes du parlement de Paris*. 2 vols. Paris, 1863-1867.

Brunel, Clovis, ed. *Les plus anciennes charters en langue provençale. Recueil des pièces originales antérieures au XIIIe siècle publiées avec une étude morphologique*. Paris, 1926.

Caesarius of Heisterbach. *Dialogus miraculorum*. Ed. J. Strange. 2 vols. Cologne, 1851.

Canso – Chanson de la croisade albigeoise. Ed. Eugène Martin-Chabot. Les classiques de l'histoire de France au moyen-âge. 3 vols. Paris, 1931-1973.

——. Ed. Paul Mayer. 2 vols. Paris, 1875-1879.

Corpus Iuris Canonici. Ed. Ae. Friedberg. 2 vols. Leipzig, 1879-1881.

Devic, Claude, and J. Vaissete. *Histoire générale de Languedoc*. 15 vols. Toulouse, 1872-1893.

Dossat, Yves, ed. *Saisimentum comitatus Tholosani*. Paris, 1966.

Douais, Céléstin, ed. *Cartulaire de l'abbaye de Saint-Sernin de Toulouse*. Paris and Toulouse, 1887.

——. *Documents pour servir à l'histoire de l'inquisition dans le Languedoc*. 2 vols. Paris, 1900.

——. *Documents sur l'ancienne province de Languedoc*. 2 vols. Toulouse and Paris, 1901-1904.

——. *Travaux pratiques d'une conférence de paléographie*. Toulouse, 1900.

Du Bourg, Antoine. *Ordre de Malte. Histoire du grand prieuré de Toulouse*. Toulouse, 1893.

Fournier, Jacques. *See* Benedictus XII, pope.

Fournier, Pierre-Fr., and Pascal Guébin, eds. *Enquêtes administratives d'Alphonse de Poitiers. Arrêts de son parlement tenu à Toulouse et textes annexes.* Paris, 1959.

Galabert, François. *Album de paléographie et de diplomatique.* Toulouse, 1912.

Gallia Christiana in provincias ecclesiasticas distributa in qua series et historia archiepiscoporum, episcoporum et abbatum regionum omnium quas vetus Gallia complectebatur, ab origine ecclesiarum ad nostra tempora deducitur. 16 vols. Paris, 1715-1865. – Volume 13 (Provinciae Tolosana et Trevirensis) edited by J. Thiroux.

Gervais of Canterbury. *The Chronicle of the Reigns of Stephen, Henry II., and Richard I.* Rolls Series 73, part 1. London, 1879.

Gilles, Henri, ed. *Coûtumes de Toulouse (1286) et leur premier commentaire (1296).* Toulouse, 1969.

Gonnet, Giovanni, ed. *Enchiridion fontium Valdensium.* Turin, 1958. – Only vol. 1 published to date.

Gregory IX, pope. *Les régistres de Grégoire IX.* 4 vols. Paris, 1890-1955.

Guiraud, Jean, ed. *Cartulaire de Notre-Dame de Prouille.* Paris, 1907.

Guy, Bernard. *Bernardus Guidonis de fundatione et prioribus conventuum provinciarum Tolosanae et Provinciae ordinis predictorum.* Ed. P. A. Amargier. In *Monumenta ordinis fratrum praedictorum historica,* vol. 24. Rome, 1961.

———. *Practica inquisitionis.* Ed. Célestin Douais. Paris, 1886.

———. *Manuel de l'inquisiteur.* Ed. G. Mollat. 2 vols. Paris 1926-1927. – A partial Latin text and French translation of the *Practica*.

La Faille, Germain. *Annales de la ville de Toulouse depuis la réunion de la comté de Toulouse à la couronne.* 2 vols. Toulouse, 1687-1701.

Léonard, Émile. *Catalogue des actes de Raimond V.* Nîmes, 1932.

Limouzin-Lamothe, Raymond. *La commune de Toulouse et les sources de son histoire 1120-1249.* Paris and Toulouse, 1932.

[Mary of Oignies.] *De B. Maria Oigniacensi.* In *Acta sanctorum,* June vol. 5 [23 June], pp. 542-572.

Matthew Paris. *Vita sancti Stephani archiepiscopi Cantuariensis.* Ed. Felix Liebermann. In idem, *Ungedruckte anglo-normannische Geschichtsquellen,* pp. 323-329. Strasbourg, 1879.

Molinier, Auguste, ed. *Correspondance administrative d'Alphonse de Poitiers.* 2 vols. Paris, 1894-1900.

Pelisson, William. *Chronicon.* Ed. Charles Molinier. Aniché, 1881.

———. ———. Ed. Célestin Douais. Paris, 1881. – All references are to this edition unless there is reason to mention that by Molinier.

Percin, Jean Jacob. *Monumenta conventus Tolosani ordinis fratrum praedicatorum primi ex vetustissimis manuscriptis originalibus transcripta et sanctorum ecclesie patrum placitis illustrata.* Toulouse, 1693.

Puylaurens, William of. *Chronica Magistri Guillelmi de Podio Laurentii.* Ed. Jean Duvernoy. Paris, 1976.

Roger of Hoveden. *Chronica.* Rolls Series 51. 4 vols. London, 1868-1871.

Saige, Gustave. *Les Juifs de Languedoc antérieurement au xive siècle*. Paris, 1881.

Vaux-de-Cernay, Pierre de. *Historia Albigensis*. Ed. Pascal Guébin and Ernest Lyon. 3 vols. Paris, 1926-1939.

Vitry, Jacques de. *The Exempla or Illustrative Stories from the Sermons Vulgares of Jacques de Vitry*. Ed. Thomas Frederick Crane. New York, 1890; rprt. 1971.

——. *Lettres de Jacques de Vitry*. Ed. R. B. C. Huyghens. Leiden, 1960.

C. Secondary Sources

Abels, Richard and Ellen Harrison. "The Participation of Women in Languedocian Catharism." *Mediaeval Studies* 41 (1979) 215-251.

Alphandéry, Paul. *Les idées moralez chez les hétérodoxes latins au début du xiiie siècle*. Paris, 1903.

Andrieu, Michel. *Le pontifical romain au moyen-âge*. 4 vols. Studi e testi 86-88, 99. Vatican City, 1938-1941.

Biraben, Jean-Noël. "La population de Toulouse au xive et au xve siècles." *Journal des Savants* (1964) 284-300.

Blanc, Alphonse. *Le livre de comptes de Jacme Olivier, marchand narbonnais du xve siècle*. Paris, 1899. – Only vol. 2, part 2 was ever published.

Borst, Arno. *Die Katharer*. Stuttgart, 1953.

Boutaric, Edgard. *Saint Louis et Alfonse de Poitiers: Étude sur la réunion des provinces du Midi et de l'Ouest à la couronne et sur les origines de la centralisation administrative, d'après des documents inédits*. Paris, 1870.

——. "Organisation judiciaire du Languedoc au moyen-âge." *BEC* 16 (1855) 200-230, 532-560; 17 (1856) 97-122.

Boyer, Georges. *Mélanges I: Mélanges d'histoire du droit occidental*. Paris, 1962.

Bressolles, Gustave and Ad. Jouglar. "Étude sur une charte inédite de 1270 contenant les statuts de la réformation du comté de Toulouse." *Recueil de l'Académie de Législation de Toulouse* 9 (1860) 309-380.

Castaing-Sicard, Mireille. *Les contrats dans le très ancien droit Toulousain, x^e-xiiie siècle*. Toulouse, 1959.

Catel, Guillaume. *Histoire des comtes de Tolose, avec quelques traitez et chroniques anciennes, concernans la mesme histoire*. Toulouse, 1623.

——. *Mémoires de l'histoire du Languedoc, curieusement et fidelement recueillis de divers autheurs grecs, latins, français et espagnols, et de plusieurs titres et chartes tirés des archifs des villes et communautez de la mesme province et autres circonvoisines*. Toulouse, 1633.

Cau, Christian. *Histoire des rues de Toulouse: Index et tables*. Marseille, 1981. – See Chalande, Jules.

Cau-Durban, D. *L'abbaye de Mas d'Azil*. Foix, 1896.

Chalande, Jules. *Histoire des rues de Toulouse – Monuments, institutions, habi-*

tants. 3 parts. Toulouse, 1919, 1927 and 1929; rprt. Marseille, 1982. – See also Cau, Christian.

Cohn, Norman. *The Pursuit of the Millennium*. 2nd ed. New York, 1961.

Contrasty, Jean. *Histoire de Saint-Jory, ancienne seigneurie féodale érigée en baronnie par Henri IV*. Toulouse, 1922.

Dossat, Yves. *Les crises de l'inquisition toulousaine au XIIIᵉ siècle, 1233-1273*. Bordeaux, 1959.

——. "Les vaudois méridionaux d'après les documents de l'inquisition." *CdeF* 2 (1967) 207-226.

Douais, Célestin. "Les hérétiques du comté de Toulouse dans la première moitié du XIIIᵉ siècle d'après l'enquête de 1245." *Bulletin théologique, scientifique et littéraire de l'Institut catholique de Toulouse*, n.s. 2 (1892) 160-173, 206-209.

Du Faur, A. *Pibrac: histoire de l'église, du village et du château*. Toulouse, 1882.

Duvernoy, Jean. *Le Catharisme: La religion des Cathars*. Toulouse, 1976.

Evans, Austin P. "Social Aspects of Medieval Heresy." In *Persecution and Liberty, Essays in Honor of George Lincoln Burr*, pp. 93-116. New York, 1931.

Fiorelli, Piero. *La tortura giudiziaria nel diritto comune*. 2 vols. Rome, 1953-1954.

Fliche, Augustin, Victor Martin, et al. *Histoire de l'église depuis les origines jusqu'à nos jours*, Vol. 10: *La Chrétienté romaine (1198-1274)*. Paris, [1950].

Gérard, Pierre. "Le cartulaire des Capdeniers." *Recueil des actes du 123ᵉ congrès d'études de la fédération des sociétés académiques et savantes de Langue-doc-Pyrénées-Gascogne* (1956) 1-19.

Gilles, Henri. "L'enseignement du droit en Languedoc au XIIIᵉ siècle." *CdeF* 5 (1970) 204-229.

Griffe, Elie. *Les débuts de l'aventure cathare en Languedoc, 1140-1190*. Paris, 1969.

Grundmann, Herbert. *Religiöse Bewegungen im Mittelalter: Untersuchungen über die geschichtlichen Zusammenhänge zwischen der Ketzerei, den Bettelorden und der religiösen Frauenbewegung im 12. und 13. Jahrhundert und über die geschichtlichen Grundlagen der deutschen Mystik*. 2nd ed. Hildesheim, 1961.

Guébin, Pascal. "Les amortissements d'Alfonse de Poitiers, 1247-1270." *Revue Mabillon* (1925) 80-106, 133-144, 293-304; (1926) 27-43.

Guiraud, Jean. *Histoire de l'inquisition au moyen âge*. Paris, 1935.

Higounet, Charles. "Le style de 1ᵉʳ Avril à Toulouse au XIIᵉ et au XIIIᵉ siècle." *AduM* 49 (1937) 157-177.

Jouglar, A. "Monographie de l'abbaye de Grandselve." *MSAM* 7 (1853-1863) 179-242.

Koch, Gottfried. *Frauenfrage und Ketzertum im Mittelalter: Die Frauenbewegung im Rahmen des Katharismus und des Waldensertums und ihre sozialen Wurzein*. Berlin, 1962.

Kolmer, Lothar. *Ad capiendas vulpes: Die Ketzerbekämpfung in Südfrankreich in der ersten Hälfte des 13. Jahrhunderts und die Ausbildung des Inquisitionsverfahrens.* Bonn, 1982.

Lahondès, Jules. *Toulouse chrétienne: l'église Saint Étienne, cathédrale de Toulouse.* Toulouse, 1890.

Lambert, Malcolm. *Medieval Heresy: Popular Movements from the Bogomils to Hus.* New York, 1976.

Lejeune, Rita. "L'évêque de Toulouse Foulques de Marseille et la principauté de Liège." In *Mélanges Félix Rousseau*, pp. 433-448.

Le Roy Ladurie, Emmanuel. *Montaillou, ville occitan de 1294 à 1324.* Paris, 1975.

Lubac, Henri de. *Corpus mysticum.* Paris, 1944.

Magnou, Elisabeth. *L'introduction de la réforme grégorienne à Toulouse (fin XIᵉ-début XIIᵉ siècle).* Toulouse, 1958.

Maisonneuve, Henri. *Études sur les origines de l'inquisition.* Paris, 1942.

Manteuffel, Taddeusz. *Naissance d'une hérésie: les adepts de la pauvreté volontaire au moyen-âge.* Paris, 1970.

Meusnier, J. "Fondation et construction d'un collège universitaire au XIVᵉ siècle, le Collège de Périgord à Toulouse." *AduM* 63 (1951) 211-220.

Molinier, Charles. "La question de l'ensevelissement du comte de Toulouse Raimond VI en terre sainte (1222-1247)." *Annales de la faculté des lettres de Bordeaux*, n.s. 2 (1885) 1-92.

Mot, G. *Le moulin du château narbonnais de Toulouse, 1182-1600.* Carcassonne, 1910.

Mulholland, (Sister) Mary Ambrose, BVM. "Statutes on Clothmaking: Toulouse 1227." In *Essays in Medieval Life and Thought*, ed. John Hine Mundy, et al., pp. 167-180. New York, 1955.

Mundy, John Hine. "Charity and Social Work in Toulouse 1100-1250." *Traditio* 22 (1966) 203-288.

——. "Une famille Cathare: Les Maurand." *Annales: ESC* (1974) 1211-1223.

——. "The Farm of Fontanas at Toulouse: Two Families, a Monastery, and a Pope." *BMCL* n.s. 11 (1981) 29-40.

——. *Liberty and Political Power in Toulouse, 1100-1230.* New York, 1952.

——. "The Origins of the College of Saint-Raymond at the University of Toulouse." In *Philosophy and Humanism*, ed. Edward P. Mahoney, pp. 454-461. Leiden, 1976.

——. "Urban Society and Culture: Toulouse and Its Region." In *Renaissance and Renewal in the Twelfth Century*, ed. Robert L. Benson and Giles Constable with Carol D. Lanham, pp. 229-247. Cambridge, Mass., 1982.

——. "Un usurier malheureux." In *Hommage à M. François Galabert*, pp. 117-125. Toulouse, 1957.

——. "Village, Town, and City in the Region of Toulouse." In *Pathways to Medieval Peasants*, ed. J. A. Raftis, pp. 142-190. Toronto, 1981.

Ourliac, Paul. "Les sauvetés du Comminges: Étude et documents sur les villages fondés par les Hospitaliers dans la région des côteaux Commingeois." In his *Études d'histoire du droit médiéval*, pp. 31-111. Paris, [1979].

Prat, Geneviève. "Albi et la peste noire." *AduM* 64 (1952) 17-25.

Puybusque, G. A. de. *Contribution à l'histoire du vieux Toulouse. Généalogie de la famille de Puybusque*. Toulouse, 1902.

Richardot, H. "Le fief roturier à Toulouse." *RHDFÉ* 4ᵉ sér. 14 (1935), 307-358, 495-569.

Röhricht, Reinhold. *Regesta regni Hierosolymitani 1097-1291*. Innsbruch, 1893.

Selge, K. V. "Pauvres catholiques et Pauvres réconciliés." *CdeF* 2 (1967) 227-243.

Sicard, Germain. *Aux origines des sociétés anonymes: Les moulins de Toulouse au moyen-âge*. Paris, 1953.

Somerville, Robert. "The Case against Berengar of Tours – A New Text." *Studi Gregoriani* 9 (1972) 53-75.

Stronski, Stanislaw. *Le troubadour Folquet de Marseille*. Krakow, 1910.

Thouzellier, Christine. *Catharisme et valdéisme en Languedoc à la fin du xiiᵉ et au début du xiiiᵉ siècle*. Paris, 1966.

——. "La répression de l'hérésie." In *La chrétienté romaine (1198-1274)*, ed. A. Fliche, Ch. Thouzellier and Y. Azais, pp. 291-340. Histoire de l'Église, 10. Paris, 1950.

——. *Une somme anti-Cathare: Le "Liber contra Manicheos" de Durand de Huesca*. Louvain, 1964.

Vicaire, Marie-Humbert. *Dominique et ses prêcheurs*. Paris and Fribourg, 1977.

——. "Les Vaudois et Pauvres catholiques contre les Cathars." *CdeF* 2 (1967) 244-272.

Wakefield, Walter. "The Family of Niort in the Albigensian Crusade and before the Inquisition." *Names* 18 (1970) 97-117, 286-303.

——. *Heresy, Crusade, and Inquisition in Southern France*. Berkeley and Los Angeles, 1974.

Werner, Ernst. *Pauperes Christi*. Leipzig, 1956.

Wolff, Philippe. *Les "estimes" Toulousaines des xivᵉ et xvᵉ siècles*. Paris and Toulouse, 1956.

——, et al. *Nouvelle histoire de Toulouse*. Toulouse, 1974.

Index

This index contains the names of the institutions, persons and places mentioned in this monograph. Only section or subdivision A of Part Two. Chapter 6 is not repeated here. The reader is warned that the personal names listed here refer only to names, not persons. Aimeric de Castronovo, for example, refers to several Aimerics of this family, and the same is true throughout the index. Lastly, exceptions apart, craft, trade, and status titles both of men and women are only given for the persons listed in the amnesty of 1279 or other documents concerning that piece. The bracketed numbers in boldface refer to the entries in the Royal Amnesty of 1279 (pp. 80-115), not to page numbers.